A Dictionary of the Roots and

Combining Forms of Scientific Words

By

Tim Williams B.Sc. M.Sc. Ph.D.

Assistant Professor in the Department of Applied Foreign Languages,

at Asia University

Taiwan

First published in 2005 by Squirrox Press
6 Hayes Lane Fakenham,
Norfolk NR21 9ER
England

Paperback ISBN 1-4116-5793-4

CONTENTS

PREFACE

The increase in popular science series on television, the information available over the internet and the rising interest in many areas of science has stimulated the desire in many to acquire an understanding of the language of science. Many fields of science have thus become areas of knowledge available to an ever-increasing number of people from an ever-widening educational background. It is for these people that this dictionary has been produced.

One of the major problems for any scientist, or aspiring scientist, is the understanding of the origins and thus the meaning of the technical terms that they come across on a daily basis. Almost all scientific words, from fields as diverse as Astronomy and Helminthology, use terms and names derived from Greek or Latin; with many more from the former than from the latter, and many of us, although we may well be conversant with the Latin names of species and the Greek-derived technical terms, are unable to explain the meaning behind them. This compilation is an attempt to remedy this by providing the roots of the most common words.

Apart from the main body of the dictionary, there has also been included a listing of adjectival forms of geographical names, some common terms for animals, plants and structures; activities and habitats, shapes, sizes, colours, textures, patterns, numbers, quantity, direction and location, parts of the year and chemical elements.

New terms are being added every day to the scientific vocabulary and the temptation to continue adding information had to be realistically constrained by publishing timetables. The proofreading of this work has been a major task in itself and any errors or omissions that remain are exclusively my own.

Suggestions for improvement and additions are always welcome, as is notification of errors. The author can be contacted at timwilliams@asia.edu.tw

A Brief Introduction to Scientific Latin and Greek

One of the major problems for any scientist, or aspiring scientist, is understanding the origins and thus the meaning of the technical terms that they come across on a daily basis. Most of the words used in the sciences are derived from Greek or Latin; with many more from the former than from the latter, and many of us, although we may well be conversant with the Latin names of species and the Greek-derived technical terms, are unable to explain the meaning behind them. In this dictionary an attempt is made to remedy this by providing the roots of the most common words.

Thus, for example, if we are confronted with the word **CROSSOPTERYGII**; look up the first part of the word **crosso**, which gives:

cross -o, (Gr. κροσσος) fringe/tassel

then look up the remaining part of the word **pterygii**, which gives:

pterygi, (Gr. πτερυγιον) a little wing or fin.

Knowing we are considering a fish name, the name is resolved as, **tassel-finned fish**. Similarly, having discovered that *platy-* is from the Greek for *flat* (πλατυς), *cnemis* is from the Greek for *legging* (κνημη), *latus* is Latin for *broad* and *pes* in Latin means *a foot*; the damselfly *Platycnemis latipes* is obviously the one with flat legs and broad feet.

Not only does an awareness of the roots of a scientific name bring that particular name to life, in many cases it also helps to form a useful mental picture. Many such roots are common to many scientific terms, and once the meaning of these roots is understood their occurrence in words subsequently encountered will immediately suggest the meanings of the new words.

Transliteration

Transliteration is the process of rendering the letters and sounds of one language into those of another. The recommended transliteration of the classic Greek alphabet of twenty-four letters plus diphthongs into Latin and ultimately into English is demonstrated as follows.

Vowels and Consonants

	Greek		English	Pronunciation
Alpha	Α, α	=	A, a	as in h*a*t
Beta	Β, β	=	B, b	as English
Gamma[1]	Γ, γ	=	G, g	as in *g*ot
Delta	Δ, δ	=	D, d	as English
Epsilon	Ε, ε	=	E, e	as in p*e*t
Zeta	Ζ, ζ	=	Z, z	as in s*d*/z (wis*d*om)
Eta[2]	Η, η	=	E, e	as in h*ai*r
Theta	Θ, θ	=	Th, th	as in *th*igh
Iota[3]	Ι, ι	=	I, i (sometimes J, j)	as in p*i*t
Kappa[4]	Κ, κ	=	K, k, C, c	as English
Lambda	Λ, λ	=	L, l	as English
Mu	Μ, μ	=	M, m	as English
Nu	Ν, ν	=	N, n	as English
Xi	Ξ, ξ	=	X, x	as English
Omicron	Ο, o	=	O, o	as in p*o*t
Pi	Π, π	=	P, p	as English
Rho[5]	Ρ, ρ	=	R, r	as English
Sigma[6]	Σ, σ, ς	=	S, s	as in *s*ing
Tau	Τ, τ	=	T, t	as English
Upsilon[7]	Υ, υ	=	U, u, Y, y	as in p*u*t
Phi	Φ, φ	=	F, f	as English
Chi	Χ, χ	=	Ch, ch	as in lo*ch*
Psi	Ψ, ψ	=	Ps, ps	as in la*ps*e
Omega[8]	Ω, ω	=	O, o	as in s*aw*

[1]Gamma becomes *n* before γ, κ, ξ, χ:

γγ = *ng*, as in στρογγυλος (strongylus), γαγγλιον (ganglion)
γκ = *nc*, as in σφιγκτηρ (sphincter), εγκεφαλος (encephalus)
γξ = *nx*, as in φαλανξ (phalanx), σαλπιγξ (salpinx)
γχ = *nch*, as in κογχη (concha), ρυγχος (rhynchus)

[2]Epsilon and eta are not distinguished in transliteration, nor is there any way of deciding from a transliterated word which letter is meant. However, eta at the end of most nouns becomes *a*, as in Ανδρομεδη (Andromeda), κομη (coma), θεκη (theca), but there are exceptions, e.g. ψυχη (Psyche), νικη (Nike).

[3]It is common now to use *i* before a consonant, as in *Ichneumon, icon*, and in almost all instances (exceptions: *major, majestas*) before a vowel in a post-initial syllable (*socialis, vaccinium*); and a J before an initial vowel (*janitor, justitia*). The initial *i* is kept if the word is still essentially Greek and has an *i* sound as an initial syllable, e.g. *ion*.

[4]Kappa is retained in many English words (*karyotype, keratin, ketone, krypton, plankton, skeleton*, etc.)

[5]In compound words the initial ρ of the second term is doubled after a vowel, as in αιμορραγια (haemorrhage), καταρριν (catarrhin, hook-nosed), πλατυρρινος (platyrrhinos, broad-nosed) but remains single after a diphthong, as in ευρις (eurhis - with a good nose), χιμαιρα (chimaera/chimera). In some words the double ρρ results from the euphonic assimilation of the ν to ρ in the prefixes αν- (an-) and συν- (syn-). initial ρ = rh, medial ρρ = rrh

[6]The final 's' is always ς. Initial σ, medial σ and final ς are not distinguished in transliteration.

[7]Upsilon (ypsilon or hypsilon) is normally transliterated as '*y*', but in some cases it has been maintained as '*u*' (μυραινα - muraena - moray, τυμβος - tumba - tomb). It is kept as '*u*' in the diphthongs *au, eu, ou*. Initial υ = y

[8]Omicron and omega are not distinguished in transliteration, nor is there any way of deciding from a transliterated word which letter is meant except sometimes in the final ov, ος, ων, ως.
ov = *um*, as in χρυσανθεμον (chrysanthemum), αρον (arum) and = *on*, as in νευρον (neuron), γαγγλιον (ganglion), μικρον (micron).
ος = *us*, as in ιππος (hippus), ποταμος (potamus) and = *os*, as in κοσμος (cosmos), λογος (logos).
ων = *on*, as in σιφον (siphon), χιτων (chiton).
ως = *os*, as in ερως (eros), ρινοκερως (rhinoceros)

Diphthongs and other double letters

A diphthong consists of two vowels written together and pronounced as a single vowel. In some older texts *ae* and *oe* may be represented as Æ, æ, Œ and œ.

Greek	Transliteration	Pronunciation
αι	ai, ae, e (preferably e)	as in high
αυ	au	how
ει/ηι	ei or i (preferably i)	as in height
ευ/ηυ	eu	as in feud ('e-oo')
οι/ωι	oe, oi, e (preferably oe)	as in boy
ου	ou, u (preferably u)	as in too
υι	yi	as in suite
αη	ae (not a diphthong)	
γγ	ng	as in finger
ov	final ov = um	
ος	final ος = us	

When changing a Greek word to a corresponding Latin or Latinized form, the ending of the word is usually changed to the corresponding Latin ending in the nominative of the same gender. The Latin plural is also used.

Masculine ending: Greek -ος, Latin -*us*. As in δακτυλος = dactylus (a finger). Pl. *dactyli*
Feminine ending: Greek -η, Latin -*a*. As in θηκη = theca (case). Pl. *thecae*
Neuter ending: Greek -ov, Latin -*um*. As in κροταλον = crotalum (rattle). Pl. *crotali*.

General rules for pronunciation of scientific names

Vowels.   All vowels are pronounced. At the end of a word the pronunciation is long (*e* as in meet, *i* as in mite, *o* as in rope, *u* as in cute) except *a*, which has an *uh* sound, as in idea. The vowel in the final syllable has a short sound (*a* as in flat, *e* as in let, *i* as in hit, *o* as in slot, *u* as in put) except *es*, which is pronounced *ease*.

Diphthongs.   As above.

Consonants.   When derived from Greek, *Ch* as *k* (as in chameleon), when derived from other languages, *Ch* as in chocolate.
C has a soft sound (*s* as in lice) when it is followed by *ae, e, oe, i* or *y*. It has a hard sound (*k*, as in cat) when followed by *a, o, oi,* or *u*.

G has a soft sound (*j* as in *gin*) when followed by *ae, e, i, oe,* or *y*; and a hard sound (*g* as in *go*) when followed by *a, o, oi,* or *u*.

The initial consonant is not pronounced in words beginning with *ps, pt, ct, cn, gn,* or *mn*. However, when these combinations occur within a word the first letter is pronounced

An initial *x* is pronounced as *z*, and as *ks* when it occurs elsewhere in the word.

A double c followed by *i* or *y* is pronounced *ks*.

Accent   The accented syllable is either the penultimate syllable (one before the end) or the antepenultimate syllable (one before the one before the end). In long words there may well be a secondary accent on a syllable near the beginning of the word.

For a detailed, entertaining and excellent discussion of the composition of scientific words see Brown, R.W. (1956). *Composition of Scientific Words*. Smithsonian, Stern, W.T. (1972) *Botanical Latin*, and Gotch, A.F. (1995). *Latin Names Explained. A Guide to the Scientific Classification of Reptiles, Birds & Mammals*. Blandford.

ABBREVIATIONS

abbrev.	abbreviation	MDu	Middle Dutch
adj. suf.	adjectival suffix	ME.	Middle English
ad lib.	ad libitum (as much as one likes)	medic.	Medical
AFr.	Anglo-French	MedL.	Medieval Latin
alt.	alternative	metaph.	metaphorically
Amer. Ind.	American Indian	Mex.	Mexican
Am. Sp.	American Spanish	MG.	Middle German
Ar.	Arabic	Mongl.	Mongolian
AS.	Anglo Saxon	MHG.	Middle High German
assim.	assimilated	MLG.	Middle Low German
augm.	augmentative	mod.	modern
Aus.	Australian	Mod.L.	Modern Latin
Bol.	Bolivian	myth.	mythology/mythological
Br.	Brazilian	NL.	New Latin
Carib.	Caribbean	Norw.	Norwegian
cf.	confer ('compare')	obs.	obsolete
chem.	chemical	OE.	Old English
cogn.	cognate with	OFr.	Old French
comp.	comparative	OHG.	Old High German
cont.	contraction	ON.	Old Norse
Da.	Danish	orig.	origin/original
den.	denoting	partic.	particularly
deriv.	derived from	perh.	perhaps
dial.	dialect	Pers.	Persian
dim.	diminutive	pert.	pertaining to
deriv.	derived from/derivation	Peru.	Peruvian
Du.	Dutch	Pg.	Portuguese
e.g.	exempli gratia (for example)	pl.	plural
Eng.	English	poet.	poetical/poetically
erron.	erroneous/erroneously	Pol.	Polish
esp.	especially	Pr.	Provençal
etc.	et cetera (and so forth)	prec.	preceding
fem.	feminine	pref.	prefix
fig.	figuratively	prep.	preposition
Fr.	French	prob.	probably
Gallo-Rom.	Gallo-Roman	Rom.	Roman, Romance
Ger.	German	Rus.	Russian
Gmc.	Germanic	SAf.	South African
Gr.	Greek	SAm.	South American
Hb.	Hebrew	SAm.Sp.	South American Spanish
Hind.	Hindu	Sc.	Scottish
Ice.	Icelandic	Skr.	Sanskrit
i.e.	id est (that is)	Sp.	Spanish
IE.	Indo-European	Sin.	Sinhalese
imit.	imitation/imitative	sing.	singular
ind.	indicating	spec.	specifically
It.	Italian	suf.	suffix
L.	Latin	super.	superlative
LG.	Low German	Sw.	Swedish
LL.	Late Latin	Tp.	Tupi
L.OE.	Late Old English	Turk.	Turkish
Mal.	Malayan	Uncert.	uncertain
Malag.	Malagasy	unkn.	unknown
masc.	Masculine	var.	variation
MdfL.	Modified Latin		

THE DICTIONARY

A

a- ab- abs-, (L.) off/from/apart/away/out
a- an, (Gr. α- αν-) not/there is not/without
-a, (L.) feminine termination for many adjectives
aages, (Gr. ααγης) unbroken/hard
aapto, (Gr. ααπτος) invincible/unapproachable
aato, (Gr. αατος) insatiable
abact, (L. abactus) driven away/aborted
abdit, (L. abditus) hidden/concealed
abdo abdit, (L. abdere) to put away/remove/hide/secrete
abdo, (L. abdomen) the belly
abduc, (L. abducere) to lead away/carry off
abeba, (Gr. αβεβαιος) uncertain/wavering/fickle
abelt, (Gr. αβελτερος) silly/stupid/foolish
aberr, (L. aberrare) to stray/wander
abet, (OFr. abeter) help
abhor, (L. abhorreo) dislike/shrink from
abie, (L. abies) the silver fir (*Pinus picea*)
abien, (L. abire) to depart
abil, (L. habilis) easy to be handled
abject, (L. abiecto) despair/a throwing away
ablat, (L. ablatus) removed/taken away
able, (L. habilis) apt/fit/expert
-able -ible -uble -ble, (L. -bilis) tending to be/capable of/worthy of
ablechro, (Gr. αβληχρος) weak/feeble
ablemo, (Gr. αβλεμης) feeble
ableps, (Gr. αβλεψια) blindness
ablus, (L. ablusus) different
ablut, (L. abluere) to wash
aboethet -o -us, (Gr. αβοηθητος) hopeless/incurable
abolla, (L. abolla, Gr. αβολλα) a cloak of thick woollen cloth
abolo -s, (Gr. αβολος) uncast/unshed
aborigin, (L. aborigineus) ancestral/native/original
abort, (L. abortus) untimely birth
abro, (Gr. αβρος) dainty/delicate/pretty/soft/graceful/splendid/luxurious
abram, (Gr. αβραμις) a kind of fish
abras, (L. abradere) to scrape off/shave
abroch -os, (Gr. αβροχος) dry/waterless
abrot, (Gr. αβρωτος) uneatable
abrot, (Gr. αβροτης) splendour/luxury/charm
abrot -os, (Gr. αβρωτος) uneatable/not eaten
abrum, (L. abrum) a holder
abrum, (L. abrumpere) to break off
abrupt, (L. abruptus) torn off/steep/precipitous
abs, (L.) off/from/apart/away/out
abscess, (L. abscessus) a purulent tumour
abscis, (L. abscidere) to cut off
absit, (L. absiti) distant/gone away
abstemi, (L. abstemius) moderate/temperate
abund, (L. abundare) to abound/to overflow/to be rich
abyss, (Gr. αβυσσος) unfathomed/bottomless pit/deep sea
-ac, (Gr. ακος/ακη/ακον) of/belonging to
ac, (L.) pref. assim. form of L. *ad-* before *c* (k) *qu.* at/to/towards
ac, (Mod.L.) with

aca, (Gr. ακα) softy/gently

acaeno, (Gr. ακαινα) thorn/spine

acaleph -a -o, (Gr. ακαληφα) the sting, as of a nettle

acallo, (Gr. ακαλλνς) ugly/without charms

acalypho, (Gr. ακαλυφης/ακαλυπτος) uncovered/unveiled

acalypto, (Gr. ακαλυπτος/ακαλυφης) uncovered/unveiled

acaman -to, (Gr. ακαμαντος) unresting/untiring

acanth -a -o, (Gr. ακανθα) thorn/prickle/spine

acanthiz, (Gr. ακανθης) thorny

acanthus, (Gr. ακανθος) a prickly plant (Acanthaceae)

acar -i, (LL. acarus Gr. ακαρι) a mite

acar, (Gr. ακαρης) short/small/tiny

acat -i -um, (Gr. ακατιον) a light boat/a woman's shoe

acaul -us, (Gr. ακαυλος) without a stalk

acced, (L. accedere) to support

accele, (L. accelerare) to quicken/hasten

accens, (L. accensus) kindled/excited/set on fire

accinct, (L. accinctus) well girdled/equipped/armed

accip, (L. accipere) to accept/receive

accipit, (L. accipiter) a hawk

accliv, (L. acclivis) uphill/steep

accol -a, (L. accola) neighbour

accre, (L. accrescere) to increase

ace -o, (Gr. ακεομαι) heal/quench/repair/staunch/cure/remedy/relief

-acea, (L. -aceus) suf. meaning: of/belonging to/having the nature of

-aceae, (L.) suf. used in botanical nomenclature to indicate a family name

acedo, (Gr. ακηδης) careless/negligent/harmless/unburied

aceo, (Gr. ακος/ακεος) cure/remedy

-aceous, (L. -aceus) suf. denoting: of the nature of/belonging to

acer, (L. acer) sharp/cutting/the maple tree (*Acer* spp.)

acer, (L. acris/acre) pointed/pungent/stinging/sharp/sour

acerat, (L. acerosus) full of chaff/mixed with chaff

acerb-, (L. acerbus) bitter/harsh

acerv, (L. acervus) a mass/heap

acest -o, (Gr. ακεσιος) healing/curing

acestr -a, (Gr. ακεστρα) darning needle

acet, (L. aceta) vinegar

acetab, (L. acetabulum) a vinegar cup/the socket of the hip joint

-aceum, (L. aceus) suf. denoting 'of the nature of'/'belonging to'

-aceus, (L. -aceus) suf. denoting 'of the nature of'/'belonging to'

ach, (Gr. αχος) pain/distress/grief/sorrow

achan, (Gr. αχανης) mute (with astonishment)/yawning/wide-mouthed

achen, (Gr. αχην) poor/needy

achet a, (Gr. αχετας/ηχετης) clear-sounding/musical/shrill/chirping (of cicada)

achly -o -s, (Gr. αχλυεις) dark/gloomy/dismal

achor -us, (Gr. αχωρος) homeless/without a resting place

achoreut, (Gr. αχορευτος) melancholy/joyless

achoro, (Gr. αχωρ/αχορος) scurf/dandruff

achos, (Gr. αχος) pain/grief/sorrow/distress

achrest, (Gr. αχρηστος) useless/unprofitable

achr -omat -ost, (Gr. αχρωατος) without colour

achther, (Gr. αχθηρης) annoying/burdensome

achth -o -s, (Gr. αχθος) burden/load/distress

achyr -o um, (Gr. αχυρον) chaff/bran

aci -do -us, (Gr. ακις) a point/barb/needle

-acias, (NL. acias) -tendency

acicul, (L. aciculum) a small needle
acid, (L. acidus) sour
acid -no, (Gr. ακιδνος) weak/feeble/insipid
acin, (Gr. ακαινα) a thorn/goad
acin, (L. acinus) berry
acina, (L. acinaces) short sword
acinet, (Gr. ακινητος) motionless/unmoved/steadfast
acinus, (L. acinus) a berry/grape
-acious, (Eng.) abounding in
-acis, (Gr. -ακις) a point/barb
acli -d -s, (L. aclys) a small javelin
aclysto, (Gr. ακλυστος) sheltered
acmae -o, (Gr. ακμαζω) flourish/abound in
acme, (Gr. ακμη) the highest point of anything/point/edge/prime/climax
acmeto, (Gr. ακμητος) untiring/unwearied
-acmon, (Gr. ακμων) anvil/pestle/head of battering ram
acniso, (Gr. ακνισος) lacking in fat/lean/meagre/spare
aco, (Gr. ακος) cure/remedy/relief
acoca, (Gr. ακωκη) a sharp point
acoet -es, (Gr. ακοιτης) bedfellow/husband/wife
acolo, (Gr. ακολος) a morsel/a little bit
acoluth -o, (Gr. ακολουθος) following after/succeeding
aconio, (Gr. ακονιας) a kind of fish
aconit -um, (L. aconitum Gr. ακονιτον) monk's hood, a poisonous plant (*Aconitum*)
acont -i -um -o, (Gr. ακωντιον) small javelin
acoresto, (Gr. ακορεστος) insatiable/unsatisfied
acost -a, (Gr. ακοστη) barley
acous, (Gr. ακουω) hear
acoustic, (Gr. ακουστικος) pert. hearing
acr -e-a, (Gr. ακρα/ακρη) highest or farthest point/end/extremity
acr -i, (L. acri-) sharp/keen
acranto, (Gr. ακραντος) futile/fruitless/idle
acras, (Gr. ακρασια) incontinence/intemperance/bad mixture
acraspeda, (Gr. ακρασπδος) without fringes
acrato, (Gr. ακρατος) pure/unmixed/undiluted
acremono, (Gr. ακρεμον) a bough/branch/spray
acri -d -s, (Gr. ακρις) hilltop/mountain peak/locust/grasshopper
acrib -o, (Gr. ακριβεια) exactness/precision
acrido, (Gr. ακρις/ακιδος/ακριδιον) a locust/grasshopper/cricket
acris, (Gr. ακρις) hill top/mountain peak
acrit -o, (Gr. ακριτος) unarranged/confused/disorderly/indistinguishable
acro, (Gr. ακρον/ακρος) height/top/extremity/pointed/apex/summit
act -a -e -i, (Gr. ακτη) coast/beach/sea-shore/headland/promontory
actaeo, (Gr. ακταιος) on the coast or shore
acti -n -s, (Gr. ακτις) a ray/beam (of sun)
actit -o -es, (Gr. ακτιτης) of or inhabiting the sea shore/coast dweller
actuos, (L. actuosus) active
acu -s, (L. acumen) a sharp point/a point/cunning
acul -us, (L. aculeus) a prickle/sting/point
aculea, (L. aculeate) stinging
acumin, (L. acuminatus) sharpened
acus, (L. acus) needle/bodkin
-acus, (L. acus) suf. 'in connection with'
acut, (L. acutus) sharpened/pointed/acute
acylo, (Gr. ακυλος) an acorn of the holm oak (*Quercus ilex*)
ad, (L.) prep. & pref. at/to/towards/into. AS suf. - towards

-ad, (Gr. -αδ L. -ad) suf. 'to'/towards/near

adam, (L. adamas Gr. αδαμας) unconquerable - hence the hardest of metals/diamond

adamast, (Gr. αδαμαστος) untamed/unconquered

adap, (L. adaperire) to fully open

adapt, (L. adaptare) to fit to

adduct, (L. adductus) stretched/strained/contracted

ade, (Gr. αδεια) abundance

-ad, -ade, (L.) suf. pertaining to/relating to/akin to/made of

adeag, (Gr. αιδοια) genitals

adecto, (Gr. αδεκτος) not received/incredible

adel -o, (Gr. αδηλος) obscure/concealed/invisible

adelph -o, (Gr. αδελφος) a brother/kinsman/colleague

-aden, (Gr. αδην) suf. a gland

adep -s, (L. adeps) fat/grease/lard

adept, (L. adeptus) proficient

adephag -o, (Gr. αδηφαγος) gluttonous/greedy

aderco, (Gr. αδερκης) invisible/unexpected

adercto, (Gr. αδερκτος) not seeing

-ades, (Gr. -αδες) a patronymic suf. ind. 'son of', 'descendant of'

adet -o, (Gr. αδετος) free/loose

adhe, (L. adhaerere) to cling to/stick to

adico, (Gr. αδικος) injurious/unjust

adir, (L. adire) to approach

adit, (L. aditus) entrance

adminicul -or, (L. adminiculum) a support/prop

adnat, (L. adnatus) united with/joined to

adnex, (L. adnectere) to bind to/to connect with

adoceto, (Gr. αδοκητος) unexpected

adocimo, (Gr. αδοκιμος) false/spurious/base/not legal/unsatisfactory

adol -o, (Gr. αδολος) honest/guileless

adolesc, (L. adolescere) to grow up

adore -us, (L. adoris) a type of grain

adorno, (L. adornatus) decorate/embellish

ados, (Gr. αδος) loathing/satiety

adox -o, (Gr. αδοξος) obscure/ignoble/despised

adr -o, (Gr. αδρος) thick/stout/bulky

adran, (Gr. αδρανης) feeble/impotent

adria, (Gr. Αδριας) the Adriatic

adras, (L. adradere) to shave/scrape

adul -a, (L. adulare) to flatter/fawn/cringe before

adult, (L. adultus) fully grown/grown up

adulter, (L. adulterare) to corrupt/pollute/defile

adun -at, (Gr. αδυνατεω) without strength

adunc, (L. aduncus) bent inwards

adust, (L. adustus) burnt/sunburnt/tanned

adve, (L. advehere) to carry to

adven, (L. advenire) to arrive

adventit, (L. adventitius) extraordinary

advert, (L. advertere) turn towards

ae see also **ai, e, oe**

-ae, (L. -ae) suf. making forms plurals

-ae, -aea, -eaum, -aeus, (L.) suf. of/ belonging to/pertaining to

-aeresis, (Gr. αιρεσις) suf. taking

aechm -a, -o, (Gr. αιχμη) point of a spear/arrow

aeci -a, di, (Gr. αικια) torture/assault/suffering/outrage

aed -es -i, (L. aedes) a building/room/temple/the cell of bees

aed, (Gr. αιδοια) the genitals

aedeag, (NL. aedeag) the genitals

aedes, (Gr. αηδης) disagreeable/unpleasant/nauseous

aedo, (Gr. αιδως) reverence/awe/shame

aedoe -o, (Gr. αιδοιος) having a claim to regard, reverence, compassion

aedon, (Gr. αηδων) nightingale

aefter, (AS.) farther away/behind

aegi, (L. aegis) a shield/protection/bulwark

aegi-, (Gr. αιγι-) goat-

aegial -o -us, (Gr. αιγιαλος) sea-shore/beach

aegis, (Gr. αιγις) the shield of Zeus

aegith, (Gr. αιγιθος) possibly a linnet, or similar bird

aegl, (Gr. αιγλη) a nymph/daughter of Jupiter and Neaera

aegl, (Gr. αιγλη) radiance/splendour/glory

aego, (Gr. αιγος) a goat

aegro, (L. argrere) to be sick

aegypio, (Gr. αιγυπιος) a vulture

aegypt -us, (L. Aegyptus) Egypt

aei, (Gr. αει) pref. ever/always/for ever

aelino, (Gr. αιλινος) mournful/plaintive

aell -a -o, (Gr. αελλα) stormy wind/whirlwind/whirling motion

aeluro, (Gr. αιλουρος) a cat

aema [heme], (Gr. αιμα) blood

aema, (Gr. αημα) wind/blast

aen -o, (Gr. αιηος) dreadful/destructive

aene, (L. aeneus) bronze coloured

aeno, (Gr. αινος) tale/story/dread/horror

aeol, (Gr. αιολος) quick-moving/nimble/wriggling

aeol, (L. Aeolus Gr. Αιολος) the god of the winds/changing/variable

aeon, (Gr. αιων) a period/age/eternity

aeoreto, (Gr. αιορητος) suspended/hovering

aep, (Gr. αιπος) lofty/high/tall

aephnidio, (Gr. αιφνιδιος) sudden/quick/unforeseen

aepsero, (Gr. αιψηρος) quick/sudden/speedy

aepy-, (Gr. αιπος) pref. high/lofty/steep/tall

aequ, (L. aequor) flat surface e.g. sea/plain/desert

aequa -bil -li, (L. aequus) equal

aequoreus, (L. aequoreus) of any smooth surface

aer -ar -e, (L. aeris) copper and the alloy of copper, bronze

aer, (Gr. αηρ) the air/atmosphere

aergos, (Gr. αεργος) idle/not working

aersi, (Gr. αειρω) lift up/raise/in the air

aerugino, (L. aeruginosus) greenish

aesal -r -ro, (Gr. αισαλων) a kind of hawk (prob. *merlin*)

aesch -o, (Gr. αισχυνη) shame/dishonour

aesch -ro, (Gr. αισχροτης) ugliness/deformity

aescul -us, (L. aesculus) the winter or Italian oak, the horse chestnut (*Aesculus hippocastanum.*)

aesio, (Gr. αισιος) auspicious/opportune/lucky

aest, (Gr. αιστος) unseen

aest, (L. aestas) summer

aesth -es -esis, (Gr. αισθησις) sensation/perception

aesth -et, (Gr. αισθητης) perceiver

aestiv, (L. aestivus) pert, summer

aestus, (L. aestus) heat/fervour/passion/unrest

aesylo, (Gr. αισυλος) godless/evil/unseemly

aesyro, (Gr. αισυρος) agile/light as air

aet -o -us, (Gr. αετος) eagle as a bird of omen/as a standard
aet, (Gr. αιτιον) a cause
aeta, (L. aetas) age/life-time/aged
aeth, (Gr. αηθης) unusual/strange/unwonted
aethal -o -us, (Gr. αιθαλους) smoky/sooty
aethero, (Gr. αιθεριος) the upper atmosphere/on high/heavenly
aethi, (Gr. αιθος) burnt
aethio, (Gr. αιθιοψ/αιθοψ) sunburnt/fiery-looking/fiery/black/scorched
aetho, (Gr. αιθων) fiery/burning/flashing/glittering
aethrio, (Gr. αιθριος) fair/clear/bright (of weather)
aethyctero, (Gr. αιθυκτηρ) rushing violently/darting
aetio, (Gr. αιτιος) causing/responsible for
aevum (evum), (L. aevum) lifetime/age
aexi, (Gr. αεξω) increase/grow/exalt
aezeno, (Gr. αιζηος) strong/active/lusty
af, (L.) pref. assim. form of L. ad- before f, at/to/towards
afer, (L. afer, afra, afrum, africus) African
affer, (L. afferre) to bring
affin, (L. affinis) related
ag, (L.) pref. assim. form of L. ad- before g, at/to/towards
aga, (Gr. αγαν) very/very much/too much
agaeo, (Gr. αγαιος) enviable/leading the procession
agall, (Gr. αγαλλω) glorify/exalt
agalli -d -s, (Gr. αγαλλις) dwarf iris
agalma, (Gr. αγαλμα) glory/delight/pleasing gift
agan -o, (Gr. αγανος) mild/gentle
agan, (Gr. αγαν) very much/too much
aganactico, (Gr. αγανακτικος) irritable/peevish/vexed
agano, (Gr. αγανος) broken/sticks broken for firewood
aganos, (Gr. αγανος) mild/gentle
agao-, (Gr. αγαομαι/αγαμαι) to wonder
agap -a, (Gr. αγαπαω) show affection/persuade/caress
agap -et -etos, (Gr. αγαπη) love (in a wide sense)
agaric -um, (L. agaricum) fungus
agast -o, (Gr. αγαστος) admirable
agastor, (Gr. αγαστωρ) near kindsman/brother
agath -is, (Gr. αγαθις) a ball of thread
agath -o, (Gr. αγαθος) good/gentle/brave/valiant
agau, agav, (Gr. αγαυος) illustrious/noble/glorious
age, (L. agere) to drive
-age, (Fr.) suf. collection of/condition.state
agel -a, (Gr. αγελη) a herd/flock
agel -aeo -o, (Gr. αγελαιος) gregarious/belonging to a herd
agel, (L. agelus) small field
agen -e -i, (Gr. αγενης) unborn/uncreated
agenio, (Gr. αγενειος) beardless/boyish
-ager, (L. ager) suf. land/field
agera, (Gr. αγηραος - αγηρασια) ageless/undecaying - eternal youth
agerochos, (Gr. αγερωχος) high minded/lordly/arrogant
agetos, (Gr. αγητος) admirable/wonderful
agglomer -at, (L. agglomerare) add to/join to
agglut -in -at, (L. agglutinare) to glue on
aggre, (L. aggressus) attacked
aggregat, (L. aggregare) to add to (a flock)
agil, (L. agilis) agile/nimble
agitat, (L. agitare) to vex/agitate/harry

agla -i -o -us, (Gr. αγλαος) splendour/shining/bright/beautiful

agleuco, (Gr. αγλευκης) sour/not sweet/harsh

agm -a -ato -et, (Gr. αγμα) a fragment/fracture

agm -en -in, (L. agmen) a stream

agn -i -us, (L. agnus) a lamb

agno, (Gr. αγνος) pure/chaste/holy

agnoi -a, (Gr. αγνοια) ignorance/lack of perception/mistake

agnost -o, (Gr. αγνωστος) unknowing/unknown/forgotten/unfamiliar

ago, (Gr. αγω) lead/fetch/carry/bring/guide

ago, (L. agere) to set in motion

-ago, (L. -ago) having the nature of/resemblance/connection/property possessed (a common botanical suffix)

agog -ue, (Gr. αγωγος) leading/guiding/drawing/attracting

agon -is, (Gr. αγωνιστης) champion

agon, (Gr. αγων) assembly/contest/struggle

agonos, (Gr. αγονος) unfruitful/barren

agor, (Gr. αγορα) assemblage/market place

agos, (Gr. αγος) chief/leader/pollution/guilt

agost -o, (Gr. αγοστος) flat of the hand/arm

agr -, (Gr. αγρα) hunting/the chase/quarry/prey/booty

agr -i -o, (Gr. αγριος) wild

agr -i -o, (L. agri Gr. αγρος) field/land in cultivation

agraulos, (Gr. αγραυλος) dwelling in the field

agrephn, (Gr. αγρειφνα) harrow

agrest -, (L. agrestis) of the fields and country/wild/rustic

agreu -o, (Gr. αγρευω) take by hunting/hunt after/pursue

agreu -s -t, (Gr. αγρευτης) a hunter

agricola, (L. agricola) farmer

agrip, (Gr. αγριππος) wild olive

agrost -es, (Gr. αγρωστης) wild/hunter/a kind of spider

agrostis, (Gr. αγρωστις) dog's tooth grass

agrycto, (Gr. αγρυκτος) not to be spoken of

agrypno, (Gr. αγρυπνος) sleepless/watchful

aguro, (Gr. αγουρος) a youth

agyia, (Gr. αγυια) a highway/street

agyrto, (Gr. αγυρτος) got by begging

ai see also **ae, e, oe,**

ai, (Gr. αει-) always/ever

aichm -a -o, (Gr. αιχμη) point of a spear/arrow

aido, (Gr. αιδως) reverence/awe/shame

aidoi, (Gr. αιδοια) the genitals

aiet -o, (Gr. αιετος) eagle as a bird of omen/as a standard

aig, (Gr. αιγειος/αιγαγρος) goat/wild goat

aigeir -o -us, (Gr. αιγειρος) the black poplar (*Populus nigra*)

aigial -o -us, (Gr. αιγιαλος) sea shore

ailur, (Gr. αιλουρος) a cat

aiphyll -o, (Gr. αειφυλλος) evergreen

air -o, (Gr. αιρω) to raise/carry/start/exalt

aist, (Gr. αιστος) unseen

ait, (Gr. αιτιος) causing

aithales, (Gr. αειθαλης) evergreen

aithyi, (Gr. αιθυια) a diving bird, prob. *shearwater*

-aix, (Gr. αιξ) goat (prob. *ibex*)/a water bird of goose kind/fiery meteor

akis, (Gr. ακις) needle/barb/arrow/dart/splinter

akt -a -e -i, (Gr. ακτη) the coast

al, (Ar.) the

al, (L.) pref. assim. form of L. *ad-* before *l*, at/to/towards
ala, (L. ala) wing
alace, (L. alacer) lively/active/animated
alalos, (Gr. αλαλος) speechless/dumb
alaos, (Gr. αλαος) blind/invisible/imperceptible
alapadno, (Gr. αλαπαδνος) easily exhausted/feeble/weak
alast, (Gr. αλαστος) unforgettable/unceasing/avenging/insufferable
alatus, (L. alatus) winged
alaud -a, (L. alauda) the lark
alazon, (Gr. αλαζων) vagrant/charlatan/quack/braggart
alb -i -id, (L. albus) white
album -en -in, (L. album) white (of an egg)
albus, (L. albus) white
alc -ae, (Gr. αλκη) strength/prowess/courage
alc -es, (L. alces) the elk
-alca, (Ice. alka) the auk
alced -in -o, (L. alcedo) the kingfisher
alcim -o, (Gr. αλκιμος) stout/brave/fortifying
-alcyon, (Gr. αλκυων) the kingfisher
-ale, (L.) suf. pertaining to/having the nature of/quality/condition of
-alector, (Gr. αλεκτωρ) a fowl/cock
alectr -o, (Gr. αλεκτρος) unwedded
aleiph, (Gr. αλειφαρ) unguent/anointing oil/oil/fat
aleo, (Gr. αλεος/αλεεινος) warm/hot
aleos/eleos, (Gr. αλεος/ηλεος) distraught/crazed/foolishly
-aleos, (Gr. -αλεος) suf. pertaining to
-ales, (L.) suf. used in botanical nomenclature to form the names of plant orders
alet -o, (Gr. αλητης/αλητεια) wanderer/wandering
alet, (Gr. αλετης/αλετος) grinder/grinding
aleth -o, (Gr. αλεθεια) truth
aleur -o -um (Gr. αλευρον) flour/wheat meal/barley meal
alex -o, (Gr. αλεξω) to ward off/keep off/turn away
alexeter, (Gr. αλεξητηρ) a protector (from plague)/defender
aleyr -o, (Gr. αλευρον) flour/wheat meal/barley meal
alg -a -o, (L. alga) seaweed
alg -e -ia -o, (Gr. αλγησις) sense of pain
alg -e, (L. algere) to be cold
ali, (L. alibi) elsewhere
alia, (Gr. αλια) meeting/assembly
alibas, (Gr. αλιβας) dead body/dead river/dead wine
alibilis, (L. alibilis) nourishing
alien, (L. alienus) belonging to another place/foreign
aliger, (L. aliger) winged
alikt -o, (Gr. αλτικος) good at leaping
aliment, (L. alimentum) food
alimmato, (Gr. αλειμμα) fat/oil/unguent (used in anointing)
-alio, (Gr. αλιος) suf. of the sea
-alis-, (L.) suf. 'in connection with'/'relating to'.
alism -a, (Gr. αλισμα) water plantain (*Alisma plantago*)
aliso, (Gr. αλεισον) a cup/goblet
aliso, (Gr. αλεισος) the hip-socket
alist -us, (Gr. αλλιστος) inexorable
alit -us, (L. alitus) nourish
alit, (Gr. αλιτημα) sin/offence
aliu, (L. alius) other/different
alka, (Gr. αλκη) bodily strength

alkali, (Ar. al-kali) soda ash/alkali
alla -nt -o, (Gr. αλλας) a sausage
allact, (Gr. αλλακ-) change/vary
allagm -a, (Gr. αλλαγμα) something taken or given in exchange
allago, (Gr. αλλαγη) change/exchange/barter
allass -o, (Gr. αλλασσω) change/alter/exchange
allat -a, (L. allatum) aided
allax -i, (Gr. αλλαξις) exchange/barter/interchange
allel-, (Gr. αλληλ-) one other/to one another/mutual
alli -um, (L. alium/allium) garlic/onion
allo -i, (Gr. αλλοιος) another sort or kind/different
allo, (Gr. αλλος) another/other/different/wrong/bad/unworthy
allo, (Gr. αλλως) otherwise/at random
alloth, (Gr. αλλοθι) elsewhere
allotr -o, (Gr. αλλοτριος) of or belonging to another/foreign/strange
alluv -i, (L. aluvius) washed against
alm, (L. almus) nourishing/refreshing
aln -or -us, (L. alnus) the alder
aloco, (Gr. αλοξ/αυλαξ) a furrow
-aloe, (Gr. αλοη) bitter aloes (*Aloe vera*)
alope -c -x, (Gr. αλοπηξ) the fox (*Canis vulpes*)/a large bat
alp -estr -in, (L. Alpes) the Alps
alpha, (Gr. αλφα α A) first letter of the Greek alphabet
alphit -o -um, (Gr. αλφιτα) barley meal
als -o -us, (Gr. αλσος) a (sacred) grove/glade
als, (L. alsius) frosty/cold
alsin -a, (Gr. αλσινα) lich-wort (*Parietaria lusitanica*)
alt -i, (L. altus) high/great
alter, (L. alter) the other (one of two)
altern, (L. alternus) one after another
althae, (Gr. αλθαινω) to heal
althos, (Gr. αλθος) a healing/medicine
alti, (L. altilis) fattened up
altr, (L. altr-) other
altri -c -x, (L. altrix) nourisher/foster-mother/nurse
aluc -o, (L. alucus/ulucus) a screech owl
alucin -a, (L. alucinor) to wander in the mind/dream
alucit -a, (L. alucita) a gnat
alul -a, (L. alula) little wing
alut -a, (L. aluta) a soft leather
alv -i -us, (L. alvus) the belly/womb/beehive/ship's hold
alve -ol -us, (L. alveolus) small pit/cavity/socket
alycto, (Gr. αλυκτος) to be shunned
alypos, (Gr. αλυπος) without pain/without pain or sorrow/harmless
alysc, (Gr. αλυσκω) flee/shun/escape
alysmo, (Gr. αλυσμος) restlessness/disquiet/anguish
alyss, (Gr. αλυσσω) restless/uneasy
alytos, (Gr. αλυτος/αλλυτος) continuous/unbroken
alyxis, (Gr. αλυξις) escape
am -a -an -at, (L. amo) love/loving/loved
ama, (Gr. αμα) at once/at the same time/together
ama, (Gr. αμη) shovel/hod/water bucket
amabil -i, (L. amabilis) amiable/loveable
amaen, (L. amoenus) pleasant/attractive/charming
amal -o, (Gr. αμαλος) soft/weak
amalg -am, (Mod.L. amalgama) a soft mass
aman -s -t, (L. amans/amantis) loving/fond/affectionate

amanit, (Gr. αμανιται) a kind of mushroom (or fungus)
amar -a, (Gr. αμαρα) trench/conduit/channel
amar, (L. amarus) bitter/pungent/disagreeable
amaranth, (Gr. αμαραντινος) unfading/imperishable (of the amaranth - *Amaranthus* sp.)
amarus, (L. amarus) bitter
amarygm -a -ato, (Gr. αμαρυγμα) sparkle/twinkle/flashing/radiant
amat, (L. amo) loved
amath -i, (Gr. αμαθης) ignorant/stupid/unmanageable
amath -o -us, (Gr. αμαθος) sand
amaur -o, (Gr. αμαυρος) dark/hardly seen/obscure
amax -i -o, (Gr. αμαξα) chassis of a wagon, also the wagon
amb -i -o, (L. ambo) both/two together
amb -o, (L. ambire) to walk/to go round
amb, (Gr. αμβον) raised platform
ambi -c -co, (Gr. αμβιξ) a spouted cup/beaker
ambi-, (L. ambi-) pref. on both sides/around/round about
ambig -u, (L. ambiguus) doubtful
ambit, (L. ambitus) going round/circuit/bribery
ambl -y, (Gr. αμβλυς) blunt/dull/feeble
amblo -s -t, (Gr. αμβλωμα) abortion
ambon, (Gr. αμβων) ridge/crest/rim
ambro -s -sia, (Gr. αμβροσια) the food of the gods
ambul, (L. ambulare) to walk
ambust, (L. amburere) to burn round/scorch
amby -co -x, (Gr. αμβυξ/αμβιξ) a spouted cup
ameb -a -o, (Gr. αμοιβη) change/exchange/alternation
amel, (ME.) enamel
ament -um, (L. amentum) a strap/thong/shoe lace/catkin
amer, (Gr. αμεριστος) undivided
amer-, American
ametor, (Gr. αμητωρ) motherless
ametos, (Gr. αμητος) harvest
-amia, (Gr. αμια) a kind of fish
amiant -o, (Gr. αμιαντος) unspotted/pure/undefiled
amic, (L. amicus) friendly/favourable to
amict, (L. amicire) to clothe/wrap round/cover/conceal
amicto, (Gr. αμικτος) unmixed/pure/immiscible
amis, (Gr. αμις) chamber pot
amm -o -us, (Gr. αμμος) sand/sandy place/race course
-amma -to, (Gr. αμμα) knot/noose/halter
ammon, (Gr. Αμμονις) Libyan
ammoni, (Gr. αμμωνιακος) of Ammon. Used for a salt and gum obtained from a region
     of Libya near the temple of Ammon [Jupiter]. Hence *gum-ammoniacum*.
amn -o -us, (Gr. αμνη) a lamb
amni -s, (L. amnis) a steam/river
amnio -n -t, (Gr. αμνιον) a bowl in which the blood of victims was caught/foetal
     membrane/lamb
amoeb -a -o, (Gr. αμιοβη) change/exchange/barter
amoen, (L. amoenus) pleasant/attractive/charming
amolgaeo, (Gr. αμολγαιος) of milk
amolgos, (Gr. αμολγος) the dead of night
amomos, (Gr. αμωμος) blameless/unblemished/perfect
amorphos, (Gr. αμορφος) shapeless/misshapen/unsightly
amoto, (Gr. αμοτος) furious/savage
ampel -o -us, (Gr. αμπελος) any climbing plant with tendrils; esp. the grape-vine
amph -i -o, (Gr. αμφισ-) on both (all) sides/around/both ways/apart/asunder/double

amph -o, (Gr. αμφο-) both of two ways/sides/etc.

amphiblestr -um, (Gr. αμφιβλησρον) a casting net/anything thrown around

amphibol -o, (Gr. αμφιβολια) ambiguity/being attacked on both sides

amphigy, (Gr. αμφιγυος) double pointed

amphor -a, (L. amphora) two-handled, narrow-necked jar

ample -ct-x, (L. amplexus) embrace/twine around/clasp/grasp

ampli, (L. ampliare) to make wider/increase/enlarge

ampulla, (L. ampulla) a flask/bottle

amput -a, (L. amputare) to cut off/remove/diminish

ampy -c -x, (Gr. αμπυξ) a band or fillet for binding the hair

amurc, (L. amerca) dirt/dregs

amyct -ic, (Gr. αμυκτικος) scratching/biting/lacerating

amydr -o, (Gr. αμυδρος) obscure/dim/faint/vague

amygdal -a -o, (Gr. αμυγδαλη) an almond

amyl -o -um, (L. amylum Gr. αμυλον) starch.

amyn, (Gr. αμυνω) to ward off

amyst -is, (Gr. αμυστις) large cup/long draught/deep drinking

amysto, (Gr. αμυστος) profane

amyxis, (Gr. αμυξις) a scratching or tearing as a sign of sorrow

an, (Gr. αν-) pref. without/not

an, (L.) pref. assim. form of L. ad- before n, at/to/towards

ana, (Gr. ανα) on/up/up to/upon/again/backwards/back/through/throughout/
towards (in general significance opposite to cata- (κατα))

anabas, (Gr. αναβασις) a going up/ascent

anablep -o, (Gr. αναβλεπω) to look up/to look back

anachor -et -etes, (Gr. αναχωρησης) one who has retired/recluse/hermit

anachyma, (Gr. αναχυμα) an expanse

anact -o, (Gr. ανακτωρ) king/lord/master

anaedo, (Gr. αναιδης) ruthless/shameless/reckless

anaereto, (Gr. αναιρετης) destroyer/murderer

anagall -is, (Gr. αναγαλλις) the pimpernel (Anagallis arvensis)

analcido, (Gr. αναλκις) weak/feeble/impotent

analecto, (Gr. αναλεκτος) select/choice

analog -ai -y, (Gr. αναλογος) proportionate/equivalent to

ananco, (Gr. ανακη) force/necessity

anant -o, (Gr. αναντης) uphill/steep

anapetes, (Gr. αναπετης) wide open/expanded

anaphes, (Gr. αναφης) insipid/tasteless/impalpable

anapno, (Gr. αναπνεω) take breath/recover

anapt -o, (Gr. αναπτω) to hang up to/to fasten on or to a thing

anarrhich, (Gr. αναρριχησις) clambering up/scrambling up

anarsios, (Gr. αναρσιος) strange/hostile/implacable

anas, (L. anas) a duck

anassa, (Gr. ανασσα) queen/lady

anastater, (Gr. αναστατηρ) destroyer

anastomos, (Gr. αναστομωσις) outlet/opening

anat, (L. anatis) a duck

anathema, (Gr. αναθεμα) a curse/an accursed thing

anato-, (Gr. ανατο-) cut up

anatos, (Gr. ανατος) unharmed/harmless

anax, (Gr. αναξ) king/lord

anaxios, (Gr. αναξιος) worthless/unworthy/despicable/royal

anc -eps -ipiti, (L. ancipitis) two-headed

-ance, -ancy, -ence, -ency, (L. -antia, entia) suf. pertaining to/quality/state

ancep, (L. anceps) two-headed/on both sides/of two natures

anch -o, (Gr. αγχω) squeeze/embrace/strangle/throttle

anch, (Gr. αγκος) a hollow
anchi, (Gr. αγχι-) near
anchialos, (Gr. αγχιαλος) near the sea
anchist -os, (Gr. αγχιστος) close-packed
ancho, (Gr. αγχω) press tight/choke/throttle
anchyl -o, (Gr. αγκυλος) crooked
ancill -a, (L. ancilla) maid servant/female slave
ancipiti, (L. ancipitis) two-headed
ancistr -um, (Gr. αγκιστρον) fish-hook/surgical instrument
anco, (Gr. αγκος) a valley/a hollow/bend
ancon, (Gr. αγκων) elbow/any nook or bend
ancor -a, (L. ancora) an anchor
anctero, (Gr. αγκτηρ) binder/clasp
ancus, (L. ancus) servant
-ancy, -ance, -ence, -ency, (L. -antia, entia) suf. pertaining to/quality/state
ancyl -o, (Gr. αγκυλος) crooked/curved/hooked
ancylio, (Gr. αγκυλιον) a link of a chain/loop of a noose
ancyr -a, (Gr. αγχυρα) an anchor
-and, (L.) having the quality of
ander -o -um, (Gr. ανδηρον) raised bank/flower border
andren -a, (NL. andrena) a bee
andren, (Gr. ανδρηια) manliness
andro-, (Gr. ανδρο-) suf. meaning belonging to or of a man/a male
androgynos, (Gr. ανδρογυνος) hermaphrodite
-anea, -anum, -anus, (L.) suf. belonging to (often used with names of localities)
anebos, (Gr. ανηβος) youth/beardless
aneca, (Gr. ανεκας) upwards
anecto, (Gr. ανηκτος) bearable/tolerable
anell, (L. anellus) a little ring
anem -o, (Gr. ανεμος) the wind
aner, (Gr. ανηρ) a man/male
aneu, (Gr. ανευ) without/away from/far from
aneurysm, (Gr. ανευρυνσις) dilatation
anfer, (L. anferre) to take away
ang -ea -i -io -o, (Gr. αγγειον) a vessel/pail/reservoir/coffin
angel -o -us, (Gr. αγγελια) messenger
-angor, (L. angor) compression of the throat/anguish
angui -s, (L. anguis) a snake
anguill m-a, (L. anguilla) an eel/slippery customer
angul, (L. angulus) angle/corner
angust -i, (L. angustus) narrow/confined
anhel -a -it, (L. anhelo) puffing/panting
-anhinga, (Tupi *water-turkey*) the darter or snake bird (*Anhinga* spp.)
anhydro, (Gr. ανυδρος) waterless/dry
ania, (Gr. ανια) sorrow/distress/trouble
anicano, (Gr. ανικανος) incapable/insufficient
aniceto, (Gr. ανικητος) unconquered/unconquerable
anicmo, (Gr. ανικμος) without moisture/sapless
anil -i, (L. anilis) like an old woman
anil, (Gr. ανιλεως) unmerciful
anim -a, (L. anima) vital breath
animal -i, (L. animal) a living being
animo, (Gr. ανειμων) naked/unclad
aniso, (Gr. ανισος) unequal/uneven/unlike
ankyl -o, (Gr. αγκυλος) crooked/curved/hooked
ankyr -a, (Gr. αγχυρα) an anchor

annal, (L. annalis) lasting a year
annect, (L. annectere) to bind together
annel, (L. anellus) a little ring
annu -a -s, (L. annus) a year
annul, (L. anulus) a signet ring
ano, (Gr. ανω-) up/upward/above
anoecto, (Gr. ανοικτος) opened/pitiless/ruthless
anolbos, (Gr. ανολβος) wretched/luckless
anom -os, (Gr. ανομος) lawless/impious
anomal -o, (Gr. ανωμαλος) uneven/irregular/unequal/strange
anophel -es, (Gr. ανωφελης) useless/unprofitable/hurtful
anopl -o, (Gr. ανοπλος) unarmed
anopt -o, (Gr. ανοπτος) unseen
anorecto, (Gr. ανορεκτος) lacking appetite/undesired
ans -a, (L. ansa) a handle/haft
ans, (L. anser) goose
-ans -antia, -antis, (L.) suf. belonging to/having the quality of
ant-/ante, (L.) in front/before
ant-/anti, (Gr. αντι-) opposite/in opposition to/before/over/against
antenna, (L. antenna) sail-yard
anter -es, (Gr. αντηρης) opposite/
anter -o, (L. anterius) in front of/before/former
anth -e -o -us, (Gr. ανθος) a flower
anthem -is, (Gr. ανθεμις) a flower
anthi, (Gr. ανθικος) flowering
-antia, -antis, (L.) suf. belonging to/having the quality of
antholco, (Gr. ανθολκος) counterpoising/balancing/equal
anthra -co, (Gr. ανθραξ) charcoal/coal
anthren -a, (Gr. ανθρηνη) a hornet/wasp
anthrop -o -us, (Gr. ανθρωπος) a man
-anthus, (Gr. ανθος) suf. a flower
antia -do -s, (Gr. αντιας) tonsils
antiqu, (L. antiquus) coming before/earlier
antlia, (L. antlia) a pump
antrum, (L. antrum Gr. αντρον) cavity/cave
antyx, (Gr. αντυξ) edge/rim/frame/rail/orbit of a planet
anu, (L. anus) anus
anu -la, (L. anulus) a ring
-anum, -anus, (L.-anus) suf. belonging to/pertaining to (often used with names of
        localities)
aochletos, (Gr. αοχλητος) undisturbed/calm
aocno, (Gr. αοκνος) without hesitation/resolute/brave
aorato, (Gr. αορατος) invisible/unseen
aoristo, (Gr. αοριστος) indefinite/indeterminate/without boundaries
aoro, (Gr. αορος) pendulous
aort, (Gr. αορτη) the great artery
ap -ex -ic, (L. apex) summit/top/tip
ap -o, (Gr. απο) away from/down from/far from/after
ap, (L.) pref. assim. form of L. ad- before p, at/to/towards
ap- aph-, (Gr. απ- αφ-) away from/from/apart
apanast, (Gr. απαναστασις) migration/departure
apata, (Gr. απατη) cheating/fraud/guile/deceit/cunning/craft/trickery
apaust -us, (Gr. απαυστος) unceasing/insatiable
apecto, (Gr. απεκτος) unkempt/uncombed/unshorn
apeoros, (Gr. απηορος) soaring/hanging on high
aper -i -t, (L. apertus) open/uncovered

aper -o, (Gr. απηρος) unmaimed
aper, (L. aper) pig/wild boar
apestys, (Gr. απεστυς) absence
apeucto, (Gr. απευκτος) to be deprecated/abominable
apeutho, (Gr. απευθης) unknown/ignorant
aphad -os, (Gr. αφαδος) displeasing/odious
aphan -es, (Gr. αφανης) obscure/unseen/secret
aphan, (Gr. αφαντος) invisible
aphas, (Gr. αφατος) speechless
aphe, (Gr. αφη) touch/grip
aphel -o, (Gr. αφελης) smooth/even
aphet -o, (Gr. αφετος) let loose/freely ranging
aphis, (Gr. αφις) a bug
aphod -o -us, (Gr. αφοδος) departure/a going back
aphr -o -us, (Gr. αφρος) foam/slaver/froth
aphrodit, (Gr. Αφροδιτη) Venus, goddess of sexual love - born from sea-foam
aphron -o, (Gr. αφρονεω) to be foolish
aphtha, (Gr. αφθα) an infantile disease
aphthit -o, (Gr. αφθαρτος) uncorrupted/undecaying
aphthon -o, (Gr. αφθονια) plenty/abundance
aphy -o, (Gr. αφυσμος) drawing off (of liquids)
apic, (Gr. απιος) the pear tree (*Pyrus communis*)
apilo, (Gr. απειλη) boast/threat
apiro, (Gr. απειρος) ignorant/inexperienced/boundless/infinite
apis, (L. apis) a bee
apisto, (Gr. απιστος) faithless/untrustworthy/shifty
apium, (L. apium) parsley/celery
apl -o, (Gr. απλοος (απλους)) onefold/single/simple
aplat -o, (Gr. απλατος) unapproachable/terrible/monstrous
aplys -ia -io, (Gr. απλυσια) filth/filthiness/a kind of sponge (so called because it is
            difficult to clean)
apo, (Gr. απο) away from/down from/far from/after
apobletos, (Gr. αποβλητος) worthless
apoceno, (Gr. αποκενοω) exhaust/drain
apocryphus, (Gr. αποκρυφος) concealed/obscure/spurious
apocyn, (Gr. αποκυνον) dog's-bane (*Marsdenia erecta*)
apoeo, (Gr. αποιος) without quality/inert
apolecto, (Gr. απολεκτος) chosen
apolos, (Gr. απολος) immovable
apono, (Gr. απονος) without toil or trouble/easy/painless
apophys -is, (Gr. αποφυσις) an offshoot/side-shoot/outgrowth/prominence
aporrhegma, (Gr. απορρηγμα) fragment
apositos, (Gr. αποσιτος) hungry/having nothing to eat
aposphax, (Gr. αποσφαξ) broken off/abrupt
apotheca, (Gr. αποθηκη) storehouse/magazine/refuge
apotmetos, (Gr. αποτμητος) cut off
apotmos, (Gr. αποτμος) unlucky/ill-starred
apotomos, (Gr. αποτομος) cut off abruptly/sheer
apoxyros, (Gr. αποξυρος) sharp/sheer
apoxys, (Gr. αποξυς) tapering
apparat, (L. appare) to prepare/provide
append -ic, (L. appendix) an appendage/addition
appet -it, (L. appetitio) desire/longing for
applanat, (NL. applanatus) flattened
apri, (L. aper) a wild boar
apric, (L. apricus) open to the sun/sunbathe

apsi -s -d, (Gr. αψις) juncture/loop/arch/vault
apt -o, (L. aptare) to fit to/to adjust
apteno, (Gr. απτην) unfledged/unable to fly
apto, (Gr. απτος) tangible
aptus/aptatus, (L. aptus) appropriate/fit/suitable
apud, (L. apud) at/near/in/with/among
apuro, (Gr. απουρος) far away/distant
aqua -ri -tic, (L. aqua) water/of water
aquil -a, (L. aquila) an eagle
aquilo -ni, (L. aquilo) the north/north wind
ar, (L.) pref. assim. form of L. *ad-* before *r*, at/to/towards
ara -eo -i, (Gr. αραιος) thin/narrow/weak/slight
arab -o, (Gr. αραβος) a rattling/gnashing of teeth
arabi, (L. Arabia) Arabia
arach -is, (Gr. αραχιδνα) the ground-pea (*Lathyrus amphicarpos*)
arach -os, (Gr. αραχος) wild vetch (*Vicia sibthorpii*)
arachn -a -i -o, (Gr. αραχης) a spider/a spider's web
arad -os -us, (Gr. αραδος) a disturbance/palpitation
aragmo, (Gr. αραγμος) rattling/clashing/clattering
aram, (L. aramus) unbranched
arane -a -i, (L. aranea) a spider/a spider's web
arasso, (Gr. αρασσω) strike hard/dash to pieces
arat -i -or, (L. aratum/arator) a plough/ploughman
arbor, (L. arbor) tree
arbut -us, (L. arbutus) the strawberry tree (*Arbutus* spp.)
arc -i -o -us, (L. arca) a little chest/box/coffin
arc -i -o -us, (L. arcus) a bow (archery)/arch/vault/rainbow
arc, (Gr. αρκυς) hunter's net
arc, (L. arcuatus) curved
arcadi -a -an, (L. arcadia) ideally rustic/a mountainous region of the Peloponnesus
arcan, (L. arcanus) shut/closed/silent/secret
arceto, (Gr. αρκετος) sufficient/satisfactory
arch -a -ae -e -i, (Gr. αρχη) a beginning/origin/first cause
arch -ae -eo, (Gr. αρχαιος) ancient/antiquated
arch -aeo -eo, (Gr. αρχαιος) ancient/primitive
arch -o -us -y, (Gr. αρχος) chief/leader/rectum/anus
archeg, (Gr. αρχεγονος) original/primal
archi-, (Gr. αρχι-) chieftain/principal/master/first
archo, (Gr. αρχω) begin
archo, (Gr. αρχων) ruler/commander
-archy, (Gr. αρχω) rule/govern
arcio, (Gr. αρκιος) sure/certain/enough/sufficient
arctic, (Gr. αρκτικος) arctic/northern
arcto, (L. Arctos Gr. Αρκτος) the greater and lesser bears (constellations)/pole star/ north/the brown bear (*Ursus arctos*)
arcy -us, (Gr. αρκυς) hunter's net
ard -e -o, (Gr. αρδω) water/watered/foster/cherish/pour forth
ard -i -is, (Gr. αρδις) arrow point/arrow/sting
-ard, -art, (Fr.) suf. highest quality/excessiveness/one who/that which
arde -a, (L. ardea) a heron (*Ardea* spp.)
arden, (L. ardere) to be on fire/to burn/to glow
ardm -o -us, (Gr. αρδομς) watering-place
ardo, (Gr. αρδω) water/watered/irrigated
ardu, (L. arduus) steep/towering/lofty/difficult
are -a, (L. area) a level or open space
-are, -aris, (L.) pertaining to
area, (L. arere) to be dry with thirst or drought

aren -a, (L. harena/harenosus) sand/a sandy place
arent, (L. aerentis) dry/thirsty
areo -la, (L. areola) a small open space
areo, (Gr. αρειος) warlike/martial/bold
areolate, (L. areolatus) with small open spaces
aresc, (L. arescere) to become dry
aresto, (Gr. αρεστος) acceptable/pleasing
arete, (Gr. αρητε) excellence/goodness/virtue
arethusa, (L. Arethusa) a fountain/a nymph
arg -o, (Gr. αργος) shining/glistening/white
argel -eo, (Gr. αργαλεος) troublesome/vexatious/painful
argem -a -at, (Gr. αργεμον) a white spot in the eye
argemon, (Gr. αργεμωνη) the wind-rose (*Papaver argemone*)
argent -at -e, (L. argentum) silver
argent, (L. argentum) silver
argest, (Gr. αργεστης) clearing/brightening/the north-west wind
argi -a, (Gr. αργια) idleness/laziness/leisure/rest
argi, (Gr. αργια) leisure
argill -o -us, (Gr. αργυλλος) white clay/potter's earth
argyr -o -us, (Gr. αργυρεος) silver
ari-, (Gr. αρι-) much/very
arid, (L. aridus) dry/arid
arie -s, (L. aries) a ram/battering ram
arill, (NL. arillus) a cover/wrapper
ariono, (Gr. αρειων) better/stouter/braver
-arion, (Gr. -αριον) dim. suffix
-aris, -are, (L.) pertaining to
arisemo, (Gr. αρισημος) notable/plain/visible
arist -a -i -o, (L. arista) a bristle
arister -a - os, (Gr. αριστερος) left/on the left
aristo, (Gr. αριστος) best
arithm -o, (Gr. αριθμος) a number/amount/sum
arithm-, (Gr. αριθμητος) few in number/easily counted/of no account
-arium, - arius, (L. arium) a place were something is done or kept
-arius, (L. arius) suf. pertaining to/having he nature of
arma -t, (L. armatus) heavily armed
armill -a, (L. armilla) a bracelet
arn -o -us, (Gr. αρνος) prob. a lamb
arnacis, (Gr. αρνακις) a sheepskin coat
arneuter, (Gr. αρνευτηρ) tumbler/acrobat/diver
aro -t, (Gr. αροτος) ploughing/arable
arog, (Gr. αρωγος) helper
aroli -um, (NL. arolium) a roll of cloth
aroma, (Gr. αρωμα) spice/aromatic herb
arot -o -r -ro, (Gr. αροτος) crop
aroto, (Gr. αρωτος) arable
arpact -es, (Gr. αρπακτης) robber
arqua -t, (L. arquatus) rainbow colours
arrect, (L. arrectus) upright/pointing upwards
arrhecto, (Gr. αρρηκτος) unbroken/invulnerable/unploughed
arrhemo, (Gr. αρρημων) silent/without speech
arrhen -o, (Gr. αρρην/αρσην) male/manly/vigorous
arrhenes, (Gr. αρρηνης) fierce/savage
arrheto, (Gr. αρρητος) inexpressible/unutterable/unspoken
arrhicho, (Gr. αρριχος) a wicker basket
arrhogo, (Gr. αρροξ) without cleft/unbreached/unbroken

arrhost, (Gr. αρρωστια) ill health
arrog, (L. arrogare) to claim for oneself/assume
ars -is, (Gr. αρσις) raising/lifting
arsen, (Gr. αρσην) male/masculine/mighty/tough
arsio, (Gr. αρσιος) fitting/right
-art, -ard, (Fr.) suf. highest quality/excessiveness/one who/that which
artam -o -us, (Gr. αρταμος) a butcher/cook/murderer (metaph.)
artane, (Gr. αρτανη) rope/noose/halter
artem -ia, (Gr. αρτημια) soundness/health
artema, (Gr. αρτημα) a pendant/earring
Artemis, (Gr. Αρτεμις) the goddess Diana (goddess of the hunt)
artemis, (Gr. αρτεμισια) wormwood (*Artemisia arborescens*)
arteri -a -o, (Gr. αρτηρια) the wind-pipe (trachea)/artery
arthmo, (Gr. αρθμος) a bond/friendship/union
arthr -o -um, (Gr. αρθρον) joint/jointed
arthro-, (Gr. αρθροω) fastened by a joint
arthrod es, (Gr. αρθρωδες) well jointed
arti -os, (Gr. αρτιος) even/complete/perfect
artic -ul, (L. articulus) small joint
arto-, (Gr. αρτος) a cake or loaf of wheat-bread
artus, (L. artus) joint
-arum, (L.) suf. belonging to
arundi -n, (L. harundo) a reed
arv -al -ens -um, (L. arvus) land/region/country
arvensis, (L. arvensis) of the fields or cultivated land
arvina, (L. arvina) fat/suet/lard
arx, (L. arx) stronghold/bulwark/fortress/citadel/castle/height/peak
-ary, (L. -arium) suf. a place were something is kept
as, (L.) pref. assim. form of L. *ad-* before s, at/to/towards
asbol -o -us, (Gr. ασβολος) soot
asc -i -o -us, (Gr. ασκος) a leather/hide bag
ascalaph -us, (Gr. ασκαλαφος) perh. an owl
ascalo, (Gr. ασκαλος/ασκαλευτος) unhoed/unweeded
ascar -i, (Gr. ασκαρις) a worm in the intestines
ascaulo, (Gr. ασκαυλης) a bagpiper
asce -o -t, (Gr. ασκησις) exercise/practise/training/mode of life
ascelo, (Gr. ασκελης) dried up/withered/worn out
ascend, (L. ascendere) to mount/ascend/go up
-ascens, (L.) the process of becoming
ascetico, (Gr. ασκητικος) laborious/rigorous practice/austere
asceto, (Gr. ασκητος) ornamented
aschemo, (Gr. ασχημων) misshapen/ugly/unseemly/shameful
ascheto, (Gr. ασχετος) ungovernable/unmanageable
ascholo, (Gr. ασχολος) busy/engaged
asci -a, (L. ascia) carpenter's axe
ascid -i -ium, (Gr. ασκιδιον) little bag
ascio, (Gr. ασκιος) unshaded/shadowless
ascit -us, (L. acitus) alien/foreign/acquired
asclepi -us, (Gr. Ασκληπιος) a god of physicians or medicine
asco -us (Gr. ασκος) bladder/bag
-ase, suf. taken from *diastase* (Gr. διαστασις, separation) and used in naming enzymes e.g. lactase maltase etc.
aselgo, (Gr. ασελγης) lewd/licentious/wanton
asell -us, (L. asellus) a little ass
asem -i -o, (Gr. ασημος) without mark/indistinct/meaningless/unnoticed
asero, (Gr. ασηρος) irksome/causing discomfort/causing disgust

asil -us, (L. asilus) the gad-fly
asilla, (Gr. ασιλλα) a yoke for carrying pails
asin -us, (L. asinus) an ass/a blockhead
asine, (Gr. ασινης) unhurt/unharmed/undamaged/harmless/innocent
-asio, (L. asio) a horned owl (*Asio* spp.)
asios, (Gr. ασιος) muddy
asmeno, (Gr. ασμενος) pleased/glad
asodes, (Gr. ασοδης) muddy/slimy/suffering from nausea
asoto, (Gr. ασωτος) abandoned/profligate
asp -is, (Gr. ασπις) a round shield
aspala, (Gr. ασπαλαξ) the blind rat (*Spalax typhlus*)
aspalath -us, (Gr. ασπαλαθος) a spinous shrub (*Alhagi maurorum*) yielding a fragrant oil
aspalieus, (Gr. ασπαλιευτης) an angler
aspect, (L. aspectus) look/appearance
asper -g -s, (L. aspergo) sprinkling/spraying
asper, (L. aspera) rough
asphal, (Gr. ασφαλης) steadfast/firm/immovable
aspi -s, (L. aspis) an adder (*Vipera berus*)/snake
aspid -a, (Gr. ασπις) shield/Egyptian cobra - asp (*Naja haje*)
aspre -d -t, (L. aspreta) rough/uneven
assicul -us, (L. assiculus) little axis
assul -a, (L. assula) a shaving/chip
ast, (Gr. αστηρ) a star/meteor
astac, (Gr. αστακος) lobster
-aster, (Gr. αστηρ) a star/meteor
-aster, -astra, -astrum, (L.) suf. inferiority/incomplete resemblance/wildness/
          diminutive
-astes, (Gr. αστης) singer/one who (does something)
asthen, (Gr. ασθενεια) weakness/feebleness/sickness
asthma, (Gr. ασθμα) short-drawn breath
astico, (Gr. αστικος/αστυκος) a city or town/urbane
-asto, (Gr. -αστυς) augmentative suf. (-huge etc.)
astr -o -um, (Gr. αστηρ) a star/meteor
-astrum, (L.) dim suf. with derogatory implications
astrabe, (Gr. αστραβη) a mule's saddle
astragal -o -us, (Gr. αστραγαλος) one of the vertebrae of the neck/ball of the ankle
          joint/dice/prism of wood/the milk vetch (*Orobus niger*)/ear ring
astragalus, (Gr. αστραγαλος) vertebra/the anklebone/wrist/knuckle bones used as dice
astrap -a -e, (Gr. αστραπη) lightning
astrape, (Gr. αστραπη) flash of lightening
astrepto, (Gr. αστρεπτος) inflexible/rigid
astut, (L. astutus) adroit/clever/cunning/crafty
asty, (Gr. αστειος) town/city/town-bred/polite/charming
asyneto, (Gr. ασυνετος) stupid/witless
asynteles, (Gr. ασυντελης) useless
asyphelo, (Gr. ασυφηλος) headstrong/foolish
at, (L.) pref. assim. form of L. *ad*- before *t*, at/to/towards
-ata, (L.) suf. used to form the names of animal divisions
-ata, -atam, -atus, (L.) suf. provided with/having the nature of/pertaining to
atacto, (Gr. ατακτος) disordered
atalant -o, (Gr. αταλαντος) equal/equivalent to
atalo, (Gr. αταλος) tender/delicate
atav, (L. atavi) in general - an ancestor
atecmarto, (Gr. ατεκμαρτος) baffling/obscure/uncertain/inconsistent
atel -e -o, (Gr. ατελης) incomplete/indeterminate/ineffectual/imperfect
ateleut, (Gr. ατελευτος) endless/eternal

atemel, (Gr. ατημελης) neglected/neglectful/careless
atenuat, (L. attenuatus) weakened/meagre/unadorned
ater, (L. ater) black/dark/dead-black/gloomy/sad
atero, (Gr. ατηρος) baneful/mischievous/ruinous
aterpes, (Gr. ατερπης) joyless
athanat -os, (Gr. αθανατος) undying/immortal
ather -o, (Gr. αθηρ) chaff/a barb
athesmo, (Gr. αθεσμως) unlawful/lawless
atheto, (Gr. αθετος) wasted/useless/incompetent
athicto, (Gr. αθικτος) untouched/chaste
athl -o -um, (Gr. αθλον) prize/contest/conflict/struggle
athlet, (Gr. αθλερτης) combatant/champion
athro, (Gr. αθροος) collective/crowded
athymo, (Gr. αθυμος) fainthearted/spiritless/
-atica, -aticum, -atius, (L.) suf. a place of growth/collection of/condition/state
-aticum, (L.) suf. - collection of/condition/state of being
-atile, -atilis, (L.) suf. found in (usually in reference to habitats)
atimo, (Gr. ατιμος) without honour/dishonoured
atlas, (Gr. Ατλας) Atlas, the Titan holding up the pillars of heaven
atm -i -ido -o -os -us, (Gr. ατμιζω) smoke/steam/vapour
atmen, (Gr. ατμην) slave/servant
atmenia, (Gr. ατμενια) slavery
atmet, (Gr. ατμητος) uncut/undivided/not carved
atom, (L. atomus, Gr. ατομος) uncut/indivisible/a small particle
atonos, (Gr. ατονος) relaxed/not taut/languid
atopo, (Gr. ατοπος) strange/marvellous/odd
atr -i, (L. atritas) blackness
atracto, (Gr. ατρακτος) spindle/arrow
atrament -um, (L. atramantum) any black fluid
atrapos, (Gr. ατραπος) short cut/path
atrat, (L. atratus) clothed in black (in mourning)
atreco, (Gr. ατεκης) strict/precise/exact
atresto, (Gr. ατρεστος) fearless/not trembling
atri -um, (L. atrium) entrance hall
atri-, (L. ater) black
atro -c -x, (L. atrox) terrible/fearful/cruel/horrible
atro-, (L. ater) black
attac -us, (Gr. αττακης) a kind of locust
attagen -is, (L. attagen) the black partridge or francolin (*Tetrao orientalis*)
-atus, (L. -atus) suf. 'provided with'
atyphos, (Gr. ατυφος) modest/not puffed up
atyzel, (Gr. ατυζηλος) frightful
au, (Gr. αυ) again/once more/on the contrary/backward
auant, (Gr. αυαντη) wasting/atrophy
auchem -a, (Gr. αυχημα) boasting/pride
auchen -o -us, (Gr. αυχην) throat/neck/isthmus/mountain pass
auchm -o, (Gr. αυχμος) drought/thirst/meagerness
auct -i -or, (L. auctor) an originator/cause/founder/author/ancestor/supporter
auctumn -i -us, (L. auctumnus) autumn/autumnal
aucup -al -i, (L. aucupatio) bird-catching/fowling
aud -ac -en, (L. audacia) daring/courage/audacity/impudence
audi -en -t, (L. audire) to hear
augm -en -in, (L. augmen) an increase/growth
augur, (L. augur) soothsayer/prophetess
aul -a -i, (Gr. αυλη) courtyard/hall
aul -o -us, (Gr. αυλος) any wind instrument/any tube

aulac, (Gr. αυλαξ) a furrow

aulon, (Gr. αυλων) hollow between hills or banks/channel/trench/pipe/furrow

aur -a -o, (L. aura) air/breath

aur -ar -at -e -i, (L. aurum/aurarius) gold/golden

aur -i -icul -is -it, (L. auris) ear

auranti, (NL. aurantiacus) orange-coloured

auricul -o, (L. auricula) lobe of the ear

auriga, (L. auriga) charioteer/driver

aurit -ud, (L. auritus) long-eared

auror -a, (L. aurora) dawn

aurum, (L. aurum) gold

auscult -a, (L. auscultare) to hear attentively

auster -us, (L. austerus) harsh/rough/stern/gloomy/sour (taste)

auster, (L. auster) the south wind

austr -ali, (L. australis) southern

aut -o, (Gr. αυτος) self

autumn -ali, (L. autumnus) autumn/autumnal

aux -e -o, (Gr. αυξη) growth/increase

auxili -ari, (L. auxilium) help/aid/assistance

avar -i, (L. avarus) covetous/greedy/desirous

avena, (L. avena) oats/wild oats

avers, (L. aversari) to turn away from/shun/avoid

averv, (LL. avervus) heap

avi -a -s, (L. avis) a bird

avid, (L. avidus) longing for/vehemently desiring

avit, (L. avitus) very old/ancestral/of a grandfather

-ax, (L.) suf. inclining to/apt to

axi -s, (L. axis) an axle/axis

axilla, (L. axilla) armpit

axio, (Gr. αξιος) worth/(man's) rank/value

axiom, (Gr. αξιωμα) self-evident principle

axo -n, (Gr. αξων) axle

az -ale, (Gr. αζω) dry up/parch/groan/sigh/breath hard

azo-, (Gr. αζωος) lifeless

azyg -o, (Gr. αζυγος) unpaired/unwedded

B

babax, (Gr. βαβαξ) a chatterer

babulus, (L. babulus) a babbler

bac -a, bacc -a, (L. baca/bacca) a berry/olive/pearl

bacch -an -e, (Gr. Βακχος) Bacchus, god of wine/wine/anyone inspired/frantic/a
branch/a garland

bacelo, (Gr. βακηλος) a eunuch/womanish

bacill -um, (L. bacillum) a little staff

bact -er -ia, (Gr. βακτηριον) a small rod/staff

bactro, (Gr. βακτρον) staff/cane

bacul -um, (L. baculum) rod/staff/walking stick

badi -i -t, (Gr. βαδισις) walking/going

badius, (L. badius) brown/chestnut-coloured

baen -o, (Gr. βαινειν) to go/walk/step/advance

baeo, baio, (Gr. βαιος) little/small/humble

baeto, (Gr. βαιτη) a coat of skin/tent of skins

baetygo, (Gr. βαιτυξ) a leech
bagoa, (Gr. βαγωας) a eunuch (a Persian word)
bajul, (L. baiulus) a porter
bal -i -o, (Gr. βαλλω) to throw/cast/hurl/shoot
balaen -a -i -o, (L. balaena Gr. φαλαινα) a whale
balan -o -us, (Gr. βαλανος) an acorn/something acorn-shaped/a date/iron peg/bolt-pin
balane -i -u, (Gr. βαλανειον) bath/bathing room
balanti -um, (Gr. βαλαντιον) bag/pouch/purse
balatro, (L. balatro) a buffoon/jester
balb, (L. balbus) stammering
balbus, (L. balbus) stammering
baleen, (L. balaena) whale
bali -o, (Gr. βαλιος) spotted/dappled/swift
balist -a, (L. ballista) catapult/the missile thrown
ball -o, (Gr. βαλλω) to throw/cast/hurl/shoot
ballism, (Gr. βαλλιζω) dance/jump about
ballot -a, (Gr. βαλλωτη) a labiate herb - the black hoarhound/horehound (*Ballota nigra*)
balne -ari -o, (L. balneum) bath/bathing place
balsam -o -um, (Gr. βαλσαμον) an aromatic herb (*Chrysanthemum balsamita*)/the balsam
          tree (*Mecca balsam*)
balteat, (L. balteus) a girdle to hold a weapon/a woman's girdle
bam -a, (Gr. βημα) a pace/step/footstep
bap -t -tis, (Gr. βαπτιζω) plunge/dip
baphe -us, (Gr. βαφευς) a dyer
bapto, (Gr. βαπτος) dipped/dyed
bar -o -us, (Gr. βαρος) weight/burden/load/pressure
bar -o -y, (Gr. βαρυς) heavy (in weight)/grievous/oppressive/severe
bar -os, (Gr. βαρος) a weight/burden/load
barb -a, (L. barba) the beard
barbar -o, (L. barbarus Gr. βαρβαρος) foreign/strange/uncultivated/rough
barbit, (Gr. βαρβιτος) a kind of lyre
bard, (L. bardus Gr. βραδυς) stupid/dull/slow
barema, (Gr. βαρημα) burden/load
bari -do -s, (Gr. βαρις) flat-bottomed boat
barys, (Gr. βαρυς) heavy/impressive/grave
bas -a -eo -i -o, (L. basis) base/pedestal
bas -i -o, (Gr. βασις) base/foundation wall/step
basan -i -ism -ist -o, (Gr. βασανιζω) examine closely/investigate/torture
bascano, (Gr. βασκανος) a sorcerer/bewitcher
basil -e -ic, (Gr. βασιλ -ευς -εια) king/chief/prince/queen/princess/royal
basm -o -us, (Gr. βασμος) a step/metaph. degree/rank
bass, (LL. bassus) low/deep
bassar -a -is, (Gr. βασσαρα) fox/impudent woman/courtesan
bat -es, (Gr. βατες) one that treads/walks/haunts
bat -o -us, (Gr. βατος) bramble (*Rubus fruticosus*)/blackberry/thorn-bush
bat -o -us, (Gr. βατος) passable/accessible
batalo, (Gr. βαταλος) anus/rump/stammerer
bate -i, (Gr. βατης) a walker
bater, (Gr. βατηρ) threshold
bathm -o -us, (Gr. βαθμος) a step/stair/threshold; metaph. degree/rank
bathr -o -um, (Gr. βαθρον) base/pedestal/stage/scaffold/throne
bathy, (Gr. βαθυς) deep/high/strong/violent/copious/abundant
bati -s, (Gr. βατις) a skate or ray
batia, (Gr. βατια) bush/ticket
batrach -o -us, (Gr. βατραχος) a frog
batt -o, (Gr. βαττος) stammerer

batyle, (Gr. βατυλη) female dwarf
bauca, (Gr. βαυκαλιον) a narrow-necked vessel (that gurgles)
bauco, (Gr. βαυκος) prudish/affected
bauno, (Gr. βαυνος) furnace/forge
baxis, (Gr. βαξις) oracular saying/report/rumour
bdella, (Gr. βδελλη) a leech
bdelycto, (Gr. βδελυκτος) disgusting/abominable
bdelygma -to, (Gr. βδελυγμα) abomination
bdelyr -o, (Gr. βδελυρια) beastly/coarse/objectionable
bdesm -a, (Gr. βδεσμα) stench
bdol -o us, (Gr. βδολος) stench/stink
beatus, (L. beatus) happy/blessed
bebaeo, (Gr. βεβαιος) firm/steady/steadfast/durable
bebel -o, (Gr. βεβηλος) profane/uninitiated
bebr -o, (Gr. βεβρος) stupid
bech -ic -o, (Gr. βηχος) a cough
beco, (Gr. βεκος) bread
bel -o -us, (Gr. βελος) arrow/dart/sting/also any weapon or engine of war
belemn -o, (Gr. βελεμνον) javelin
bell, (L. bellus) pretty/handsome/charming
bell -ac -at -i -ic, (L. bellum) war/duel between two
bellat, (L. belator/bellatrix) a warrior/female warrior
bellis, (L. bellis) a daisy
bellum, (L. bellum) war/contest between two
bellus, (L. bellus) pretty/handsome/charming
belon, (Gr. βελονη) an arrow head/needle/dart/a pipe-fish (*Sygnathus* sp.)
belt, (Gr. βελτιων) better/more excellent
beltist, (Gr. βελτιστος) best/most excellent
belu -a -i, (L. belua) a large beast/monster/brute
bemb -e -i -ic -x, (Gr. βεμβιξ) a whipping top/cyclone/whirlpool/buzzing insect
bembro, (Gr. βεμβρος) stupid
bene, (L. bene) well/good/excellent/honourably/properly
benetes, (Gr. βενετειος) blue
benign, (L. benignus) kind/friendly/liberal/generous
benth -ic -o -us, (Gr. βενθος) depths of the sea
beran, (AS.) to bring forth
bero -e, (Gr. Βεροη) ocean nymph (daughter of Oceanus)
beryll -o -us, (Gr. βηρυλλος) a gem of sea-green colour
bessa, (Gr. βησσα) a wooded glen/drinking cup
besti -a, (L. bestia) a beast
bet -a, (L. beta) a vegetable, beet
beta, (Gr. βητα β B) second letter of the Greek alphabet
betonica, (L. betonica) wood betony (*Betonica* spp.)
betul -a, (L. betula) the birch (*Betula* spp.)
beuth -os, (Gr. βευδος) a woman's dress
bex -i, (Gr. βηξ) cough
bi, (L. bis) twice/double
biaio, (Gr. βιαιος) forcible/violent
biarco, (Gr. βιαρκες) supplying/life-giving
biast -es, (Gr. βιαστης) forceful/mighty/potent
bib -e -ul, (L. bibere) to drink
bibi, (L. bini) a pair
bibio, (LL. bibio) an insect
bibli -o -um, (Gr. βιβλιον) a book
biblio, (Gr. βιβλος/βυβλος) Egyptian papyrus/paper/book
bibrosco, (Gr. βιβρωσκω) eat/be eaten/be bitten/worm-eaten

bibul, (L. bibulus) fond of drinking
bico, (Gr. βικος) jar/cask/drinking bowl/a measure
bienn, (L. biennium) a space of two years
bili -s, (L. bilis) gall/bile/anger/displeasure
-bilis, (L.) suf., tending to be/capable of/worthy of/having the quality of
bilix, (L. bilix) having a double thread
bimus, (L. bimus) lasting for two years/two years old
bin, (L. bini) twofold/of pairs of things
binarius, (L. binarius) of two
bio -o -t, (Gr. βιον) living
bion, (Gr. βιωναι) to live
bios -is, (Gr. βιωσις) living/way of life/manner of life
bios, (Gr. βιος) life/lifetime
biota, (Gr. βιοτη) life
biotic, (Gr. βιωτικος) pertaining to life
birr -us, (L. birrus Gr. βιρρος) a type of cloak
bis, (L. bis) twice/double
bittac -o -us, (Gr. βιττακος) a parrot
bitum -en -in, (L. bitumen) asphalt/pitch
blab, (Gr. βλαβη) harm/damage/hurt
blaber -o, (Gr. βλαβερος) harmful/noxious/hurtful
blac -ic -o, (Gr. βλακικος) stupid/lazy/sluggish
bladar -o, (Gr. βλαδαρος) flaccid
bladder, (AS. blaedre) bladder
blaes -o, (Gr. βλαισος) crooked/bent/distorted/dishonest
blaesus, (L. blaesus) lisping/stammering/speaking indistinctly
blamma, (Gr. βλαμμα) harm/damage
blano, (Gr. βλανος) blind
blaptico, (Gr. βλαπτοκος) hurtful/mischievous
blasphem, (Gr. βλασφημεω) slander/speak profanely
blast -em -o -us, (Gr. βλαστος) a bud/shoot/sucker
blasta, (Gr. βλαστη) growth
blastem, (Gr. βλαστημα) offshoot/offspring
blatero, (L. blaterare) to babble/chatter
blatt -a, (L. blatta) a cockroach
blatte, (Gr. βλαττα) purple
blaut, (Gr. βλαυτη) a slipper
blechado, (Gr. βληχας) a bleater
blechn -o -um, (Gr. βληχνον) the male fern (*Dryopteris felix-mas*)
blechr -o, (Gr. βληχρος) gentle/faint/dull/sluggish/slight/small
blema, (Gr. βλημα) a coverlet/cast of dice
blemma -to, (Gr. βλεμμα) look/glance
blenn -o -us, (Gr. βλεννυς) slime/a kind of fish
blenn -us, (L. blennus Gr. βλεννος) simpleton/drivelling fellow
blep -o -sis, (Gr. βλεπησις) look/glance/eyesight
blep -o, (Gr. βλεπω) see/have power of sight/look (e.g. look terrible/look longingly)
bleph -ar -id -is -o, (Gr. βλεφαρις) eyelash
bleph, (Gr. βλεφαρον) eyelid
blepo, (Gr. βλεπος) look/see
bleps -is, (Gr. βλεψις) seeing
blet -os, (Gr. βλητος) stricken/palsy-stricken/stricken by disease
bletron, (Gr. βλητρον) a fastener/band/hoop
blisso/blitto, (Gr. βλισσω/βλιττω) steal honey from a hive/steal/rob
blit -o -um, (L. blitum) a tasteless herb used in salads
blitas, (Gr. βλιτας) a worthless woman
blite, (L. bliteus) insipid/silly

blosis, (Gr. βλωσις) arrival/presence

blosyr -o, (Gr. βλοσυρος) hairy/shaggy/bristling/burly/grim/fearful

blothr -o, (Gr. βλωθρος) tall

bly -s -sm, (Gr. βλυσις) bubbling up

bo -a -i, (L. boa) water serpent

bo -ar -o -s -v, (L. boarius) relating to cattle/an ox/a cow

boama, (Gr. βοαμα) shriek/cry

boete, (Gr. βοητης) clamorous

boeth -os, (Gr. βοηθος) assisting/auxiliary

bol -ac -ax, (Gr. βωλαξ) clod of earth/lump of something

bol -o -us, (Gr. βωλος) clod/lump of earth

bol, (Gr. βολις) a missile/javelin/sounding-lead/anything thrown

bola, (Gr. βολη) a throw

bolb -o -us, (Gr. βολβος) a bulb/onion/bulbous root

bolet -us, (L. boletus) a kind of mushroom

bolido, (Gr. βολιδος) a missile/javelin

bolit -o -um -us, (Gr. βολιτον) cow dung

bolo, (Gr. βολος) a throw with a casting net/the thing caught

bolus, (Gr. βωλος) clod/lump of earth

bolus, (L. bolus) a throw, as of a fishing net or dice

bom -o -us, (Gr. βωμος) raised platform/stand/tomb/cairn

bomaco, (Gr. βομαξ) beggar/ribald/coarse

bomb -us, (Gr. βομβος) booming/humming/buzzing

bomba -c -x, (LL. bombax) cotton

bomby -c -x, (Gr. βομβυξ) silk worm (*Bombyx mori*)/wasp-like insect/silk garment

bombyli -us, (Gr. βομβυλιαζω) a buzzing insect: humble bee, gnat, mosquito

bomo, (Gr. βωμος) base/platform/tomb/cairn

bomoloch -o -os, (Gr. βωμολοχος) beggar/toady/small jackdaw

bon, (L. bonitas) goodness/excellence/kindness/integrity

bonas, (L. bonasus) a kind of buffalo - the wisent (*Bos bonasus*)/the ruffed grouse (*Bonasa umbellus*)

boo -p, (Gr. βοωπις) ox-eyed

bor -a -i, (Gr. βορα) food/meat

borag, (LL. borago) borage (*Borago officinalis*)

borass -o -us, (Gr. βορασσος) the spadix of the date, with immature fruit

borbor -o -us, (Gr. βορβοριζω) mud-like

bore -al, (Gr. βορεας L. boreas) north wind/the north/northern

boreus, (Gr. βωρευς) pickled mullet

boro, (Gr. βορος) devouring/gluttonous

bos, (Gr. βους/βως) bullock/bull/ox/cow

-bos, (L. bos) bullock/bull/ox/cow

bosc, (Gr. βοσκας) feeding

bosi -s, (Gr. βοσις) food/fodder

bostrich -o, (Gr. βοστρυχηδον) curly/like curls

bostrych -o, (Gr. βοστρυχος) curl/lock of hair/anything twisted or wreathed/winged insect

botan -a, (Gr. βοτανη) pasture/fodder/herb/weeds

botaur -us, (NL. botaurus) a bittern (*Botaurus* spp.)

bothr -i -o -us, (Gr. βοθρος) trench/pit/hole/trough/hollow/grave

bothy -n -nos, (Gr. βοθυνος) trench/pit/hole/trough/hollow/grave

botr -io -y -yo -ys (Gr. βοτρυς) bunch of grapes

botul -us, (L. botulus) a sausage

bou, (Gr. βους) bullock/bull/ox/cow

boub -on, (Gr. βουβαστις) the groin

boubal -o -us, (Gr. βουβαλος) the buffalo

boubal, (Gr. βουβαλις) an African antelope (*Bulbalis mauretanica*)

bouno, (Gr. βουνος) mound/small hill
bov, (L. bovis Gr. βους) an ox/cow/bull
brabeut, (Gr. βραβευτης) an umpire/judge
bracat, (L. bracatus) wearing breeches
brach, (Gr. βραχυς) short/few/little
brachi -o -um, (Gr. βραχιων) the arm
brachi, (L. bracchium) fore-arm
brachi-, (Gr. βραχυ-) short-/shortness of -
brachist -o, (Gr. βραχυτης) shortness/narrowness/smallness
bracte -a, (L. bractea) a thin metal plate/gold leaf
brad -o -y, (Gr. βραδυς) slow/dull/sluggish
branch -i -ium -o -um, (Gr. βραγχια) fins/gills/hull of a ship
branch, (Gr. βραγχος) a gill/a fin
brassic -a, (L. brassica) cabbage
brastes, (Gr. βραστης) earthquake
brastos, (Gr. βραστος) a boiling up
brechm -o -us, (Gr. βρεχμα) top of head/parietal bones
brecho, (Gr. βρεχω) wet/soak
bregma, (Gr. βρεγμα) top of head/parietal bones
brenth, (Gr. βρενθος) of stately bearing/arrogance
breph -o, (Gr. βρεφος) foetus/the new-born/foal, whelp, cub, etc.
bret, (Gr. βρετας) wooden image of a deity
brev, (L. brevis) short
briar -o -os, (Gr. βριαρος) strong
brime, (Gr. βριμη) strength/might
brimos, (Gr. βριμωσις) indignation
brith -o -y, (Gr. βριθυς) heavy
britho, (Gr. βριθω) to be heavy/weighed down/laden/full
briz -o, (Gr. βριζω) to be sleepy/nod/slumber
broch -o, (Gr. βροχος) noose/slip knot/snare
brochet, (Gr. βροχετος) rain/moistening/steeping
brochth, (Gr. βροχθος) throat
brom -a -ato, (Gr. βρωμα) food/meat
brom -o -us, (Gr. βρομος) oats
brom -o -us, (Gr. βρωμος) stink/foul-smell
bromeli, (NL. bromelia) pineapple
bromet, (Gr. βρομητης) brayer/ass
bromi -o, (Gr. βρομιος) noisy/boisterous
bromos, (Gr. βρωμος) stench
bronch -i -o -us, (Gr. βρογχος) the windpipe/trachea
bront -a -o, (Gr. βροντη) thunder
brosis, (Gr. βρωσις) meat/pasture/taste/flavour/corrosion/rust
brot -o -us, (Gr. βροτος) a mortal man
brot -o -us, (Gr. βρωτος) to be eaten
brote -o, (Gr. βρωσιμος) eatable
brotic, (Gr. βρωτικος) voracious/gnawing
broton, (Gr. βρωτον) food/meat
brotos, (Gr. βροτος) mortal man
bruch -us, (Gr. βρυκω/βρυχω) to eat greedily/gobble
brum -al, (L. brumalis) of the shortest day/wintry
brunne, (LL. brunneus) brown
brut, (L. brutus) heavy/immovable/dull/insensible
bry, (Gr. βρυω) to swell or teem with
bryc -h -ho -o, (Gr. βρυχαομαι) roar/bellow/death-cry
brychio, (Gr. βρυχιος) from the depths of the sea/deep
bryco, (Gr. βρυκω/βρυχω) to eat greedily/gobble

brygm -o, (Gr. βρυγμος) bitting/chattering/shivering/gnashing
bryo, (Gr. βρυον) moss/swell or teem with/grow luxuriantly
bryon, (Gr. βρυον) oyster-green
bu- L. pref. (Gr. βου-) large/huge/great/monstrous
bubal -us, (Gr. βουβαλος) the buffalo
bubo, (L. bubo) an owl
bubon, (Gr. βουβων) the groin/glands
bubul, (L. bubulus) of cows or oxen
bucc, (L. bucca) the cheek
buccin, (L. buccina/bucina) a crooked trumpet/shepherd's horn/military trumpet
bucer, (L. buceros) horned
bucolic, (Gr. βουκολικος) pastoral/rustic
bufo, (L. bufo) toad
bul -es, (Gr. βουλη) determination/will/counsel
-bula, -bulum, (L.) suf. an instrument of means
bulb -us, (L. bulbus) onion/bulb
buleuto, (Gr. βουλευτος) devised/plotted
bulga, (L. bulga) leather knapsack
bulim, (Gr. βουλιμια) ravenous hunger
bull -a, (L. bulla) bubble/round swelling/boss/stud
-bulum, (L.) suf. ind. tool/instrument
bumastus, (Gr. βουμαστος) having large grapes/large breasts
bun -o -us, (Gr. βουνος) hill/mound/alter/blood clot
-bundus, -bunda, -bundum, (L.) suf. denoting continuation/augmentation/increased
          quality
buprest -is, (Gr. βουπρηστις) a beetle poisonous to cattle
burra, (L. burra) nonsense/a trifle
burranicum, (L. burranicum) a vessel for milk
burricus, (L. burricus) a small horse
bursa, (Gr. βυρσα) ox-hide/hide/skin
bursa, (L. bursa) pouch
-bus, (L.) having the quality of
bust -um, (L. bustum) funeral pile
buteo, (L. buteo) the buzzard
butom -us, (Gr. βουτομον) a sedge (*Carex riparia*)
butyr -um, (L. butyrum) butter
byas, (Gr. βυας) the eagle owl (*Bubo bubo*)
byblis, (Gr. Βυβλις) a nymph
byblo, (Gr. βυβλος) papyrus
bycano, (Gr. βυκανη) a spiral trumpet/a horn
bycto, (Gr. βυκτης) a swelling/blustering/hurricane
byo, (Gr. βυω) stuff full of/plug with/stow away
byrr, (L. byrrh) red/flame coloured
byrs -a -o, (Gr. βυρσα) ox-hide/hide/skin
bysma, (Gr. βυσμα) plug/bung
byss -o -us, (Gr. βυσσος) depths of the sea
byss, (Gr. βυσσος) fine flax/fine linen
byth -o, (Gr. βυσοος) bury/plunge/sink/submerge
bythi -os, (Gr. βυθος/βυθιος) in the depths of the sea/sunken

C

caball -us, (L. caballus) a pack horse
cac -a -h, (Gr. κακ-) pref. bad/badly done/bringing bad/etc.
cac, (Gr. κακη) wickedness/vice/cowardice/baseness of spirit.

caca, (Gr. κακη) badness/baseness/cowardice
cacali -a, (Gr. κακκαλια) the colt's foot (*Mercurialia tomentosa*)
cacatu, (Mal. kakatoe/kokatua) the cockatoo
cachinn -a, (L. cachinnus) loud laughter/splashing of the sea
cachleco, (Gr. καχληξ) gravel/shingle/a pebble on a stream bed
cachr -i -y -ys, (Gr. καχρυς) parched barley/winter bud
cachryo, (Gr. καχρυς) parched barley/a winter bud/catkin
caco -a, (Gr. κακκη) human excrement
cacoc, (Gr. κακος) bad/evil/ugly
cact -us, (Gr. κακτος) the Spanish artichoke
cad -o us, (Gr. καδος) flask/jar/urn/pail
cad, (L. cadere) to fall/wane/decay/subside/sink
cadaver -i, (L. cadaver) a dead body/carcass
cadisco, (Gr. καδισκος) an urn for receiving ballots
caduc, (L. caducus) falling/doomed/frail/perishable
cadus, (Gr. καδος) jar/jug
cae-, see also ce, coe
caec, (L. caecus) blind/hidden/unseen/obscure/dark
caecili -a, (L. caecilia) a kind of lizard
caed -o, (L. caedere) to cut down/strike/beat/kill
caela -t, (L. caelare) to engrave/carve/emboss
caen -o, (Gr. καινος) new/recent/fresh
caenis, (Gr. καινις) a knife
caenum, (L. caenum) filth/mud/mire
caero, (Gr. καιρος) the right time/place/proportion
caerule, (L. caeruleus) azure/sky-blue
caesari, (L. caesariatus) hair/long-haired
caesi, (L. caesius) bluish-grey
caesp -es -it, (L. caespes) a turf/a sod
caffer, (NL. caffra/caffrum) see *kafir*
cal -o, (Gr. καλλος) beauty
cal, (L. calere) to be warm
calam -o -us, (L. calamus Gr. καλαμος) cane/reed/reed-pipe
calamistr -um, (L. calamister) a curling iron for hair
calamit, (L. calamitas) loss/failure/misfortune/damage
calandr -us, (Gr. καλανδρος) a kind of lark
calath -isc, -o -us, (Gr. καλαθος) a wicker basket, narrow at the base
calc -ar -e -i, (L. calcar) a spur/stimulus/incitement
calc -i, (L. calx) the heel/lime/limestone
calcan -e, (L. calcaneum) the heel
calce, (L. calceus) a shoe
calceat, (L. calceatus) a covering for the foot (shoe as opposed to sandal)
calcitr, (L. calcitrare) to strike with the heel/kick
calcul -us, (L. calculus) a little stone
cald, (L. caldarius) concerned with warming/warm water
cale, (L. calere) to be warm/hot/inflamed/excited
calen, (L. calescere) to become warm
calend, (L. calendae) first day of the Roman month/a month
calf, (AS. caelf) the young of cattle and some other mammals
cali -a -o, (Gr. καλια) wooden house/cabin/hut/barn/shrine/bird's nest
cali -c -x -y, (L. calix) goblet/cup/cooking vessel
calid, (L. calidus) warm/hot/fiery/passionate
calidri -s, (deriv. Gr. σκαλιδρις) a spotted shore bird (sandpiper/sanderling - *Calidris*)
calig -a, (L. caliga) a stout shoe/soldier's boot
caligin, (L. caliginosus) foggy/misty/dark
calim, (Gr. καλυμμα) a covering
calipt -o, (Gr. καλυπτος) covered/wrapped around/enveloping

calix, (L. calix) goblet/cup/cooking vessel
call -e -i -o, (L. callum) hard or thick skin/toughness/insensibility
callaea, (Gr. καλλαιον) a cock's comb/wattles/tail feathers
calli, (Gr. καλλι-) suf. giving the idea of *beautiful* e.g. Callichthyis - a beautiful fish
calli, (Gr. καλλιον) more beautiful
callid, (L. callidus) dextrous/skilful/sly/cunning
callis -to, (Gr. καλλιστος) most beautiful
callis, (L. callis) narrow track/footpath/trail
callo, (Gr. καλλος) beauty
callun, (Gr. καλλυνω) beautify/gloss over/sweep clean
callyntro, (Gr. καλλυντρον) broom/brush
calm, (Gr. καυμα) burning heat (esp. of sun)/heat of the day
calo, (Gr. καλον) a billet of wood
calo, (Gr. καλος) virtuous/beautiful
calor -i, (L. calor) warmth/heat/glow/passion/excitement/ardour
calpi -d -s, (Gr. καλπις) pitcher/urn
caltha, (L. caltha) plant, prob. a marigold
calumn, (L. calumnia) trick/deceive/artifice/pretence
calv, (L. calva) the bald scalp
calva, (L. calvaria) the skull
calx, (L. calx) the heel/lime/limestone
caly -c -x, (Gr. καλυξ) covering/seed pod
calymm, (Gr. καλυμμα) head covering/hood/veil
calyps -o, (Gr. καλυψω) a nymph (she that conceals)
calypt, (Gr. καλυπτηρ) covering/sheath/lid/tile
calyptr -a, (Gr. καλυπτρα) veil/head-dress
camaco, (Gr. καμαξ) pole/prop/shaft
camato, (Gr. καματος) toil/labour/trouble/distress
cambr -, (L. Cambria) Wales
camel -o -us, (Gr. καμηλα) camel
camer -a -o, (L. camera Gr. καμερη) anything with a vaulted or arched covering/
            vault/chamber
camilo, (Gr. καμιλος) rope
camin -us, (Gr. καμινος) furnace/oven/kiln
camp -a -o, (Gr. καμπη) caterpillar
camp -o -s -so -to, (Gr. καμπη) bending/winding/flexion
camp -os -us, (Gr. καμπος) a sea-monster
camp -us, (L. campus) field/plain/level space
campan, (L. campana) bell
campestr, (L. campester) of fields
campho, (Gr. καμπτω) bend/curve
campsio, (Gr. καμψιον) little case/little casket
campto, (Gr. καμπτιεν) to bend/turn/flexible
campus, (L. campus) a field/plain
campylo, (Gr. καμπυλη) a crooked staff
camur, (L. camur) turned inward/hooked/curved
camus, (Gr. κημος) muzzle/nose-bag/gag
can -o -um, (Gr. κανων) straight rod/bar/weaver's rod
can -us -ut, (L. canus) whitish-grey/grey
can, (L. canus) grey-ish white/ash-coloured
canabino, (Gr. καναβινος) lean/slender
canacho, (G. καναχος) noisy
canal, (L. canalis) channel/duct
canc -er -r -ro, (L. cancer) a crab/cancer
cancell -i, (L. cancelli) a lattice/railing/grating
canchasmo, (Gr. καγχασμος) loud laughter

cand -e -id -or, (L. candidus) shining white/glittering white
candid -us, (L. candidus) shining white/radiant/bright
candidat, (L. candidatus) clothed in white
canescen, (L. canscere) to become white or hoary/to become old
cani -n -s, (L. canis) a dog
canip, (L. canipa) a fruit-basket
cann -a -ul, (Gr. κavva) reed pole/reed mat/reed fence
cannabi -s, (Gr. κavvαβις) hemp (*Cannabis sativa*)
cano -r, (L. canere) to sing or play
canon, (Gr. κavωv) a general rule/limit/boundary/measuring rod
cant, (L. cantus) a song/melody/poetry
canteri -us, (L. canterius) gelding/nag
canth -us, (Gr. κavθoς) tyre/edge/corner of eye
canthar -i -o, (Gr. κavθαρις) a kind of beetle (*Cantharis* spp.)
canthar -os, (Gr. κavθαρoς) the dung beetle (*Scarabaeus pilularius*)/a type of drinking
          cup/a type of boat
cantheli -a, (Gr. κavθηλια) panniers/any large baskets
canther, (Gr. κavθηλιoς) ass/mule/gelding
canthylo, (Gr. κavθυλη) swelling/tumour
canum, (Gr. κavωv) straight rod/bar/weaver's rod
cap -er -re, (L. caper) male goat/the smell under the armpits
cap, (L. capere) to take/capture/tempt/choose/obtain/hold/grasp/undertake
cap, (L. caput) the head
capac -i, (L. capax) broad/wide/roomy/able to hold much
cape, (LL. cappa) hood
capell -a, (L. capella) female goat
capelo, (Gr. καπηλoς) retail-dealer/huckster/tavern-keeper
caper -o, (L. caperare) to be wrinkled
caperat, (L. caperatus) wrinkled
capet -o, -us, (Gr. καπετoς) ditch/trench/hole/grave
capill -a, (L. capillus) the hair
capistr -um, (L. capistrum) a halter/muzzle
capit -i -o, (L. capitulum) a little head
capitan, (L. capitaneus) large
capn -o -us, (Gr. καπνoς) smoke
capo, (Gr. καπη) crib/manger
capr, (L. capra) she-goat
capreol -us, (L. capreolus) tendril
caprific -us, (L. caprificus) the wild fig and its fruit
caprin -us, (L. caprinus) of goats
capro, (Gr. καπρoς) wild boar
caps -a, (L. capsa) box
caps -i, (Gr. καψις) gulping/gulping down
capsul, (L. capsula) little chest
capt -o, (Gr. καπτoς) strength/vigour/courage
capt, (Gr. καπτω) gulp down greedily
capt, (L. captare) to seize/catch at/lay hold of/hunt/conduct
capul, (L. capulus) a sepulchre/coffin/a handle
caput, (L. caput) the head
capyro, (Gr. καπυρoς) dry/dried by the air/brittle/crisp/crackly (of sound)
car -a, (Gr. καρα) the head of animals/peak/top
car -ex -ic, (L. carex) rush/sedge
car, (L. carus) beloved/dear/costly
carab -us, (Gr. καραβoς) a horned beetle/prickly crustacean (crayfish)/light ship/gate
caran -g -x, (NL. carangue) a flatfish
carano, (Gr. καρανoς) a chief
carapac, (Sp. carapacho) covering

carb -o -on, (L. carbo) coal
carbas, (L. carbasus) fine Spanish flax/curtains/sails
carc -in, (L. carceris) in prison
carc, (Gr. καρις) shrimp/prawn
carcer -a, (L. caecer) prison/jail/cell
carchaleo, (Gr. καρχαλεος) rough/fierce
carchar -o, (Gr. καρχαρος) saw-like/sharp-pointed/jagged, hence a kind of shark
carcin -o, (Gr. καρκινος) a crab/a kind of shoe/an ulcer/cancer
card -i -ia -io, (Gr. καρδια) the heart
card -in -o, (L. cardo) hinge/crisis
card, (Gr. καρδια) stomach/(poetical)heart
cardin -al, (L. cardinalis) a chief/red
cardu, (L. carduus) a thistle
caren -o -um, (Gr. καρηνα) heads/mountain peaks
caret -to, (Fr. caret) turtle
cari -d -s, (Gr. καρις) a shrimp
cari -es -o, (L. cariosus) rotten/decayed
carica, (L. carica) a dried fig
caries, (L. caries) decay
carin -a, (L. carina) hull/keel/boat
cario, (L. cariosus) rotten/decayed
carisa, (L. carisa) an artful woman
caritas, (L. caritas) costliness/dearness/esteem
carn -eo -i, (L. carno) flesh/meat
carnal, (L. carnalis) fleshy
carnif -ex -ic, (L. carnifex) an executioner/hangman/murderer/tormentor
carno, (Gr. καρνον) a Gallic horn
carnos, (L. carnosus) fleshy
caro, (Gr. καρος) heavy sleep/torpor
carot -ic, (Gr. καρωτικος) stupefying/soporific
carp -o -us, (Gr. καρπος) fruit/fruits of the earth/corn/seed
carp -o -us, (L. carpus) the wrist
carpalimo, (Gr. καρπαλιμος) swift/eager/ravenous
carph -o -us, (Gr. καρφος) dry twigs/chips/straws/bits of wood
carpin -us, (L. carpinus) the hornbeam (*Carpinus* spp.)
carpt-us, (L. carpere) to pluck/pull off/select/separate
carsio, (Gr. καρσιος) crosswise
cartero, (Gr. καρτερος) strong/staunch
cartilag -in -o, (L. cartilago) cartilage/gristle
carto, (Gr. καρτος) shorn close/shortened/chopped/sliced
caruncul, (L. caruncula) small piece of flesh
carus, (L. carus) dear
cary -o -um, (Gr. καρυον) any kind of nut/stone/kernel
casa, (L. casa) cottage/cabin/hut
casc, (L. cascus) old
case -i -us, (L. caseus) cheese
casio, (Gr. κασις) brother/sister
cask, (Sp. casco) potsherd/skull/helmet
cassi -di -s, (L. cassis) a metal helmet
cast, (L. castus) pure/virtuous
castane -a, (L. castanea) the chestnut tree (*Castanea* spp.)/chestnut
castig, (L. castigare) to reprove/chasten/punish
castor, (L. castor Gr. καστωρ) the beaver (*Castor fiber*)
castr, (L. castare) to castrate
castus, (L. castus) pure
casu, (L. casus) falling/accident/opportunity
cat -a -o, (Gr. κατα) down from/down towards/down upon

catabasi, (Gr. καταβασις) way down/descent
cataclito, (Gr. κατακλιτον) a couch
cataclysm, (Gr. κατακλυσμος) flood/deluge/disaster
catacto, (Gr. κατακτος) breakable
catactrio, (Gr. κατακτρια) a spinner (particularly a woman)
cataegis, (Gr. καταιγις) hurricane/whirlwind
catagma -to, (Gr. καταγμα) fragment/breakage/fracture/flock of wool
cataleps, (Gr. καταληψις) fit/seizure/seizing/assaulting
catalysi -s, (Gr. καταλυσις) dissolving/dissolution/putting down
catant, (Gr. καταντα) downhill/below
cataract, (Gr. καταρακτης) waterfall
catarato, (Gr. καταρατος κατηρητος) cursed/abominable
catast, (L. catasta) scaffold
catax, (L. catacis) limping/lame
catelipho, (Gr. κατηλιψ/κατηλιφος) ladder/staircase/roof beam/upper story
caten -a -ari, (L. catena) chain/fetter/restraint
catepho, (Gr. κατηφης) downcast/mute/dejected
catero, (Gr. κατηρης) furnished with
cathamma -to, (Gr. καθαμμα) a knot
cathar -o, (Gr. καθαρος) spotless/pure/clear
catharmato, (Gr. καθαρμα) refuse
cathart -i, (Gr. καθαρτης) purifier/cleanser
cathedr -a, (Gr. καθεδρα) a seat/chair/throne
cathep, (Gr. καθεψειν) to digest
cathet -o, (Gr. καθετηρ) anything let down into/inserted/hanging down/perpendicular
cathism -at -ato, (Gr. καθισμα) the part on which one sits/buttocks/seat
cathod, (Gr. καθοδος) descent/going down/way down
catholic -o, (Gr. καθολικος) general/universal
catill -o, (Gr. κατιλλω) force into a narrow space/roll up/coop up
catin -us, (L. catinus) a deep dish or bowl
cato, (Gr. κατω) downwards/down from/lower
catopt -o, (Gr. κατοπτος) visible/dried up/overbaked
catoptero, (Gr. κατοπτης) a scout/spy/overseer
catoptr -o -um, (Gr. κατοπτρον) a mirror
catorycto, (Gr. κατορυκτος) buried deep
cattyo, (Gr. καττυς) a piece of leather
catul -us, (L. catulus) puppy/young animal
cau -m -s -st -t, (Gr. καυμα) burning heat (of sun)/fever heat/brand/embers
cauca, (Gr. καυκος) a type of cup
caucalias, (Gr. καυκιαλης) a type of bird
caud -a, (L. cauda) tail
caud -ex -ic, (L. caudex = codex) tree trunk/blockhead
caude, (L. caudeus) wooden
caul -i -is, (L. caulis Gr. καυλος) stem of a plant/stalk/shaft
caula, (L. caulae) a hole/opening/sheep-fold
cauma, (Gr. καυμα) burning heat (esp. of sun)/heat of the day
caunaco, (Gr. καυνακης) a thick cloak
caupo, (L. caupo) small shopkeeper/inn-keeper
caurinus, (L. Caurus) the north-west wind
caus -t, (Gr. καυσις) burning/smelting
causalido, (Gr. καυσαλις) blister/burn
causia, (Gr. καυσια) a broad-brimmed felt hat
caut, (Gr. καυτηρ) burner
cauter, (Gr. καυτηρ) branding iron/burner
cautes, (L. cautes) a rough sharp rock
cav -a -e -i, (L. cavus/cavum) hollow/hole/cave

caval, (Fr. cheval) horse
cave, (L. caverna) cave/ship's hold
cavill -a, (L. cavilla) jesting/scoffing
caesm, (Gr. κεασματα) chips/splinters
ceanoth -us, (Gr. κεανωθος) the corn thistle (*Carduus arvensis*)
ceb -o -us, (Gr. κηβος) a long-tailed monkey (?a mangabey)
cebl -a -o, (Gr. κεβλη) head
ceblo, (Gr. κεβλος) a dog-faced baboon (?*Papio cynocephalus*)
cec, (L. caecus) blind/hidden/unseen/obscure/dark
cecheno, (Gr. κεχηνα) gaping/yawning
ceci -do -s, (Gr. κεκιδιον) little nut/ink-gall
cecibalo, (Gr. κηκιβαλος) a kind of shellfish
cecrop -i, (Gr. κεκροψ) myth. king of Athens
cecryphalo, (Gr. κεκρυφαλος) woman's hairnet/pouch or belly of a hunting net
cedemon, (Gr. κηδεμων) guardian/protector/mourner
cedno, (Gr. κεδνος) careful/diligent/trusty
cedo, (Gr. κηδος) care/concern/anxiety/grief
cedr -o -us, (Gr. κεδρος) the cedar tree (*Cedrus* spp.)/cedar wood
cei, (Gr. κει) in that place
celad -o -us, (Gr. κελαδος) poet. sound of rushing water/loud clear voice/ shout/din/
        clamour
celaeno, (Gr. κελαινος) black/dark/murky
celat, (L. celo) concealed
cele, (Gr. κηλη) tumour/hernia/rupture
celebo, (Gr. κελεβη) cup/jar
celebr, (L. celeber) famous/celebrated
celeo, Gr. (κηλεω) charm/bewitch/beguile
celeo, (Gr. κελεος) the green woodpecker (*Picus viridis*)
celeonto, (Gr. κελεοντες) the vertical beams of a loom
celepho, (Gr. κελεφος) a leper
celer -i, (L. celer) swift/quick/rapid
celest -i, (L. caelestis) heavenly
celet, (L. celo) concealed
celetico, (Gr. κηλητικος) charming
celeto, (Gr. κελης) riding-horse/fast-sailing yatch
celeusmo, (Gr. κελευσμος) order/command
celeutho, (Gr. κελευθος) road/path/journey/voyage/walk/gait
celi -a, (Gr. κοιλος) a hollow/cavity/body cavities/ventricles
celi -do -s, (Gr. κηλις) spot/stain/defilement
celib, (L. caelebs) unmarried
cell -a -i, (L. cella) room/storeroom/garret/compartment/granary
-cella, -cellum, -cellus, (L.) dim. Suf.
cellu, (L. cellula) small room
celo, (Gr. κηλον) arrow shaft
celono, (Gr. κηλωνος) a swing-beam for drawing water/male ass
celoro, (Gr. κελωρ) son/eunuch
celox, (L. celox) swift/quick/a yatch/a cutter
celyph -o -us, (Gr. κελυφος) pod/shell/sheath/encasing membrane
-cem, (Gr. κεμως) muzzle
cemet, (Gr. κοιμητηρια) sleeping-room/burial-place
cen -o, (Gr. κιονος/κοινως) recent/in common/shared/in general
cenchri, (Gr. κεγχρος) millet
cenchris, (Gr. κεγχρις) a kind of small millet-eating bird (? a bunting)
cenclo, (Gr. κηξ/κηκος) a sea-bird (? a tern)
-cene, (Gr. καινος) new/recent
cenebrio, (Gr. κενεβρειος) carrion (esp. of dead cattle)

ceneono, (Gr. κενεων) flank/the hollow between ribs and hips
cent -e, (Gr. κεντειν) to prick/sting/goad/stab
cent -en -i, (L. centum) a hundred
centau -r, (Gr. κενταυρος) Centaur/spearman
centes -is, (Gr. κεντημα) prick/dot/puncture/sting
centesim, (L. centesimus) the hundredth
cento, (L. cento) patchwork/a covering to ward off missiles or extinguish fires
centr i -o -um, (Gr. κεντρον) any sharp point/goad/spur/point/the point round which a
        circle is described
ceo, (Gr. κειω) cleave/split
ceodo, (Gr. κηωδης) fragrant/incense-like
cep -a -ol, (L. caepa) an onion
cep, (NL. ceps) head
cepaeo, (Gr. κηπαιος) of or from a garden/cultivated
cephal -a -o, (Gr. κεφαλη) head
cepheno, (Gr. κηφην) a drone/a lazy vagabond
cepo, (Gr. κηπος) a garden/orchard/plantation
cepph -us, (Gr. κεπφος) a sea-bird, perh. a storm-petrel/a feather-brained fellow
-ceps, (NL. ceps) the head
cer -a -e -i, (L. cera) wax
cera -t -o, (Gr. κερας) animal's horn
ceram -o -us, (Gr. κεραμος) potter's clay or earth/earthen vessel
cerambyc -o, (Gr. κεραμβυξ) a longicorn beetle
ceraphido, (Gr. κεραφις) a kind of locust
ceras -us, (L. cerasus) a cherry tree/cherry
cerasto, (Gr. κεραστης) horned
ceraun -o -us, (Gr. κεραυνιος) of a thunderbolt
cerc -i -is, (Gr. κερκις) weaver's shuttle/a rod/dowel
cerc -o -us, (Gr. κερκος) the tail of a beast
cercaria, (NL. cercaria) tailed
cerchne, (Gr. κερχνη) a kind of hawk, prob. a kestrel (*Falco tinnunculus*)
cercis, (Gr. κερκις) a weaver's shuttle
cercop -i -s, (Gr. κερκωψ) myth. a man-monkey/knave
cercyo, (Gr. Κερκυον) a notorious Attic robber
cerd -al, (Gr. κερδαλεος) crafty/cunning/a fox
cerdo, (Gr. κερδος) profit/gain/cunning
cere, (L. Ceres) myth. goddess of agriculture
cere, (L. cereus) waxen/the cells of a hive/wax-coloured
cereal, (L. cerealia) corn or any edible grain (from Ceres, goddess of agriculture)
cereb -r -ro, (L. cerebrum) the brain
cerebellum, (L. cerebellum) the small brain
ceresio, (Gr. κηρεσιος) deadly/pernicious
ceri, (L. cera) wax
cerin, (L. cerinus) wax-coloured/yellowish
cerio, (Gr. κηριον) honeycomb/anything pleasant
cermato, (Gr. κερματος) fragment/small coin
cern, (L. cernere) to separate/sift/distinguish/decide
cerno, (Gr. κερνος) a type of earthen dish with small pots attached
cernu, (L. cernuus) nodding/drooping slightly/falling face down
cero, (Gr. κερκος) tail
cero, (Gr. κηρος) wax/bee's wax
cerom -a, (Gr. κηρωμα) a wax-salve/ointment
cert -a, (L. cartare) to settle by contest/contend/struggle
cert -a, (L. certus) settled/resolved/decided/undoubted/certain
certhi, (Gr. κερθιος) a little bird, perh. the tree-creeper (*Certhia familiaris*)
cerule, (L. caeruleus) blue

ceruss -a, (L. cerussa) white lead
cerv -us, (L. cervus) deer/stag
cervi -c -x, (L. cervix) the nape of the neck/the neck
ceryco, (Gr. κηρυξ) herald/messenger/crier
ceryl -us, (Gr. κηρυλος) a fabulous sea-bird, perh. a male kingfisher
cesi, (L. caesius) bluish-grey
cespi, (L. caespes) a turf/sod/grassy sward
cess -a, (L. cessare) to delay/cease/be idle/lie fallow
cest -o, (Gr. κεστος) the charmed girdle of Venus (Aphrodite)/a girdle
cestr -a, (Gr. κεστρα) pickaxe/poleaxe/hammer/a kind of fish
cestro, (Gr. κεστρα) a hammer
cet -a -us, (Gr. κητος) sea monster; later a whale
cethario, (Gr. κεθαριον) a dice-box
cethido, (Gr. κεθις) ballot-box/voting urn
cetio, (Gr. κητειος) monstrous
cetr -a, (L. caetra) a short Spanish shield
cetus, (L. cetus) whale/dolphin
ceuth -o, (Gr. κευθω) cover/hide/conceal
chaem -e, (Gr. χαμαι-) on the ground/of the ground/low
chaen -o, (Gr. χαινω) gape
chaen -o, (Gr. χαινω) yawn/gape/burst with fruitfulness
chaer -o, (Gr. χαιρω) rejoice!
chaet -a -o, (Gr. χαιτη) loose, flowing hair/mane
chalar -o, (Gr. χαλαρος) slack/loose/supple/languid
chalast -o, (Gr. χαλασις) slackening/loosening/relaxation
challis -a -o, (Gr. χαλαις) hail/hail shower/storm/small pimple/tubercle
chalk -eau, (Gr. χαλκεος) of copper or bronze/brazen
chalci -d -s, (Gr. χαλκις) a bird, perh a night hawk/a migratory fish (perh. pilchard or
                sardine/a poisonous lizard/a female slave
chalepo, (Gr. χαλεπος) difficult/severe/harsh
chalic, (L. calix) goblet
chalico, (Gr. χαλιξ/χαλικος) small stone/pebble/gravel/rubble
chalin -o -us, (Gr. χαλινος) a strap/bit/thong/serpent's fangs
chalin -o, (Gr. χαλινοω) bit/bridle
chalk -o, (Gr. χαλκος) copper
chalyb -i -us, (L. chalybs) articles made of steel (horse's bit/sword/arrow tip)
chalybo, (Gr. χαλυψ) hardened iron/steel
cham -ae -e, (Gr. χαμαι-) on the ground/of the ground/low
chameleon, (Gr. χαμαιλεων) a kind of lizard (Chamaeleo spp.)
chamelos, (Gr. χαμαιλεος) on the ground/creeping/low
champs, (Gr. χαμψα) crocodile
chan -e -o, (Gr. χανων) yawn/gape
chan -o, (Gr. χανος) the mouth
chano, (Gr. χαινω) to open wide/yawn/gape
chaos, (Gr. χαος) infinite space/unformed mass
char -i -o, (Gr. χαρα) joy/delight
char, (Gr. χαρις) favour/grace
chara -c -x, (Gr. χαραξ) pointed stake/vine-prop/pole/cutting/a sea fish (bream)
chara, (L. chara) cabbage
charact -er, (Gr. χαρακτηρ) engraver/engraving tool/die/stamp
charadr -a, (Gr. χαραδρα) mountain stream/torrent/deep gully/rift/ravine
charadri -us, (Gr. χαραδριος) a bird, prob. the Norfolk plover (Charadrius spp.)
charadro, (Gr. χαραδρος) full of gullies
charagma, (Gr. χαραγμα) any engraved, cut or stamped mark
chari -s -t, (Gr. χαρις) favour/grace/beauty
chariento, (Gr. χαριεντος) graceful/beautiful/gracious

charis, (Gr. χαρις) grace/kindness/beauty
charops, (Gr. χαροψ) bright-eyed
chart -a, (L. charta) a leaf of papyrus/a paper
chasma -to, (Gr. χασμα) a yawning chasm/gulf/gaping mouth
chaulio, (Gr. χαυλιος) outstanding/projecting
chauliodont, (Gr. χαυλιοδους) with projecting teeth/tusks
chaun -o -us, (Gr. χαυνος) porous/spongy/empty/foolish
chaun -o, (Gr. χαυνοω) puff-up/fill with conceit
chauna -x, (Gr. χαυναξ) liar/braggart/impostor
cheil -o -us, (Gr. χειλος) the edge/brink/a lip/muzzle
cheim -o, (Gr. χειμα) winter/cold/frost
chein, (Gr. χεειν) to pour
cheir -o, (Gr. χειρ) the hand
chel -a -i, (Gr. χηλη) a claw/a hoof/a talon
chel -on -ona -y -ys, (Gr. χελωνη) a tortoise/turtle
cheleum -a, (Gr. χηλευμα) awl
cheleuto, (Gr. χηλευτος) plaited/netted
chelidon, (Gr. χελιδων) a swallow (Hirundinidae)
chelin -o, (Gr. χηλινος) netted/plaited
chelom -a, (Gr. χηλωμα) a notch
chelonis, (Gr. χελωνις) a lyre
chelos, (Gr. χηλος) a large chest/coffer/coffin
chelydr -o -us, (Gr. χελυδρος) an amphibious serpent/kind of tortoise
chelyne, (Gr. χελυνη) lip/jaw
chem, (Gr. χημη) yawning/gaping/a clam
chemi, (Gr. χημεια) alchemy/chemistry/a transmutation
chemo, (Ar. alchimia) pertaining to chemistry and chemical terms
chen -o, (Gr. χην) a goose (*Anser* spp.)
cheo, (Gr. χεω) to pour/melt/scatter
chera, (Gr. χηρα/χηρη) widow
cherado, (Gr. χεραδος) silt/gravel/alluvium/detritus
chermado, (Gr. χερμαδιον) a large pebble/stone/boulder
chern -e, (Gr. χερνητης) day labourer
chers -o, (Gr. χερσος) dry land/dry/hard/barren
chetos, (Gr. χητος) need/want/lack
cheum -a, (Gr. χευμα) something poured/a stream
chi, (Gr. χι χ X) twenty-second letter of the Greek alphabet
chias -m -t, (Gr. χιασμα) cross/cross piece/decussation
chil -o -us, (Gr. χειλος) lip/bill/beak/edge/rim/fodder
chili -o, (Gr. χιλιας) a thousand
chim -a -ato -o, (Gr. χειμα) winter/winter weather/cold/frost
chimaer -a, (Gr. χιμαιρα) a fire-breathing monster/she-goat
chimato, (Gr. χειμα) winter weather/cold/frost/winter/storm
chimer -a, (Gr. χιμαιρα) fire-breathing monster/she-goat
chion, (Gr. χιων) snow
chir -o, (Gr. χειρ) the hand
chirido, (Gr. χερυδριον) little hand/little arm/glove/sleeve
Chiron, (Gr. Χειρων) a centaur reputed for his skill in medicine
chironom -us, (Gr. χειρονομεω) I gesticulate
chithr, (Gr. χυθριδιον) little pot
chito, (Gr. χιτων) a tunic
chlaen -a -o, (Gr. χλαινα) cloak/wrapper
chlamy -d -do -s, (Gr. χλαμυς) a short cloak/mantle
chlan -a, (Gr. χλαινα) cloak/wrapper
chlani -do -s, (Gr. χλανις) woollen garment

chlaro, (Gr. χλαρος) gay/lively
chledo, (Gr. χληδος) mud/dirt/debris
chleuast, (Gr. χλευαστης) a mocker/scoffer
chliaro, (Gr. χλιαρος) warm (of food)/lukewarm (of people)
chlidan -o, (Gr. χλιδανος) delicate/luxurious/voluptuous
chlidono, (Gr. χλιδων) bracelet/anklet/ornament
chlo -a, (Gr. χλοη) young green corn or grass/first green shoot
chloanth, (Gr. χλοανθεο) bud/sprout
chlor -o, (Gr. χλωρος) greenish/greenish-yellow/pale green
chlorion, (Gr. χλοριων) the golden oriole (*Oriolus oriolus*)
chloris, (Gr. Χλορις) a goddess of buds and flowers
chnauma, (Gr. χναυμα) piece/slice/tit-bit
chnauro, (Gr. χναυρος) dainty
chnoe, (Gr. χνοη) the axle-box, nave or hub of a wheel
chnu, (Gr. χνους) any light, porous substance
choan -a -o, (Gr. χοανη) a funnel
choe, (Gr. χοη) a pouring-out/drink-offering
choem -e, (Gr. χαμαι-) on the ground/of the ground/low
choer -o, (Gr. χοιρος) piglet
choico, (Gr. χοικος) of earth or clay
chol -a -e -o, (Gr. χολη) gall/bile/bitter anger
chol -as -o, (Gr. χωλος) lame/halting/limping/defective
chola -d -s, (Gr. χολαδες) guts, bowels of oxen
choler -a, (Gr. χολερα) cholera
choli -c -x, (Gr. χολιξ) guts, bowels of oxen
chomato, (Gr. χωματος) dam/mound/bank
chondr -o -us, (Gr. χονδρος) coarse grains/granules/cartilage
chondrill -a, (Gr. χονδριλλη) a lump
chone, (Gr. χωνη) a funnel
chor -a, (Gr. χωρα) a space/room/place
chor -is, (Gr. χορις) separate
chor -ism -ismos, (Gr. χωρισμος) separation/separated
chor -o -eo, (Gr. χωρεω) spread abroad/disperse
chor -o, (L. chorus Gr. χορος) a dance
chord -a, (Gr. χορδη) a string (of gut)
chordeuma, (Gr. χορδευμα) sausage/black pudding
chore -o, (Gr. χορευω) dance/choral dance/of any circling motion
chore -o, (Gr. χορεω) withdraw/go/make way
choret -es, (Gr. χωριτης) an inhabitant of the country/a rustic
chori -i -o -um, (Gr. χοριον) skin/leather/membrane surrounding a foetus/any intestinal
          membrane
chori -st, (Gr. χωριστος) separable
choro, (Gr. χορος) a circling dance/a place for dancing/a choir/a troop/band
choro, (Gr. χωρος) a place/piece of ground/land country
chort -o -us, (Gr. χορτος) feeding place/farmyard/fodder
chrema -to, (Gr. χρεμα) a need/money/goods
chreo, (Gr. χρεος) debt/obligation
chres -is, (Gr. χρησις) employment/use
chres -to, (Gr. χρηστης) prophet/soothsayer/useful/serviceable
chresmo, (Gr. χρησμος) an oracle/prophet
chrisma -to, (Gr. χρισμα) ointment/unction
christ -o, (Gr. χριστος) anointed
chro -s -t -to, (Gr. χρως) colour/skin/flesh/complexion
chroa, (Gr. χροια) skin/surface/appearance/complexion
chrom -a -ato -o, (Gr. χρωμα) colour

chromo, (Gr. χρομος) neighing/noise
chron -i -o -us, (Gr. χρονος) time
chryma, (Gr. χρισμα) an unguent/salve
chrys -o -us, (Gr. χρυσος) gold
chrysal, (Gr. χρυσαλλις) gold-coloured sheath of butterflies
chthalamos, (Gr. χθαμαλος) near the ground/on the ground/low
chthon -o, (Gr. χθων) the ground/earth
chyl -o, (Gr. χυλος) juice/moisture
chym -o, (Gr. χυμος) juice/flavour
chyt -lo, (Gr. χυτλον) anything that can be poured
chyt-os, (Gr. χυτος) poured/heaped up/shed (as in discard)
chytr -a -o, (Gr. χυτρα) earthen pot/jug
cib -ar, (L. cibus) food/rations
cibdelus, (Gr. κιβδηλος) spurious/adulterated/false
cibori -um, (L. ciborium) large drinking vessel
ciboto, (Gr. κιβωτος) box/chest/coffer
cicad -a, (L. cicada) grasshopper
cicatr -ic -ix, (L. cicatrix) a scar
cichl -a, (Gr. κιχλη) a thrush (generic term)/a sea-fish (*Wrasse* spp.)
cichori -um, (Gr. κιχορα) chicory
cicindel -a, (L. cicindela) a gloworm
cicinn -o -us, (Gr. κικιννος) ringlet
cicon -i, (L. ciconia) a stork
cicut -a, (L. cicuta) hemlock
cicy -s, (Gr. κικυς) vigour/strength
cidapho, (Gr. κιδαφος) wily
cidar -i -s, (Gr. κιδαρις) turban/crown/tiara of ancient Persians
-cide, (L. caedere) to kill
cili -a -o -um, (L. cilium) an eyelash/eyelid/a small hair
-cilla, -cillum, -cellus, (L.) dim. suf.
cilliba, (Gr. κιλλιβας) a three-legged stand/shield-stand/easel
cillico, (Gr. κιλλιξ) an ox with crooked horns
cillo, (Gr. κιλλος) an ass
clm -ex -ic, (L. cimex) a bug
cimbic, (Gr. κιμβιξ) skinflint/niggard
cimeli -um, (Gr. κειμηλιον) treasure/heirloom
cimoli -a, (Gr. κιμωλια) a white clay
-cin, (L. caedere) to kill
cinaed, (Gr. κιναιδος) lewd/wanton
cincinn, (L. cincinnus) curled hair/a lock of hair
cincl -is, (Gr. κιγκλις) latticed gate
cincl -o -us, (Gr. κινκλος) the wagtail
cinct, (L. cinctum/cinctutus) girdle/girdled
cindyno, (Gr. κινδυνος) hazard/danger/venture
cine -ma -mato -s -t, (Gr. κινεσις) movement
cine, (Gr. κινησις) motion/movement
ciner -ar -e -i, (L. cinereus) ashen
cinetro, (Gr. κινητρον) ladle/stirring rod
cingul -um, (L. cingulum) girdle/sword belt
cini -s, (L. cinis) ashes
cinnabar, (L. cinnabaris) a red or vermilion pigment (red sulphide of mercury)
cinnyr -is, (Gr. κιννυριδες) a small bird
cinygm -a -ato, (Gr. κινυγμα) a floating body/anything moved about
cinyro, (Gr. κινυρος) wailing/plaintive
cio, (Gr. κις/κιος) a weevil
cion -o, (Gr. κιων) a pillar/the division of the nostrils/the uvula

cipher, (Ar. sifr) empty

cipit, (NL. ceps) the head

cippus, (L. cuippus) a stake/tombstone/palisades

circ -a -e, (L. Circe Gr. κιρκη) Circe, an enchantress

circ -a, (L. circa) round about

circ -i -in -ul, (L. circus) a ring/circle/circuit/circular figure

circ -us, (Gr. κιρκος) a type of hawk or falcon/a kind of wolf/circle/ring

circ, (L. circum) around

circinate, (L. circinatus) coiled/curled away from the apex

circum, (L. circum) round about/around

ciris, (Gr. κιρις/κιρρις) a sea-fish, prob. a species of Wrasse

ciro, (Gr. κειρω) cut short/shear/clip/cut down/waste/destroy

cirr -us, (L. cirrus) a curl/lock/ringlet

cirrh -o, (Gr. κιρρος) a tawny-orange

cirs -o -um, (Gr. κιρσος) an enlarged vein/varicose vein

cirsi -um, (Gr. κιρσιον) a kind of thistle (Cirsium spp.)

cirso, (Gr. κιρσος) a dilated vein/a varicosity

cis, (L. cis) on this side (opp. = trans)

cis, (NL. cis, from Gr. κισ/κιος) a weevil

cisero, (Gr. κισηρις) pumice-stone

ciss -o -us, (Gr. κισσος) ivy (Hedera helix)

cist -a, (Gr. κιστη) basket/hamper/voting urn

cistern -a, (L. cisterna) underground reservoir for water

cit, (L. citatus) quick/swift

citat -us, (L. citatus) swift/hastened on/incited

citer, (L. citer) near/close

cithar, (Gr. κιθαρα) a lyre

citimus, (L. citimus) nearest

citr -in -o, (Gr. κιτρινος) of a lemon tree/lemon/yellow

citta, (Gr. κιττα/κισσα) the jay, a chattering bird (Garrulus glandarius)

citus, (L. citus) swift/quick

-cium/-cion, (Gr. -κιον) a pillar/the uvula

cixallo, (Gr. κιξαλλης) a highway robber

cixi, (Gr. κικυς) poet. strength/vigour

clad -i -o -us, (Gr. κλαδος) a young branch or shoot

cladar -o, (Gr. κλαδαρος) quivering/'whippy' in the shaft/wavy

clades, (L. clades) destruction/disaster/injury

claen, (Gr. κλαιω) lament

clagero, (Gr. κλαγερος) screaming (of cranes)

clam -a-or, (L. clamare) to call/shout/cry aloud

clam, (L. clam) secretly

clamb -o, (Gr. κλαμβος) docked/cropped/deficient

clandestin, (L. clandestinus) secret/concealed/hidden

clangul -a, (L. clangor) a sound/clang/noise (of birds/trumpet)

clanio, (Gr. κλανιον) bracelet

clar -a -i, (L. clareo) to be bright/to shine/to be evident

clar, (L. clarus) clear/distinct

clas -i -m -t, (Gr. κλασις) breaking/fracture

clasm -a -ato, (Gr. κλασμα) a fragment/piece/morsel

clast -o, (Gr. κλαστος) broken in pieces

claster -i -ium, (Gr. κλαστεριον) knife for dressing vines

clathr, (Gr. κληθρα) bars/lattice/trellis/grating

claud -i, (L. claudus) limping/halting/lame

claus -us, (L. clausum) shut/close/conclude

clausto, (Gr. κλαυστος) mournful

claustr, (L. claustrum) a bolt/bar/enclosure/prison

clauthmo, (Gr. κλαυθμνος) weeping

clav -a -i, (L. clava) club/cudgel
clav -us, (L. clavus) a nail/a stripe on a tunic
clav, (L. clavis) key
-cle, (L. -culus) dim. suf.
cleav, (AS. cleofan) to cut
cledono, (Gr. κληδων) omen
clei -o -us, (Gr. κλεις) collar bone/bar/bolt/hook/key
cleis -is -to, (Gr. κλεισις) closing
cleist, (Gr. κλειστος) to be shut/closed
cleithr -um, (Gr. κλειθρον) bolt/bar for closing a door/key
clem -a -t -tis, (Gr. κληματις) vine branch/brushwood/faggots
clemato, (Gr. κλημα/κλεμμα) twig/branch/cutting
clemen-s -t, (L. clamens) mild/placid/kind/merciful
clemma -to, (Gr. κλεμμα) theft
clemmy -s, (Gr. κλεμμυς) a tortoise
cleo -to, (Gr. κλεος) rumour/report/fame/glory
clep -s -si, (Gr. κλεψ) thief
clepsydr -a, (Gr. κλεψυδρα) a water-clock
clept -o, (Gr. κλεπτω) steal/spirit away/cheat
clepto, (Gr. κλεπτω) steal
cler -i -o -us, (Gr. κληρος) something assigned by lot (piece of land)/inheritance
cleros, (Gr. κληρος) a beetle (Clerus apiarius) destructive in bee-hives
-cles, (Gr. -κλης) suf. of many Greek proper names to indicate fame/honour
clethr -um, (Gr. κλειθρον) bolt/bar for closing a door/key
clethra, (Gr. κληθρα) the alder (Alnus glutinosa)
cleto, (Gr. κλητεος) called/invited/summoned
clid -o -us, (Gr. κλεις) a key
clima -c -x, (Gr. κλιμαξ) ladder/staircase
clima -to, (Gr. κλιμα) slope/incline/climate/region/zone
climact, (Gr. κλιμακτηρ) a step of a ladder/staircase
clin -a -i -o, (Gr. κλινις/κλινη) a small couch/bed
clin -o, (Gr. κλινειν) to slant/slope/incline
clin, (L. clinare) to bend
clinat -us, (Gr. κλινω) bend/slope/slat/tend
clio -to, (Gr. κλεος) rumour/report/fame/glory
clipe -o -us, (L. clipeus) a round shield
clis -eo -i, (Gr. κλισια) hut/shed/booth/couch
clis -is, (Gr. κλισις) bending/inclination
clismo, (Gr. κλισμος) couch/inclination/slope
clisto, (Gr. κλειστος) closed/shut/barred
clitell, (L. clittellae) pack saddle/pair of panniers
clithr -o -um, (Gr. κλειθρον) bolt/bar for closing a door/key
clithrid -io, (Gr. κλειθριδιον) little keyhole/cleft/chink
clito, (Gr. κλιτος) slope/hillside
cliv -us, (L. clivus) slope
cloac -a, (L. cloaca) a sewer
clobo, (Gr. κλωβος) bird-cage
cloeo, (Gr. κλοιος) dog-collar/pillory
clogmo, (Gr. κλωγμος) a clucking sound (with which a horse is urged on)
clomaco, (Gr. κλωμαξ) a heap of stones/a rocky place
clon -us, (Gr. κλονος) violent movement/confused motion/turmoil
clon, (Gr. κλων) a twig/branch
clope, (Gr. κλοπη) fraud/theft
clopo, (Gr. κλωψ) thief
clos, (L. clausus) shut
closmat -o, (Gr. κλωσμα) thread/line/clue/thread of fate

clost -er -ri, (Gr. κλωστηρ) thread/yarn/skein
clost -o, (Gr. κλωστος) spun
clostellum, (L. clostellum) a small lock
clostero, (Gr. κλωστηρ) a spindle
clu -d -s, (L. claudere) to close
clun, (L. clunes) buttocks
clupe -us, (L. clupea) a river fish
clur -inh, (L. clurinus) pertaining to apes
clus -us, (L. clusus) shut/closed
clydon -o, (Gr. κλυδων) a wave/billow
clymeno, (Gr. κλυμενος) famous/infamous
clype -o -us, (L. clypeus) a shield
clys -is -m, (Gr. κλυσμα) drench/washed by waves
clyst -er -ero, (Gr. κλυστηρ) a syringe
clyt -o, (Gr. κλυτος) renowned/glorious/noble/splendid
clyzo, (Gr. κλυζω) wash/purge/rinse out
cmelethro, (Gr. κμελεθρον) a beam
cnapho, (Gr. κναφος) the teasel (*Dipsacus* spp.) a carding comb
cnec -o -us, (Gr. κνηκος) pale yellow/tawny
cnem -a -i -is, (Gr. κνημη/κνημις) the tibia/legging
cnepha -to, (Gr. κνεφας) darkness/twilight
cnest -i, (Gr. κνηστηρ) scraping knife
cneth -o, (Gr. κνηθω) scratch/scrape/tickle/itch
cnic -us, (Gr. κνηκος) a kind of thistle
cnid -a -o, (Gr. κνιδη) a nettle (*Urtica dioica*)
cnipo, (Gr. κνιπος) niggardly/miserly
cnism -a -ato, (Gr. κνισμος) itching/tickling
cnodal -o, (Gr. κνωδαλον) any wild animal
cnodax, (Gr. κνωδαξ) pin/pivot
cnodo, (Gr. κνωδων) a sword
cnopo, (Gr. κνοπευς) a bear (*Ursus* spp.)
cnyzemato, (Gr. κνυζημα) whimper/whine
co -l -m -n, (L. cum) with/together
coagul, (L. coagulum) curdle
coal -es, (L. coalesere) to grow together/to take root/to grow
coarct, (L. coarctare) to press together
cobalo, (Gr. κοβαλος) rogue/knave
cobelo, (Gr. κωβηλη) needle
cobit, (Gr. κοβιτ) a gudgeon-like fish
cocc -i -o -us, (Gr. κοκκος) grain/berry/a kernel
coccin, (L. coccineus) scarlet
coccy -g -x -z, (Gr. κοκκυξ) a cuckoo (from its cry)
cochl -ea, (L. cochlea) snail/snail shell/spiral/spoon
cochli, (Gr. κοχλιας) a spiral-shelled snail
cod -eia -ia, (Gr. κωδεια) the head/the head of a poppy
cod -ex -ic, (L. codex) a ledger
coda, (L. cauda) tail
codio, (Gr. κωδιον) dim. of κωας, fleece
codon, (Gr. κωδων) a bell
coec, (L. caecus) blind/hidden/unseen/obscure/dark
coel -i -o, (Gr. κοιλος) hollow
coeles -t, (L. caelestis) heavenly
coelia, (Gr. κιολια) belly/intestines
coelo -m, (Gr. κοιλωμα) a hollow/a cavity
coemema, (Gr. κοιμημα) sleep
coen -o, (Gr. κοινος) in common/common

coepio, (L. coepere) to begin
coeran, (Gr. κοιρανος) ruler/leader/commander
coereb, (Br. coereba) a kind of bird (*Coereba flaveola*)
coerule, (L. caeruleus) azure
coet -o, (Gr. κοιτος) resting place/bed/sleep
coffin, (Gr. κοφινος) basket
coilia, (Gr. κοιλια) the belly/bowels/intestines
coit -us, (L. coitio) a coming together/meeting/sexual union
coite, (Gr. κιοτη) bed/lair/nest/pen/fold/lodging
coito, (Gr. κοιτος) resting place/bed/sleep
col -o -on, (Gr. κολον) colon
col -o, (Gr. κολος) curtailed
col -o, (Gr. κωλον) member of the body/limb
col, (L. colere) to inhabit/dwell
col-, (L. cum) together
-cola, (L. colere) dweller/inhabitant
colaco, (Gr. κολαξ) flatterer
colapt -o, (Gr. κολαπτω) peck (of birds)/strike (of a horse's hoof)/carve/engrave/
        hew/cut/chisel
colasto, (Gr. κολαστης) a punisher
cole -o, (Gr. κολεος) a sheath
colero, (Gr. κολερος) short-woolled
coli -o -us, (Gr. κολιος) the green woodpecker (*Picus viridis*)
colic -o, (Gr. κωλικος) suffering in the colon
colinus, (Nahuatl (Mex.) zolin) the bobwhite (*Colinus virginianus*)
coll -a, (Gr. κολλα) glue
coll -i, (L. collum) neck/throat
collari, (L. collare) a chain for the neck
collat, (L. collate) bring together/compare
collet, (Gr. κολλητος) glued together/closely joined
colli -s, (L. collis) hill/high ground
collicul, (L. colliculus) little hill
collig -at, (L. colligat) bound together
collin, (L. collis) a hill/high ground
collod, (Gr. κολλωδες) glue-like/viscous
collopo, (Gr. κολλα) glue
collum, (L. collum) neck/throat
collyr -a, (Gr. χολλυρα) roll of coarse bread/cake
colo -bo, (Gr. κολοβος) curtailed/docked/shortened
colocynth -a, (Gr. κολοκυνθη) round gourd (*Cucurbita maxima*)
colon -i -y, (L. colonia) farm/settlement
colon -ic, (Gr. κολον) the colon; part of the large intestine
colono, (Gr. κολωνος) hill/mound/barrow
colophon -o, (Gr. κολοφων) summit/top/finishing touch
color -i, (L. color) colour/tint/hue
colos, (Gr. κολος) curtailed/docked
coloss -o, (Gr. κολοσσιαιος) colossal/gigantic
-colous, (L. colere) to inhabit/dwell
colp -o -us, (Gr. κολπος) bosom/vagina/womb/fold of a garment
colub -er -t, (L. coluber) a snake
columb -a, (L. columba) a pigeon/dove
column -a, (L. columna) column/pillar
-colus, (L. colere) to inhabit/dwell
colus, (L. colus) a distaff
colymato, (Gr. κωλυματος) hindrance
colymb -is, (Gr. κολυμβις) a diver/diving bird, prob. the grebe (*Podiceps* spp.)

colymb -o, (Gr. κολυμβαω) dive/plunge headlong/swim
colythro, (Gr. κολυθρον) a ripe fig
colythro, (Gr. κολυθρος) a testicle
colytico, (Gr. κωλυτικος) hindering/checking/preventing
com-, (L. cum) together
coma, (Gr. κωμα) deep sleep
coma, (L. coma Gr. κομη) hair
comaco, (Gr. κωμαξ) debauchee
comast, (Gr. κωμαστης) reveller
comatus, (L. comatus) with long hair/shaggy/hairy
combo, (Gr. κομβος) roll/band/girth
comi -d, (Gr. κομιδη) care bestowed/supplies
comis, (L. comis) courteous/kind/friendly
comisto, (Gr. κομιστης) caretaker/guardian
comma, (Gr. κομμα) a piece/coinage/embellishment/stamp
commis, (L. commisura) joining together/connection/joint/knot
commo, (Gr. κομμος) dirge/lamentation
commod, (L. commodus) suitable/obliging/fitting
commun, (L. communis) common/general
commus, (Gr. κομμος) lamentation/adornment/molar teeth
como, (Gr. κωμος) revel/festivity
comos, (L. comosus) hairy/with long hair/downy
comp -o, (L. κομπος) din/clash/boast/vaunt
compell, (L. compellere) to force/impel
compil, (L. compilare) to plunder/bundle together
compl, (L. complere) to fill up
compo, (Gr. κομπος) din/clash/boast/vaunt
compress, (L. comprimere) to compress
comps -o, (Gr. κομψος) refined/gentlemanly/smart/clever
compt, (L. comptum) adornment (esp. of the hair)
comytho, (Gr. κωμυς) bundle/sheath of hay/branch of laurel
con -o -us, (Gr. κωνος) cone
con, (L. cum) with/together
conabo, (Gr. κοναβος) ringing/clashing/din
conario, (Gr. κωναριον) the pineal gland (a cone-shaped structure)
conaro, (Gr. κοναρος) fat/well-fed
conch -a -o, (L. concha Gr. κογχη) a shell
conchyli -o -um, (Gr. κογχυλιον) any mollusc or its shell
conchyli -o, (Gr. κογχυλιος) purple
condit, (L. conditum) put away/stored out of sight/hidden/withdrawn
condyl -o -us, (Gr. κονδυλος) a knuckle
cong -er, (L. conger Gr. κογγυος) a sea or conger eel
congelo, (L. congelare) to freeze/stiffen/thicken
conger -o -es -um, (L. congerere) to carry together/bring together/collect
coni -co -o -um, (Gr. κωνος) a cone/pine cone/peak of a helmet
coni -di -o -s, (Gr. κονις/κονια) dust/sand/louse egg
coniat -o, (Gr. κονιατος) plastered/daubed
conium, (Gr. κωνειου) hemlock
coniv, (L. conivere) to wink/blink
conjug, (L. conjugare) to join together
connar -us, (Gr. κονναρος) a prickly evergreen
connecto, (L. conexio) binding/fastening/joining
conno, (Gr. κοννος) beard/a trinket
conopo, (Gr. κωνωψ) gnat/mosquito
conor, (L. conor) to undertake/endeavour
conspers, (L. conspergere) to spinkle

cont -o -us, (Gr. κοντος) a punting pole/crutch/goad
contabesc, (L. contabesco) to waste away
contigu, (L. contiguus) adjoining/contiguous/near
conto, (Gr. κοντος/κονδος) short
contr -a -o, (L. contra) opposite/over/against
contumac, (L. contumax) stubborn/obstinate/firm/unyielding
conul, (L. conuli) a little cone
conus, (L. conus) cone/peak of a helmet/pine cone
convall -is, (L. convallis) a valley shut in on all sides
convolv, (L. convolvere) to roll together/intertwine
cop -a -e -i, (Gr. κωπη) oar/oar handle
cop -o, (Gr. κοπος) striking/beating/suffering/toil
copa, (L. copa) hostess of a wine shop
coph -o, (Gr. κωφος) blunt/dull/obtuse/mute/deaf
copi, (Med. L. copiare) copy
copia, (L. copia) abundance/plenty
copid, (Gr. κοπις) chopper/cleaver
copio -s, (L. copiosus) richly provided/wealthy
copo, (Gr. κοπος) striking/beating/suffering/fatigue
copr -o -us, (Gr. κοπρος) dung
copt -o, (Gr. κοπτω) smite/cut off/chop off/strike/beat
copul -a, (L. copulare) to link/join/couple
copula, (L. copula) link/bond/thong/grappling iron
cor, (L. cor) heart/mind
cor -i -o, (Gr. κορις) a bug/a kind of fish
cor-, (L. cum) with/together
cora -c -co -x, (Gr. κοραξ) crow or raven
corall -i -um, (Gr. κοραλλιον) coral
corb -i -is, (L. corbis) little basket
corchor -us, (Gr. κορχορος) the blue pimpernel (*Anagallis foemina*)/jute (*Corchorus*
        olitorius)/fat
cord -i, (L. cordis) the heart
cord, (L. chorda Gr. χορδη) cord
cordul/cordyl -e -i, (Gr. κορδυλη) a cudgel/truncheon/swelling
core, (Gr. κορη) a girl/maiden/young wife/puppet/pupil of the eye
corem -a, (Gr. κορημα) a broom/sweepings/refuse
coremato, (Gr. κορηματος) sweepings/refuse
coreo, (Gr. κορις) a kind of bug
corethr -um, (Gr. κορηθρον) a broom
cori -a -um, (L. corium) hide/leather
corm -o -us, (Gr. κορμος) tree trunk/log
corn -e, (L. corneus) horn/horny
corni -c -x, (L. cornix) the crow (*Corvus corone*)
cornu, (L. cornu) horn/drinking horn
coro, (Gr. κοροκοσμιον) pupil of the eye
coro, (Gr. κορος) satiety/surfeit
coroll -a, (L. corolla) a little crown or garland/wreath
coron -a, (L. corona) crown
corono, (Gr. κορονος) curved/crooked
corp -or -u, (L. corpora) a body
corpusc, (L. corpusculum) a little body/a small particle
correct, (L. corrigo) make straight/set right/improve
corrugat, (L. corrugare) to wrinkle up
corrupt, (L. corruptus) spoilt/damaged/corrupt
corso, (Gr. κορση) side of the head/temple
cort -ex -ic -ico, (L. cortex) bark/rind/shell
corthyo, (Gr. κορθυς) heap

cortin -a, (L. cortina) a round kettle/cauldron
corusco, (L. coruscus) a flash of light/twinkling
corv -us, (L. corvus) a crow/raven
coryc -o -us, (Gr. κωρυκος) leathern sac/wallet/scrotum
corycaeo, (Gr. κωρυκαιος) a spy
corycido, (Gr. κωρυκις) a gall on elm (*Ulmus*) leaves
corycus, (Gr. κωρυκος) a leather punch-bag
coryd -o -us, (Gr. κορυδος) the crested lark (*Galerida cristata*)
corydal -is -us, (Gr. κορυδος) a lark, esp. the crested lark (*Alauda cristata*)
coryl -us, (L. corylus) a hazel-tree (*Corylus avellana*)
corymb -us, (Gr. κορυμβος) uppermost point/top of a hill/cluster of fruit or flowers
coryn -a -et, (Gr. κορυνη) club/mace/shepherd's staff
coryno, (Gr. κορυνη) a club/mace/shepherd's staff
coryph -a, (Gr. κορυφη) head/top/top of head/top of mountain etc.
corys, (Gr. κορυς) helmet/scalp of a lion
coryst -es, (Gr. κορυστης) a warrior/helmeted man
coryth-us, (Gr. κορυθος) crested
corytho, (Gr. κορυθος) helmet
coryz -a, (Gr. κορυζα) mucous discharge from the nose; metaph. drivelling/stupidity
cos, (L. cos) any hard flinty stone/grindstone
coscin -i -um, (Gr. κοσκινον) a sieve
cosm -o, (Gr. κοσμος) well ordered/regular/moderate
cosmet -o, (Gr. κοσμητος) regular/well arranged/trim
cosmetro, (Gr. κοσμητρον) a broom
cosmo, (Gr. κοσμος) order/universe/government
cost -a, (L. costa) a rib/a side
cost -um, (L. costum Gr. κοστος) an eastern aromatic plant used as a spice
cosymbo, (Gr. κοσυμβος) fringe
cotalis, (Gr. κωταλις) pestle/ladle/stirrer
cothono, (Gr. κωθων) a drinking vessel
cothurn -us, (Gr. κοθορνος) a high boot/buskin
coticula, (L. coticula) a touchstone
cotilo, (Gr. κωτιλος) babbling/chattering/prattling/twittering
cotin -us, (Gr. κοτινος) wild olive tree
coto, (Gr. κοτος) grudge/hate/wrath
cott -us, (Gr. κοττος) a river fish/a horse
cottid, (Gr. κοττις) the cerebellum/occiput
coturni -c -x, (L. coturnix) a quail
cotyl -a -ed -o, (Gr. κοτυλη) a small cup or vessel/socket (esp. the hip)/cavity
cotyledon, (Gr. κοτυληδων) a cup-shaped hollow
cox -a -o, (L. coxa) the hip bone
crabro -n, (L. crabro) a hornet
cracc -a, (L. cracca) a kind of pulse (*Cracca spicata*)
cracen -t, (L. cracentis) slender/graceful/neat
cractico, (Gr. κρακτικος) noisy
-cracy, (Gr. κρατος) strength/might/power
cradalo, (Gr. κραδαλος) quivering
crado, (Gr. ηραδη) the quivering spray at the end of a branch (esp. of fig)
craepno, (Gr. κραιπνος) swift/rushing
crageto, (Gr. κραγετης) screamer/chatterer
cram, (AS. crammian) stuff/crowd/pack
cramato, (Gr. κραματος) a mixture/alloy
cramb -o, (L. crambe) cabbage
crambaleo, (Gr. κραμβαλεος) dry/parched/roasted
crambo, (Gr. κραμβος) dried/parched/roasted
cran -o -us, (Gr. κρανος) helmet/ships' ram

cranao, (Gr. κραναος) rugged/rocky

crang -o -on, (Gr. κραγγων) a kind of shrimp, prob. *Squilla mantis*

crani -a -o -um, (Gr. κρανιον) the skull/the head

cranter, (Gr. κραντηρ) one that accomplishes/ruler

cranter, (Gr. κραντηρες) the wisdom teeth

crapul -a, (L. crapula) drunkenness/hangover

cras -i, (Gr. κρασις) a mixing

crasped -o, (Gr. κρασπεδον) edge/border/margin

crass, (L. crassus) thick/dense/solid/misty/heavy/dull/uneducated

crastin, (L. crastina/us) tomorrow/of tomorrow

crat -ero -i -o -us, (Gr. κρατερος) strong/stout/valiant/mighty

crat -i -o, (Gr. κρατος) strength/might/power

crataeg -us, (Gr. κραταιγος) a thorn (*Crataegus* spp.)

crater -a, (L. cratera) a large bowl

cratero, (Gr. κρατερος) strong/stout/mighty

crati, (L. cratis) a wicker frame or basket

crato, (Gr. κρατερος) strong/stout/mighty

craty, (Gr. κρατερος) strong/stout/mighty

crauro, (Gr. κραυος) brittle

cre -a -o, (Gr. κρεας) flesh/meat/carcass

cre -as -at -o, (Gr. κρεας) flesh/meat/carcass

creagro, (Gr. κρεαγρα) a meat-hook

crebr, (L. crebra) thick/crowded together/close/repeated/numerous/frequent

crecto, (Gr. κρεκτος) struck to sound (as of musical instruments)

credit, (L. credo) believe/trust

cregyo, (Gr. κρηγυος) good/useful/agreeable

crem -a -o, (Gr. κρεμαστος) hung/hanging

crem -a, (L. cremare) to burn/consume by fire

-cremaster, (Gr. κρεμαστηρ) a suspender (muscles by which the testicles are suspended)

cremasto, (Gr. κρεμσατος) hung/suspended

cremat -us, (L. cremare) to burn/consume by fire

cremathro, (Gr. κρεμαθρα) a rope or basket for hanging things up

cremno, (Gr. κρημνος) precipice/crag/overhang

cren -a -o, (κρηνη) a well/a spring

cren -a -ul, (L. crena) notch/incision

creo-, (Gr. κρεο-) flesh-

creper, (L. creper) dark/obscure/uncertain

crepi -do -s, (Gr. κρηπις) foundation/shoe/half-boot

crepit, (L. crepitaculum) a rattle

crepuscul, (L. crepusculum) dusk/twilight

cresc, (L. crescere) to grow/increase

cret -a, (L. creta) chalk/a kind of fuller's earth

-cret, (L. cernere) to sift/separate

creta, (Gr. κρητη) Crete

cretus, (L. cretus) separated/sifted/distinguished

crex, (Gr. κρεξ) a long-legged bird, perh. a corn-crake (*Crex crex*) or ruff (*Philomachus pugnax*)

crib -ell -r, (L. cribellum) a sieve/little sieve

crib -r, (L. cribrum) a sieve

cribano, (Gr. κριβανος) an earthen vessel wider at the bottom than at the top

cric -o -us, (Gr. κρικος (κιρκος)) a ring/a circle

crimno, (Gr. κριμνον) coarse barley meal

crin -o -um, (Gr. κρινον) a lily

crin -o, (Gr. κρινειν) to separate/divide/choose

crini -s, (L. crinis) the hair/tail of a comet

crio, (Gr. κριος) a ram (animal)/sea monster

crionto, (Gr. κρειων) ruler/lord/master
crisi -s, (Gr. κρισις) decision/judgement/separating/dispute
crisp, (L. crispus) curly/trembling/quivering
crissum, (L. crissum) a bird's rump
crista/crysta, (L. crista) crest/plume/tuft
crith -a -o, (Gr. κριθη) barley
crithmo, (Gr. κρηθμον) samphire (*Crithmum maritimum*)
criti -c, (Gr. κριτος) chosen/separated/selected
croc -, (Gr. κροκος) the saffron (*Crocus sativus*)/the colour of saffron
croc -e, (Gr. κροκυς) thread/flock/nap/pebble
croc-, (Gr. κροκη) thread
crocalo, (Gr. κροκαλη) sea-shore/beach
crocido, (Gr. κροκυς) nap/downy fibres
crocino, (Gr. κροκινος) yellow
crocodil -us, (Gr. κροκυδιλος) the crocodile
crocydo, (Gr. κροκυς) nap/downy fibres
crogmo, (Gr. κρωγμος) the cawing of a crow (*Corvus* spp.)
cromaco, (Gr. κρωμαξ) a heap of stones
cromy -o -um, (Gr. κρομυον) an onion (*Allium cepa*)
cron, (Gr. Κρονος) Saturn (former ruler of heaven and earth)
cropio, (Gr. κροπιον) a scythe/bill-hook
cross -o, (Gr. κροσσος) fringe/tassel
cross, (Gr. κροσσαι) battlements/steps
crotal -um, (Gr. κροταλον) a castanet/rattle
crotaph -us, (Gr. κροτηφος) side of the forehead/temples
crotaphid -o, (Gr. κροταφις) a pointed hammer
croteo, (Gr. κροτεω) knock/strike/clap/gnash/hammer/rattle/clash
crotic, (Gr. κροτειν) to beat
croto, (Gr. κροτος) a rattling noise
croto, (Gr. κροτων) a tick (*Ixodes ricinus*)/castor oil plant (*Ricinus communis*)
crotono, (Gr. κροτωνη) a gall on trees/fragments of bronchial cartilage
croz, (LL. crocia) a crook/hook
cru -c -x, (L. crux) a cross
cru, (L. cruor) blood (from a wound)
cruci, (L. crucio) torture/torment/a cross
crud -us, (L. crudus) bloody/raw/uncooked/rough
crudesc, (L. crudesco) becoming hard/violent
cruent, (L. cruento) to make bloody/stain with blood
-crum, (L. -crum) suf. signifying instrument/tool
crum, (L. crumen) a purse
crumen -a, (L. crumena) a leather money-bag/store of money
cruor, (L. cruor) blood
cruor, (L. cruor) blood (esp. flowing from a wound)
crupper, (OFr. croupe) buttocks
crur -a, (L. crus/crura) shin/shin bone/leg
crus, (L. crus) leg/shank
crust, (L. crusta) crust/shell/bark/mosaic
crustico, (Gr. κρουστικος) striking/butting
-crux, (L. crux) a cross
cry -mo -o, (Gr. κρυος) ice/frost/cold
crybel -o, (Gr. κρυβηλος) hidden
cryo, (Gr. κρυος) icy cold/frost
cryph, (Gr. κρυφα) secretly/obscurely
cryps, (Gr. κρυψις) hiding/concealment
crypt -o, (Gr. κρυπτος) hidden/secret/concealed
cryst -allo, (Gr. κρυσταλλος) rock-crystal

ctameno, (Gr. κταμενος) killed
ctedono, (Gr. κτηδων) a fibres of the heart/layers of slate/gills of a mushroom
ctein, (Gr. κτεινω) to kill/slay/slaughter
ctemato, (Gr. κτημα) property/possession
cten -idi -iz -o, (Gr. κτεις/κτενος) a comb
ctet, (Gr. κτητος) acquired
ctilo, (Gr. κτιλος) tame/obedient/docile
ctisto, (Gr. κτιστος) established/built
cton -o, (Gr. κτονος) murder
ctypo, (Gr. κτυπεω) a loud noise
cub, (Gr. κυβη) cube
cub, (L. cubito) lie down
cubiculum, (L. cubiculum) sleeping-room
cubile, (L. cubile) couch/bed/den/lair/nest/kennel
cubit, (L. cubitus) elbow
cubitus, (L. cubitus) reclined
cubo, (Gr. κυβοειδης) cube-like
cucuj, (Br. cucuj) a kind of beetle
cucul -i -us, (L. cuculus) a cuckoo
cucull, (L. cucullus) a hood/cowl
cucum -er -is, (L. cucumis) a cucumber
cucurbit -a, (L. cucurbita) a gourd
cud, (L. cudere) to beat on/pound/thresh
-cul -a -um -us, (L.) dim. suf.
culcit, (L. culcita) pillow/cushion/bolster
cule -us, (L. culeus/culleus) a leather sac/a liquid measure
-culex, (L. culex) a gnat/midge
-culic, (L. culicis) gnat/mosquito
culin -a, (L. cilina) a kitchen
cull, (L. colligere) to collect
culm -en -in, (L. culmen) summit/roof
culm -us, (L. culmus) stalk/thatch
culp -a, (L. culpa) fault/blame
cult, (L. cultus) tilling/cultivation/tending
cultell, (L. cultellus) little knife
cultr, (L. culter) razor/ploughshare/knife
cultus, (L. cultus) cultivated/tilled
culus, (L. culus) rump
cum -a -ato, (Gr. κυμα) wave/billow/anything swollen (as if pregnant)
cum, (L. cum) with/together
cumb, (L. cumbens) lying down
cumer, (L. cumera) a corn-bin/box
cumul -o, (L. cumulus) a heap/pile
cun -a, (L. cunae) a cradle/nest
cunabul, (L. cunabula) a cradle/earliest abode
-cunda, -cundum, -cundus, (L.) increased quality/aptitude/tendency towards
cune -i -us, (L. cuneus) wedge/wedge-shaped
cunicul -us, (L. cuniculus) a rabbit/underground passage/mine
cunn -us, (L. cunnus) a prostitute/the vulva
cupedi, (L. cuppedia) dainties/tit-bits
cupho, (Gr. κουφος) light/nimble/airy/easy
cupid, (L. cupiditas) eager desire/passionate longing
cupr -i -o -um, (L. cupreus) coppery
cupul -a, (L. cupula) little tub/cask/butt
cura, (L. cura) care/attention
curcu, (Ar.) orange coloured
curculio -n, (L. curculio) a weevil/corn weevil

curidio, (Gr. κουριδιος) wedded/nuptial
curido, (Gr. κουρις) razor/shears
curimo, (Gr. κουριμος) shorn
curo, (Gr. κουρος) boy/youth/twigs
curr -en, (L. currere) to run
curso -r, (L. cursor) runner/courier
curt -i, (L. curtus) shortened/mutilated/defective
curt -o, (Gr. κυρτος) bulging/swelling/humped/convex/curved/bent/arched
curv -i, (L. curvare) to bend/arch/curve
cus, (L. cudere) to beat
cuspi -d -s, (L. cuspis) point/lance/spear
custod, (L. custodis) guardian/watchman/keeper/attendant
cut -ane -i -ic, (L. cutis) skin/surface
cyam -o, (Gr. κυαμος) a bean/pebble
cyan -e -i -o, (Gr. κυανος/κυανεος) blue/dark blue
cyaro, (Gr. κυαρ) hole/orifice/eye of a needle
cyath -us, (Gr. κυαθος) a cup
cybe, (Gr. κυβη) head (of mushroom)
cybebo, (Gr. κυβηβος) stooping/with the head bent
cybele, (Gr. Κυβελη) a goddess of nature
cybelido, (Gr. κυβηλις) cleaver/axe
cybern, (Gr. κυβερνητης) steersman/pilot/guide/governor
cybister, (Gr. κυβιστητηρ) tumbler/diver/one who pitches headlong
cybo, (Gr. κυβος) a cube, esp. a cubical die
cycethro, (Gr. κυκηθρον) a ladle/agitator
cycl -o -us, (Gr. κυκλος) a circle/ring/wheel
cycli, (Gr. κυκλιον) small wheel
cyclo -sis, (Gr. κυκλωσις) an encircling/enclosing
cyclop, (Gr. κυκλωψ) myth. a one-eyed giant
cyd -o, (Gr. κυδαλιμος) glorious/renowned
cydon -i, (Gr. κυδωνεα) the quince (Pyrus cydonia)
cydro, (Gr. κυδρος) glorious/noble
cyem -a -ato -i, (Gr. κυημα) an embryo/foetus
cyesi -o -s, (Gr. κυησις) pregnancy/conception
cygn -o, (Gr. κυκνος) a swan/a kind of ship
cygn -us, (L. cygnus) a swan
cylichn -a, (Gr. κυλιχνη) a small cup/small pot
cylico, (Gr. καλιξ) cup
cylind -ro, (Gr. κυλινδρος L. cylindrus) rolling stone/tumbler/cylinder
cylisto, (Gr. κυλιστος) a roll of papyrus/rolled
cylix, (Gr. καλιξ) cup
cyll -o, (Gr. κυλλος) club-footed/deformed/crooked
cylo, (Gr. κυλον) a region under the eye
cym -a -ato -o, (Gr. κυμα) a wave/foetus/embryo/anything swollen
cymado, (Gr. κυμας) a pregnant woman
cymb -a -i -o, (Gr. κυμβιον) small cup/small boat
cyndalo, (Gr. κυνδαλος) a wooden peg
cynip -s, (Gr. κυνιψ) a kind of gall-fly (name coined by Linnaeus)
cyno-, (Gr. κυνο-) dog (combining form)
cyns, (Gr. κυνσις) pregnancy
cynth, (Gr. υακινθος) hyacinth
cynthia, (Gr. Κυνθια) a goddess of the moon
cyo, (Gr. κυος) foetus
cyon, (Gr. κυων) dog/bitch
cypar -is, (Gr. κυπαρισσιας) the cypress tree (Cupressus spp.)
cypasado, (Gr. κυπασσις) a short frock or tunic

cypell, (Gr. κυπελλον) a big-bellied drinking-vessel/goblet/cup

cyper -us, (Gr. κυπηρος) the sedge/rush (*Cyperus rotundus*)

cyph -o, (Gr. κυφος) bent/stooping/bowed forward/hunchbacked

cyphell -a, (Gr. κυφελλα) the hollows of the ears/clouds of mist

cypho, (Gr. κυφος) bent/humped/humpback

cypo, (Gr. κυπη) a kind of ship

cypr -ae -i -o, (Gr. κυπρις) Venus//love/passion

cyprid, (Gr. κυπριδιος) lovely

cyprin -o -us, (Gr. κυπρινος) a carp

cypsel, (Gr. κυψελη) any hollow vessel/chest/box/bee-hive

cypto, (Gr. κυπτω) bend forward/stoop

cyr -io -o, (Gr. κυριος) authority

cyrbasio, (Gr. κυρβασια) a Persian hat with a peaked crown

cyrebio, (Gr. κυρηβια) bran/husks

cyri -o, (Gr. κυριος) authoritative/decisive/valid/lord/master

cyrillio, (Gr. κυριλλιον) a narrow-necked jug

cyrmato, (Gr. κυρμα) prey/booty/plunder

cyrt -o, (Gr. κυρτος) bulging/swelling/humped/convex/curved/bent/arched

cyst -i -o, (Gr. κυστις) bladder/sac/cell

cyst -is -o, (Gr. κυστις) the bladder/a bag/pouch

cystho, (Gr. κυσθος) the female pudenda (*pudenda muliebria*)

cyt -e -o -us, (Gr. κυτος) a hollow/any hollow container/a cell

cytido, (Gr. κυτις) small chest/trunk

cyto, (Gr. κυτος) a hollow place/vessel/container

cyttar, (Gr. κυτταρος) a cell of a honeycomb

cyuro, (Gr. κυουρα) a plant used to produce abortion

D

da, (Gr. δα-) intensifying prefix - very

daceto, (Gr. δακητον) a biting animal

dacn -o, (Gr. δακω) a bite/sting (actual & metaph.)

dacry -m -o, (Gr. δακρυον) a tear/gum - sap (which drops like a tear)

dactyl -o -us, (Gr. δακτυλος) a finger/toe

dado, (Gr. δαδος) firebrand/torch/pine-wood

daedal, (L. daedalus) skilful/variegated

daeo, (Gr. δαιος) hostile/destructive/wretched

daetro, (Gr. δαιτρος) a carver of meat

dagma, (Gr. δηγμα) bite/sting

daict, (Gr. διακτηρ) slayer/murderer

dalero, (Gr. δαλερος) burning heat

dall, (Gr. δαλλει) be vicious

dalo, (Gr. δαλος) firebrand/beacon light/torch

-dama, (L. damma/dama) a fallow dear/chamois/antelope

damart -o, (Gr. δαμαρτος) wife/spouse

Danae, (Gr. Δαναοι) the Greeks

danist -a, (Gr. δανειστης) money lender/creditor

danos, (Gr. δανος) a gift/loan/debt

dapan -o, (Gr. δαπανος) extravagant/expensive

daped -um, (Gr. δαπεδον) a level surface/floor/ground/soil

daph, (L. Daphne) daughter of the river god Peneus

daphn -a -i, (Gr. δαφνη) the sweet bay tree (*Laurus nobilis*)

daphoen -o, (Gr. δαφοινος) bloody (colour)
dapid -do -s, (Gr. δαπις) a carpet/rug
dapsil, (Gr. δαψιλεια) abundance/plenty
dapt -es, (Gr. δαπτης) eater/bloodsucker (of gnats)
dart -o, (Gr. δαρτος) flayed/stripped
das -i -y, (Gr. δασυς) hairy/thick with hair/rough/shaggy
dasci -o, (Gr. δασκιος) thick-shaded/heavily-shaded/dark
dascyll, (Gr. δασκιλλος) a kind of fish
dasmo, (Gr. δασμος) tribute/tax
daso, (Gr. δασος) a thicket/copse/shagginess
daspleto, (Gr. δασπλητις) horrid/frightful
dasyll, (Gr. δασυλλις) a bear
dasys, (Gr. δασυς) hairy/shaggy/rough/thick with leaves
daterio, (Gr. δατηριος) dividing/distributing
dato, (Gr. δατεομαι) distribute/divide
daucus, (Gr. δαυκος) an umbelliferous plant, also the wild carrot (*Daucus corota*)
daul -o, (Gr. δαυλος) thick/shaggy
de-, (L. de-) down from/from/about/away
dealbo, (L. dealbare) to whitewash/plaster
debil -i, (L. debilis) powerless/feeble/weak
deca -do, (Gr. δεκα) ten
decan, (Gr. decanus) chief of ten
decem, (L. decem) ten
decen -t, (L. decentia) propriety/comeliness
decid -u, (L. decidere) to fall down/fall off
decim, (L. decimus) a tenth
decipio, (L. decipere) to catch/cheat/deceive
decipul, (L. decipula) snare/trap
decis, (L. decisis) cut off
declin, (L. declinare) to bend away/deviate/decrease
declivi, (L. declivis) bent or inclined downwards/sloping
deco, (Gr. δηξ/δηκος) a wood-worm
decor, (L. decor) elegant/grace/beauty
dect -o, (Gr. δεκτος) received/accepted/grasped
dectes, (Gr. δηκτης) a biter
dectic, (Gr. δηκτικος) fit for or capable of receiving/biting/pungent
decumben, (L. decumbens) lying down/reclining
decuss -i, (L. decusso) an intersection of two lines/the letter 'X'
dedal, (L. daedalus) skilful/variegated
degma -to, (Gr. δηγμα) a sting/bite
dehisc, (L. dehisco) gape/open/split down
dei, (L. deus) god
deil -e, (Gr. δειλη) afternoon/day, as opposed to night
deimat, (Gr. δειματοω) frighten
dein -o, (Gr. δεινος) terrible/fearful/frightful/venerable/dangerous
deio -s, (Gr. δειος) enemy
deipn -o, (Gr. δειπνον) a meal/food/provender
deira, (Gr. δειρη) the neck/the throat
del -e -o, (Gr. δηλος) manifest/visible/evident
dele -t, (L. deletum) blot out/efface/destroy/annihilate
deleato, (Gr. δελεαρ) bait/an incitement
delect -us, (L. delectus) choice/a choosing
delect, (L. delectare) to divert/attract/delight
delemo, (Gr. δηλημων) baneful/noxious
delic -at -io, (L. delicatus) dainty/nice/soft/tender
deliquesc, (L. deliquescere) to liquefy/melt/dissolve/vanish

delir, (L. delirus) silly/crazy/doting

delos, (Gr. δηλος) evident/clear/visible

delph -i -y, (Gr. δελφυς) womb

delpha -c -x, (Gr. δελφαξ) a young pig

delphi -n -s, (Gr. δελφις) a dolphin

delphic -o, (Gr. δελφιξ) a tripod

delphini -um, (Gr. δελφινιον) temple of Apollo Delphinios/the larkspur (*Delphinium ajacis*)

delphy -s, (Gr. δελφυς) the womb

delta, (Gr. δελτα δ, Δ) fourth letter of the Greek alphabet/triangular

dem -o -us, (Gr. δημος) people/district/commons/fat

demat -o, (Gr. δεμα) band/clamp/tow-rope

deme, (Gr. δεμας) the living body

demers, (L. demergere) to plunge

demi, (L. dimidius) half

demiss, (L. demissus) hanging down/drooping/feeble

demn -i, (Gr. δεμνιον) a bed/bedding

demo, (Gr. δημοδες) abundant

demono, (Gr. δαιμων) an inferior divinity/an evil spirit/a malignant being

dempt, (L. demptus) taken away

den -s, (L. dens) tooth/prong

den, (AS. denn) lair

denaeo, (Gr. δηναιος) long-lived/long-continued

dendr -o -on -um, (Gr. δενδρον) a tree

denno -s, (Gr. δεννος) reproach

dens, (L. densus) thick/close

dent -i -o, (L. denticulum) little tooth

dental, (L. dentalia) the share-beam of a plough

dentat, (L. dentatus) with teeth

deo, (L. deus) god

deon -to, (Gr. δεον) duty/that which is binding

deorsus, (L. deorsus) downward

depas -tr, (Gr. δεπας) goblet/chalice

deph -o, (Gr. δεφω) knead

depilis, (L. depilis) lacking hair

deplanat, (L. planus) flattened

depress, (L. depressus) pressed down

der -a/ deir -a, (Gr. δειρη) neck/throat/collar/gully

derbios, (L. derbiosus) scabby

derco, (Gr. δερκομαι) see clearly

dergmato, (Gr. δεργμα) look/glance/thing seen/sight

deris, (Gr. δερις) battle/contest

derm -a -ato -o, (Gr. δερμα) the skin/hide

dero -s, (Gr. δερος) poetical for skin/hide

dero -s, (Gr. δηρος) long time/too long (time)

derobios, (Gr. δηροβιος) long-lived

derris, (Gr. δερρις) a skin/leather covering/curtain

dertr -um, (Gr. δερτρον) a membrane which contains the bowls

des-, (L. de-) suf. ind. from/down/of/bend from/turn aside

desert, (L. desertus) forsaken/abandoned/deserted/lonely/solitary

deses, (L. deses) idle/lazy/inactive

designat, (L. designatio) designation/marking out

desis, (Gr. δεσις) binding together/bundling

desm -a -i -io -o, (Gr. δεσμα) a band/chain/bond/fetter/ligament

desmido, (Gr. δεσμις) bundle/package

desmo, (Gr. δεσμος) a band/chain/bond/fetter/spell/charm

desmot -es, (Gr. δεσμωτης) a captive/prisoner
desud, (L. desudare) to sweat profusely
det -ic, (Gr. δετος) bound
dete, (Gr. δετη) faggot/torch
detha, (Gr. δηθα) for a long time
detis, (Gr. δετις) a head of garlic/torch
detos, (Gr. δετος) bound/a fetter/sheath
detrit, (L. detritus) rubbed off
deuma -to, (Gr. δευμα) soaked/steeped in/boiled
deuo, (Gr. δευω) wet/drenched
deus, (L. deus) god
deuso, (Gr. δευσοποιεω) to dye/stain
deust -us, (L. deustus) burned up
deutero, (Gr. δευτερος) the second
deversor, (L. deversorius) inn/lodging/refuge
devex-us, (L. devexus) sloping/descending
dex, (Gr. δηξ) a worm in wood
dexio, (Gr. δεξιος) on the right hand side/fortunate/skilful/clever
dexis, (Gr. δηξις) bite/biting
dextr, (L. dexter) on the right/skilful
di -a, (Gr. δια) through/throughout/right through/apart/separate
di -s, (L. dis-) prefix, between/away from
di, (Gr. δι-) pref. two-/double-
diabath -ra, (Gr. διαβαθρα) ladder/ship's gangway/drawbridge
diabol -o, (Gr. διαβολη) slanderous/quarrel/enmity/devilish
diabrotico, (Gr. διαβρωτικος) corrosive/eating through
diadem -a, (Gr. διαδημα) crown/especially the band which went round the turban of a
             Persian king.
diadoch -o -us, (Gr. διαδοχος) a successor
diadrom -o, (Gr. διαδρομη) running across/passage through/wandering
diadysis, (Gr. διαδυσις) passage/passing through
diaeres -is, (Gr. διαιρεσις) division/dissection/distinction
diaet, (Gr. διαιτα) dwelling
diago, (Gr. διαγω) carry over/draw through/draw apart/divert/force apart
dialy -s -sis, (Gr. διαλυσις) separating/parting/disbanding/dissolution
diamper -es, (Gr. διαμπερες) piercing/continuously/for ever
diapedes, (Gr. διαπηδησις) leaping or starting through
diapegma, (Gr. διαπηγμα) crossbar/partition
diaphano, (Gr. διαφανης) transparent/distinct
diaphor -o, (Gr. διαφορα) difference/variance/disagreement
diaphragm, (Gr. διαφραγμα) partition wall/the muscle sheet separating the thorax from
             the abdomen.
diaphyge, (Gr. διαφυγη) refuge/means of escape
diaptyxis, (Gr. διαπτυξις) spreading out fanwise
diarrhea, (Gr. διαρροια) a flowing through/diarrhoea
diasphax, (Gr. διασφαξ) any opening made by violence/a rocky gorge
diastatos, (Gr. διαστατος) divided/separated
diastema -to, (Gr. διαστημα) aperture/interval/difference
diastol, (Gr. διαστολη) separation/dilatation (of lungs)/fencing off
diastroph -o, (Gr. διαστροφη) twisting/distortion/perversion
diateles, (Gr. διατελης) continuous/incessant
diathesi -us, (Gr. διαθεσις) placing in order/arrangement/state/condition
diatribe, (Gr. διατριβη) a wearing away/pastime/study/discourse
diazoma -to, (Gr. διαζωμα) a girdle/bandage/isthmus/layer of atmosphere
dibam -o, (Gr. διβαμος) on two legs
dibol -o, (Gr. διβολος) double pointed/in two pieces

dic-/dex, (Gr. δηξ) wood-worm

dicaeo, (Gr. δικαιος) decent/just/civilised

dicell -a, (Gr. δικελλα) two-pronged mattock

dicer -o, (Gr. δικερος) two-horned

dich -o, (Gr. διχα) in two/in two ways/asunder/apart/at variance

dicha-, (Gr. διχο-) in two/asunder/separately

dichas -is, (Gr. διχασις) division/halving

dichel -o -us, (Gr. διχηλος) with two pincers, prongs or claws/cloven-hoofed

dichthad, (Gr. διχθαδιος) double

dicr -o, (Gr. δικροος) forked/cloven

dicran -o, (Gr. δικρανον) pitchfork/two-pointed/two-headed

dicrot -o, (Gr. δικροτος) double-oared/double-beating (of heart)

dict, (L. dictare) to say often/dictate

dicty -o -um, (Gr. δικτυον) a net

dicyrt -o, (Gr. δικυρτος) two-humped (of the Bactrian camel - *Camelus bactrianus*)

did -i -o, (L. didere) to divide/distribute

didym -o, (Gr. διδυμος) testicle/twin/double/two fold

dielo, (Gr. δειελος) of the evening

dieneco, (Gr. διενεκης) continuous

dieresis, (Gr. διαιρεσις) division/dissection/distinction

dieress, (Gr. διερεσσειν) to swing about

diero, (Gr. διηρης) double

diesthio, (Gr. διησθιω) eat through/consume/corrode

diet, (Gr. διαιτα) course of life/way of living

difflu, (L. diffluere) to flow in different directions

digest, (L. digesta) methodically arranged/divided and disposed/dispersed

digit -al -i, (L. digitus) a finger or toe

digmato, (Gr. δειγμα) sample/specimen/pattern

dign, (L. dignus) worthy/deserving/suitable/fitting

dilat, (L. dilatare) to spread out/extend

dilect, (L. dilectus) beloved/dear

dilemm -a, (Gr. διλημμα) an ambiguous proposition

dilo, (Gr. δειλη) afternoon/evening

dimidi, (L. dimidius) halved/divided

dimin, (L. deminutio) lessening/diminution

dimo, (Gr. δειμος) fear/terror

din -o, (Gr. δεινος) powerful/terrible/fearful

dineo, (Gr. δινηεις) eddying/whirling

dino, (Gr. δινος) rotation/a whirl/an eddy

dino, (Gr. δινος) whirling/rotation

dio-, (Gr. διο-) divine/from the gods/god-like

dioche, (Gr. διοχη) distance/interval

diocto, (Gr. διωκτος) pursued/banished

diogma, (Gr. διωγμα) chase/pursuit

-diol, (Gr. διολου) altogether/always

diopter, (Gr. διοπτηρ) spy/scout/an optical instrument

diorygma, (Gr. διορυγμα) canal/channel

diota, (L. diota) a two-handled wine-jar

diphet, (Gr. διφητωρ) searcher

diphro, (Gr. διφρος) a chariot/seat

diphthera, (Gr. διφθερα) leather/prepared hide

diphy, (Gr. διφυης) two-fold/double

dipl-, (Gr. διπλοη) fold

diplo, (Gr. διπλοος) two-fold/double

dipn -o -um, (Gr. δειπνον) a meal/food/provender

dips -a -i, (Gr. διψη) thirst

dipsacus, (Gr. διψακυς) the teasel (*Dispacus* spp.)

dir -o, (Gr. δειρη) the neck

dir, (L. dirus) fearful/horrible/dire

dirado, (Gr. δειρας) the ridge of a chain of hills

dirept, (L. direptus) plundered/ravaged/raped

diribit, (Gr. διριβιτορ) a separator/sorter

dirig, (L. dirigere) to arrange/to direct

dirus, (L. dirus) fearful/ominous

dis, (L. dis-) prefix, separately/apart/in different directions

dis-, (Gr. δισ-) twice-

disaleo, (Gr. δεισαλεος) filthy

disc -i -o -os -us, (Gr. δισκος) a round plate

dischides, (Gr. δισχιδης) cloven hoofed/cloven/divided

discors, (L. discordis) disagreeing/inharmonious

disi, (Gr. δεισι-) fear

dissit, (L. dissitus) apart/remote

disso, (Gr. δισσος) two-fold/double

dist -ad -al, (L. distare) to stand apart

distagmo, (Gr. δισταγμος) doubt

distich -o, (Gr. διστιχος) of two rows/lines

distolo, (Gr. διστολος) in pairs

ditto/disso, (Gr. διττο-/δισσο-) twice/doubly

diurn, (L. diurnus) of the day/lasting for a day

divaric -a, (L. divaricare) to stretch apart/spread apart

diversi, (L. diversitas) contradiction/difference/diversity

divert, (L. diverticulum) a by-way

diverto, (L. divertere) to turn different ways

dix -o, (Gr. διξοος) forked/cleft

dmeto, (Gr. δμητος) tamed

dnophero, (Gr. δνοφερος) dark/gloomy/murky

doc -o -us, (Gr. δοκος) a wooden beam or bar/shaft

doca, (Gr. δοξα) glory

doce, (Gr. δοκεω) expect/seem

doce, (Gr. δοκη) vision/fancy

doch -i, (Gr. δοχη) receptacle/reception/entertainment

dochm -i -o, (Gr. δοχμιος) across/slanting

doci -l, (L. docilis) teachable/docile

docim, (Gr. δοκιμαζω) test/assay/prove

doct, (L. doctor) teacher

dodeca, (Gr. δωδεκα) twelve

dodo, (Pg. doudo) simpleton

dogma -t, (Gr. δογμα) opinion/belief/decision/judgement

dol, (L. dolium) wine cask

dolabr -a, (L. dolabra) pick-axe

dolat, (L. dolatus) hewn/cut

doler -o, (Gr. δολερος) deceitful/treacherous

doli -o -um, (L. dolium) a large jar/wine cask

dolich -o, (Gr. δολιχος) long

dolio, (Gr. δολιος) deceitful/treacherous

dolo -m -p, (Gr. δολομηδης) wily/crafty

dolo, (Gr. δολο-) subtle

dolo, (Gr. δουλος) a slave

dolon, (Gr. δολων) dagger/stiletto/pike

dolopo, (Gr. δολοψ) ambusher

dolor, (L. doloris) pain/grief/sorrow

dolos -us, (L. dolosus) cunning/deceitful/crafty

dom -o -us, (Gr. δομος) house/room/chamber
doma -to, (Gr. δωμα) house
domestic, (L. domesticus) of the house/native (as opposed to foreign)
domin -ic -us, (L. dominus) the master of a house/lord/master
dona -c -x, (Gr. δοναξ) a reed/arrow shaft/shepherd's pipe/fishing rod
dona, (L. donare) to give/to present
donesi, (Gr. δονεω) shake (in wind)/disturb/terrify/excite/buzz of bees
-dont, (Gr. οδους) a tooth
dor -a -o, (Gr. δορα) skin/hide
dor, (Gr. δορυ) spear/hunting spear
dorat -ium, (Gr. δορατιον) small spear
dorca -do -s, (Gr. δορκας) an antelope or gazelle
dorea, (Gr. δωρεα) a gift
dori -d -s, (Gr. δορις) a sacrificial knife, a sea nymph
dorm -it, (L. dormer) to sleep
doron, (Gr. δωρον) a gift/offering
doros, (Gr. δορος) leather bag/wallet
dors -o -um, (L. dorsum) the back/ridge/ledge
dory -t, (Gr. δορυ) beam/shaft/hunting-spear
dosi, (Gr. δοσις) giving/a gift/legacy
dox -a, (Gr. δοξα) expectation/notion/opinion/judgement
draba, (Gr. δραβη) the Arabian mustard plant (*Lepidium draba*)
drac -aen -o -on, (L. draco) water snake/serpent/dragon
drachm -a, (Gr. δραχμη) a weight/a silver coin
drag, (Gr. δρακων) a huge serpent
dragm -a, (Gr. δραγμα) handful/sheaf
dragmo, (Gr. δραγμος) grasping
dram, (Gr. δραμημα) running/course
drama -t, (Gr. δραμα) duty/action/stage effect
drapet -es, (Gr. δραπετης) a fugitive (esp. runaway slave)
dras -t, (Gr. δρασις) strength/efficiency/action
drasmo, (Gr. δρασμος) running away/flight
drasteri, (Gr. δραστηριος) activity/energy/active
drepan -i -um, (Gr. δρεπανη) a sickle/scythe
drepto, (Gr. δρεπτος) plucked
dril, (Gr. δριλος) worm/penis
drimy, (Gr. δριμυς) piercing/sharp/keen/pungent/bitter/fierce
drios, (Gr. δριος) copse/wood/thicket
drom -a -ae -aeo -i -o, (Gr. δρομας) running/racing/whirling/any quick movement/a
　　　　place for running
drom -us, (Gr. δρομευς) runner
dros -o, (Gr. δροσος) dew/pure water
droser -o, (Gr. δροσερος) dewy/watery/fresh/tender/soft
drup -a, (Gr. δρυπετης) an over-ripe olive/a stone-fruit
dry -o -s, (Gr. δρυς) the oak (sacred to Zeus)
drya, (Gr. δρυας) a wood nymph
dryas, (L. Dryas) a wood or tree nymph
drym -o -us, (Gr. δρυμος) an oak-coppice/woodland/forest
dryphacto, (Gr. δρυφακτος) a railing/latticed partition
drypis, (Gr. δρυπις) a kind of thorn
drypt -o, (Gr. δρυπτω) a tear (as in cut)/strip
du -o, (L. duo/duos) two
dubi, (L. dubius) doubtful/wavering in opinion
duc -t, (L. ductus) bringing
ducer, (L. ducere) to lead/marry
ductil, (L. ductilis) that which may be led or drawn out thin

dul -io -o, (Gr. δουλος) a slave/bondsman
dulario, (Gr. δουλαριον) little female slave
dulc -i, (L. dulcis) sweet/pleasant/delightful/agreeable
dule, (Gr. δουλη) female slave
dulio, (Gr. δουλιος) servile/slavish
dulos, (Gr. δουλος) enslaved
dum -us, (L. dumetum) a thorn brake/thicket
duo, (L. duo) two
duodec -im, (L. duodecim) twelve
duoden -i, (L. duodeni) twelve each
dupl -ex -ic -o, (L. duplex) double/deceitful
duplic, (L. duplicare) to double
dupo, (Gr. δυοπος) any dead, heavy sound/a thud
dur -a -o, (L. dura) hardship/hard/tough/strong/enduring
dura, (L. durare) to make hard/to endure
dux, (L. ducis) leader
dwarf, (AS. dweorg) little/short/low
dya -d -s, (Gr. δυας) two
dymant, (Gr. δειματοω) I frighten
dyn -am -amo -ast, (Gr. δυναμις) strength/might/power
dyo, (Gr. δυο) two/two together
dyo, (Gr. δυω) sink/plunge in/go into/enter
dys, (Gr. δυσ-) un-/mis- (with notion of hard/bad/unlucky)
dyschimo, (Gr. δυσχιμος) dangerous/fearful/troublesome
dyschro, (Gr. δυσχρως) discoloured/of a bad colour
dysco, (Gr. δισκος) disc
dysis, (Gr. δυσις) setting of sun or stars/the west/hiding place
dysmiko, (Gr. δυσμικος) western
dysode, (Gr. δυσωδης) foul-smelling/stinking
dysporo, (Gr. δυσπορος) scarcely passable
dyspsycto, (Gr. δυσψυκτος) tolerant of the cold
dystherat, (Gr. δυσθηρατος) hard to catch
dyt -as -es, (Gr. δυτης) a diver/burrower

E

e, (refer also to ae, ai, o, oe)
e-, (L.) prefix (before s and d) without/not/lacking/from out
-eae, (L.) suffix used for plant tribe names
ear -in -o, (Gr. εαρ) spring/juice/blood
eb -en -o, (Gr. εβενος) ebony
ebaeo, (Gr. ηβαιος) little/a few
eben -o -us, (Gr. εβενος) the dark heart wood of many species of *Diospyrus*
ebrius, (L. ebrius) drunk
ebur -ne, (L. ebur) ivory
ec-, (Gr. εκ- L. ex-) from/out of/away from
ecaton, (Gr. εκατον) a hundred/very many
ecbleto, (Gr. εκβλητος) cast overboard/thrown away/rejected
eccli, (Gr. εκκλινης) inclined outwards/bent outwards
eccopto, (Gr. εκκοπτω) cut out/fell/destroy
eccremo, (Gr. εκκρεμης) hanging/pendent
eccri -s -t, (Gr. εκκρινω) to secrete/choose/separate/expel/reject
eccroust, (Gr. εκκρουστος) beaten-out/embossed

eccye, (Gr. εκκυεω) bring forth/put forth (as in leaves)

ecdem -i -io, (Gr. εκδημος) away from home/abroad

ecdy, (Gr. εκδυμα) that which is put off a skin/garment

ecdy, (Gr. εκδυω) strip off/to get out of

ecdys -is, (Gr. εκδυσις) a slipping out/escape

ece -sis -tes, (Gr. οικησις) the act of dwelling/inhabiting

-eces, (Gr. -εκες) suf. ind. sharp/point/sharp edge

-ecetes, -etes, (Gr. οικετης) one who/to dwell in (often in reference to habitats)

ecgon, (Gr. εκγονος) born of/sprung from/descended from/grandchild

ech -o, (Gr. ηχω) echo/ringing sound

echel, (Fr. échelle) ladder

echem, (Gr. ηχημα) a sound

echene -i, (Gr. εχενηις) a type of fish reputed to hold ships back

echetle, (Gr. εχετλη) a plough handle

echi -dn -s, (Gr. εχιδνα) a constrictor snake/viper/monster

echin -o -us, (Gr. εχινος) sea urchin/hedgehog/spine/a large, wide-mouthed jar

echm -a -at, (Gr. εχμα) an obstruction/hindrance/bulwark/defence

echo, (L. echo Gr. εχω) echo

echth -ist -o -r, (Gr. εχθρος) hatred

echyro, (Gr. εχυρος) strong/secure

-ecious, (Gr. οικος) house/any dwelling

eciz -e, (Gr. ιοκην) to settle

eclamp, (Gr. εκλαμπρος) very bright/brilliant/distinguished

eclamps, (Gr. εκλαμψις) shining forth/brightness

ecle -c -cto -x -is, (Gr. εκλεξις) choice

eclip -s -t, (G. εκλιπης) deficient/failing/omitted/overlooked

eclog, (Gr. εκλογη) choice/selection/collection of tribute

ecnomo, (Gr. εκνομος) outlawed/unlawful/monstrous

eco-, (Gr. οικος) house/any dwelling place

ecpaglo, (Gr. εκπαγλος) wondrous/terrible/violent

ecphor, (Gr. εκφοριον) that which is brought forth

ecphyad, (Gr. εκφυης) abnormally developed/projecting/extraordinary

ecphyas, (Gr. εκφυας) appendage/outgrowth/branch (of blood vessel)

ecphymato, (Gr. εκφυματος) an eruption of pimples

ecpomato, (Gr. εκπωματος) beaker/drinking cup

ecro, (Gr. εκροος) outflow/issue/outlet/means of escape

ect -o, (Gr. εκτος) outside/out of/far from/free from

ecta -sis, (Gr. εκτασις) stretching out/extension/making explicit/impulse

ectemno, (Gr. εκτεμνω) cut out

ecteno, (Gr. εκτεινω) stretch out

ecthymo, (Gr. εκθυμος) spirited/ardent

ecto, (Gr. ηκτος) the sixth

-ectomy, (Gr. -εκτομη) suf. ind. excision

ectop -i -o -y, (Gr. εκτοπιζω) remove from a place/migrate/displace

ectopist -es, (Gr. εκτοπιστης) wanderer

ectro -m -s, (Gr. εκτρωμα) untimely birth

ectromo, (Gr. εκτρομος) trembling

ectyp, (Gr. εκτυπος) worked in relief/distinct

ectypho, (Gr. εκτυφος) puffed up/empty

ecze -m, (Gr. εκζεω) boil over/break out

edaph -o, (Gr. εδαφος) ground/the base/bottom/foundation

edax, (L. edax) greedy/gluttonous/destructive/consuming

ede -o, (Gr. αιδοια) the genitals

edema -t, (Gr. οιδημα) swelling/tumour

edesma, (Gr. εδεσμα) food/meat/eatables

odest oo, (Gr. οδοστης) an oator
edest, (Gr. εδεστος) to be eaten/eatable
edibil, (LL. edibilis) edible
editus, (Gr. editus) raised/high/lofty
edr -a -i, (Gr. εδρα) a seat
edulis, (L. edulis) eatable
ef-, (L. ef-) prefix (before *f*) without/not/lacking/from out
efferat, (L. efferatus) savage/wild
efferen, (L. effero) to carry out/bring out/carry away
effetus, (L. effetus) exhausted/weakened
efficax, (L. efficax) effective/efficient
effluen, (L. effluo) to flow out/pass away/vanish/be forgotten
effod, (L. effodere) to dig up/dig out
effus, (L. effusus) poured out
effusus, (L. effundo) pour out/pour forth/shed
egelid, (L. egelidus) lukewarm/tepid
egen -us, (L. egenus) needy/destitute
egeri -a, (L. egeria) a nymph
egest -us, (L. egestus) voiding/emptying
ego, (L. ego) the personal pronoun *I*
egregor, (Gr. εγρηγορτι) awake/watching
egresso, (Gr. εγρησσω) watch/awake
egretta, (Fr. aigrette) a tuft of feathers; a kind of heron - particularly the Lesser White
             Heron (*Egretta garzetta*)
-ei, (L.) of, belonging to, pertaining to
eido, (Gr. ειδος) form/shape/image/that which is seen
eidol -o, (Gr. ειδωλ) idol/image
eile, (Gr. ειλεω) to roll or twist tight up/to force together/to be rolled up together
eir -o, (Gr. ειρος) wool
eis, (Gr. εις) in/into/towards
ejacul, (L. eiaculari) to throw out/hurl out
ejulo, (L. eiulo) wail/lament
ejuncid, (L. eiuncidus) rush-like
ek-, (Gr. εκ-) from/from out of/outside/beyond/out of
eka -st -sto, (Gr. εκαστος) each
ekaton, (Gr. εκατον) a hundred/very many
-el, (L. -el/-cle) dim. suf.
elacat -a, (Gr. ηλακατη) a staff/one joint of a reed or cane
elach -ist -y, (Gr. ελαχιστος) fewest/smallest/least/shortest
elae -o, (Gr. ελαιον) oil/olive oil
elaegn -us, (Gr. ελαιαγνος) the goat's or pussy willow (*Salix caprea*)
elai -o, (Gr. ελαιον) oil/olive oil
elano, (Gr. ελανος) a species of kite
elap -s, (NL. elaps) a serpent
elaph -o -us, (Gr. ελαφος) a stag or hart (*Cervus elaphus*)
elaphr -o, (Gr. ελαφρος) light/easy to bear/nimble
elaps, (NL. elaps) a kind of snake
elasas, (Gr. ελασας) a kind of bird
elasm -o -us, (Gr. ελασμος) a plate/a metal plate/metal beaten out
elasso, (Gr. ελασσοω) make less or smaller/diminish
elast, (Gr. ελαστοκος) ductile
elat, (L. elatus) elevated/exalted/lofty
elate, (Gr. ελατη) the Grecian fir (*Abies cephalonica*)/an oar
elater, (Gr. ελατηρ) a driver/charioteer
elatin -o, (Gr. ελατινος) of the fir/made of fir or pine wood
elatr, (L. elatrare) to bark/cry out
elatri, (Gr. ελατηριος) driving/driving away

elatus, (L. elatus) exalted/high/lofty

elaun, (Gr. ελαυνω) to set in motion/to drive/ride/sail/row/advance/proceed/to draw out/beat out

elc -e, (Gr. ελκεω) pull/drag about/tear asunder

elc -o -oma -os, (Gr. ελκοω) wound/lacerate/ulcerate

elcysm, (Gr. ελκυσμος) dragging/attraction/idle fancy

elect, (Gr. εκλεκτος) selected

electoro, (Gr. ηλεκτωρ) the beaming sun/fire as an element

electr -i -on, (Gr. ελεκτρον) amber (in which the property of developing electricity was first observed)

eleg, (Gr. ελεγος) song/melody/lament

eleg, (L. elegans) choice/fine/neat

elegan -t, (L. elegantia) elegant/grace

elego -s, (Gr. ελεγος) a mourning song/poem

elench -o, (Gr. ελεγχος) a trial/test

eleo, (Gr. ελαιον) oil/olive oil

eleo-, (Gr. ελεο-) swamp-/marsh-

eleos/aleos, (Gr. ηλεος/αλεος) distraught/crazed/foolishly

eleph -as ant, (Gr. ελεφας) elephant/ivory

elephant -i -o, (ελεφας) an elephant

eleuther -o, (Gr. ελευθερος) free/free born

elibat-o, (Gr. ηλιβατας) haunting the heights

elido, (L. elidere) to strike out/dash to pieces

elig, (L. eligere) to pluck out/pick out/choose

elign -o, (Gr. ελιγμος) winding/convolution/rotary motion

elis, (L. elisi) eradicated/dashed to pieces/shattered

-elis, (L.) pertaining to/having the nature, quality or condition of

elithi -o, (Gr. ηλιθιος) idle/vain/foolish

-ell -a -um -us, (L. -ella) dim. suf.

elleips, (Gr. ελλειψις) a deficiency/falling short

ellip -s -t, (Gr. ελλιπης) leaving out/defective/wanting/failing/elliptical (in grammar)

ellob, (Gr. ελλοβιον) an earring

ellobo, (Gr. ελλοβος) in a pod

ellop -s, (Gr. ελλοφ) a serpent/sea fish/mute

-ellum, (L. -ellum) dim. suf.

-ellus, (L. -ellus) dim. suf.

elo -d, (Gr. ελος) marsh-meadow/marshy ground/backwater

elo -t, (Gr. ηλωτος) nail-shaped/nailed

elop -s, (Gr. ελοψ = ελλοφ) a serpent/sea fish/mute

elpido, (Gr. ελπις) hope/expectation

elu -d -s, (L. eludere) to parry a blow/ward off/evade

eludo, (L. eludere) to avoid/evade/parry

elukt, (L. eluctor) to struggle out/to surmount a difficulty

elut, (L. eluere) to wash out/clean/rinse/efface/wash away

elym -o, (Gr. ελυμος) case/quiver/millet

elyma, (Gr. ελυμα) the share-beam of a plough

elymo, (Gr. ελυμος) case/quiver/a kind of pipe

elysi -s, (Gr. ηλυσις) step/gait

elytr -o -um, (Gr. ελυτρον) sheath/covering/case

em-, (Gr. εμ-) prefix, in/within

ema, (Gr. ημα) that which is thrown /dart/javelin

emato, (Gr. εματιος) by day/daily

embal -lo -m, (Gr. εμβαλλω) throw in/throw into/put into

embaph, (Gr. εμβαφιον) a shallow vessel for sauces/a saucer

embas, (Gr. εμβας) a felt shoe/slipper

emberiz -a, (NL. emberiza) (from Swiss-German *emmeritz*) a bunting/yellow hammer

embi -a -o, (Gr. εμβιος) having life/lasting one's whole life
embi, (Gr. εμβια) lively
embio, (Gr. εμβιοω) live in/of plants - become established/take root
embol, (Gr. εμβολη) putting in/inserting/ramming/gust of wind
embol -im -o, (Gr. εμβολιμος) intercalated
embol, (Gr. εμβολος) a wedge/peg/stopper/linch-pin
embrith -o, (Gr. εμβριθης) weighty/heavy/dignified
embryo, (Gr. εμβρυον) embryo/foetus
emer -a, (Gr. ημερα) a day
emero-, (Gr. ημερο-) for a day/by day
emet -i -o, (Gr. εμετος) vomiting/sickness
emetic, (Gr. εμετικος) provoking sickness
-emia, (Gr. αιμα) blood
emico, (L. emicare) to appear suddenly/spring out/become apparent
emigro, (L. emigrare) to move out/migrate
eminen, (L. eminere) to project
eminus, (L.) at a distance/from afar
emmel -eia, (Gr. εμμελης) in tune/harmonious/melodious/graceful/elegant
emmen -a -o, (Gr. εμμηνος) lasting a month/monthly/the menses of women
emmeno, (Gr. εμμενης) steadfast
emmochlio, (Gr. εμμοχλιον) a socket for a bar
emmochtho, (Gr. εμμοχθος) toilsome
emolli, (L. emollire) to soften/to make mild
emosyne, (Gr. ημοσυνη) skill in throwing or shooting
empedos, (Gr. εμπεδος) firm/steadfast/firm set
emphrax -i -is, (Gr. εμφραξις) stoppage/obstruction
emphys, (Gr. εμφυσαω) blow in/inflate/breathe upon
emphyt -o, (Gr. εμφυτος) inborn/natural/planted/implanted
empi -d -us, (Gr. εμπις) a gnat/mosquito
empir -o, (Gr. εμπειρικος) experienced
empis, (Gr. εμπις) a mosquito/gnat
emplastr, (Gr. εμπλαστρος) salve/mortar
emplecto, (Gr. εμπλεκτος) inwoven
empodio, (Gr. εμποδιος) at one's feet/hindering/impeding
empres -i -m, (Gr. εμπρησις) burning/inflammation
empusa, (Gr. Εμπουσα) a hobgoblin
empy -ems, (Gr. εμπυημα) abscess
empyema, (Gr. εμπυημα) suppuration, esp. internal
empyr, (Gr. εμπυρευω) set on fire
emulsi, (L. emulgere) to milk out/exhaust/drain out
emy -d -s, (Gr. εμυς) a fresh-water tortoise or turtle
en, (Gr. εν) within/on/upon/in/at/'to put in a state of'
enali -o, (Gr. εναλιος) in the sea/on the sea/of the sea/marine
enall -a -agm, (Gr. εναλλαγη) interchange/variation
enallax, (Gr. εναλλαξ) crosswise/alternately/interlacing/in inverted order/upside
        down
enallo, (Gr. εναλλος) changed/contrary
enamma, (Gr. εναμμα) a garment/covering
enant -i, (Gr. εναντα) opposite/over against
enantio, (Gr. εναντιος) opposite side/face to face/opposite direction
enapo, (Gr. εναπο-) in
enargma, (Gr. εναργμα) a phenomenon/evident facts
enargo, (Gr. εναργης) visible/manifest
encarsi, (Gr. εγκαρσιος) oblique/athwart
-ence, -ency, -ancy, -ance, (L. -antia, -entia) pertaining to/quality/state
encephal -o -us, (Gr. εγκεφαλος) within the head/brain

ench -o -us, (Gr. εγχος) a spear
enchely -s, (Gr. εγχελυς) an eel
enchiridio, (Gr. εγχειριδιον) a dagger/hand-knife/handbook/handle
encho, (Gr. εγχος) a spear/lance/weapon
enchy, (Gr. εγχεω) to pour in/be poured in
enchym -a, (Gr. εγχυμα) infusion
-ency, -ence, -ancy, -ance, (L. -antia, -entia) pertaining to/quality/state
encyclio, (Gr. εγκυκλιος) circular/round/periodical
encyo, (Gr. εγκυος) pregnant
-end, (L.) having the quality of
end -o, (Gr. ενδον) within/inner
endem, (Gr. ενδημος) native to somewhere/at home
endico, (Gr. ενδικος) right/fair/just
endio, (Gr. ενδιος) at midday
endo, (Gr. ενδον) within
endoxo, (Gr. ενδοξος) held in esteem or honour
endym -a -ato, (Gr. ενδυμα) garment/covering
endysi -s, (G. ενδυσις) entry/putting on/dressing
enelico, (Gr. ενηλιξ) in the prime of manhood
enem -a, (Gr. ενεμα) injection
eneos, (Gr. ενεος) dumb/senseless/stupid/silent
ener -o, (Gr. ημερος) tame/(of animals)/cultivated (of plants)/civilised (of man)
energ, (Gr. ενεργω) to work/be active
eneter, (Gr. ενετηρ) a syringe
engion, (Gr. εγγιων) nearer
engisto, (Gr. εγγιστος) nearest
engraul -is, (Gr. εγγραυλις) a small fish
engy, (Gr. εγγυς) near/nearly
engy, (Gr. ενγυ) narrow
enhydr -is, (Gr. ενυδρις) the sea otter (*Enhydra lutris*)/a water snake
enhydr -o, (Gr. ενυδρο-) living in water
enic -o, (Gr. ενικος) single/individual/exhibiting unity
enicmo, (Gr. ενικμος) humid
enisk -o, (Gr. ηνικος) small thong/small strap
enixus, (L. enixus) strenuous/eager/zealous
enkephal, (Gr. εγκεφαλον) that which is in the head/brain
enne -a, (Gr. εννεα) nine
eno, (Gr. οινος) wine
enochlesis, (Gr. ενοχλησις) annoyance
enod, (L. enodis) without knots/smooth/clear/plain
enope, (Gr. ενοπη) an earing
enope, (Gr. ενοπη) crying, shouting (as of birds)/war-cry/battle-cry
enopios, (Gr. ενωπιος) face to face
enoplo, (Gr. ενοπλος) armed/in arms
enoptron, (Gr. ενοπτρον) a mirror
enosis, (Gr. ενοσις) shaking/quake
-ens -e -is, (L. -ensis) suf. ind. belonging to (usually with locality/place name)
ensis, (L. ensis) a sword
enstatico, (Gr. ενστατικος) stubborn/opposing/resisting
ent -o, (Gr. εντος) within/inside
entas -is, (Gr. εντασις) tension/straining/exertion
entatico, (Gr. εντατικος) stimulating/sexually vigorous
entaxis, (Gr. ενταξις) insertion
entele, (Gr. εντελης) perfect/complete/full
entelech, (Gr. εντελεχεια) full/complete reality/actuality
enter -o -um, (Gr. εντερον) a piece of gut

enthet -ic -o, (Gr. ενθετικος) implanting
-entia, -ens, -entis, (L.) having the quality of, belonging to
entimo, (Gr. εντιμος) honoured/prized
entom -a -o -on, (Gr. εντομον) an insect
entoma, (Gr. εντομη) slit/groove/notch/incision
entomo-, (Gr. εντομος) to cut up as sacrifices/victims
enton -i -o, (Gr. εντονος) sinewy/violent (of wind)/intense/vehement/eager
entrop, (Gr. εντροπη) turning towards
-enus, (L.) suf. ind. pertaining to/one who/belonging to
enydr -is, (Gr. ενυδρις) the sea otter (*Enhydra lutris*)/a water snake
enygr -o, (Gr. ενυγρος) watery/aquatic/in the water/wet/damp
enystron, (Gr. ηνυστρον) the fourth chamber of the ruminant stomach
eo -s, (Gr. ηως) dawn/morning/early
eol -i -o, (Gr. αιολο-) impersonation of the wind/quick moving
eolo -s, (Gr. αιολος) changeful
eon, (Gr. αιων L. aeon) a lifetime/an age
eos, (Gr. ηως) dawn/morning/early/east
epachthes, (Gr. επαχθης) heavy/ponderous/burdensome/grievous
epacmo, (Gr. επακμος) in full bloom
epacr -o, (Gr. επακρος) pointed at the end
epact, (Gr. εκαπτος) adventitious/foreign/strange/alien
epactero, (Gr. επακτηρ) hunter/fisherman
epactio, (Gr. επακτιος) on the shore
epacto, (Gr. επακτος) imported/acquired
epaeto, (Gr. επαιτης) a beggar
epagog -o, (Gr. επαγωγος) bringing on/attractive/alluring
epallel -o, (Gr. επαλληλος) in sequence
epan -et -i, (Gr. επανιημι) let loose at/let go/relax
epan, (Gr. επανω) on the upper side
epaul -o, (Gr. επαυλος) dwelling/home/fold for cattle at night
epedan -o, (Gr. ηπεδανος) weak/infirm
epeetan -o, (Gr. επηετανος) sufficient/ample/abundant
epeir -o -us, (Gr. ηπειρος) terra firma, esp. the mainland of Western Greece/later, a
            continent
epelis, (Gr. επηλις) a cover/lid
epelys, (Gr. επηλυς) a stranger/foreigner
epelyx, (Gr. επηλυξ) overshadowing
ependy -ma -tes, (Gr. επενδυμα) a tunic/upper garment
epenthes -is, (Gr. επενθεσις) insertion/application (of something)
eperato, (Gr. επηρατος) lovely/charming
eperop, (Gr. ηπεροπευς) cheat/deceive
epete, (Gr. ηπητης) repairer
epeter, (Gr. ηπητηριον) needle
ephapt -o, (Gr. εφαπτω) to grasp/hold/touch/reach/attain/fasten on
epheb, (Gr. εφεβος) grown up youth/manhood
ephel -is, (Gr. εφηλις) a freckle/rough spot on the face/rivet
ephemer -i -o, (Gr. εφημεριος) lasting for one day
ephesti, (Gr. εφεστιος) at home/at one's own fireside/domestic
ephestris, (Gr. εφεστρις) an outer garment/wrapper
ephicto, (Gr. εφικτος) easy to reach/attainable
ephimer, (Gr. εφιμερος) desired/delightful
ephippi -us, (L. ephippium) a saddle
ephodo, (Gr. εφοδος) approach/entrance/attack
epholcio, (Gr. εφολκιον) an appendage/a small boat towed behind a ship
ephydr -o, (Gr. εφυδρος) moist/rainy/abounding in water/living on the water
ephyr -a, (Gr. Εφυρα) old name for Corinth

epi, (Gr. επι) on/upon/at/by/near/in addition

epial -o -us, (Gr. επιαλος) nightmare (as a throttling demon)

epibathra, (Gr. επιβαθρα) a ladder/steps/stairs

epiblem -a -ato, (Gr. επιβλημα) a covering/tapestry/patch

epicauto, (Gr. επικαυτος) burnt at the tip

epicharis, (Gr. επιχαρις) pleasing/charming

epicoeno, (Gr. επικοινος) common to many/promiscuous

epicrato, (Gr. επικρατες) master

epicrio, (Gr. επικριον) sailyard/yard-arm

epicuro, (Gr. επικουρος) assister/ally/mercenary troops

epidemi -o, (Gr. επιδημιος) among the people/epidemic

epiderm, (Gr. επιδερμις) outer skin/web of a water-bird's foot

epidos -is, (Gr. επιδοσις) contribution/largess/increase/advance

epier -a, (Gr. επιηρα) pleasant/grateful

epilep -s -t, (Gr. επιλεψις) clasping/taking hold of/claiming

epilept -o, (Gr. επιληπτικος) epileptic

epilineut, (Gr. επιλινευτης) one who catches with nets

epimach -o, (Gr. επιμαχος) assailable/contended for/equipped for battle

epimek, (Gr. επιμηκης) oblong/longish/far-stretching

epimethes, (Gr. επιμηθης) thoughtful

epimol, (Gr. επιμολος) invader

epiolo, (Gr. ηπιολος) a moth

epios, (Gr. ηπιος) gentle/kind/mild/soothing

epipast -o, (Gr. επιπαστος) sprinkled over/a kind of cake

epiped -o, (Gr. επιπεδος) on the ground/level/flat

epiphor -a, (Gr. επιφορα) extra pay/an addition/growth by assimilation

epiphor -o, (Gr. επιφορος) carrying towards/leaning towards/sloping

epiplo, (Gr. επιπλοον) fold of the peritoneum/omentum

epiplo, (Gr. επιπλοος) sailing after/sailing against (an enemy)

epipol -a, (Gr. επιπολα) commonplace

epipole, (Gr. επιπολη) a surface

epiptygma, (Gr. επιπτυγμα) a flap/operculum

epir -o -us, (Gr. ηπειρος) terra firma, esp. the mainland of Western Greece/later, a continent

epirrhyto, (Gr. επιρρυτος) running/overflowing/abundant

episio, (Gr. επισιον) the pubic region

epistem, (Gr. επιστημη) knowledge/science/understanding/skill

epistol, (Gr. επιστολη) a letter/anything sent by messenger

epistroph, (Gr. επιστροφαδην) turning this way and that/wheeling/vehemently/ attention

epithalam -i, (Gr. επιθαλαμιος) nuptial

epithe -ca -m -s -t, (Gr. επιθετος) added/additional/annexed/adventitious/fictitious

epithema, (Gr. επιθημα) a cover/lid/arrow shaft

epithet, (Gr. επιθετος) additional

epithym -i, (Gr. επιθυμος) desirous

epiton, (Gr. επιτονιον) the peg for tightening the strings of an instrument

epitrop, (Gr. επιτροπη) guardian/a reference/arbiter

epoch, (Gr. εποχη) pause/stoppage/station

epomidi -o, (Gr. επωμιδιος) on the shoulder

epops, (Gr. εποψ) the hoopee (*Upupa epops*)

epos, (Gr. επος) word/tale/speech

epsilon, (Gr. εψιλον, ε Ε) fifth letter of the Greek alphabet

epstasi -s, (Gr. επστασις) stopping/stoppage/sluggishness of flow

ept -a, (NL. epta) seven

epul -um, (L. epulum) a banquet/feast

epulot, (Gr. επουλος) scar over/heal

epy, (Gr. αιπος) tall/high
equ -a -i, (L. aequus) equal
equestr, (L. equester) relating to horsemen/horse-soldiers
equin, (L. equinus) relating to horses
equit -an, (L. equitare) to ride
equu -s, (L. equus) a horse
er, (Gr. ερα) the earth
-er, (L. -er) suf. ind. an agent
era, (L. aera) an age
erag, (L. erga) towards
eran -o, (Gr. ερανος) a friendly society/a contribution/favour/service
erann -o, (Gr. εραννος) lovely (of places, seldom of people)
erasmi, (Gr. ερασμιος) lovely/pleasant/beloved/desired
erast -es -o, (Gr. εραστης) lover/admirer
erat -o, (Gr. ερατος) lovely (of places and things)
ereb -o -us, (Gr. Ερεβος) myth. a place of nether darkness/darkness
erechth/erichth, (Gr. ερεχθω) rend/break/shiver
erect, (L. erectus) upright/raised/high/elevated/alert/anxious
ereid, (Gr. ερειδω) to support/strengthen/urge
erem -a -aeo, (Gr. ηρεμα) quietly/gently/calmly
erem -i -o, (Gr. ερημια) a desert/lonely place
eremit, (Gr. ηρεμιτης) a hermit
eremno, (Gr. ερεμνος) murky/black/dark
eremo, (Gr. ερημος) lonely/solitary
erepsis, (Gr. ερεψις) roofing
erept, (L. ereptio) snatching/taking by force
-eres, (Gr. -ηρης) adj. suf.
eresis, (Gr. αιρεσις) taking/receiving/acquisition of power
eret -mo, (Gr. ερετμος) rowing
ereth -ist -iz, (Gr. ερεθιζω) I rouse to anger
ereun, (Gr. ερευνα) inquiry/search/exploratory operation
erg -asia -o, (Gr. εργασια) work/business/productive labour (e.g. of bees)
erg, (Gr. εργον) work/activity
ergastul, (L. ergastulum) workhouse for debtors or slaves
ergat -es -o, (Gr. εργατης) a worker
ergod, (Gr. εργωδης) irksome/troublesome
ergot, (OFr. ar(i)got) a cocks spur
ergot, (L. ergot) a fungus (*Claviceps purpurea*)
eri, (Gr. εαρινος) of spring/spring-time
eri, (Gr. εριον) wool
eri, (Gr. ηρι) early/in the morning
eri-, (Gr. ερι-) strengthening prefix = very, much
-eria, (L.) suf. denoting: place where/place for
eric -a, (Gr. ερεικη) heath
erici -n -us, (L. ericius) a hedgehog (*Erinaceus europaeus*)
erigeron, (Gr. εριγερων) early-old, a type of groundsel (*Senecio vulgaris*)
erin, (Gr. ερινεος) woollen
erineo, (Gr. ερινεος) the wild fig (*Ficus* sp.)
erio, (Gr. εριον) wool
eriole, (Gr. εριωλη) hurricane/whirlwind
erioxyl, (Gr. εριοξυλον) cotton
eripho, (Gr. εριφος) a young goat
eripne, (Gr. εριπνη) a cliff/crag/any sheer ascent
eripsimo, (Gr. ερειψιμος) thrown down/in ruins
eris -m -t, (Gr. ερις) strife/quarrel/contention
erisma -t, (Gr. ερεισμα) prop/stay/support

eristalis, (L. eristalis) an undefined precious stone
eristico, (Gr. εριστικος) fond of strife or battle
eritho, (Gr. εριθος) a hired servant/day-labourer
eritmo, (Gr. εριτμος) precious/highly-prized
erizoo, (Gr. εριζωος) long-lived
ermineus, (L. ermineus) white, like ermine
ern -o, (Gr. ερνος) young sprout/shoot/offspring
erneum, (L. erneum) a cake baked in an earthen pot
erno, (Gr. ερνος) a sprout/shoot/offspring
erod -i, (Gr. ερωδιος) a heron, prob. the common heron (*Ardea cinerea*)
eros, (Gr. ερως) love/desire/the god of love
eros, (L. erodere) to wear away
eros, (L. erosus) eaten away/consumed
erot -e -em, (Gr. εροταω) a question/a challenge (of sentries)
erot-, (Gr. ερωτ-) love-
erotyl, (Gr. ερωτυλος) a loved one/a darling
erpe -s -t, (Gr. ερπετον) an animal which moves on all fours
erpes, (Gr. ερπης) shingles
erpo, (Gr. ερπω) creep/crawl/move slowly
err -an -at, (L. erratus) wandering about/straying
ers -ae -e, (Gr. ερση) dew/rain drops/metaph. of any fresh, young or tender thing
eruca, (L. eruca) caterpillar
eructo, (L. eructare) belch/vomit/eject
-erum, (L.) of, belonging to, pertaining to
erupt, (L. eruptio) bursting forth/an attack
erycin -a, (L. Erycinus) the goddess Venus
eryg -e -ma -mos, (Gr. ερυγη) a belching
erygmelo, (Gr. ερυγμηλος) a loud bellowing
eryma, (Gr. ερυμη) fence/guard/defence
eryo, (Gr. ερυω) drag/draw/pull
erysi-, (Gr. ερυθρος) red
erythr -o, (Gr. ερυθρος) red
-es, (Gr. -ες) suf. ind. an agent/dooer of an action
es-, (Gr. εσ-, εισ-) into/to/towards
esca, (L. esca) victuals/bait/tit bits
-escens -is -e, (L. -escent) a participle ending signifying beginning of/becoming/
              inceptive (often equivalent to the English *-ish*)
eschar, (Gr. εσχαρα) hearth/fireplace/brazier
eschar, (Gr. εσχαρος) perhaps a kind of sole
eschar, (Gr. εσχαροω) ulcerate/to be caustic
eschat -o, (Gr. εσχατος) farthest/uttermost/extreme
eschyn, (Gr. αισχυνω) disfigure/dishonour/disdain/shame
escul -us, (L. aesculetum) the winter or Italian oak (*Aesculus* spp.)/an oak forest
esculen -t, (L. esculentus) edible
-ese, (L.) of, pertaining to, originating in, inhabitant of
csmo, (Gr. εσμος) a swarm of bees/something which settles
cso-, (Gr. εσω) within/inward
esod, (Gr. εισοδος) a way in
esophag -o -us, (Gr. οισοφαγος) the gullet
esor/estrix, (L. esor/estrix) an eater
esot-at, (Gr. εσωτατος) innermost
esoter, (Gr. εσωτερικος) inner/esoteric
-esque, (Fr. (It. -esco)) like in manner or style
-ess, (OFr. -esse) feminine suffix
-essa, (L. /Gr. -essa; -issa) feminine suffixes
essed, (L. esseda) a two-wheeled war-chariot

-cssus, (NL. -essus) dim. suf.

essymen, (Gr. εσσυμενος) hurrying/eager/impetuous

est -es, (Gr. εσθιω) I eat/devour/consume

esth -es, (Gr. εσθης) clothing/clothes

esthem -ato, (Gr. αισθησις) perception

esthesi -o, (Gr. αισθησις) sensation/perception

esthet, (Gr. αισθετος) sensible/perceptible

-esthi, (Gr. εσθιω) I eat/devour/consume

esthlo, (Gr. εσθλος) good/brave/stout

estival, (L. aestivus) of summer

-estr -is, (L. -estris) suffix ind. a place of growth/dwelling/belonging

estr -o -us, (Gr. οιστρος) gadfly/metaph. a sting/goad/anything that torments/a frenzy

estri, (Gr. εστρις) thrice

estrix, (L. estrix) a female eater

estu -a, (L. aestus) boiling/agitation/seething/dizziness/perplexity

estuar, (L. aestuarium) estuary/firth/creek

esurio, (L.) to be hungry/to hunger/to desire food

-et, -ette, -ot, (Fr.) dim. suffixes

eta, (Gr. ητα ε E) seventh letter of the Greek alphabet

eteo, (Gr. ετεος) true/genuine

-etes, (Gr. -ετες) a dweller/one who dwells

etesi -us, (Gr. ετησιος) yearly/lasting a year

eth -er, (L. aether) the upper air/(poet.) heaven

etha, (Gr. εθας) customary/usual/tame

ethel -o, (Gr. εθελω) wish/will

etheo, (Gr. ηθεος/ηθιος) an unmarried youth/unmated

ether -i, (Gr. αιθηρ) the upper air/the heavens

ethic, (Gr. ηθικος) moral/moral character/tactful

ethio -p, (Gr. αιθιοψ) burnt-face/Ethiopian/African

ethiro, (Gr. εθειρα) hair/mane

ethisma, (Gr. εθισμα) habit/custom

ethm -o -us, (Gr. ηθμος) sieve/strainer/colander

ethma, (Gr. εθμη) vapour

ethn -o, (Gr. εθνος) number of people living together/band of comrades/nation/flock, swarm, etc.

etho, (Gr. εθος) a custom/usage/habit

etho, (Gr. ηθος) haunts or abodes of animals

etio, (Gr. αιτιος) responsible for

etiol -ate, (Fr. étioler) pale/whitened/blanched

etno, (Gr. ετνος) a thick soup of pease or beans

etor, (Gr. ητορ) the heart/seat of life

etos -io, (Gr. ετωσιος) fruitless/in vain

etos, (Gr. ετος) year

etr -a -o, (Gr. ητρον) the abdomen, esp. lower part/belly of a pot/pith of a reed

etrio, (Gr. ητριον) warp/a thin, fine cloth

etron, (Gr. ητρον) abdomen, esp. the lower part/pith of a reed

-ett, -a -um -us, (NL) dim. suf.

-ette, -et, -ot, (Fr.) dim. suffixes

-etum, (L.) a place of collective growth

-etus, (L. -etus) having the nature of

etym -o, (Gr. ετυμος) true

eu, (Gr. ευ-) pref. good/well/pleasing/easily

-eua, -eum, -eus, (L.) made of/having the resemblance of (in material/colour)

euch, (Gr. ευχη) prayer/vow/curse

eucrato, (Gr. ευκρατος) well-tempered/temperate

eucrato, (Gr. ευκρατως) firmly/fast

eudi -o, (Gr. ευδιος) calm/clear/fine/warm/mild/peaceful/gracious

eudoro, (Gr. ευδωρος) generous

eugene, (Gr. ευγενης) well-born

euido, (Gr. ευειδης) shapely/beautiful

eulab, (Gr. ευλαβεια) discretion/caution/godly fear/timidity

eule, (Gr. ευλη) a worm/maggot

euloncho, (Gr. ευλογχος) fortunate/propitious

-eum, (NL. -eum Gr. -ειον) a place where

eumaro, (Gr. ευμαρης) easy/convenient

eumeco, (Gr. ευμηκης) tall/considerable/great

eumen, (Gr. ευμενης) kindly

eunuch, (Gr. ευνουχος) a castrated person/a guardian of women/of dates without
        stones

euonym, (Gr. ευονυμιος) of good name/honoured/prosperous/fortunate

eupatori -um, (Gr. ευπατοριον) agrimony

eupet, (Gr. ευπετης) favourable/fortunate

euphem, (Gr. ευφημια) use of words of good omen/auspiciousness

euphon, (Gr. ευφωνια) a pleasing sound

euphorbi -a -um, (Gr. ευφορβια) spurge (*Euphorbia* spp.)

euphrasia, (Gr. ευφρασια) good cheer

euphue, (Gr. ευφυης) shapely/graceful/clever

euphy, (Gr. ευφυης) well-grown/shapely/well-ordered/graceful

euporia, (Gr. ευπορια) plenty/ease

eur -o, (Gr. Ευρος) the East wind

eur -o, (Gr. ευρος) breadth/width

eurax, (Gr. ευραξ) on one side/sideways

eurhopo, (Gr. ευρωπος) inclining or sliding easily

eurin, (Gr. ευριν (ευρις)) with a good nose

eurip, (Gr. ευριπος) any strait or channel where the flux and reflux is violent

euro -t, (Gr. υερως) mould/dank decay

euro-, European

eury, (Gr. ευρυς) wide/broad/spacious

-eus -eutes, (Gr. ευς/ευτης) one who/an agent

eusomat, (Gr. ευσωματος) sound in limb/able-bodied/well-grown

eustachi, Eustachio, an Italian anatomist

eutact, (Gr. ευτακτεω) to be orderly/behave well

eutel, (Gr. υετελεια) cheapness/meanness/shabbiness

-eutes -eus, (Gr. ευς/ευτης) one who/an agent

euthem, (Gr. ευθεμων) tidy inhabits/harmonious

euthen, (Gr. ευθηνια) abundance

euthicto, (Gr. ευθικτος) clever/quick/to the point

euthy, (Gr. ευθυς) straight/direct

euthym -o, (Gr. υεθυμος) kind/generous/cheerful

eutolmo, (Gr. ευτολμος) courageous

evacu -a, (L. vacare) to be empty/void

evan -escen -id, (L. evanidus) vanishing/passing away

evani -o, (Gr. ευανι) making trouble easily

evect, (L. evectus) carry out/carry up/sail away/ride away

evectic, (L. ευεκτικος) good health/wholesome

evexus, (L. evexus) rounded at the top

evidens, (L. evidens) clear/plain/visible

evira, (L. evirare) to castrate

evirat, (L. eviratus) effeminate/weak

evol -ut, (L. evolvere) to unroll

evuls, (L. evulsio) a pulling out (as of teeth)

evum (aevum), (L. aevum) lifetime/age

ex-, (L. ex-) prefix - without/not/lacking/from out/out of
exacerb, (L. exacerbare) to irritate/provoke/exasperate
exaesio, (Gr. εξαισιος) extraordinary
exagger, (L. exaggerare) to heap up/enlarge/increase
examen, (L. examen) swarm/throng/crowd/shoal
examma, (Gr. εξαμμα) handle
exanclo, (L. exanclare) to exhaust/drain/suffer/endure to the end
-exanthema, (Gr. εξανθημα) eruption/efflorescence/pustule
exarat, (L. exarare) to plough up/dig up
exastis, (Gr. εξαστις) fringe
excert, (L. exsertus) protruding/put forth
excetra, (L. excetra) a snake/viper - as term of abuse
excipulum, (L. excipulum) receptacle/vessel
excit -o, (L. excitare) arouse/call forth/provoke
excresc, (L. excrescere) to grow up/spring up
excret, (L. excretus) separate/sift/sort/throw out
excubit, (L. excubitor) guard/sentinel
excult, (L. excultus) adorned/polished
exeche, (Gr. εξεχε-) prominent
exeden, (L. exedo) devour/consume/wear down/exhaust
exedro, (Gr. εξεδρος) away from home/extraordinary/out of/away from
exhib, (L. exhibere) to produce/show/display/exhibit
exhil -ar, (L. exhilare) to make cheerful
exhomil, (Gr. εξομιλος) strange/unfamiliar/alien
exi, (Gr. ηξις) coming
exi, (L. exigere) to drive out/drive away/drive through/complete
exigu, (L. exiguus) small/little/scanty/short (of time)
exil -i, (L. exilitas) thinness/meagerness/weakness
exit, (L. exitus) a going out/a way out
exitelo, (Gr. εξιτηλος) lessening/fading
exitiosus, (L. exitiosus) destructive/fatal/deadly
exo, (Gr. εξο) outside/going out/out of
exocho, (Gr. εξοχος) jutting out/projecting/eminent
exod -o -us, (Gr. εξοδος) way out/a going out
exoeno, (Gr. εξοινος) drunken
exole, (Gr. εξολεθρευω) ruined/completely destroyed
exolet, (L. exoletus) mature
exorm -i, (Gr. εξορμη) going out/expedition
exoter -o, (Gr. εξωτερικος) external/belonging to the outside
exotic -o, (Gr. εξωτικος) foreign/outlying/alien
expio, (L. expare) to appease
explicat, (L. explicatio) an unfolding/uncoiling
expul, (L. expulare) to drive out
exsp -e -es, (L. exspes) without hope
exsula, (L. exsulis) an exile
extern -o, (L. externus) outside/external
extim, (L. extimus) farthest away/outermost
extra, (L. extra-) beyond/outside/more
extrem, (L. extremus) outermost
extrins, (L. extrinsecus) from the outside/on the outside/outwardly
extrors, (L. extrarius) outward/external/extrinsic
exu, (L. exuere) to strip off/to deprive of
exuber, (L. exuberare) prolific/abundantly productive
exud, (L. exudare) to sweat
exust, (L. exustio) a burning up/conflagration
exuv -i, (L. exuere) to strip off
exygr -o, (Gr. εξυγρος) watery/liquid

F

fab -a -ella, (L. faba) a bean
fabul -a, (L. fabula) talk/conversation/story/fable
fac -et -es -ia, (L. facies) aspect/face/appearance
fac, (L. facere) to make
faci, (L. facil) easy
facin, (L. facinus) a deed or action, esp. a misdeed/crime
factio, (L. factiosus) busy/factious
factiti, (L. factitare) to make/to do frequently
factum, (L. factum) act/deed
facula, (L. facula) a little firebrand
-facula, (L. facula) a little torch (dim. of L. *fax*)
facult, (L. facultas) possibility/feasibility/ability/capacity
faec -i, (L. faeces) dregs
fag -a -us, (L. fagus) the beech tree (*Fagus* spp.)
fal -c -x, (L. falx) a sickle/scythe
fala, (L. fala/phala) scaffold/a wooden tower from which missiles were thrown
falc -o, (L. falco) a falcon
falcat, (L. falcatus) sickle-shaped/hooked
falcul, (L. falcula) little hook
falisc, (L. falsica) a rack in a manger
fallac, (L. fallax) deceitful/treacherous/false/fallacious
fals -i, (L. falsus) wrong/mistaken/misled/untrue
falx, (L. falx) sickle/bill-hook
fam -eli -in, (L. famelicus) hungry/famished
famex, (L. famex) bruise
famil, (L. familia) a family/household
famul -us, (L. famulus) a house-servant/slave
fan, (AS. fann) fan
fantas, (L. phantasia) phantom/delusion/fancy/caprice
fanum, (L. fanum) a temple
farc, (L. farctus) stuffed
farcim, (L. farcimen) a sausage
farin -a, (L. farina) flour
-farius, (L. -farius) suf. ind. multiplication in numbers or parts
fasc, (L. fascis) a bundle/pack
fasci -a, (L. fascia) a band/head-band/bandage/woman's girdle
fasciat, (L. fasciatus) banded
fascin -o, (L. fascinare) to bewitch
fasciola, (L. fasciola) a little bandage
fascis, (L. fascis) a bundle/packet/sheaf
fast, (L. fastus) pride/arrogance
fastig -at -o, (L. fastigatus) pointed/sharpen to a point
fastigi -um, (L. fastigium) pointed/sloping down/slanting/gable/slope/depth/dignity
fat, (AS. faett) fat/grease/lard
fateor, (L. fateor) confess/admit/allow
fatig -o, (L. fatigare) to weary
fatisc, (L. fatiscere) to crack
fatu, (L. fatuitas) foolishness/silliness
fauc -es -i, (L. fauces) throat/narrow passage
faun, (L. Faunus) the god of the woods, also of herdsmen.
faust, (L. faustus) favourable/fortunate/lucky
fauto, (L. fautor) a patron/promoter
faux, (L. faux/fauces) throat/pharynx
fav -o -us, (L. favus) a honeycomb
favill -a, (L. favilla) glowing ashes/embers/spark

faviss, (L. favissa) a cellar or reservoir of a temple
favon -i, (L. favonius) the west wind which blew at the beginning of spring
favus, (L. favus) a honeycomb
fawn, (AS. fagnian) rejoice/flatter
fax, (L. fax/facis) torch/firebrand
febr -i, (L. febris) fever
februo, (L. februum) purify/expiate
fec -i -ul, (L. faeces) dregs
fecund, (L. fecundus) fruitful/prolific
feli -n -s, (L. feles) a cat
felic -it -itas, (L. felicitas) happiness/good fortune/success
felix, (L. felix) happy
fell, (L. fel/fellis) the gall bladder/gall/bile
fellat, (L. fellator/fellatrix) a sucker
felo, (L. feles) a cat/robber
fem -or -oro -ur, (L. femur) the thigh
femin, (L. femina) a female
femur, (L. femur) thigh
fen, (L. fenare) to bridle
fence, (L. defensus) protect/guard
fenestr -a, (L. fenestra) window
feng -o, (Gr. φεγγω) make bright/shine/gleam
fenisec -a, (L. faeniseca) a mower/countryman
fenum, (L. faenum) hay
fer -a, (L. fera) a wild animal
fer, (L. ferire) to strike/knock/smite
-fer, (L. ferre) to bear/bring/move/produce/plunder
feral, (L. feralis) of the dead
ferax, (L. ferax) fertile/fruitful/prolific
ferculum, (L. ferculum) a frame/litter/bier/tray
feria, (L. feria) holiday/festival
ferin, (L. ferinus) of wild animals/of the wilderness
ferment, (L. fermentum) leaven/yeast
fero -c -x, (L. ferox) courageous/war-like/brave/wild/unbridled/arrogant
-ferous, (L. ferre) to bear/bring /move/produce/plunder
ferr, (L. ferrum) iron
ferrugin, (L. ferrugineus) rust-coloured/dusky
ferrugo, (L. ferrugo) rust
ferrul, (Fr. ferrule) a ring/bracelet
fertil, (L. fertilis) fertile/fruitful
ferul -a, (L. ferula) fennel (*Foeniculum vulgare*)/a stick/cane/goad
ferus, (L. ferus) wild/uncultivated/rough/savage
ferv -en -id -or, (L. ferventis) glowing/hot/heated/fiery
fess, (L. fessus) weary/tired/exhausted
fest, (L. festus) joyful/merry/of a holiday
festin, (L. festinare) to hasten/hurry/accelerate
festuc -a, (L. festuca) a stalk/straw/stem
fet -i -us, (L. fetus) the offspring while in the womb/that which is brought forth
fetal, (L. fetalium) birthday
feti -d, (L. fetere) to stink
fetus, (L. fetus) pregnant/fertile/fruitful
-fex, (L. facere) suf. denoting a maker
-fiber, (L. fiber) a beaver (*Castor fiber*)
fibr -in -o, (L. fibra) fibre/nerve/band
fibul -a, (L. fibula) broach/pin/buckle/clamp
fic -o -us, (L. ficus) the fig tree (*Ficus* spp.)
-fic, (L. -fic) suf. ind. make/cause
fic-a -ation, (L. facere) to make

fict, (L. fictus) feigned/false
fictil, (L. fictilis) earthen/made of clay
-ficus, (L. ficus) suf. denoting making/doing/causing
ficus, (L. ficus) the fig tree (*Ficus* spp.)
-fid, (L. findere) to split/cleave
fide -l -n, (L. fidelitas) faithfulness
fidel -i, (L. fidelia) an earthenware pot or vase
fidi, (L. fides) a lute
fidic -in, (L. fidicen) lute player
fiend, (AS. feond) enemy/foe
fier, (L. fieri) to become/happen
fig, fix, (L. figere) to fasten/fix
figul -a, (L. figulus) a potter
figulinus, (L. figulinus) pertaining to pottery
figur -a, (L. figura) form/shape/figure
fil -i -o -um, (L. filum) a thread
fili -a, (L. filia/filius) daughter/son
fili -c -x, (L. felix) a fern
filum, (L. filum) a thread
fim -us, (L. fimus) manure
fimbri -a, (L. fimbriae) fringe/border/edge
fin -a -i, (L. finis) boundary/limit/border/end
fin, (AS. finn) fin
find, (L. findere) to split/cleave
finit -i, (L. finitimus) adjoining/bordering
firm, (L. firmus) strong/stable/constant/true
fisc -us, (L. fiscus) a basket/money bag/purse/state treasury
fish, (AS. fisc) fish
fiss -i -ur, (L. fissus) a cleft
fissil -is, (L. fissilis) that can be cloven or split
fissur, (L. fissura) a split/chink.
fistuc -a, (L. fistuca) a type of beetle/rammer/pile-driver
fistul -a -i, (L. fistula) a pipe/tube/flute
fix -us, (L. fixus) immovable/fast
facc -id, (L. flaccidus) flabby/weak/languid
flabell -a, (L. flabellum) a small fan
flabella, (L. flabellare) to fan
flabr, (L. flabrum) breezes/blasts of wind
flagell -um, (L. flagellum) a small whip
flagr -an, (L. flagrantia) a burning/blazing/glittering
flamen, (L. flamen) a priest
flamm -ei, (L. flammeum) a bridal veil
flamm, (L. flamma) a flame/blaze/blazing fire
flamme, (L. flammeus) fiery/fame-coloured/fiery-red
flat, (L. flatus) blowing/blast/breathing
flav, (L. flavus) yellow/golden
fleb -il, (L. flebilis) tearful/doleful/lamentable
flect -o, (L. flectere) to bend/turn/curve
fledge, flie, (Ger. fleuzan) to fly
flet, (L. fletus) wept/lamented
fleur, (Fr. fleur) flower
flex -i -u, (L. flexus) bending/turning/pliant
flict, (L. flictus) struck/beaten
flig, (L. fligere) to beat down/dash down
flo, (L. flare) to blow/blow forth
flocc, (L. floccus) a lock of wool
flor -a, (L. Flora) goddess of flowers and spring
florid, (L. floridus) flowery/fresh/blooming**

flos, (L. flos) a flower/ornament
floscul -us, (L. flosculus) a little flower
flu, (L. fluere) to flow/wave
fluctu, (L. fluctuor) waver/toss about
fluen -t, (L. fluens) flowing/fluent
fluito, (L. fluitare) to float/undulate
flum -en -in -ini, (L. flumen) river/stream/stream of anything
fluvi -a, (L. fluvius) a river/stream
flux, (L. fluxus) a flowing
foc -i -us, (L. focus) fireplace/hearth/house family/home/a point
fod, (L. fodere) to dig/dig up/stab
fodien -t, (L. fodere) digging
fodina, (L. fodina) a pit/mine
foed, (L. foedus) a league/agreement
foed, (L. foedus) filthy/ugly/abominable
foenisec -a, (L. faeniseca) a mower/countryman
foeten, (L. foetidus) having a bad smell/stinking/fetid
foetus, (L. foetus) a foetus/fetus
foli -a -um, (L. folium) a leaf
folli, (L. follis) a sac/bag/bellows/puffed out cheeks
follicul, (L. folliculus) a little bag or sac
foment -um, (L. fomentum) a warm lotion/poultice
fomes, (L. fomes) tinder/kindling wood/a genus of fungi (order Agaricales)
fon -s -t -tan, (L. fons/fontis) a spring/fountain/origin/source
fon, (Gr. φονος) murder/slaughter/homicide
fora, (L. foratus) bored
foram -en -in, (L. foramen) an opening
forast, (L. frasticus) out of doors
forcip -i, (L. forceps) tongs/forceps
ford, (L. fordus) pregnant/a cow in calf
foren -s, (L. forensis) of the forum/public
foresc, (L. floresco) blossoming/flourishing
forf -ex -ic -icis, (L. forfex) shears/scissors
forficat, (L. forficatus) scissors-shaped/forked
fori -s, (L. foris) a door/out of doors/outside
form -a, (L. forma) shape/form/beauty
formic -a, (L. formica) an ant
formid, (L. formido) dread/terror
formos, (L. formosus) beautiful
formul, (L. formula) rule/method
forn -ac -ax, (L. fornax) oven/kiln
forn -ic -ix, (L. fornix) an arch/vault/arcade/brothel
fornic, (L. fornicatus) vaulted
fors, (L. fors) chance/luck
fort -i, (L. fortis) strong/powerful/robust/stout
fort, (L. fortuna) luck/chance
fortax, (L. fortax) carrier/bearer
fortis, (L. fortis) strong/powerful/brave
fortuit, (L. fortuitus) accidental/casual chance occurrence
forum, (L. forum) an open public place/market place
forus, (L. forus) a ship's gangway/tiers of cells in a beehive/block of seats in the theatre
foss -a, (L. fossa) a ditch
fossil, (L. fossilis) dug up
fossor, (L. fossor) a digger
fotus, (L. fotus) a warning
fove -a, (L. fovea) a pit/pitfall/depression
fracid, (L. fracidus) overripe/soft/mellow
fract, (L. fractus) broken/dashed

frag -a, (L. fragum) the strawberry (*Fragaria* spp.)
fragil, (L. fragilis) frail/fragile/brittle
fragm -en -in, (L. fragmentum) a piece broken off
fragor, (L. fragor) a loud noise/crash/crack
fragos, (L. fragosus) broken/rough/uneven
fragr -an, (L. fragrare) to emit a smell/fragrant
framb -es -oes, (L. framboes) the raspberry (*Rubus* spp.)
frang, (L. frango) break/break in pieces/shatter
frat -er -r, (L. frater) brother
fratercul -us, (L. fraterculus) little brother
fraud -a, (L. fraudare) to cheat/defraud/deceive/swindle
fraxin -us, (L. fraxinus) an ash tree (*Fraxinus* spp.)/spear or javelin
fregat -a, (It. fregata) a frigate
frem -it, (L. fremere) to roar/murmur/growl
fren -a -at -um, (L. frenum) a bridle/reins/bit/curb
fret, (L. fretum) strait/channel/estuary
fret, (L. fretus) a strait/an interval/spring (season)
fret, (L. fretus) trusting to/relying on/confiding in
friable, (L. friabilis) easily broken
frict, (L. fricare) to rub/rub down
frig -er -id -or, (L. frigidus) cold/cool/chilly
frig, (L. frigus) cold/coldness/winter
frigid, (L. frigidus) cold/stiff/feeble/spiritless/lifeless
frigo, (L. frigere) to roast/parch
fritill -us, (L. fritillus) a dice box
frivol, (L. frivolus) trifling/worthless
fron, (L. frons) forehead/brow/front
frond -e -i, (L. frons) a leaf/foliage
front, (L. frontis) front
fruc, (L. frux) fruit/crops/result/value
fruct -i -us, (L. fructus) a fruit
frug, (L. frux) fruits/success
frugal, (L. frugalis) economical/thrifty/honest
frugi, (L. frugi) useful/honest/discrete/moderate
frument -um, (L. frumentum) corn/grain
frustr, (L. frustra) in error/mistaken/in vain/without reason
frustul -um, (L. frustum) a bit/piece/morsel
frut -ex -ic, (L. frutex) a shrub/bush
frux, (L. frux/fruges) fruit/produce
fry, (L. frigere) parch/roast
fuc -i -us, (L. fucus Gr. φυκος) rock-lichen/rouge/disguise/a drone
fucat, (L. fucatus) coloured/painted
fug -i, (L. fugere) to flee/run away/avoid
fuga -ci -x, (L. fugax) runaway/swift/fleeting
fugit, (L. fugitivus) fleeing/flying
fulcim, (L. fulcimen) prop/support
fulcr -um, (L. fulcrum) foot (of a couch)/a support/prop
fulg -en -i, (L. fulgere) to flash/shine/lighten/glitter/gleam
fulg -or -ur, (L. fulgor) lightening/glitter/brightness
fulic -a, (L. fulica) a coot (*Fulica* spp.)
fulig -in, (L. fuligo) soot
fulm -en -in, (L. fulmen) a thunderbolt/stroke of lightening
fult, (L. fultura) prop/support
fulv, (L. fulvus) tawny/yellowish-brown/reddish-yellow
fum, (L. fumus) smoke
fun -al -i -is, (L. funalis) attached to a rope/a trace-horse/the thong of a sling
funct, (L. functio) a performance/performing/executing
fund -a -i, (L. funda) a sling/missile

fund, (L. fundare) to found
fund, (L. fundere) to pour out/spread out
fund, (L. fundus) the bottom
fundat, (L. fundatus) firm/grounded
fundibulum, (L. fundibulum) funnel
fundit, (L. funditus) from the bottom/completely/entirely
fundul, (L. fundulus) piston
fune -bri -re, (L. funebris) funeral/funereal/deadly/destructive
fung -i -us, (L. fungus) a mushroom/fungus
funi -cul -s, (L. funis) a rope/cord/line
fur -en, (L. furenter) furiously
furc -a, (L. furca) a two-pronged fork
furcip, (L. forceps) pincers
furfur, (L. furfur) bran/scurf/scales
furi -os, (L. furiosus) raging/raving/mad/furious/maddening
furn -ari -us, (L. furnus) an oven/bakehouse
furor, (L. furor) madness/raving/insanity
furtiv, (L. furtivus) stolen/secret/concealed
furunc, (L. furunculus) a sneak thief/pilferer
furvus, (L. furvus) dark-coloured/dusky/black
fus -i, (L. fusus) a spindle/spread out/wide
fusc, (L. fuscus) dusky/tawny/dark
fuscina, (L. fuscina) a trident
fusilis, (L. fusilis) liquid/molten/soft
fust -i -is, (L. fustis) a stick/staff/cudgel
fust, (L. fustis) staff/cudgel/club
fusus, (L. fusus) a spindle
futil, (L. futilis/futtilis) brittle/vain/worthless
futuo, (L. futuere) to copulate

G

gacino, (Gr. γακινας) earthquake
gad, (Gr. γαδος) a kind of fish
gaea, (Gr. γαια) the earth/one's country
gaes -o, (Gr. γαισον/γαισος) a kind of javelin
gagates, (Gr. γαγατης) lignite/jet
gala -ct -cto, (Gr. γαλα) milk
gala, (Gr. γαλη) polecat/weasel
galag, (Wolof (W. Sudanese lang.) golokh, a lemur-like primate
galat -ea -hei, (Gr. Γαλαται) a sea nymph
galathen, (Gr. γαλαθηνος) young/tender
galax -i, (Gr. γαλαξαιος) milky/milk-white
galax, (LL. galaxias) a kind of fish
galb -an -in, (L. galbinus) greenish-yellow
galb, (L. galbulus) cypress nut
galbe, (L. galbeum) an arm band/arm bandage
gale -a -i, (Gr. γαλεη) a marten/weasel/polecat
gale -a, (L. galea) helmet
galen -a, (Gr. γαληνη) stillness/calm/calmness/serenity
galen, (Gr. γαληνη) an ore of lead (lead sulphide)
galeo -d, (Gr. γαλεος) a shark/a marten
galer -o, (Gr. γαλερος) cheerful

galer, (L. galerum) a skull cap/wig

galid, (Gr. γαλιδευς) a young weasel

galium, (Gr. γαλιον) bedstraw (*Galium* spp.)

gall -a, (L. galla) the oak apple/gall-nut

gall -in -o -us, (L. gallus) a cock/chicken

gallic, (L. gallicula) a Gallic shoe

galvan -i -o, (L. Galvani) of physiological electrical currents (Luigi Galvani, Italian physiologist)

gam -o -us, (Gr. γαμος) marriage/union

gambro, (Gr. γαμβρος) a relative by marriage

gamel, (Gr. γαμελιος) nuptial

gamet -o, (Gr. γαμετης) a spouse/husband

gamma, (Gr. γαμμα γ Γ) third letter of the Greek alphabet

gammar -us, (L. gammarus) a kind of lobster

gamos, (Gr. γαμος) marriage/union

gamphel, (Gr. γαμφηλαι) jaws of animals/beaks

gamps -o, (Gr. γαμψος) curved/crooked/bent

-gamy, (Gr. γαμος) marriage/reproduction

gan -eo -o -os, (Gr. γανος) brightness/sheen/gladness/joy

gan -eon -ium, (L. ganium) brothel or low eating-house

gangamo, (Gr. γαγγαμον) a small round net

gangli -on, (Gr. γαγγλιον) a little tumour

gangren, (Gr. γαγγραινα) gangrene/mortification

gannio, (L. gannire) to yelp/snarl/growl

gap, (ON. gapp) open/yawn/gape

gar, (AS. gar) spear

gargal -is -o, (Gr. γαργαλιζω) tickle/titillate

garin, (Gr. γαρινος) a kind of fish

garrul, (L. garrulus) talkative/chattering/babbling

gast -er -ero -r -ro, (Gr. γαστηρ) stomach/belly/paunch/womb

gaud -e -i, (L. gaudeo) to rejoice

gaul, (Gr. γαυλος) a water-bucket/milk-pail

gaur -o, (Gr. γαυροω) proud/arrogant

gaus -o, (Gr. γαυσος) crooked/bent outwards

gausap, (L. gausape) a shaggy woollen garment or cloth

gavial -is, (NL. gavialis) a crocodile (*Gavialis gangeticus*)

gavis, (L. gavisus) causing delight

gaza, (Gr. γαζα) treasure/riches

ge -o, (Gr. γεα) earth/land/soil/home

gegon, (Gr. γεγωνος) loud-sounding/sonorous

geiss -o, (Gr. γεισσον) the cornice

-geiton -o, (Gr. γειτων) neighbour/borderer

gel, (L. gelare) to congeal

gelasim -o, (Gr. γελασιμος) laughable/ridiculous

gelasin, (Gr. γελασινος) a dimple

gelast, (L. γελασις) laughing

gelat, (L. gelatio) frozen/stiffened

gelech, (Gr. γηλεχης) sleeping on the ground

gelgi, (Gr. γελγις) a head of garlic

gelid, (L. gelidus) icy-cold/frosty/chilling

gelo, (Gr. γελος/γελως) laughter

gelo, (L. gelare) to freeze

gem, (L. gemma) bud/jewel

gemin, (L. geminus) double/twin

gemit, (L. gemitus) groan/sigh

gemm -a -ul, (L. gemma) bud/jewel

gemo, (Gr. γεμος) load/freight
gen -e -ei -i, (Gr. γενειον) a beard/the chin
-gen -e -es -ic, (Gr. -γενης) suf. ind. production/producing/forming
gen -er, (L. generare) to beget/produce/bring to life
gen, (Gr. γεν-) produce
gen, (Gr. γενναω) to generate/produce/beget
gen, (L. gens) a clan/tribe/race/nation
-gena, (L. gena) the cheeks/chin
gene -a -o -s, (Gr. γενεσις) birth/descent/origin/race/an engendering/an origin
gene -sis, (Gr. γεννησις) a begetting/producing
gener -o, (L. genero) to beget/produce
genet, (Gr. γενετης) ancestor/begetter/father
geneth, (Gr. γενεθλη) race/stock/family/offspring
genethli, (Gr. γενεθλιος) birthday
geni -o, (Gr. γενειον) the chin/jaw/beard/lion's mane
-genic, (Gr. γενεσις) producing
genico, (Gr. γενικος) generic
genicul, (L. geniculum) little knee/knotty
genit -i -o, (gignere) to beget
gennaeo, (Gr. γενναιος) noble/excellent
geno, (Gr. γενος) race/nation/a descendant
-genous, (Gr. γενεσις) producing
gens/gent, (L. gens) a clan/tribe/race/nation
gentle, (L. gentilis) of the same clan
genu, (L. genu) the knee
genus, (L. genus Gr. γενος) birth/race/type/kind/descent
geny -o -s, (Gr. γενυς) lower jaw/chin
-geny, (Gr. γενεσις) producing
geo, (Gr. γεω-) earth-
georgyo, (Gr. γεωργικος) a farmer
gephyr -a -o, (Gr. γεφυρη) a bridge
ger -o, (L. gerere) to carry/bear
-ger, (L. -gerous) suf. ind. bear/carry/perform
gera -s -t, (Gr. γηρας) old age
geran, (Gr. γερανος) a crane (bird)
geraro, (Gr. γεραρος) dignified/honoured/majestic
germ, (L. germen) bud/sprig
germen, (L. germen) bud/seed/graft
germin, (L. germinare) to sprout
gero, (Gr. γερο-) pref. carrying the idea of old/venerable/etc.
geron, (Gr. γερων) old man/elder
-gerous, (L. -igerous) in use always/ever present
gerr -ho -i -o, (Gr. γερρον) anything made of wicker-work esp. a shield
gerra, (L. gerrae) trifles/nonsense
gerul, (L. gerulus) a porter
gery -o, (Gr. γηρυω) sing/say/speak/cry/utter
gest, (L. gestare) to bear/carry
gethosyn, (Gr. γηθοσυνος) glad/joyful
geus -i -t, (Gr. γευσις) sense of taste/tasting/taste/flavour
ghost, (AS. gast) soul/spirit
gibb -er -us, (L. gibbus) a hump
giga -n -nto, (L. gigas) giant
gigart, (Gr. γιγαρτον) a grape seed
gigne, (L. gignere) to beget/to give birth to
gigno, (Gr. γιγνωσκω) perceive/know
gilb/gilv, (L. gilbus/gilvus) pale yellow

gingiv -a, (L. gingiva) the gum (of mouth)

ginglar, (Gr. γιγγλαρος) a flute/fife

ginglism -o -us, (Gr. γιγγλισμος) a tickling

ginglym -o -us, (Gr. γιγγλυμος) a hinge

gingras, (Gr. γιγγρας) a small Phoenician flute

girdle, (AS. gyrdel) belt

gisso, (Gr. γεισσον) eaves/cornice/hem/border

gito, (Gr. γειτων) neighbour

gizzard, (L. gigerium) entrail, particularly of birds

glab, (L. glaber) bald/smooth

glaci -a, (L. glacies) ice

gladi -a -us, (L. gladius) a sword

glaes, (L. glaesum/glessum) amber

glager, (Gr. γλαλερος) full of milk

glamyr, (Gr. γλαμυρος) bleary-eyed/watery

glan -d -i -s, (L. glans) an acorn/gland

glanos, (Gr. γλανος) hyena

glaphyr -o, (Gr. γλαφυρος) hollowed/polished/smooth/delicate/neat/dainty

glare -a -o, (L. glarea) gravel (shingle)

glaris, (Gr. γλαρις) a chisel

glauc -o, (L. glaucus) sea-green/bluish-green

glaucidi -um, (Gr. γλαυκιοων) glare fiercely/glare blindly

glaux, (Gr. γλαυξ) the little owl (*Athene noctua*) from its glaring eyes

gle -a -o, (Gr. γλοια) glue

gleb -a, (L. gleba) a lump or clod of earth/soil/land

glen -o, (Gr. γληνη) a socket/the pupil of the eye/eye-ball/a puppet

gleno, (Gr. γλενος) gaudy things/playthings

gless, (L. glessum/glaesum) amber

gleuco, (Gr. γλευκος) sweet new wine/sweetness

gli -a -o, (Gr. γλοια) glue

glis/gliris, (L. glis/gliris) the dormouse (*Glis glis*)

glischr -o, (Gr. γλισχρος) sticky/sticking close/mean/shabby

glob -o -us, (L. globus) sphere/globe

gloch -i -is, (Gr. γλωχις) a point/nail/arrow barb/stigma of saffron

gloe -a -o, (Gr. γλοια) glue

gloi -o, (Gr. γλοια) glue

glom -er -us, (L. glomerare) to form into a ball

glom, (L. glomus) a ball/a ball of thread

gloom, (AS. glom) twilight

glori -a, (L. gloria) fame/renown/glory

gloss -a -o, (Gr. γλωσσα) the tongue

glott -i -o, (Gr. γλωττα) the tongue

glottis, (Gr. γλωττις) the entrance of the windpipe

glox, (Gr. γλωξ) a beard of wheat

glubo, (L. glubo) a strip of bark/peel/skin

gluc/glyc, (Gr. γλυκυς) sweet

glum -a, (L. gluma) hull/husk/bract

glut -e -eo, (Gr. γλουτος) the rump/buttocks

glut -i, (L. gluten) glue

glut -i, (L. glutire) to swallow/gulp down

gluten, (L. gluten) glue

glutin, (L. glutinis) glue

glutio, (L. glutire) to devour/swallow

glyc -er -o, (Gr. γλυκυς) sweet

glycy, (Gr. γλυκυς) sweet

glymma -to, (Gr. γλυμμα) engraved figure/inscription

glyp -h -ho -t -to, (Gr. γλυφα) carving/engraving
glyph, (Gr. γλυφις) notch of an arrow/the arrow
gnamp -to, (Gr. γναμπτω) bend
gnaph -o -us, (Gr. γναφος) the prickly teasel
gnaphalo, (Gr. γναφαλλον/γναφαλον) wool
gnarus, (L. gnarus) knowing/acquainted with
gnash, (ON. gnastan) grind the teeth together
gnat, (AS. gnaet) fly
gnath -o -us, (Gr. γναθος) the jaw/mouth
gnesi, (Gr. γνησιος) lawful/legitimate/genuine
gnom -a -o, (Gr. γνωμη) mark/token/thought/judgement
gnome, (NL. gnomus) a fabled diminutive being
gnomon, (Gr. γνωμων) expert witness/carpenter's square/pointer of sun dial
gnoph -o, (Gr. γνοφος) darkness/storm-clouds
gnorim -o, (Gr. γνοριμος) well-known/familiar/distinguished
gnos -is -t -tic, (Gr. γνωστος) knowable/common knowledge
gnot, (Gr. γνωτος) known/well known
gnytho, (Gr. γνυθος) cave/pit/hollow
go, (AS. gan) move
gobi -us, (Gr. γωβιος) a type of small fish
goeto, (Gr. γοητης) sorcerer/wizard
goit, (L. gutter) throat
goleos, (Gr. γωλεος) hole
gomph -o -us, (Gr. γομφος) a large wedge-shaped bolt
gomphi -o, (Gr. γομφιος) a molar tooth
gomphia, (Gr. γομφιασις) toothache
gomphos, (Gr. γομφωσις) bolted together
gon -e -idi -o -y, (Gr. γονη) seed/offspring
gon -i -ia -io, (Gr. γωνια) corner/angle/solid angle
gon -y, (Gr. γονυ) the knee
gonat, (Gr. γονατιον) little knee
gone, (Gr. γονευειν) to beget
goneu, (Gr. γονευω) produce
gongro, (Gr. γογγρος) excrescence/swelling/conger-eel
gongyl, (Gr. γογγυλος) round
gongylis, (Gr. γογγυλις) a turnip (Brassica campestris)
gongylos, (Gr. γογγυλος) ball/round/sphere
gonia, (Gr. γονια) angle
gonidi, (Gr. γονιδιον) little offspring
gonim -o, (Gr. γονιμος) productive/fertile/fruitful
gonio, (Gr. γωνια) angle/corner
gono, (Gr. γονος) that which is begotten or produced/young animals/fruit
gonu, (Gr. γονυ) the knee
gony, (Gr. γενυς) lower jaw
-gony, (Gr. γονος) offspring/seed/produce
gordi, (Gr. γορδι) a type of knot
gorg -o, (Gr. γοργος) terrible/fearful/fierce
gorge, (L. gurges) abyss/whirlpool/eddy
gorgyra, (Gr. γοργυρα) drain/sewer
goro, (Fr. gorge) throat
gorytos, (Gr. γωρυτος) quiver
gossypi -um, (L. gossypion) cotton
grabat, (L. grabatus) small couch/bed
grabio, (Gr. γραβιον) torch
gracil, (L. gracilis) slender
grad -a, (L. gradus) pace/step/rank/position/slope/grade

grall -a -ato -in, (L. grallae) stilts
gram -en -in, (L. gramen) grass
gram/gramma, (Gr. γραμμα) a written character/a line/stroke/inscription/drawing
gran -io -um, (L. granum) grain/seed
granat, (L. granatum) with many seeds
grand -i, (L. grandis) large/great
grand -in -o, (L. grando) hail/a hailstone
granilos, (L. granulosa) grainy
granum, (L. granum) grain/seed
grao, (Gr. γραυς) old/an old woman
-graph, (Gr. -γραφος) written
graph, (Gr. γραφειν) to write/sketch/draw
graps -i, (Gr. γραψαιος) a crab
grapt, (Gr. γραπτος) written on /painted on
grassat, (L. grassator) vagabond/idler/footpad
grastis, (Gr. γραστις) grass/green fodder
grat -i, (L. gratia) pleasantness/attraction/favour/esteem/regard
gratus, (L. gratus) beloved/agreeable/pleasing
grav -e -i, (L. gravis) heavy/weighty/important
gravid, (L. gravidus) pregnant/loaded/filled
gravis, (L. gravis/gravidus) heavy/laden/pregnant
greg -ar -i, (L. gregare) to collect into a flock/herd
greg, (L. grex) flock/herd
gregar, (L. gregarius) common
gremi -um, (L. gremium) lap/bosom/(fig.) womb
gress, (L. gressus) a step
-grex, (L. grex) flock/herd
gripeus, (Gr. γριπευς) fisherman/maker of fishing nets
griph -o, (Gr. γριφος) fishing-basket/riddle/anything intricate
grise, (Mod.L. griseus) grey/pearl-grey
gromph, (Gr. γρομφας) an old sow
grono, (Gr. γρωνος) eaten out/hollowed out/cavernous
grosph -o -os, (Gr. γροσφος) a type of javelin
gross, (L. grossus) thick/coarse/big/unripe fig
grossul -a -ar, (NL. grossularia) the gooseberry (*Ribes* spp.)
gru -i -s, (L. grus) crane (bird)
grum -a, (L. grumus) hillock/little heap
gry, (Gr. γρυ) a grunt
grylismo, (Gr. γρυλισμος) a grunting
gryll -us, (L. gryllus) a grasshopper
grylo, (Gr. γρυλος) a pig/porker
grymea, (Gr. γρυμεα) a bag/chest
gryno, (Gr. γρυνος) a fagot/firebrand
gryp -o, (Gr. γρυπος) hook-nosed/aquiline/hooked/curved
grysmo, (Gr. γρυσμος) a grunting
gryte, (Gr. γρυτη) a vanity-bag/frippery
guan, (Inca (Quechuan) huanu) dung
gubern -a, (L. gubernaculum) a rudder/helm/direction/management
gubernator, (L. gubernator) a pilot/steersman/governor
gul -a, (L. gula) the gullet/throat
gulos, (L. gulosus) gluttonous
gumm -i, (L. gummi) gum (resin)
guno, (Gr. γουνος) high ground
gurg -it, (L. gurges) whirlpool/eddy/abyss
gurugust, (L. gurgustium) hut/hovel
gust -a -us, (L. gustare) to taste/relish
gutt -a, (L. gutta) a drop/spot

-**guttur -i**, (L. guttur) windpipe/throat
guttus, (L. guttus) a narrow-necked flask
gya, (Gr. γυης) the beam of a plough
gyale, (Gr. γυαλας) a Megarian cup
gyalo, (Gr. γυαλον) a hollow
gyalo, (Gr. γυαλος) a cubical stone
gyg -es, (Gr. γυγης) the white tern (*Gygis alba*)
gyio, (Gr. γυιον) a limb
gyio, (Gr. γυιος) lame
gylio, (Gr. γυλοις) an elongate wallet/hedgehog
gymn -o, (Gr. γυμνος) uncovered/naked/bare/unarmed
gyn -a -e -eco -o, (Gr. γυνη) a woman/female
gynaec, (Gr. γυναικος) of women
gyp -s, (Gr. γυψ/γυπος) a vulture
gyps -o, (Gr. γυψος) chalk/gypsum/cement
gyr -a -o, (L. gyrare) to revolve
gyr, (L. gyrus) circuit/ring/circle
gyrgatho, (Gr. γυργαθος) a wicker basket
gyrin -o -us, (Gr. γυρινος) a tadpole
gyrin, (Gr. γυρινη) a kind of cake
gyris, (Gr. γυρις) the finest meal
gyro, (Gr. γυρος) rounded/curved/crooked/ring/circle

H

haben, (L. habena) a thong/strap/rein
habil, (L. habilis) convenient/expert/handy
habit -at, (L. habitare) to inhabit/dwell
habit, (L. habitus) appearance/bearing/nature/character
habra, (Gr. αβρα) a favourite slave
habro-, (Gr. αβρος) dainty/delicate/pretty/soft/graceful/splendid/luxurious
habrynt, (Gr. αβρυντης) a coxcomb (a cap worn by a jester)
hacten, (L. hactenus) as far as this/so far/hitherto
hades, (Gr. Αιδης) the lower world
hadr -o, (Gr. αδρος) thick/stout
hadryn, (Gr. αδρυνω) ripen/mature
haed -us, (L. haedus) a young goat/kid
haem -a -ato -o, (Gr. αιμα) blood
haemul, (Gr. αιμυλος) wheedling/wily
haemulo, (Gr. αιμυλος) flattering/wheedling
haer -esi, (Gr. αιρεσις) taking/receiving
haereto, (Gr. αιρετος) chosen/elected
haes, (L. haesitare) to stick fast/hesitate/stammer
haet, (L. haetere) to stick to/cling to
hagi -o, (Gr. αγιος) sacred/holy/devoted to the gods
hagno, (Gr. αγνος) pure/chaste/holy
hal -a -e -it, (L. halare) to breathe/exhale
hal -o, (Gr. αλος) sea/salt/salt water
halcyon, (Gr. αλκυων) myth. bird identified with the kingfisher
hales, (Gr. αλης) thronged/crowded
hali -o, (Gr. αλιος) of the sea
hali, (Gr. αλιν) the sea

hali, (Gr. αλς) salt/brine

halia, (Gr. αλια) an assembly or meeting of people

halia, (Gr. αλια) saltcellar

haliaet -e -us, (Gr. αλιαετος) a sea-eagle; prob. the osprey (*Pandion haliaetus*)

halieutes, (Gr. αλιευτης) a fisherman

halimo, (Gr. αλιμος) of or belonging to the sea

halin -o, (Gr. αλινος) saline/made of or from salt

halio, (Gr. αλιος) of the sea

haliphthoro, (Gr. αλιφθορος) a pirate

halit, (L. halitus) breath/exhalation/vapour

hallo, (Gr. αλλος) another/other/different/wrong/bad/unworthy

hallu -c -x, (L. hallux) the big toe

halma -to, (Gr. αλμα) spring/leap/jump/pulsation

halmyro, (Gr. αλμυρος) salty/briny/distasteful

halo-, (Gr. αλος) sea/salt

halosimo, (Gr. αλωσιμος) easy to take or conquer

halter, (Gr. αλτηρες) weights used to give impetus in leaping

haltic, (Gr. αλτικος) good at leaping/nimble

halurgo, (Gr. αλουργος) sea-purple/purple

halys -i -is, (Gr. αλυσις) chain/link/bond

ham -at -i, (L. hamus) a hook/hooked

-ham, (AS. ham) home/enclosure

hama, (Gr. αμα) at once/at same time/together

hamadry -s -d, (L. Hamadryas) a wood nymph

hamamel -is, (Gr. αμαμηλις) the medlar (*Mespilus germanica*)

hamartin -a, (Gr. αμαρτια) a failure/fault/sin/error

hamat, (L. hamatus) hooked/crooked

hamaxa, (Gr. αμαξα) a wagon/wagon-load

hamma, (Gr. αμμα) anything tied, e.g. a knot/noose/halter/link

hamma, (Gr. αμμα) mother/foster mother/nurse

hammil, (Gr. αμιλλα) contest/conflict

hamu, (L. hamus) a hook/a coat of mail/a fish hook/hawk's talon

hamul, (L. hamulus) little hook

hapal -o, (Gr. απαλος) soft/gentle/tender

hapax, (Gr. απαξ) once/once only

haphe, (Gr. αφη) lighting/kindling/touch/grip/infection

hapl -o, (Gr. απλως) simply/plainly/absolutely

haplo, (Gr. απλοος) simple/simplex/single/onefold

haplom -a, (Gr. απλωμα) something unfolded/a coverlet/an expanse

hapso, (Gr. αψος) juncture/joint

hapto, (Gr. απτω) to touch/grasp/hold/seize/fasten

haptra, (Gr. απτρα) wick

harbor, (Ger. herberge) shelter for soldiers

haren, (L. harena) sand/arena

harilo, (L. hariolus) soothsayer/prophet

harma, (Gr. αρμα) a chariot, esp. a war chariot

harmo -s, (Gr. αρμος) a fastening/a fitting/a joint/bolt/shoulder joint

harmoni, (Gr. αρμονια) musical scale/agreement/harmony

harmost, (Gr. αρμσοτος) adapted/suitable/well-fitted

harp -e -i, (Gr. αρπη) sickle/scythe/scimitar/perh. shearwater (*Puffinus* spp.)

harpa, (L. harpa) sharp

harpa, (LL. harpa) a harp

harpac -t, (Gr. αρπακτηρ) a robber

harpag -i, (Gr. αρπαγονις) a grappling-hook

harpal -eo, (Gr. αρπαλεος) devouring/greedy/alluring

harpax, (Gr. αρπαξ) robbing/rapacious

harpe, (Gr. αρπη) an unknown bird of prey/sickle/elephant-goad
harped -o, (Gr. αρπεδονη) cord/thread/yarn
harpeza, (Gr. αρπεζα) hedge
harpis, (Gr. αρπις) a half-boot/foundation
harpy, (Gr. Αρπυιαι) a monster, half bird and half woman (personification of whirlwinds or hurricanes)
haruspex, (L. haruspex) soothsayer/
hast -a, (L. hasta) a spear/pike/javelin
hathr -o, (Gr. αθρους) in crowds, heaps or masses/together
haust -or -r, (L. haurire) to drain/to draw up/to drain/absorb/exhaust/weaken/waste
heauto, (Gr. εαυτου) of oneself
hebdom -at, (Gr. εβδοματος) seventh
hebe -t, (Gr. εβετικος) juvenile/puberty
hebe, (L. hebes) blunt/dull
hebetat, (L. hebetatus) dulled/blunted/weakened
heca, (Gr. εκας) afar/far off/far way from
hecasto, (Gr. εκαστος) each/every
hecat -o -on, (Gr. εκατον) a hundred
hecate, (Gr. Εκατη) goddess of magic and witchcraft
hecato, (Gr. εκατον) a hundred
hecelo, (Gr. εκηλος/εκαλος) at rest/at ease
hecist -o, (Gr. ηκιστος) least/gentlest/slowest
hect -o, (Gr. εκτος) from outside/without/beyond
hectico, (Gr. εκτικος) habitual
hecto, (Gr. εκτος) sixth
hecusio, (Gr. εκουσιος) voluntary
hecyro, (Gr. εκυρος) father-in-law
hed -i -o, (Gr. εδος) seat/abode/dwelling place
hede, (Gr. εδητυς) meat/food
hede-, (Gr. ηδυμος) sweet/pleasant
hedeosm -a, (Gr. ηδυοσμος) sweet-smelling
heder -a, (L. hedera) ivy
hedno, (Gr. εδνον) a wedding gift/bride-price
hedolio, (Gr. εδωλιον) seat/abode
hedon, (Gr. ηδονη) pleasure/joy/delight
hedos, (Gr. εδος) seat/abode/base/foundation
hedr -a -io, (Gr. εδρα) a seat/chair/bench
hedus, (L. haedus) a young goat
hedy, (Gr. ηδυμος) sweet
hegemon, (Gr. ηγεμων) leader
hegeto, (Gr. ηγετης) a leader
hekist, (Gr. ηκιστος) gentlest/slowest/least
hel -a -eo -o, (Gr. ελος) swamp/marsh/marsh meadow
hela, (Gr. ειλη) sun's warmth
helco, (Gr. ελκος) a wound/sore/ulcer/loss
helco, (Gr. ελκος) wound/sore/ulcer
helcto, (Gr. ελκτος) draw/drag/tensile
heleio, (Gr. ελειος) of or in the swamp/marsh
helene, (Gr. ελενη) a torch/wicker basket
heleo, (Gr. ελεος) mercy/compassion
heli -a -o, (Gr. ηλιος) the sun
helic -o, (Gr. ελιξ) rolled/twisted/winding/spiral/convolution/whirl/eddy/tendril/coil/curl
helict, (Gr. ελικτος) rolled/twisted/wreathed
heligma -to, (Gr. ελιγματος) fold/wrapping/curl of hair
heligma, (Gr. ελιγμα) whirling/rolling/a curl

helino, (Gr. ελινος) a vine tendril
helio, (Gr. ηλιος) the sun
heliso, (Gr. ηλισκος) a little nail
helix, (Gr. ελιξ) a spiral/coil
hell -a -ado -en, (Gr. Ελλην) Greece
hellu -o, (L. helluo) a glutton/squanderer
helmin -s -th, (Gr. ελμινθ) a worm
helo, (Gr. ελω) grasp
helor, (Gr. ελωρ) spoil/booty/prey
helos, (Gr. ελος) swamp/marsh/marsh meadow/backwater
helos, (Gr. ηλος) a nail/knot/callus/wart
helot, (Gr. ειλωτης) a (Spartan) surf
heluor, (L. helluo) a glutton/squanderer
helv, (L. helvus) yellow/bay-yellow/tawny
helxis, (Gr. ελξις) a drawing/dragging/trailing
hem -a -ato -ia -o, (Gr. αιμα) blood
hemat, (Gr. αιματιτης) an iron ore/blood-like
hemedapo, (Gr. ημεδαπος) native
hemer -a -o, (Gr. ημερη) a day
hemer, (Gr. ημερος) tame
hemi, (Gr. ημι-) half-
hemiono, (Gr. ημιονος) half-ass (a mule)
hemitomo, (Gr. ημιτομος) a kind of cup
hen -i, (Gr. ενικος) single/individual
hen -o, (Gr. ενος) a year old/a year
hendeca, (Gr. ενδεκα) eleven
henic -o, (Gr. ενικος) single
henicm -o, (Gr. ενικμος) humid
heniko, (Gr. ηνικος) driver
henion, (Gr. ηνια) rein/bit/bridle/any leather thong
heno, (Gr. ενος) a year old/a year
heolo, (Gr. εωλος) stale
heort -io, (Gr. εορτη) feats/festival/holiday
heothino, (Gr. εωθινος) in the morning/early/eastern
hepa -r -t -to, (Gr. ηπαρ L. hepar) the liver
hephtho, (Gr. εφθος) boiled/refined/lanquid
hepial -o -us, (Gr. ηπιαλος) a night-mare
hepset, (Gr. εψητος) boiled
hept -a, (Gr. επτα) seven
hera, (Gr. Ηρα/Ηρη) wife of Zeus
heracle, (Gr. Ηρακλεης) Hercules (myth. hero)
herb -a -i -o, (L. herba) a green plant/grass
herc -o -us, (Gr. ερκος) barrier/fence/enclosure
hered, (L. hereditas) heirship
herma -to, (Gr. ερμα) a support/prop/stay/beam
herma, (Gr. ερμα) reef/sunken rock
hermaphrodit, (Gr. ερμαφροδιτος) combining both sexes/with both male and female
            organs
herme, (Gr. Ερμης) Hermes, the messenger of the gods
hermin -o -s, (Gr. ερμιν/ερμις) bed post
herni -a, (L. hernia) a rupture
hero, (Gr. ηρως) a hero
herodi, (Gr. ερωδιος) a heron, prob. the grey heron (*Ardea cinerea*)
herpest, (Gr. ερπηστης) creeper /stalker
herpet -o, (Gr. ερπετον) reptile/creeping thing
herse, (Gr. ερση) dew

hesis, (Gr. εσις) sending forth/aiming at
hesit -a, (L. haestatio) sticking fast/hesitation/stammering
hesmos, (Gr. εσμος) swarm/flock
hesper -o, (Gr. εσπερος) at evening/the evening star/western
hesper, (Gr. εσπερα) the evening/nightfall/the west
hesso, (Gr. εσσων) inferior/weaker/less/worse
hestho, (Gr. εσθης) clothing/raiment/a garment
hestia, (Gr. εστια) hearth/fireside/house
hestico, (Gr. ηστικος) agreeable/pleasing
hesto, (Gr. ηστος) glad
hesych -o, (Gr. ησυχος) quiet/still/gentle/cautious
hesychast, (Gr. ησυχαστης) a hermit
heta -er -ir, (Gr. εταιρος) comrade/companion/messmate
heter -o, (Gr. ετερο-) the other/different/one of two
heterosis, (Gr. ετερωσις) alteration
hetoemo, (Gr. ετοιμος) ready/prepared
heur, (Gr. ευρετικος) inventive/ingenious
heuresi, (Gr. ευρεσις) discovery/invention
hex -a, (Gr. εξ) six
hex -i -io -is -y, (Gr. εξις) state or habit of mind, body/trained or acquired habit
hiameno, (Gr. ειαμενη) a meadow/a river-side pasture
hiat -us, (L. hiatus) a cleft/opening
hibern, (L. hibernaculum) winter quarters
hibern, (L. hibernum) winter
hibernia, (L. Hibernia) Ireland
hibisc -us, (Gr. ιβισκος) the marsh mallow (*Athaea officinalis*)
hicano, (Gr. ικανος) able/competent
hiceto, (Gr. ικετης) suppliant/pilgrim
hidro, (Gr. ιδρως) sweat/exudation of trees
hidry -s -t, (Gr. ιδρυω) to be seated/settle down
hiem -al, (L. hiemalis) wintry/stormy
hier -o, (Gr. ειρο-) sacred
hiera -c -x, (Gr. ιεραξ) a hawk/falcon
hierarch, (Gr. ιεραρχικος) belonging to the priesthood
hil -um, (L. hilum) a trifle/'not in the least'
hilao/eo, (Gr. ιλαος/ιλεος) kind/gracious
hilar, (L. hilaris) cheerful/merry/blithe/gay
hilasmo, (Gr. ιλασμος) atonement
hilla, (L. hillae) the small intestine of animals/a kind of sausage
hilum, (L. hilum) a trifle/not in the least
himant -o, (Gr. ιμαντωδης) furnished with straps/leathery/fibrous/sinewy
himantop -us, (Gr. ιμαντοπους) spindle-shanked
himas, (Gr. ιμας) any leathern strap or thong
himasthle, (Gr. ιμασθλη) a whip/any thong
himat -um, (Gr. ιματιον) an outer covering/cloak
himato, (Gr. ιμα/ειμα) an over-garment/rug
himer -o, (Gr. ιμερος) longing/yearning/desire/love
himonia, (Gr. ιμονια) a well-rope
hinn, (L. hinnus) a mule
hinnio, (L. hinnire) to neigh/to whinny
hinnul, (L. hinnuleus) a young stag (L. hinnulea - a young hind)
hio, (Gr. Ιω) the moon
hipp -e -o -us, (Gr. ιππος) a horse/mare
hippari -um, (Gr. ιππαριον) a pony/statuette of a horse
hippocamp -us, (Gr. ιπποκαμπος) a sea monster with a horse's body and a fish's tail
hira, (L. hira) a gut/intestine

hirc -in -us, (L. hircinus) a male goat
hircto, (Gr. ειρκτη) a prison/enclosure
hircus, (L. hircus) a male goat/a goat-like smell
hirne -a, (L. hirnea) a can/jug
hirp -ex -ic, (L. (h)irpex) a harrow
hirrit, (L. hirritus) the snarl of dogs
hirsut, (L. hirsutus) covered with hair/rough/shaggy/prickly/unadorned
hirtus, (L. hirtus) shaggy/rough/hairy/prickly
hirud -in -o, (L. hirudo) a leech
hirund -o, (L. hirundo) a swallow
hisc -o, (L. hiscere) to open/split open/gape
hisma, (Gr. ισμα) foundation/seat
hispan -i, (L. Hispania) Spain/Spanish
hispid, (L. hispidus) bristly/hairy/rough
hist -er -ri, (L. histrio) an actor
hist -o, (Gr. ιστος) web/tissue
histero, (Gr. ιστερος) latter/coming after/behind
histi -o -um, (Gr. ιστιον) web/cloth/sheet/sail
histo, (Gr. ιστος) anything set upright/a mast/beam/spider's web
histor -i, (L. historia) inquiry/history/narrative
histrio -ni, (L. histrio) an actor
hiulc -us, (L. hiulcus) gaping/split/open
hizema, (Gr. ιζημα) settling down/sinking
hod -o -us, (Gr. οδος) a way/path/road/entrance
hodego, (Gr. οδηγος) guide/teacher
hodiern, (L. hodiernus) of today
hol -o, (Gr. ολος) whole/entire/complete
holc -o, (Gr. ολκος) a furrow/trail/track/trace
holcado, (Gr. ολκας) a towed ship
holcimo, (Gr. ολκιμος) ductile
holcio, (Gr. ολκειον) a large bowl
holmo, (Gr. ολμος) a hollow seat/drinking vessel/mortar
hom -eo -io -o -oeo -oio, (Gr. ομοιος) alike/shared in common/resembling
hom -in -ini -o, (L. hominis) a man
homado, (Gr. ομαδος) noise/din
homalo, (Gr. ομαλος) even/level/uniform
homaulo, (Gr. ομαυλος) living together/companion
homelix, (Gr. ομηλιξ) of the same age
homelys, (Gr. ομηλυς) companion
homero, (Gr. ομερος) pledge/security/hostage
homichlo, (Gr. ομιχλη) mist/fog/steam
homiletico, (Gr. ομιλητικος) affable
homilo, (Gr. ομιλος) crowd/throng
homo, (Gr. ομος) one and the same/common
homo, (L. homo) man
homolog, (Gr. ομολογος) agreeing/corresponding
homoro, (Gr. ομορος) neighbouring/marching with
-hood, (AS. had), condition/state of
hopl -o -um, (Gr. οπλον) a tool/implements of war/arms/armour
hople, (Gr. οπλη) hoof
hoplist, (Gr. οπλιστης) armed
hoplit, (Gr. οπλιτης) heavy-armed warrior
hoplon, (Gr. οπλον) a tool/implements of war/arms/armour
hora, (L. hora) an hour
horama, (Gr. οραμα) a visible object/a scene
horco, (Gr. ορκος) an oath

horde -um, (L. hordeum) barley
horia, (L. horia) a small fishing boat
horimo, (Gr. ωριμος) seasonable/timely/ripe
horio, (Gr. ωριος) in season
horisto, (Gr. οριστος) definable
horiz, (Gr. οριζων) separating circle/horizon
horme, (Gr. ορμη) impetus/onrush/onset/assault
hormetico, (Gr. ορμετικος) impetuous/impulsive/exciting/stimulating
hormo, (Gr. ορμος) cord/chain/necklace/collar
hormon, (Gr. ορμαινω) excite/set in motion/rouse
hornotin, (L. hornotinus) of the present year
horo, (Gr. ορος) boundary/landmark
horo, (Gr. ωρος) year/season/time
horr -i -ib, (L. horribilis) horrible/frightful/dreadful
horre -n -s, (L. horrendus) horrible/frightful/dreadful
horre -um, (L. horreum) a barn/storehouse/granary
horre, (L. horrere) to bristle/stand on end/to shudder at/to dread
horrid, (L. horridus) rough/shaggy/bristly
hort -i -us, (L. hortus) a garden
hort, (L. hortamen) an encouragement/exhortation
hortativ, (L. hortativus) encouraging
hosio, (Gr. οσιος) holy/hallowed
hosp -it, (L. hospes) host/guest/stranger
hosti, (L. hostis) public enemy/stranger
hum -at -i, (L. humus) the ground/earth/soil/bury
humect, (L. humectus) moist/damp
humer -o -us, (L. humerus) the shoulder
humesc, (L. humesco) grow moist/become wet
humid -i, (L. humor) moisture/fluid
humifus -us, (L. humifusus) low/procumbent
humil -i, (L. humilis) on the ground
humil -i, (L. humilitas) lowness/shallowness/insignificance
humor, (L. humor) moisture/fluid
humus, (L. humus) earth/ground/soil
hy -aen -en -o, (Gr. υαινα) the striped hyaena (*Hyaena striata*)/a kind of antelope
hy -al, (Gr. υοειδης) Y-shaped
hyal -i -in -o, (Gr. υαλος) glass/crystalline stone/transparent
hybo, (Gr. υβος) humped
hybrid -a, (L. hibrida) a mongrel/hybrid/cross
hybris, (Gr. υβρις) wanton violence/outrage/insolence
hyco, (Gr. υκης) a sea-fish
hydat -in, (Gr. υδατινος) watery/wet/moist
hydr -a -i -o, (Gr. υδωρ) water
hydra, (Gr. υδρα) a fabulous water-serpent
hydra, (Gr. υδραινω) bathe
hydrargyr -o -us, (Gr. υδραργυρος) quicksilver (mercury)
hydria, (Gr. υδρια) a water-pot/jug/ewer
hydro, (Gr. υδροχοος) pouring
hydro, (Gr. υδωρ) water
hydrophor, (Gr. υδορφορος) carrying water
hyem -al, (L. hiemalis) winter
hyen -a, (Gr. υαινα) the striped hyaena (*Hyaena striata*)/a kind of antelope
hyet -o, (Gr. υετια) rainy weather
hyeto, (Gr. υετος) rain
hyg -ei -ie -io, (Gr. υγιαινω) be healthy/be of sound mind
hygr, (Gr. υγρος) wet/moist

hyios, (Gr. υιος) a son
hyksos, (Gr. υκσως) a dynasty of Egyptian nomad kings
hyl -a -o, (Gr. υλη) material/a forest/woodland
hylact, (Gr. υλακτεω) bark/bay/howl/yelp/bark or snarl at
hylia, (Gr. υλια) a shoe's sole
hylist, (Gr. υλιστηρ) a colander/filter
hylo, (Gr. υλο-) wood-
hylurg -o -us, (Gr. υλουργος) carpenter/woodsman
hymen -o, (Gr. υμην) a membrane
hynis (hynnis), (Gr. υνιη) a ploughshare
hyo, (Gr. υοειδης) Y-shaped/U-shaped
hyos, (Gr. υος-) pig/hog
hypato, (Gr. υπατος) highest/uppermost
hypenanti, (Gr. υπεναντιος) opposite/set against
hypene, (Gr. υπηνη) a moustache
hyper -o, (Gr. υπερ-) (in a general sense) from above/over/excessive
hyper -o, (Gr. υπερωα) palate
hyperbore, (Gr. υπερβορεοι) a people of the extreme north
hypero, (Ionic Gr. υπερωη) above
hyperos, (Gr. υπερος) a pestle
hyph -a -o, (Gr. υφη) a web/spider's web
hyphaem -o, (Gr. υφαιμος) suffused with blood/blood-shot
hyphaen, (Gr. υφαινω) contrive/plan/compose
hyphalo, (Gr. υφαλος) submerged
hyphant, (Gr. υφαντης) weaver
hyphesson, (Gr. υφησσων) smaller/less/of lesser stature
hypho, (Gr. υφη) a web/spider's web
hyphydr, (Gr. υφυδρος) under water/full of water/dropsical/of a diver
hypno, (Gr. υπνος) sleep
hypnom, (Gr. υπονομος) a waterpipe
hypo, (Gr. υπο-) (in a general sense) from under/below/'not quite like'
hypocrite, (Gr. υποκριτης) interpreter/actor/pretender
hyponom, (Gr. υπονομος) undermined/underground/mine/water pipe/conduit
hypopion, (Gr. υπωπιον) a black eye/any bruise
hypothesis, (Gr. υποθεσις) a foundation
hypothet, (Gr. υποθετικος) suggesting
hypozoma, (Gr. υποζωμα) diaphragm/midriff
hyps -elo -i -o, (Gr. υψηλος) high/lofty/stately/proud
hyptio, (Gr. υπτιος) supine/anything turned downside up
hyra -c -x, (Gr. υρακος) a shrew-mouse
hyrcha, (Gr. υρχη) a pickle-jar
hyricho, (Gr. υριχος) a wicker basket/hand basket
hyrtane, (Gr. υρτανα) a pot lid
hys, (Gr. υς/συς) a hog
hysginon, (Gr. υσγινον) a crimson or scarlet vegetable dye
hysma, (Gr. υσμα) rain
hysmine, (Gr. υσμινη) fight/battle/combat
hyssos, (Gr. υσσος) a javelin
hyster, (Gr. υστερα) womb
hyster, (Gr. υστερεω) come later/lag behind/fall below/lack
hysteres, (Gr. υστερησις) late arrival
hystero, (Gr. υστερος) after/behind
hystri -c -x, (Gr. υστριξ) a porcupine
hythlos, (Gr. υθλος) idle talk/gossip/nonsense

I

-i, (L.) of/belonging to/pertaining to
-ia, (Gr. -ια) suf. den. pertaining to/condition/names of countries, diseases
iacho, (Gr. ιαχω) shout/cry/shriek
iachr -o, (Gr. ιαχρος) melted/softened/calm
ialemo, (Gr. ιαλεμος) a dirge/lament/wail
ialto, (Gr. ιαλτος) sent forth
iama -to, (Gr. ιαμα) remedy/medicine
ianth -in, (Gr. ιανθινος) violet-coloured
iaphetes, (Gr. ιαφετης) an archer
iapy -g -x, (Gr. Ιαπυξ) the west-northwest wind
-ias, (Gr. -ιας), ind. a close connection
-iasis, (Gr. ιασις) healing/mode of healing/remedy/cure/mending/refining
iaspis, (Gr. ιασπις) jasper
iati, (Gr. ιατικος) healing
iatr -a -ic -o -us, (Gr. ιατρος) doctor/surgeon/physician/healer
iatreus -is, (Gr. ιατρεια) medical treatment
ibano, (Gr. ιβανον) a water-bucket
iber -i -ia, (Gr. Ιβηρες) Spain/Spaniards
iberi -d -s, (Gr. ιβηρις) the pepperwort (*Lepidium* spp.)
ibex, (L. ibex) a kind of goat/chamois
ibi -d -s, (L. ibis) the ibis (*Threskiornis aethiopica*) a sacred bird of the Egyptians
ibidem, (L. ibidem) in the same place/in the same matter
ibis, (Gr. ιβις) a sacred bird of the Egyptians
-ible, (L. -bilis) suf. ind. capable of/having the quality of
ibyctero, (Gr. ιβυκτηρ) leader in a war song
ibyx, (Gr. ιβυξ) a crane
-ica, -icum, -icus, (L.) belonging to
icano, (Gr. ικανος) competent/sufficient
icel -o, (Gr. ικελος) like/resembling/in the same way as
ichn -i -o, (Gr. ιχνος/ιχνιον) track/trace/footstep
ichneum, (Gr. ιχνευμων) a tracker/mongoose/wasp
ichor, (Gr. ιχωρ) juice/serum/whey
ichthy -o -s, (Gr. ιχθυς) a fish
ichthy, (Gr. ιχθυς) a fish
-ician, (Fr. -icien) suf. ind. one who specialises in or practices
-icle, (L.) dim. suf.
icma -le, (Gr. ικμαλεος) damp/wet/full of fluid
ico, (Gr. εικος) likely/probable/reasonable
icon, (L. icon) an image
icos -a -i, (Gr. εικοσι) twenty
-icosa, -icosum, -icosus, (Gr. -ικοσα/ικοσον/ικοσος) ind. ability or fitness
icoto, (Gr. εικοτως) fairly/reasonably
icrio, (Gr. ικρια) platform/stage/scaffold/theatre benches
-icter -i -o -us, (Gr. ικτερος) yellowish/jaundiced
icti -s, (Gr. ικτις) the yellow-throated marten (*Martes flavigula*)
ictico, (Gr. εικτικος) fielding/pliable
ictin -us, (Gr. ικτινος) a kite/a kind of wolf
ictus, (L. ictus) a blow/stroke/stab
-icula -iculus -icus, (L.) dim. suf.
-id/ide, (L. -idus) suf. ind. having the nature of
-ida -idum -idus, (L.) suf. ind. a state or action
-ida, (L.) suf. used to form the names of some animal orders
-ida, -idum, -idus, (L.) ind. a state of action in progress/having the nature of

-idae, (Gr. -ιδες) a patronymic suffix used in zoological nomenclature to indicate a family name

idalimo, (Gr. ειδαλιμος) shapely/comely

idano, (Gr. ιδανος) fair/comely

idea, (Gr. ιδεα) appearance/semblance/nature/species/kind

idechtho, (Gr. ειδεχθης) ugly/repulsive/putrid

idem, (L. idem) the same

idemono, (Gr. ειδεμων) expert/skilled

iden, (L. idem) the same

ident -i, (L. identidem) repeatedly

ideo, (Gr. ειδος) form/shape/physique

ideo, (Gr. ειδω) to perceive mentally/to see/know

-ides, (Gr. -ιδης) suf. ind. son of/descendent of/resemblance

idetico, (Gr. ειδητικος) knowable/capable of geometric representation

-idia, -idium, -idius, L. and Gr. (-ιδια, -ιδιον) dim. suf.

idico, (Gr. ειδικος) specific/special

idio, (Gr. ιδιος) one's own/private/pert. to oneself

-idion, (Gr. -ιδιον) dim. suf.

idmono, (Gr. ιδμων) skilled/expert

ido, (Gr. ειδος) resemblance/form

ido, (Gr. ιδιω) sweat/cold sweat

idol -o, (Gr. ειδωλ-) phantom/ghost/idol

idr -o, (Gr. ιδροω) sweat

idri, (Gr. ιδρις) experienced/knowing/skilful

-idus, (L.) having the nature of

idylo, (Gr. ειδυλος/ειδημων) expert

iena, (Gr. ιεναι) to go

-ies, (L.) ind. a thing formed

-ifer -ous, (L. ferre) to bear/bring/move/produce/plunder

igdis, (Gr. ιγδις) mortar

-igerous, (L. -igerous) in use always/ever present

ign -e -i, (L. ignis) fire/glow/glitter

ignav, (L. ignavus) inactive/listless/cowardly

ignobil, (L. ignobilis) unknown

ignot, (L. ignotus) unknown/strange

ignya, (Gr. ιγνυα) a ham

-igo, (L. -igo) resemblance/connection/property possessed (a common botanical suffix)

il/im/in/ir, (L.) pref. in/into/for/contrary/not/without/on

ilapinasto, (Gr. ειλαπιναστης) feaster/guest

ile, (Gr. ιλη) troop/band of men

ilea, (Gr. ειλεω) to wind/turn around

ilema -t, (Gr. ειλημα) veil/covering/wrapper/coil/arch/vault/cellar

iletico, (Gr. ειλητικος) wriggling

ilex/ilic, (L. ilex) the holm oak (*Quercus ilex*)

ilia, (L. ilia Gr. ιλια) intestines/gut/loin/flank

ilingo, (Gr. ιλιγξ) whirlpool/whirling/agitation

ilipodo, (Gr. ειλιποδης) with a rolling gait

-ilis, (L. -ilis) adjectival suffix denoting capability - 'able to'

ilium, (L. ilium) groin/flank

-ill -a -um -us, (L.) dim. suf.

ill -a -aen -is -os, (Gr. ιλλαινω) look awry/squint

illas, (Gr. ιλλας) a rope/band

illat, (L. illatio) drawing a conclusion/inferred

illici, (L. illicium) allure/enticement/attraction

illigat, (L. illigare) to fetter/entangle

illot, (L. illotus) unwashed/dirty

-illum, (L.) dim. suf.

illumina, (L. illuminatus) light up/embellish

-illus, (L.) dim. suf.

illusi, (L. illusio) mocking

illustr -a -i, (L. illustratus) made clear/bright/distinguished

ily -o -us, (Gr. ιλυς) mud/slime/dregs

ilymato, (Gr. ειλυματος) a wrapper

im/in/il/ir, (L.) pref. in/into/for/contrary/not/without/on

-ima, -imum, -imus, (L.) super. suf.

imag -in -o, (L. imago) an image/copy/likeness

imb -er -r, (L. imber) shower/rain/rain-cloud

imbecill, (L. imbecillitas) weakness/feebleness

imberbis, (L. imberbis) beardless

imbric -a -i, (L. imbrex) a tile/roof tile

imbricat, (L. imbricatus) overlapping like roof tiles

imbut, (L. imbuere) to wet/steep/saturate/stain/taint

imitat, (L. imitari) to imitate

imitor, (L. imitari) to copy/mimic/replace

imman, (L. immanis) enormous/monstrous

immens, (L. immensus) vast/boundless

immit, (L. immitis) harsh/rough/sour

immun -i -o, (L. immunis) exempt from a service/free

immund, (L. immundus) unclean/impure/foul

impar -i, (L. impar) unequal/uneven

impast, (L. impastus) hungry/unfed

impavid, (L. impavidus) fearless/intrepid/undaunted

imped, (L. impedio) hinder/prevent

impen, (L. impennae) featherless

impenden, (L. impendens) overhanging/imminent

impens, (L. impensus) ample/great/strong

imperat, (L. imperator) commander-in-chief/general/ruler

impero, (L. impero) command

imperv, (L. impervius) impassable/impenetrable

impet -us, (L. impetus) an attack/onset

impex, (L. impexus) uncombed/uncouth

impiger, (L. impiger) diligent/active

impilium, (L. impilium) a soft shoe

impingo, (L. impingere) to trust/drive against

impius, (L. impius) wicked/undutiful/disloyal

implex, (L. implexus) plaited/entwined

implicat, (L. implicare) to involve/entangle

impluvium, (L. impluvium) an opening in the roof of a Roman house

impotens, (L. impotens) powerless/weak

-imus, (Gr. -ιμος) suf. ind. pertaining to/having the quality of

imus, (L. imus) lowest

-in/-ine, (L. -inus) chem. suf. used for names of neutral substances

in/im/il/ir, (L.) pref. in/into/for/contrary/not/without/on

ina, (from Gr. ις) fibre

-ina, (L.) dim. suf.

-ina, -inum, -inus, (L.) likeness, belonging to

-ina, (L.) suf. used to form the names of some animal orders or suborders

-inae, (L. -inae) a suffix used in zoological nomenclature to indicate a subfamily or in botanical nomenclature to indicate a subtribe

inaequal, (L. inaequalis) unequal/uneven/various

inan -i, (L. inanis) empty/void

inauris, (L. inauris) an earring

incan, (L. incanus) quite grey/hoary

incert, (L. incertus) uncertain/doubtful/not sure

incest, (L. incestus) impure/defiled/sinful
incho, (L. incohare) to begin/to take in hand
incien, (L. inciens) pregnant
incil -i, (L. incilis) a ditch/trench
incipient, (L. inceptare) to begin
incis, (L. incisus) cut into/cut open
inclus, (L. inclusio) confinement
incol -a, (L. incola) an inhabitant
incrass, (L. incrassare) to thicken
incu -s, (L. incus) anvil
incub, (L. incubare) to lie in or on
incubus, (L. incubus) a nightmare/male demon
inculco, (L. inculcare) tread down/cram/force upon
incurv, (L. incurvare) to curve
incus, (L. incus) an anvil
indago, (L. indagare) to track down/investigate/explore
index, (L. index) one that informs or indicates/a sign/a token
indi, (L. indicum) indigo (the colour and the dye)
indic, (L. indico) I show/point out
indig, (Sp. indico Gr. ινδικον L. indicum) Deep violet-blue
indigen, (L. indigena) native/a native
indigen, (L. indigere) to want/need/require
indo-, Indian/indigo
indoles, (L. indoles) native quality/character/talents
indu -s, (L. induere/indusium) to put on/an undergarment
inductura, (L. inductura) a covering/coating
industri, (L. industria) diligence/industry
-ine/-in, (L. -inus) chem. suf. used for neutral substances
-inea, -ineum, -ineus, (L.) ind. Material/colour
-ineae, (L.) suffix used in botanical nomenclature to indicate a suborder
inebri -at, (L. inebrare) to intoxicate
inept, (L. ineptia) foolish behaviour/absurdness
iner, (L. iners) idle/sluggish/unskilful
inerm -is, (L. inermis) unarmed/undefended
iners, (L. inertis) untrained/unskilful
inesco, (L. inescare) to entice/deceive/allure with a bait
infan -s, (L. infans) a little child
infan -t, (L. infantia) inability to speak/want of elegance
infarct, (L. infarcio) to cram in/to stuff in
infect, (L. infectus) dyed/stained/tainted
infelic, (L. infelicitas) unhappiness/misfortune/ill-luck
infero, (L. inferus) from below/beneath/of the lower world
infest, (L. infestus) hostile/unsafe
infim, (L. infimus) lowest
inflat, (L. inflatus) swollen/puffed up
inflect, (L. inflectere) to bend in
infloresc, (L. inflorescentia) being to bloom
influen, (L. influere) to flow into
infra, (L. infra) below/beneath/underneath
infract, (L. infractio) broken/weakened
infucat, (L. infucatus) coloured
inful -a, (L. infula) a bandage/band
infund -o, (L. infundere) to pour in, on or over
infundibul, (L. infundibulum) a funnel
infus, (L. infusus) poured in to
infuscat, (L. infuscare) to make dark/to blacken
infusorium, (L. infusorium) a vessel
ingen -s, (L. ingens) vast/enormous/monstrous/large

ingluv, (L. ingluvies) a bird's crop/a stomach

inguin, (L. inguen) groin/abdomen

inhib, (L. inhibere) to restrain/hinder

ini -a -o -um, (Gr. ινιον) the back of the neck/occipital bone/occiput

-ini, (Gr. ινις) son or daughter

-ini, a suffix used in zoological nomenclature to indicate a tribe

iniquus, (L. iniquus) uneven/unjust

-init, (L. initiare) to initiate

-inium, (Gr. -ινιον) dim. suf.

innoc -en -u, (L. innocens) harmless/inoffensive/innocent

-ino -d, (Gr. ινωδες) fibrous/sinewy

inocul -a, (L. inoculatio) an engrafting/implant

inops, (L. inops) poor/weak/helpless

-inos, (Gr. -ινος), of/made of

inquilin -us, (L. inquilinus) a tenant/lodger

inquino, (L. inquinare) to pollute/stain

inscitus, (L. inscitus) ignorant/awkward/stupid

insect, (L. insecare) to cut into/notched

insem, (L. inseminare) to sow into

inser, (L. insertus) joined

insess, (L. insessor) 'sitters upon'

insidi, (L. insidiae) an ambush/snare/trap/deceit/plot

insignis, (L. insignis) remarkable/notable/distinguished

insipid, (LL. insipidus) tasteless

in situ, (L. in situ) in place

instar, (L. instar) a likeness/form/image

instig -a, (L. instigare) stimulate/goad/incite

insul -a, (L. insula) an island

intact, (L. intactus) untouched/chaste

integ -r, (L. integer) complete/whole/entire/intact/renewed

inter, (L. inter) between/among/amid

interaneum, (L. interaneum) gut/intestine

intercal, (L. intercalaris) inserted

interdict, (L. interdictum) a prohibition

intergeriv, (L. intergerivus) placed between

interit, (L. interitus) destruction/ruin

interluv, (L. interluvies) a strait

intern, (L. internus) within/inside

interstit, (L. intersistere) to stand between

interul, (L. interulus) inward/inner

intestin um, (L. intestinus) inward/internal/the intestines

inti, (L. intimus) innermost/deepest/most profound

intim -a, (L. intimus) innermost

intort, (L. intortus) twisted/tangled

intr -a -o, (L. intra) within/inside

intric, (L. intricare) to confuse/entangle

intrins, (L. intrinsecus) inwardly/inside

intro, (L. intrare) to go in/enter

intromit, (L. intromittere) to send in or cause to enter

intror, (L. introsus) inwards

intum, (L. intumescere) to swell

intus, (L. intus) within

inuncat, (L. inuncatus) hooked together

inunct, (L. inunctus) anointed/oiled/smeared

inundat, (L. inundatus) flooded/overflowed

-inus, (L. -inus) like/in the manner of/belonging to

inust, (L. inustus) burnt in/branded/imprinted

invagin, (MedL. invaginare) to sheath

invas -o, (L. invasor) intruder
invectiv, (L. invectivus) scolding/abusive
invert, (L. invertere) to turn upside down
invict, (L. invictus) unconquered
involucr -um, (L. involucrum) a covering/wrapper
involut, (L. involutus) rolled up/enveloped/wrapped up/covered
Io, (Gr. Ιω) the moon/daughter of Inachus, a stream god
iochmos, (Gr. ιωχμος) rout
iod -i -o, (Gr. ιοειδης) violet-like
-iol -a -um -us, (L. -iolum) dim. suf.
-ion, (Gr. -ιον) dim. suf.
-ion, Gr. -ιον), ind. occurrence
-ion, -sion, -tion, (L.) act/process/result/state of/having the nature of
ion, (Gr. ιον) violet (*Viola odorata*)/(generally) any flower /alone
ionisco, (Gr. ιωνισκος) softly/effeminately
ionth -o, (Gr. ιονθος) young hair/hair root
iops, (Gr. ιωψ) a small fish
-ior, (L. -ior) comp. suf.
ioro, (Gr. ιωρος) a guard/keeper
ios, (Gr. ιος) poison (as of serpents)/venom of a mad dog
ios, (Gr. ιος) rust/verdigris
iota, (Gr. ιωτα ι I) ninth letter of Greek alphabet/anything very small
iotoco, (Gr. ιοτοκος) poison-bearing/venomous
ip -o -s, (Gr. ιψ) a worm/wood-worm
iphi-, (Gr. ιφι-) strong-
iphthim, (Gr. ιφθιμος) stout/strong/powerful/stately
ipn -o, (Gr. ιπνος) oven/furnace/kitchen/lantern/dunghill/privy
ipo-, (Gr. ιπο-) worm-
ipse, (L. ipse) self
ipsi, (NL. ipsi) same
ipsis, (Gr. ιποω) a pressing/a squeezing
ir/im/il/in, (L.) pref. in/into/for/contrary/not/without/on
ira -sc, (L. ira) wrath/anger/ire/violence/rage
iren, (Gr. Ειρηνη) goddess of peace
iri -d -do -s -t, (Gr. ιρις) a rainbow/a messenger between the gods/any bright-coloured
　　　　circle surrounding another body/iris of the eye/the plant genus *Iris*.
iris, (L. Iris) goddess of the rainbow
irmo, (Gr. ειρμος) series/sequence
Iro, (Gr. Ιρος L. Irus) a proverbial name for a beggar
irono, (Gr. ειρων) dissembler
irretit, (L. irretitus) caught in a net
irrig -a -u, (L. inriguus) watering/irrigating/refreshing
irris -i -or, (L. inrisus) mockery/laughter/derision
irritabil, (L. inritabilis) easily roused
irrito, (L. inritare) to provoke/stimulate/excite
irror -a, (L. inrorare) to moisten
irrup, (L. inrumpere) to break in/burst in/rush in
is, (Gr. εις) toward/into
is, (Gr. ις) strength/force/nerve/a muscle
-is, (L.) adj. suf. meaning with, having the nature of
-is, (Gr. -ις), ind. a close connection
isati -s, (Gr. ισατις) woad, a plant (*Isatis tincoria*) producing a dark blue dye
-isca, -iscum, -iscus, (L.) dim. suf.
ischas, (Gr. ισχας) a dried fig
ischi -a -o -um, (Gr. ισχιον) the hip/hip-joint
ischn -o, (Gr. ισχνος) reduced/weak/dry/withered

ischo, (Gr. ισχω) keep back/restrain/hold/stay/stop

ischy -r -ro, (Gr. ισχυρος) strong/powerful/forcible/violent/severe

-iscus, (Gr. -ισκος) dim. suf.

-ise, (L. -itia) suf. ind. make/give/act

-ish, (AS. isc/Gr. -ισχ), denoting origin/pertaining to/like

Isis, (Gr. Ισις L. Isis) an Egyptian goddess of fertility

isis, (Gr. Ισις) an Egyptian goddess

-isk, (Gr. -ισκος) dim. suf.

-ism, (Gr. -ισμος/-υσμος; L. -ismus) suf. forming nouns of action from verbs of
                condition/quality/result

iso -s, (Gr. ισος) equal/similar

isol -a -e, (Fr. isolé) isolated

isomer, (Gr. ισομερης) of equal length

isoped, (Gr. ισοπεδος) level

-issa, (L./Gr. -issa; -essa) feminine suffixes

-issim -a -um -us, (L. -issimus) super. suf.

ist -io -o, (Gr. ιστιον) sail/tissue/cloth/sheet/web

-ist, (Gr. -ιστ) super. suf.

-ist, (L. -ista Fr. -iste) suf. denoting ability/agent/one who

-ista, -istum, -istus, (Gr. -ιστα/-ιστον/ιστος) super. suf.

-ister, (L.) wildness, a diminutive

isthm, (Gr. ισθμος) neck/narrow passage/isthmus

-istos, (Gr. -ιστος) adj. super.

-ita, (Sp. -ita) dim. suf.

ital -o, (Gr. ιταλος) a bull

itam -o, (Gr. ιταμος) hasty/impetuous/reckless

-itas, -itia, -ities, -itudo, (L.) ind. a concept or quality

-ite/ites, (Gr. -ιτης) belonging to/like/having the nature of

itea, (Gr. ιτεα) the willow (Salix spp.)

item, (L. item) likewise/as/part of a series

-iter, (L. iter) a going/walk/way/journey/march

itera, (L. iteratio) repetition

ithagin, (Gr. ιθαγενης) original/aboriginal/genuine

ithris, (Gr. ιθρις) eunuch

ithy -s, (Gr. ιθυ-) straight

ithycteano, (Gr. ιθυκτεανος) tall/slender

itin -o, (Gr. ινεινος) made of wicker/wicker shield/target

itiner, (L. itineris) a journey

-itia, -itium, -itius, (L.) ind. result of an action

-itica, -iticum, -iticus, (L.) ind. fitness or capability for something

-itis, (Gr. ιτις/ιτης) ind. inflammation (e.g. arthritis)

-itus, (L. -itus) suf. ind. having the nature of

-ity, (Eng.), ind. a concept or quality (from L. -itas)

ity -o -s, (Gr. ιτυς) outer edge or rim of a shield/felloe of a wheel/rim of joint-socket

iul -us, (Gr. ιουλος) a multiped (maybe a wood louse (Oniscidae))/catkin

-ium, (Gr. -ιυμ) dim. suf./suf. den. quality or nature of

-ium, (L. -ium) suf. denoting a place

-ius, (Gr. -ιος), of/pertaining to

-ius, -ia, -ium, (L.) suf. attached to stems of personal/proper names

-ive, (L. -ivus) suf. den. nature/quality/action

-ivus, -iva, -ivum, (L.) capacity/ability/possession/agent

ix, (Gr. ιξ) a worm that destroys vine buds

ixal -o, (Gr. ιξαλος) bounding/springing

ixeut, (Gr. ιξευτης) a bird-catcher

ixo, (Gr. ιξωδης) sticky/clammy

ixos, (Gr. ιξος) birdlime/mistletoe/any sticky substance

ixy -s, (Gr. ιξυς) a woman's waist/loins
iygmos, (Gr. ιυγμος) shout of joy/cry of pain/shriek
iyn -g -x, (Gr. ιυγξ) the wryneck (*Jynx torquilla*)/metaph. a spell/charm
-izans, (L.) becoming like/resembling/forming
-ize, (Gr. -ιζειν) suf. ind. make/cause to be/action

J
(in Latin j = consonantal i)

jacan, (Pg. jaçanã) a bird, from SAm., a native name
jaceo, (L. iaceo) to lie/to be idle
jactans, (L. iactantia) boasting/bragging
jactus, (L. iactus) a throwing/cast
jacul, (L. iaculari) to throw/shoot at/toss/cast/hurl
jacul, (L. iaculum) a dart/javelin/casting net
jaculat, (L. iaculatrorius) throwing
jan, (L. Ianus) a two-faced deity/a door
jan, (L. ianus) a covered passage/arcade
janua, (L. ianua) a door/entrance
japonic, (NL. japonica) of Japan
japy -g -x, (Gr. Ιαπυξ) the west-northwest wind
jec -in -or -ur, (L. iecur) the liver, (as seat of passions)
jecund, (L. iucundus) pleasant/agreeable/delightful
jejun, (L. ieiunus) hungriness/emptiness
jentacul, (L. ientaculum) breakfast
jocosus, (L. iocosus) facetious
jub -a, (L. iubatus) crested/having a mane
jubar, (L. iubar) light/sunshine/splendour
jug -o -um, (L. iugum) yoke/bench/mountain ridge
jug, (L. iugare) to marry/connect
jugerum, (L. iugerum) a measure of land
jugis, (L. iugis) joined together/perpetual/continuous
juglan -s -d, (L. iuglans) the walnut/walnut tree (*Juglans* spp.)
jugul -um, (L. iugulum) the throat
julus, (L. iulus Gr. ιουλος) a multiped (maybe a wood louse (Oniscidae))/catkin
jumentum, (L. iumentum) a beast of burden
junc -us, (L. iuncus) a rush/reed
junct, (L. iunctus) joined
jung, (L. iungere) to join/unite/yoke/harness
junix, (L. iunix) a heifer
just, (L. iustus) lawful/fair
juv, (L. iuvare) to help/gratify
juvenal, (L. iuvenalis) youthful
juvenesc, (L. iuvenescere) to grow young
juxta, (L. iuxta) near to
juxtim, (L. iuxtim) next to

K

(see also **c** and **ch**)

kac, (Gr. κακ-) pref. carrying the sense of bad/badly done/bringing bad/etc.

kaca, (Gr. κακη) badness/baseness/cowardice

kaco, (Gr. κακος) bad/evil/ugly

kafir, (Ar. kafir) infidel/unbeliever

kairo, (Gr. καιρος) due measure/fitness/exact time/time period/season

kako, (Gr. κακος) bad/evil/ugly

kaleido, (Gr. καλος + ειδος) of beautiful form

kali, (Ar. qaliy) the ashes of saltwort (*Salsola kali*)

kali, (Gr. καλια) wooden house/hut/barn/nest

kalli, (Gr. καλλι-) pre. giving the idea of *beautiful* e.g. καλλι-βλεφαρος - with beautiful eyelids or beautiful eyes.

kalo, (Gr. καλον) billet of wood/timber

kalo/kallo, (Gr. καλος/καλλος) beauty

kalymm, (Gr. καλυμμα) a covering

kalypto, (Gr. καλυπτος) enveloping

kama, (Gr. καμαξ) a pole/stake/shaft of spear

kamp -a -t, (Gr. καμπτη) winding (of a river)/flexion/bending

kamp -a, (Gr. καμπη) a caterpillar

kampto, (Gr. καμπτος) flexible

kapn -o, (Gr. καπνος) smoke

kappa, (Gr. καππα κ K) tenth letter of the Greek alphabet

kary -o, (Gr. καρυον) a nut/nucleus

kata, (Gr. κατα) down from/down towards/down upon/in opposition to, (in general significance opposite to ana- (ανα)

kathar, (Gr. καθαρος) spotless/physically clean/clear/pure

kaul, (Gr. καυλος) stem/stalk

keel, (AS. ceol) ship

kel, (Gr. χηλη) a claw/a hoof/a talon

kelaen -o, (Gr. κελαινος) black/dark/murky

keli -d -s, (Gr. κηλις) stain/spot/blemish/defilement

kelo, (Gr. κηλη) tumour/rupture/hernia

kelyph -o, (Gr. κελυφος) sheath/case/pod/shell

ken -o, (Gr. κενοω) empty

kentr -o, (Gr. κεντρον) any sharp point/goad/spur/point/the point round which a circle is described

kera/cera, (Gr. κερας) animal's horn

keraum -o, (Gr. κεραυνος) a thunderbolt

kerm -es, (Ar. qirmiz) crimson

kero, (Gr. κηρος) wax/bee's wax

kilo, (Gr. χιλιοι) a thousand

kine -ma -mato -s -si -t -to, (Gr. κινειν) to move/moving/movement

kio -no, (Gr. κιων) a pillar/the uvula

klas -a, (Gr. κλασμα) fragment

klept, (Gr. κλεπτηρ) a rouge/deceiver/thief

klepto, (Gr. κλεπτω) to steal/cheat/beguile

kleronom, (Gr. κληρονομος) heir

kneph, (Gr. κνεφας) twilight/dusk/darkness

kolyon, (Gr. κωλυον) hindering

koni -o, (Gr. κονις) dust

-kont, (Gr. κοντος) punting pole

korethr, (Gr. κορηθρον) a broom

korm, (Gr. κορμος) trunk, (of tree with boughs removed)

koro, (Gr. κορος) satiety/surfeit/male infant/sprout/shoot/dark/black/pure

kotyl -o, (Gr. κοτυλη) a small cup or vessel/socket (esp. the hip)/cavity

kraur -o, (Gr. κραυρος) brittle/friable

kremast, (Gr. κρεμαστος) hanging

krypto, (Gr. κρυπτος) hidden/secret

kurt -i -o, (Gr. κυρτος) bulging/swelling/humped/convex/curved/bent/arched

kyan -o, (Gr. κυανος/κυανεος) blue/dark blue

kyll -o, (Gr. κυλλος) club-footed/deformed/crooked

kym -a -o, (Gr. κυμα) a wave/foetus/embryo/anything swollen

kyo, (Gr. κυησις) pregnancy

kypho, (Gr. κυφος) bent/stooping/bowed forward/hunchbacked

kyrio -ho -o, (Gr. κυριος) authoritative/decisive/valid/lord/master

kyst -ho -o, (κυτος) a hollow/any hollow container/a cell

L

la -o, (Gr. λαος) a people/the common man/stone

lab, (L. labium) lip

labarum, (L. labarum Gr. λαβαρον) Roman imperial standard

labe, (Gr. λαβη) a handle/haft/hilt/grasping

labe -s, (L. labes) a falling in/sinking in/fall/spot/stain/blemish/misfortune

labecula, (L. labecula) a little stain/blemish/disgrace

labell -um, (L. labellum) little lip

labeo, (L. labeo) one with large lips

labi -a -o, (L. labia) a lip

labid, (Gr. λαβις) forceps

labido, (Gr. λαβιδιον) a small pair of tweezers

labil, (L. labilis) apt to slip

labium, (L. labium) lip

labo, (L. labare) to shake/totter/sink/waver

labor, (L. labor) work/effort/toil/effort

labr -i -o, (L. labrum) lip/upper lip/edge/rim

labro, (Gr. λαβρος) furious/boisterous/turbulent/impetuous/mighty/eager/greedy

labrys, (Gr. λαβρυς) a two edged axe (for felling trees)

labyrinth -o -us, (Gr. λαβυρινθος) a labyrinth/maze

lac, (L. lac) milk

lac, (Pers. lak) lacquer

lacaro, (Gr. λακαρα) a type of tree, prob. the bird-cherry (*Prunus avium*)

lacc -o -us, (Gr. λακκος) pit/reservoir/cistern

lacca, (It. lacca) varnish/wax

lacer -at, (L. lacerare) to mangle/tear to pieces

lacerna, (L. lacerna) a kind of cloak

lacero, (Gr. λακερος) talkative

lacert, (L. lacerta) a lizard

lacert, (L. lacertus) the upper arm

lacertos, (L. lacertosus) powerful/muscular

laceryzo, (Gr. λακερυζα) a screamer/howler

lacesso, (L. lacessere) to excite/provoke/irritate

laches -i, (L. Lachesis Gr. Λαχεσις) one of the three fates/destiny

lachn -o, (Gr. λαχνος) wool/woolly

lachr -im -ym, (L. lacrima) a tear/tears/weeping

laci -d -st, (Gr. λακις) rent/torn

lacin -i -ia, (L. lacinia) a flap/fringe

lacismato, (Gr. λακισμα) something torn/in tatters
lacos, (Gr. λακος) noise
lacr -im -um, (L. lacrima) a tear/tears/weeping
lacrim, (L. lacrimare) to weep
lact -a -o, (L. lactare) to allure/wheedle/entice/dupe
lact -e -i -o, (L. lactues) of milk/milky/milk-white
lact, (L. lactare) to suckle
lactis -m, (Gr. λακτιζω) kick with heel/kick/struggle/trample
lactis, (L. lactes) small intestines/guts
lactuc -a, (L. lactuca) a lettuce
laculat, (L. laculatus) four-cornered/chequered
lacun -a, (L. lacuna) a cavity/hollow/dip/pool/pond
lacus, (L. lacus) a lake
lacustr, (L. lacustrus) of a lake
ladas, (Gr. λαδας) a young stag
laedo, (L. laedere) to hurt by striking/injure/wound
laedos, (Gr. λαεδος) an unknown type of bird
laelaps, (Gr. λαιλαψ) furious storm/hurricane
laem -o -us, (Gr. λαιμος) the throat/gullet
laemarg -o, (Gr. λαιμαργος) gluttonous/greedy
laen -a, (Gr. λαινα L. laena) a cloak
laeo, (Gr. λαιος) the left
laepho, (Gr. λαιφος) a shabby garment/piece of cloth/a sail
laepsero, (Gr. λαιψερος) light/nimble/swift
laersino, (Gr. λαερκινον) an aromatic wood
laertes, (Gr. λαερτης) a kind of ant/a kind of wasp
laesenio, (Gr. λαισενιον) a shield
laet, (L. laetus) bright/pleasant/joyful/fat/rich
laetam -en -in, (L. laetamen) dung/manure
laetma -to, (Gr. λαιτμα) depth of the sea
laev -i -o, (L. laevus) the left/left-handed/foolish
laevigat -us, (L. laevigatus) smooth/polished/beardless/bald
lafyst, (Gr. λαφυστιος) gluttonous
lag -o -us, (Gr. λαγως) a hare
lagan, (Gr. λαγανον L. laganum) a thin broad cake
lagar -o, (Gr. λαγαρος) hollow, sunken (of an animal's flanks)/slack/loose/nimble
lagen, (Gr. λαγηνος L. lagena) a flagon/flask
lagn -o, (Gr. λαγνος) lustful/lecherous
lago, (Gr. λαγως) a hare
lagynos, (Gr. λαγυνος) a flagon/flask
lailaps, (Gr. λαιλαψ) furious storm/hurricane
laim -o -us, (Gr. λαιμος) the throat/gullet
lal -i -o, (Gr. λαλεω) talk/speak/chat/prattle
lall, (L. lallare) to sing a lullaby
lama, (L. lama) slough/bog/fen
lamb -a -en, (L. lambere) (of animals) to lick/wash/bathe
lambda, (Gr. λαμβδα/λαβδα λ Λ) eleventh letter of the Greek alphabet
lamell -a -i, (L. lamella) a small plate
lament, (L. lamenta) wailing/weeping
lamia, (Gr. λαμια) a fabulous monster said to feed on man's flesh
lamin -a -i, (L. lamina) a thin plate of metal or marble/sword blade
lamna, (Gr. λαμνα) a shark
lamp -ad -as -s, (Gr. λαμπας) a torch/metaph. of the sun
lampero, (Gr. λαμπηρος) scummy/slimy
lampr -o, (Gr. λαμπρος) radiant/brilliant/bright/clear/distinct
lampyri -d -s, (Gr. λαμπυρις) a glow worm

lamyro, (Gr. λαμυρος) greedy/wanton
lan -a -i -o, (L. lana) wool/clouds/the down on leaves
lance -a, (L. lancea) a light spear/lance
lancin, (L. lanciare) to tear to pieces/to squander
langu -i, (L. langueo) to be faint/weak/languid/inert/inactive
languri -a, (L. languria) a kind of lizard
lani -a -o, (L. laniare) to tear to pieces/mangle/lacerate
lani -us, (L. lanius) a butcher/executioner
lani, (L. lana) wool/clouds/the down on leaves
lanici, (L. lanatus) woolly/wool-bearing
lanth -an -o, (Gr. λανθανω) escape notice or detection/unseen
lanu -g, (L. lanugo) down (feathers)/the down on plants
lao, (Gr. λαος) a people/the common man/stone
lapact, (Gr. λαπαξις) evacuation of the bowels/empty
lapar, (Gr. λαπαρα) the soft region of the body between ribs and hips
laparo, (Gr. λαπαρος) slack/loose
lapath -i -um, (L. lapathum) sorrel (*Rumex* spp.)
lape, (Gr. λαπη) scum
laphist, (Gr. λαφυστιος) gluttonous
laphygmo, (Gr. λαφυγμος) gluttony
laphyr -a -o, (Gr. λαφυρα) plunder
lapi -d -s, (L. lapis) a stone/boundary stone/grave stone/precious stone
lapistes, (Gr. λαπιστης) a swaggerer
lapp -a, (L. lappa) a burr
lapponic -us, (L. Lapponia) of Lapland
laps, (L. lapsare) to stumble/slip
laps, (L. lapsio) a gliding/tendency towards
laque -us, (L. laqueus) a noose/halter/snare
laquear, (L. laqueare) panelled
lar -i -us, (Gr. λαρος) a ravenous sea bird - perh. gull
larc -o -us, (Gr. λαρκος) a charcoal basket
larg, (L. largus) abundant/numerous/copious/liberal/bountiful
lari -c -x, (L. larix Gr. λαριξ) the larch (*Larix* spp.)
larin -o, (L. laridum) lard/fat
larnaco, (Gr. λαρναξ) box/chest/coffer
laros, (Gr. λαρος) agreeable/pleasant
larus, (L. larus) a gull
larv -a -i, (L. larva) ghost
laryn -g -go -x, (Gr. λαρυγξ) the larynx/gullet
lascivi, (L. lascivia) playfulness/sportivness/wantonness/licentiousness
lasio, (Gr. λασιος) shaggy with hair or wool
lass -it, (L. lassitudo) weariness/exhaustion
lass, (L. lassus) weary/exhausted
lat, (L. latus) side/flank/wide/broad
lata -g -x, (Gr. λαταξ) a drop of wine/a water-quadruped, perh. beaver (*Castor fiber*)
latebr -a -i, (L. latebra) a hiding place
laten -t, (L. latens) hidden
later -al -o, (L. lateralis) pert. the side
lateri -ci -ti, (L. latericius) made of brick
lateri, (L. later) a brick/tile
latesc, (L. latescere) to be hidden/to hide oneself
latex, (L. latex) a fluid/liquid (esp. water)
lathargo, (Gr. λαθαργος) a piece of leather
lathetico, (Gr. λαθητικος) likely to escape detection
lathr -i -idi -o, (Gr. λαθραιος) clandestine/hidden
lathyr -us, (Gr. λαθυρις) caper spurge (*Euphorbia lathrus*)
lati-, (L. lati-) broad/wide

latibul, (L. latibulum) a hiding place/refuge
latic -i, (L. laticis) a liquid/a fluid
latom, (L. lautumiae/latomiae) a stone quarry
lator, (L. lator) a bearer/proposer
latr, (L. latrare) to bark/rant
latra -n -t, (L. latratus) a barking
latra, (Gr. λαθρη) secret/clandestine/by stealth
latri, (Gr. λατρειος) to serve
latri, (Gr. λατρις) a hired servant/handmaid
latro, (Gr. λατρον) pay/hire
latro, (L. latro) hired servant/mercenary/robber/brigand
-latry, (Gr. λατρεια) divine worship
latus, (L. latus) broad/side
latypos, (Gr. λατυπος) a stone-cutter/mason
lauda, (L. laudatio) praise/commendation
laur -eat -i -us, (L. laureus) of the laurel (*Laurus nobilis*)
laura, (Gr. λαυρα) a passage/alley/lane/ *alley* or *bazaar* where women sold delicacies of
            all kinds,
laut, (L. lautus) washed/bathed/splendid/elegant/sumptuous
lavo, (L. lavare) to wash/bathe
lax -a, (L. laxare) to widen/loosen
laxeutes, (Gr. λαξευτης) a stone-cutter
lazul, (LL. lazulinus) azure/blue/ultramarine
leberi -d -s, (Gr. λεβηρις) exuvia, the skin or slough of serpents
lebes, (Gr. λεβης) a kettle/cauldron
lecan -a, (Gr. λεκαν) dish/pot/pan
lech -o, (Gr. λεχος) couch/bed/bier/bird's nest
lechri -o, (Gr. λεχριος) slanting/crosswise
leci -d -s, (Gr. λεκανη) dish/pot/pan/basin/hod
lecith -o, (Gr. λεκιθος) egg yolk
lect -icul -ul, (L. lecticula) a small bier/small litter
lect, (L. lectus) a bed/couch
lecto, (Gr. λεκτος) chosen/gathered/selected
lecyth -o, (Gr. ληκυθος) an oil-flask/casket for unguents, etc.
ledos, (Gr. λεδος) a cheap dress/a light dress
leg -a -i, (L. lex/legis) law
leg -o -us, (Gr. λεγω) choose/pick out/recount/speak
leg -o, (Gr. ληγω) stay/abate/cease
legib, (L. legibilis) read
legio, (L. legio) a body of soldiers/an army
legitim, (L. legitimus) lawful/legal
legnon, (Gr. λεγνον) border/edging
lego, (L. legare) to appoint/bequeath
lego, (L. legere) to collect/to gather together/to pick
legos, (Gr. λεγος) lewd
legum -en in, (L. legumen) a legume (e.g. pea/bean)
leich -o, (Gr. λειχω) lick
leima -c -x, (Gr. λειμαξ) meadow/garden/snail
leimo, (Gr. λειμων) meadow
leio, (Gr. λειος) smooth/smooth skinned/hairless
leip -o, (Gr. λειπω) to leave/leave remaining/leave behind
leir -o, (Gr. λειρως) pale (like a lily)
leist -o, (Gr. ληιστος) plunder
lembus, (L. lembus Gr. λεμβος) a small, swift vessel/fishing boat
lemma -to, (Gr. λεμμα) peel/husk/skin/scale
lemna, (Gr. λεμνα) a water plant

lemnisc -us, (Gr. λημνισκος) a ribbon
lemo, (Gr. λαιμος) the throat
lemur, (L. lemures) ghosts/spirits
len -s -t, (L. lentis) a lentil
leni -en -s, (L. lenis) smooth/soft/mild/gentle
leno, (Gr. ληνος) wool/fleece
lent, (L. lentus) tough/resistant/slow
lenticula, (L. lenticula) a freckle/lens
lentig -nos, (L. lentignosus) freckled
-lentus, (L. -lentus) suf. ind. full of/prone to
leo -ni -nt, (L. leo Gr. λεων) a lion
lep, (L. lepus) a hare
lepa -d -s, (Gr. λεπας) a limpet/bare rock
lepi -do -s -sma, (Gr. λεπιδος) a scale
lepi, (Gr. λεπις) shell/scale (of fish)/husk
lepid -ot, (Gr. λεπιδωτος) scaly/scaled
lepid, (L. lepidus) pleasant/agreeable
lepism, (Gr. λεπισμα) peel
lepist -a, (Gr. λεπαστη) a limpet-shaped drinking cup
lepo, (Gr. λεπος) rind/husk/scale
lepor -i, (L. leporis) a hare
lepr -a -o, (Gr. λεπρος) scaly
leps -is, (Gr. ληφις) a taking/seizing/receiving
lept -ale -ino -o, (Gr. λεπτος) slender/thin/fine/delicate/small
leptes, (Gr. ληπτης) a receiver/one who accepts
lepto, (Gr. λεπτος) peeled/fine/small/thin/delicate
lepus, (L. lepus) a hair
lepyr -o, -um, (Gr. λεπυρον) rind/shell/husk
lere -m -si, (Gr. ληρημα) nonsense/silly talk
lescho, (Gr. λεσχη) gossip/talk
lesi, (L. laesi) hurt/injure/damage/strike/knock
less, (L. lessus) cry/lamentation
lest -es -ic -o -r, (Gr. ληστης) robber/plunderer/pirate
leste, (Fr. leste) nimble/sprightly
-let, (Fr. -lette) dim. suf.
-letes, (Gr. -λετης) suf. ind. hidden
leth -arh -i -o, (Gr. ληθη) forgetfulness
leth, (L. letalis) deadly
lethal, (L. lethalis) deadly
lethar, (Gr. ληθαργικος) lethargic
letifer, (L. letifer) death-bringing
leuc -o, (Gr. λευκος) white/light/brilliant/clear
leucani, (Gr. λαυκανιη) the throat
leucom -a, (Gr. λευκομα) whiteness
lcugalco, (Gr. λευγαλεος) sad/mournful
leuko, (Gr. λευκος) light/bright/clear/distinct
leur -o, (Gr. λευρος) smooth/level/even/polished
leuster, (Gr. λευστηρ) a stoner
leva, (L. (e)levare) to raise
levator, (L. (e)levator) a lifter
levi, (L. levigare) to make smooth/light
levigat, (L. levigatus) polished
levis, (L. levis) light/mild/fickle
levo, (L. laevus) the left/to the left
levo, (L. levare) to make smooth/to polish
levo, (L. levare) to raise up/make light
lexi, (Gr. ληξις) cessation/death/decease

lexi, (Gr. λεξις) speech/diction/style/a word

liban -o -us, (Gr. λιβανος) the frankincense-tree (*Boswellia carteri*)

libas, (Gr. λιβας) anything that drops or trickles

libat, (L. libatio) pour-out/taste

libell -a, (L. libella) a carpenter's level/plummet-line

libell -us, (L. libellus) a little book/note-book

liber, (L. liber) free/independent/unencumbered

liber, (L. liber) the inner bark of a tree/a book/treatise

libera -l -t, (L. libera) free

liberi, (L. liberi) a child/the young of an animal

libethron, (Gr. λειβηθρον) a wet place

libid, (L. libido) violent desire/appetite/longing

libo, (Gr. λειβω) pour/pour forth/tears shed

libra, (L. libra) a balance/pair of scales

librar -i, (L. librarius) of books

libri, (L. liber) the inner bark of a tree/a book/treatise

libum, (L. libum) a cake

liby, (Gr. λιβυκος) strange/foreign

licha, (Gr. λιχας) the space between the forefinger and thumb

lichan, (Gr. λιχανος) the forefinger/licking

lichen, (Gr. λειχην) tree-moss/lichen

lichno, (Gr. λιχνος) gluttonous/curious/inquisitive/dainties

licin, (L. licinus) bent/turned upwards

licium, (L. licium) the thrum (in weaving, thread left at the end of the warp)

licmo, (Gr. λικμος) a winnowing fan/cradle

licno, (Gr. λικνον) a wicker basket/cradle

lictor, (L. lictor) an attendant to a Roman magistrate

lictus, (L. lictus) abandoned/forsaken

lien -i -o, (L. lien) the spleen

liga -m -t, (L. ligare) to tie/bind

ligament, (L. ligamentum) bandage

lign -e -i -um, (L. lignum) wood

lignyo, (Gr. λιγνυωδης) smoky/sooty/dark-coloured

ligo, (L. ligare) to tie/bind

ligo, (L. ligo) a mattock

ligul -a, (L. ligula) little tongue/tongue of land/tongue of a shoe

ligurio, (L. ligurire) to lick/lick up/gloat over/lust after

ligustr -um, (L. ligustrum) privet (*Ligustrum lucidum*)

ligy -r -ro, (Gr. λιγυρος) clear/shrill

ligys, (Gr. λιγυρος) sharp/clear/shrill

lili -um, (L. lilium) a lily

lim -a -o, (L. lima) a file (tool)

lim -en -in, (L. limen/liminis) threshold/entrance/home/house

lim -i -us, (L. limus/limi) slime/mud/mire

lim -o -on, (Gr. λειμων) any moist, grassy place/a meadow

lim, (L. limare) to file/polish/diminish

lim, (L. limulus) squinting/looking sideways

lima -c -x, (L. limax) a slug/snail

limaco, (Gr. λειμαξ) a meadow/garden

liman, (NL. limans) slime/mud/mire

limat, (L. limatulus) polished/refined

limb -us, (L. limbus) a border/edge/hem/fringe

limeno, (Gr. λιμην) harbour/haven/refuge

limer -o, (Gr. λιμηρος) hungry/causing hunger

limit, (L. limes) frontier/boundary/limit

limma -to, (Gr. λειμμα) remnant/residue/interval (in music)

limn -a -i -o, (Gr. λιμνη) a marshy lake/artificial lake/pool/pond/swamp/sea

limno, (Gr. λιμνωδης) marshy
limo, (Gr. λιμωδης) famished/hungry
limos, (L. limosus) slimy/muddy/miry
limpid, (L. limpidus) clear/limpid
limulus, (L. limulus) somewhat oblique/squinting
limus, (L. limus) mud/mire/slime
lin -a -ar -o -um, (Gr. λινον L. linum) flax/thread/line/cord
lin -ea-eo -o, (L. linea) a thread/line
lin -o -um, (Gr. λινον) anything made of flax/fishing net/linen-cloth
linct, (L. linctus) licked
-ling, (AS. -ling), dim., having the quality of/pertaining to
lingu -a, (L. lingua) tongue/speech
lini -m -t, (L. linere) to smear/daub
lino, (Gr. λινον) flax/anything made of flax/cord/net
lint, (L. linteum) linen/cloth esp. a sail
linter, (L. linter) a boat/skiff/wherry/trough/tub/vat
linurgo, (Gr. λινουργος) a linen-weaver
linyph, (Gr. λινυφαντικος) of or for linen-weaving
lio -t, (Gr. λειος) smooth/smooth-skinned
lip -i -o, (Gr. λιπος) grease/fat/lard/tallow
lipar -o, (Gr. λιπαρος) shiny with oil/sleek/fatty/greasy
lipaug, (Gr. λιπαυγης) dark/sunless
lipern, (Gr. λιπερνης) homeless/outcast
liph(a)em, (Gr. λιφαιμος) lacking blood/pallid
lipo, (Gr. λειπειν) to be missing or lacking something/be wanting/be left behind
lipp -i, (L. lippio) to have sore eyes/be blear-eyed
lips, (Gr. λιψ) a stream
lips, (Gr. λιψ) the south-west wind/the south/the west
lipsan -o -um, (Gr. λειψανον) remnant/remains of the dead/relic
lipsi -a, (Gr. λειψις) omission/failure/lack
liqu -e -i, (L. liquor) a fluid/liquid
lir -a, (L. lira) a ridge/furrow-slice
liri -o -um, (Gr. λειριωδης) like a lily
liro, (Gr. λιρος) bold/shameless/lewd
lis, (L. lis) contention/strife/quarrel
liss -a -o, (Gr. λισσος) smooth/poor/insolvent
listr -io -o -um, (Gr. λιστρον) tool for digging
litamen, (L. litamen) sacrifice
litan, (Gr. λιτανεια) prayer/entreaty
litarg -o, (Gr. λιταργος) running quick
-lite, (Gr. λιθος) stone
-lite, (Gr. λιτος) simple
liter -a -e -i, (L. litus) the sea-shore/beach/strand/coast
litera, (L. li(t)tera) a letter of the alphabet
lith -io -o -us, (Gr. λιθος) a stone
lithi, (Gr. λιθιζω) to resemble a stone
litig -i, (L. litigium) a quarrel/dispute/contention
lito, (Gr. λιτος) simple/frugal/paltry/petty/small
litr -a, (Gr. λιτρα) a silver coin (of Sicily)/a measure of capacity
littor -a -e -i, (L. litoreus) of the sea-shore/beach/strand/coast
littor/litor, (L. littoralis/litoralis) of the seashore
litu -us, (L. lituus) the curved staff of an augur/a curved cavalry trumpet
litur, (L. litura) erase by smearing/an erasure/correction
liturg, (Gr. λειτουργος) a public servant/minister
litus, (L. litus) the sea-shore/beach/strand/coast
lituus, (L. lituus) the curved staff or wand of an augur
lixa, (L. lixa) a camp-follower

liv -e -id, (L. lividus) bluish-grey/ashen
lixivi, (L. lixiv(i)us) made into lye/ash-coloured
lob -i -o -us, (Gr. λοβος LL. lobus) a lobe
lobat, (NL. lobatus) lobed
loc-a -o -us, (L. locus) a place/neighbourhood/region
local, (L. localis) local
loch -o -us, (Gr. λοχος) an ambush/armed band/body of troops
loch, (Gr. λοχμη) thicket/copse/lair of wild beasts
lochi -a -o, (Gr. λοχιος) of or associated with childbirth
lochm -a, (Gr. λοχμη) thicket/copse/lair of wild beasts
locul -us, (L. loculus) a little place/coffin
locus, (L. locus) a place
locust -a, (L. locusta) a locust/a kind of lobster
locutio, (L. locutio) speech/speaking
lodi -c -x, (L. lodix) blanket
loedoro, (Gr. λοιδορος) abusive/railing
loego, (Gr. λοιγος) ruin/havoc
loem -o -us, (Gr. λοιμος) a plague/pestilent
loepo, (Gr. λοιπος) remaining
loestho, (Gr. λοισθος) a beam/spar
loestho, (Gr. λοισθος) left behind/last
log -o -os -us -y, (Gr. λογος) a word/discourse/study of
loga -do -s, (Gr. λογαδην) picked/chosen
logas, (Gr. λογας) the whites of the eyes/eyes
loim -o -us, (Gr. λοιμος) a plague/pestilent
lolig -in -o, (L. lolligo) a squid/cuttlefish
lolium, (L. lolium) Darnel, a type of grass (*Lolium* spp.)
loma -to, (Gr. λωμα) a hem/fringe/border
loment -um, (L. lomentum) a face cream made of bean-meal and rice/a means of
            cleansing
lomvia, (Faroese/Danish dialect) a type of guillemot (? *Uria lomvia*)
lonch -a -o, (Gr. λογχη) spear/lance/javelin
long -i, (L. longus) long
long, (L. longus) long (time/distance/etc.)
longaev, (L. longaevus) aged/ancient
longur, (L. longurius) a long pole/rod/rail
lop -ism -o -us, (Gr. λοπος) peel/husk
lopas, (Gr. λοπας) a flat vessel/plate
loph -i -io -o -us, (Gr. λοφος) back of neck/brow of hill/crest/ridge
lophema, (Gr. λωφημα) rest (from toil)
lophido, (Gr. λοφειον) a case
lophnido, (Gr. λοφνις) a torch made from vine bark
lopo, (Gr. λωπη) cloak/mantle/robe
lopodytes, (Gr. λωποδυτης) a clothes-stealer/thief
loqu, (L. loquor) to speak
lor -um, (L. lorum) leather strap/thong
lordo, (Gr. λορδος) bent backwards
lore, (L. lorum) a thong/strap/reins/bridle
loric -a, (LL. lorica) a corselet/metal breastplate
loris, (Du. loeris) a clown
lorum, (L. lorum) strap/thong/reins/whip
lot -io -us, (L. lotum) flowed over/a washing
lot -o -us, (Gr. λωτος) a name for various plants/trees
loxo, (Gr. λοξος) slanting/oblique/crosswise/ambiguous
lubric, (L. lubricus) slippery/smooth/slimy/deceitful
luc -i, (L. lucis) light
lucan, (LL. lucanus) a type of beetle

lucaris, (L. lucaris) of a forest/a forest tax
lucern -a, (L. lucerna) lamp/oil lamp
luci -d, (L. lucidus) bright/light/clear/shining
luci -o -us, (L. lucius) the pike (*Esox lucius*)
luco, (Gr. λυκος) a wolf
lucr, (L. lucrum) gain/profit/advantage
luct, (L. loctari) to wrestle/struggle/strive/contend
luctuos, (L. luctuosus) mournful/lamentable/doleful
lucus, (L. lucus) a sacred grove or woodland
lud -i -icr, (L. ludicer) play/sportive
ludovician, (LL. ludovicianus) of Lousisiana
lue -s, (L. lues) a plague/pestilence/contagious disease
lugubr, (L. lugubris) mournful/grievous/plaintive
lum -en -in, (L. lumen) light
lumb -a -o -us, (L. lumbus) the loin
lumbric -i -us, (L. lumbricus) an earthworm
lun -a, (L. luna) the moon/the night/a month
lunul -a, (L. lunatus) crescent-shaped
lup -i -o -us, (L. lupus) a wolf
lupan, (L. lupanar) a brothel
lupin -o, (L. lupinus) wolfish/of a wolf/lupine
lupul -us, (L. lupulus) the hop plant (*Humulus lupulus*)
lura, (L. lura) a sack/the mouth of a sack
lurco, (L. lurco) a glutton
lurid, (L. luridus) pale yellow/ghastly/lurid
lusc, (L. luscus) one-eyed
luscin/luscus, (L. luscinus) one-eyed/half blind/with one eye shut
luscini -a, (L. luscinia) the nightingale (*Luscinia* spp.)
lusitanic, (L. Lusitania) of Portugal and parts of Spain
lusor, (L. lusor) a player
lusso, (Gr. λουσσον) the pith from a conifer
lusto, (Gr. λουστης) one fond of bathing
lustr, (L. lustrare) to make bright/to illuminate
lustrum, (L. lustrum) a bog/morass/lair/brothel
lusus, (L. lusus) game/sport/amusement
lut -e -i, (L. luteus) golden-yellow/orange-yellow
lut -e -i, (L. luteus) of mud or clay/dirty
luter, (Gr. λουτηρ) a bathtub
luto, (L. lutum) mud
lutr, (L. lutra) otter
lutro, (Gr. λουτρον) bath/bathing place
lutus, (L. lutus) washed
luvi, (L. luere) to wash
lux, (L. lux) light
luxa, (L. luxare) to dislocate/displace
luxur -i, (L. luxuria) exuberant growth/extravagance
ly-/lys, (Gr. λυειν) to loosen
lyc -o -os, (Gr. λυκος) wolf/a type of fish/spider/anything hook-shaped
lycaena, (Gr. λυκαινα) she-wolf
lychn -is, (Gr. λυχνις) the rose campion (*Lychnis coronaria*)
lychn -o -us, (Gr. λυχνος) a small portable lamp
lygae, (Gr. λυγαιος) shadowy/murky/gloomy
lygdo, (Gr. λυγδος) white marble
lygero, (Gr. λυγερος) plaint/flexible
lygi -sm, (Gr. λυγισμος) bending/twisting (as of a willow)
lygi, (Gr. λυγη) twilight
lygistes, (Gr. λυγιστης) a basket-maker

lygm, (Gr. λυγξ) hiccough/an ineffectual retching

lygo, (Gr. λυγος) a twig/pliant rod

lygr -o, (Gr. λυγρος) baneful/mournful/mischievous

lyma, (Gr. λυμα) moral filth/defilement

lymantri, (Gr. λυμαντηριος) injurious/destructive

lyme, (Gr. λυμεων) injury from

lymph -a -o, (L. lympha) pure water/spring water/nymphs of the spring

lymphat -i -o, (L. lymphatus) raving/mad/frantic

lyn -c -x, (Gr. λυνξ) a lynx (Felis lynx)

lyngo, (Gr. λυγξ) hiccough/an ineffectual retching

lyo, (Gr. λυω) to loosen/slacken/untie/release/weaken/dissolve/demolish/dismiss

lyp -e -ero -o, (Gr. λυπηρος) painful/distressing/causing sorrow/causing pain

lypr -o, (Gr. λυπρος) distressful/wretched/poor

lyr -a -i, (Gr. λυρα) a lyre

lys -i -is -io, (Gr. λυσις) dissolving/loosening/setting free

lyss -a -o, (Gr. λυσσα/λυττα) madness/rage/martial rage/rabies

lyt -o, (Gr. λυτος) something which may be untied

lyter, (Gr. λυτηρ) a deliverer/arbitrator

lythr -o -um, (Gr. λυθρον) blood/gore/venom of a hydra

lytro, (Gr. λυτρον) a ransom

lytt -a, (Gr. λυττα) madness/rage/martial rage/rabies

M

-ma, (Gr. -μα), the result of an action

macar -i -o, (Gr. μακαρια) happiness/bliss

macell -a, (Gr. μακελλα) a mattock/pick axe with one point

macer -a, (L. macerare) to soften/make weak

macer, (L. maceria) a garden wall

mach -a -i -o, (Gr. μαχη) battle/combat/struggle/fight

macha -er -ir, (Gr. μαχαιρα) a dagger/dirk/sacrificial knife/shears

machetico, (Gr. μαχητικος) warlike/quarrelsome/pugnacious

machin -a, (L. machina) any machine/catapult/ballista

machlo, (Gr. μαχλος) lustful/lewd

maci -a, (L. macies) thinness/leanness/poverty/barrenness

macr -o, (Gr. μακρος) long/tall/lofty/large/far stretching

macraeo, (Gr. μακραιων) long-lived/long-lasting

mact, (L. mactare) to magnify/honour

mact, (L. mactare) to slay/smite

mactr -a -i, (Gr. μακτρα) a kneading trough

mactus, (L.) honoured/glorified/rewarded with [something]

macula -t, (L. macula) spot/stain/fault/mesh

mad -e -id, (L. madidus) wet/moist/wet with tears/drunken

madar -o, (Gr. μαδαρος) bald

madesc, (L. madescere) to become wet

madre, (Sp. madre) mother

maduls, (L. madulsa) a drunkard

maeeu -si -sio, (Gr. μαιευσις) childbirth

maen -a -ad -as, (Gr. μαινας) raving/frantic/excited

maen -a -i, (Gr. μαινη) a sprat (Maena vulgaris)

maest, (L. maestus) sad/mournful/dejected

magadis, (Gr. μαγαδις) a harp-like instrument of 20 strings/a Lydian flute

magado, (Gr. μαγας) the bridge of the cithara (a lyre)

magan -ar, (Gr. μαγγαναριος) conjurer/mechanical engineer

magdal -i, (L. magdalium) a cylindrical figure/pill

magir, (Gr. μαγειρος) a slaughterer/butcher/cook

magis, (Gr. μαγις) a dish/plate/platter/cake

magist -er -r, (L. magister) master/chief/head/teacher

magma, (Gr. μαγμα) a thick unguent

magn -i, (L. magnus) large/great

magne -to, (Gr. μαγνητις λιθος) the load stone/a magnet

mai -a -o, (Gr. μαια) foster-mother/midwife/female doctor/a type of crab

maieu -si -sio, (Gr. μαιευσις) childbirth

maior, (L. maior) great/large

maira, (Gr. Μαιρα) name of the dog-star (the *Sparkler*)/shine/sparkle

majalis, (L. maialis) a gelded boar

major, (L. maior) great/large

makr -o, (Gr. μακρος) large/tall/high/deep/long/far/remote

mal -a, (L. mala Gr. μηλον) jaw bone/cheek bone

mal -e -i -ign, (L. malignus) malicious/malignant/ill-disposed/wicked/bad/evil/
　　　　barren/wrong/imperfect

mal -i -us, (L. malum) an apple or any similar fruit (quince, peach, pomegranate)

mal -o, (Gr. μαλλος) a flock of wool/woolly

mal(l)el, (LL. malella) little jaw bone/little cheek bone

mala, (Gr. μαλα) very/exceedingly

malac -h -i -o, (Gr. μαλακια) softness/moral weakness

malaco, (Gr. μαλακος) soft/gentle/mild

malari, (It. mal - aria) bad - air

malax, (Gr. μαλαξις) softening

malc, (Gr. μαλκιος) freezing/benumbing

male, (L. male) bad/evil/wrong

maledic, (L. maledicus) abusive/scurrilous

malero, (Gr. μαλερος) fierce/raging/violent/fiery

maliasm -us, (Gr. μαλιασμος) a contagious disease (glanders)

malign, (L. malignus) bad/malevolent

malist, (Gr. μαλιστα) most

malit, (L. malitia) badness/wickedness/vice

mall -o -us, (Gr. μαλλος) flock of wool/tress of hair

malle -us, (L. malleus) a hammer

mallo, (Gr. μαλλον) more

malo, (Gr. μαλος) slender

malth -a -aco -e -o, (Gr. μαλθα) soft wax/a mixture of wax and pitch

malum, (Gr. μηλον) metaph. of the cheeks/breasts

malum, (L. malum) an apple/peach/pomegranate/quince

malus, (L. malus) bad/evil

malv -a, (L. malva) the mallow (*Malva* spp.)

mam -ma, (L. mamma) breast

mamilla, (L. mamilla) nipple

mammal -i, (L. mammalia) mammal

man -o, (Gr. μανος) loose/open/rare/spares/infrequent

man, (L. manus) a hand

mana, (L. manabilis) flowing/penetrating

manc, (L. manca) incomplete/defective/maimed/crippled/lame

mancep, (L. manceps) a purchaser at auction/farmer/contractor

manciol, (L. manciola) little hand

mancip, (L. mancipium) a taking in hand (a legal form of sale and purchase)

-mancy, (Gr. μαντεια) prophetic power/oracle

mand, (L. mandere) to chew/eat/devour/consume

manda, (L. mandare) to order/command/entrust

mandal, (Gr. μανδαλος) a bolt/bar
mandibul, (LL. mandibulum) the lower jaw
mandra, (Gr. μανδρα) an enclosed space/byre/fold
mandragor, (Gr. μανδραγορας) the mandrake (*Mandragora officinalis*)/belladonna (*Atropa belladonna*)
manduc, (L. manducare) to chew
mandya, (Gr. μανδυα) a woollen cloak
manes, (Gr. μανης) a kind of cup/small bronze figure/a slave
mangan -eu, (Gr. μαγγανευτης) an impostor
mani -a, (Gr. μανιας) frantic/mad
mani, (L. manus) the hand
manicat, (L. manicatus) sleeved/with long sleeves
manifest, (L. manifestus) clear/distinct/visible
manipul, (L. manipulatim) in bundles/handfuls
manis, (L. manes) a ghost
mann -o -us, (Gr. μαννος) necklace
manna, (Gr. μαννα) frankincense powder or granules
manno, (Gr. μαννος) necklace
mannus, (L. mannus) a small, swift, Gallic horse
mano, (Gr. μανος) rare/happening rarely
mansio, (L. mansio) a station/halting place/stage
mansu, (L. mansus) bitten/chewed
mansuet, (L. mansuetus) tame/mild/soft/gentle/quiet
mant, (Gr. μαντις) a prophet
mant, (Sp. manto/manta) cloak/blanket
mantell -um, (L. mantel(l)um) a cloak/covering
mantha, (Gr. μανθανω) understand
manti -d -s, (Gr. μαντις) diviner/seer/prophet/the praying mantis (*Mantis religiosa*)
mantic, (L. mantica) wallet/knapsack
mantill, (Sp. mantilla) a light cloak
mantissa, (L. mantis(s)a) a make-weight/a small addition
manu -s, (L. manus) the hand
manubri -um, (L. manubrium) a handle
mapal, (L. mapalium) an African hut
mappa, (L. mappa) napkin/towel
maps, (Gr. μαψ) in vain/without result/falsely
mar -i, (L. mare) the sea
marant, (Gr. μαρανσις) dying or fading away/wasting away
marasm, (Gr. μαρασμος) withering
maraugia, (Gr. μαραυγια) dazzling of the eyes/loss of sight
marc -esc -id, (L. marcesco) to begin to droop/to grow feeble
marc -us, (L. marculus) a small hammer
marcid, (L. marcidus) withered/shrivelled
marcus, (L. marcus) a large hammer
marg -in -o, (L. marginare) to border/make a border
marg, (L. margo) edge/margin
margar, (Gr. μαργαρωδης) pearl-like
margarit -es, (Gr. μαργαριτης) a pearl
margo, (Gr. μαργος) furious
marian, (L. Maria) of Mary
marilo, (Gr. μαριλη) charcoal embers/coal dust
marin, (L. marinus) of the sea
marit -a, (L. maritus) conjugal/relating to marriage/a husband/a lover
maritim, (L. maritimus) marine/maritime
marm -ar -or, (Gr. μαρμαρος) marble
marpt -o, (Gr. μαρπτω) seize/take hold of
marra, (L. marra) a hoe

mars -ipo -upi, (Gr. μαρσυπος) a pouch/bag
marsup, (L. marsupium) a pouch
marti, (L. Martis) Mars, the god of war, husbandry, shepherds and seers
mas, (L. mas) the male
maschal, (Gr. μασχαλη) the arm-pit
mascul -in, (L. masculinus) male/masculine
mascul, (L. masculus) male
masesi, (Gr. μασησις) chewing
mass -a -o, (L. massa) a lump/a mass of something
masset -er, (Gr. μασητηρ) a chewer
massul -a, (L. massula) a little mass
mast, (Gr. μαστευω) seek/search/crave/need/strive
masta -c -x, (Gr. μασταξ) the jaws/mouth
maste, (Gr. μαστηρ) seeker
masthle, (Gr. μασθλης) a leather whip
mastic, (L. masticare) to chew
mastiche, (Gr. μαστιχη) a resin from the mastich tree (*Pistacia* spp.)
mastig -ia, (L. mastigia) a scoundrel
mastig -o, (Gr. μαστιξ) a whip
masto, (Gr. μαστος) a woman's breast/nipple
masturba, (L. masturbari) to practise self-abuse
mastus, (Gr. μαστος) the breast
mat -aeo -eo, (Gr. ματαιος) vain/empty/idle/foolish/rash/profane
matar, (L. mataris) a Celtic javelin
mataxa, (Gr. μεταξα) raw silk
mater, (Gr. μητηρ L. mater) mother
math, (Gr. μαθη) learning/knowledge
mathali, (Gr. μαθαλις) a kind of cup or measure
matr -i -o, (L. mater) mother
matri -c -x, (L. matrix) a female used in breeding/parent stem/a place where something
              is generated/the womb/uterus
matron, (L. matrona) a married woman/wife/noble lady
matt, (L. matta) a mat of rushes
mattea, (Gr. ματτυη) a (meat) delicacy
matul, (L. matula) a vessel/pot/simpleton
matur, (L. maturus) ripen/quicken/hasten/timely
matutin, (L. matutinus) early in the morning/of the morning
maulis, (Gr. μαυλις) a bawd/procuress
maur -o, (Gr. μαυροω) darken/blind/make dim/make obscure
max -i -im, (L. maximus) the largest/greatest
maxill -a -i, (L. maxilla) upper jaw/jaw bone
maxim, (L. maximus) greatest
maz -ia -o, (Gr. μαζα) cake/lump/mass/ball/amalgam
me, (Gr. μη) not - a negative used in prohibitions
meandr, (Gr. μαιανδρυς) sinuous/winding/twisting
meat -us, (L. meatus) motion/course/passage
mecasmo, (Gr. μηκασμος) bleating
mechan -i -o, (Gr. μηχανη) a contrivance/instrument/machine
mecist -o, (Gr. μηκιστος) tallest/greatest/longest/farthest
meco, (Gr. μηκος) length/height
mecon -i -o, (Gr. μηκων) poppy (*Papaver somniferum*)
meconid, (Gr. μηκωνιδιον) little poppy
mecopt, (Gr. μηκοπτερα) longwing
mecyn -o, (Gr. μηκυνω) lengthening/prolong/delay
medam, (Gr. μηδαμινος) worthless
meddix/medix, (L. meddix/medix) a caretaker/curator/magistrate

medeol, (L. Medea) a sorceress
medi -a -o, (L. medius) middle/in the centre/neutral
mediast, (L. mediastinus) a drudge/menial
mediat, (L. mediator) arbitrator/umpire
medic -a -o, (L. medicari) to heal/cure
mediocr, (L. mediocris) moderate/ordinary
medo, (Gr. μεδω) protect/rule over/guard
medull -a, (L. meddula) the middle/marrow of bones/inmost part/pith
medusa, (Gr. Μεδουσα) Medusa (one of the Gorgons)
meg -a -alo, (Gr. μεγας) great/vast/tall/large
megar -on -um, (Gr. μεγαρον) a large room/hall/chief room/bedchamber/sanctuary
megisto, (Gr. μεγιστο-) greatest/largest/most blest
mei -o, (Gr. μειον/μειων) smaller/less/lesser/too small
meios -is, (Gr. μειωσις) diminution/lessen
meioti, (Gr. μειοτης) minimising
meiz -o, (Gr. μειζον-) greater/larger
meko, (Gr. μηκος) length/height/stature/magnitude
mel -es -id, (L. meles) badger
mel -i -it -ito, (Gr. μελι) honey
mel -o, (Gr. μελος) a limb/song/melody
mel -oe -oi, (Gr. μηλη) a probe
mel, (L. mel) honey
mela, (Gr. μελας) black/dark/gloomy
melaen, (Gr. μελαινω) blacken/to dye black
melan -o, (Gr. μελανο-) black-
melan, (L. melas) black
melas, (Gr. μελας) black/dark/dark in colour
melathron, (Gr. μελαθρον) roof/ceiling/lair/cage
meldo, (Gr. μελδω) soften by boiling
meleagri -s, (Gr. μελεαγρις) the Guinea-fowl (*Numida meleagris*)
meledono, (Gr. μελεδωνος) attendant/guardian
meleo, (Gr. μελεος) idle/useless/miserable
meletero, (Gr. μελετηρος) diligent
melia, (Gr. μελια) an ash tree (*Fraxinus ornus*)/an ashen spear
melic, (Gr. μελικος) musical/melodious
melichr -o, (Gr. μελιχρως) honey-coloured
melicto, (Gr. μελικτης) a flute player
meligery, (Gr. μελιγηυρς) melodious/sweet-voiced
melin, (Gr. μελινος/μειλινος) ashen
melior, (L. melior) better
melism, (Gr. μελισμα) a song/air/melody/lyric poetry
melism, (Gr. μελισμος) dismembering/dividing
meliss -a, (Gr. μελισσα) honey-licker/honey bee/bee
melit -o, (Gr. μελιτο-) honey-
melizo, (Gr. μελιζω) sing/modulate/celebrate in song
mello, (Gr. μελλο-) be about to do/about to be
mellum, (L. mellum) a dog-collar
melo -n, (Gr. μηλον/μαλον) apple/any tree-fruit
melo, (Gr. μελος) a limb/musical phrase
melo, (Gr. μηλον) sheep or goat
melod -i, (Gr. μελωδια) singing/chanting
melolonth -a, (Gr. μηλολονωη) the cockchafer (*Melolontha melolontha*)
melos, (Gr. μελωσις) probing
melotri -di, (Gr. μηλωτριδιον) a small probe/probe (a wound)/sound (the bladder)
melyr -is, (Gr. μελιρους) a kind of beetle (Melyridae)
memat -o, (Gr. μεματος) desired

membra -c -x, (Gr. μεμβραξ) a kind of cicada
membran -a, (Gr. μεμβρανα) a parchment/skin
membran -a, (L. membrana) a thin skin/membrane/film
membrum, (L. membrum) a part/limb/member of the body
meme, (Gr. μιμημα) a copy
memnoni, (L. memnonis) Memnon, a king of Ethiopia; hence brownish-black
mempsis, (Gr. μεμψις) blame/reproof/censure
men -o, (Gr. μην) month
mena -do, (Gr. μηνη) the moon
menda -c -x, (L. mendacium/mendax) a lie/falsehood
mendic, (L. mendicus) poor/beggarly
mene, (Gr. μηνη) the moon/silver
mene, (Gr. μηνιαιος) monthly/the menses of women/a month long
meneto, (Gr. μενετος) patient/inclined to wait
meni, (Gr. μηνις) wrath/anger
menin -g -go -x, (Gr. μενιγξ) a membrane
menis, (Gr. μηνις) wrath
menisco, (Gr. μηνισκος) crescent-shaped/a small moon
meno, (Gr. μενω) to remain/stand fast
mens -a, (L. mensa) a table
mens -e -i, (L. mensis) a month
mens, (L. mensor) a measurer/surveyor
mens, (L. mentis) the mind/understanding/reason/intellect
menstru, (L. menstrualis) monthly
mensur, (L. mensura) a measuring/amount/proportion/measure
ment -a -i, (L. mentis) the mind/understanding/reason/intellect
ment -al, (L. -amentum) suf. ind. 'materials for something'
ment -i -um, (L. mentum) the chin
menth -a, (L. menta/mentha) mint
mentul -a, (L. mentula) the penis
-mentum, (L.) action/means/result/condition/tool
meny, (Gr. μηνυτηρ) informer/guide
mephit -i -is, (L. mephitis) a foul odour from the earth/malaria
mer, (L. meracus) pure/unmixed
meracus, (L. meracus) pure/unmixed
mercator, (L. mercator) merchant/shopkeeper
mercur, (L. mercurius) Mercury (the Grecian messenger of the gods)
merd -a, (L. merda) excrement/dung
mere -t, (L. merere) to deserve/earn/obtain
-mere, -meri, -mero, -merous, (Gr. μερος/μερις) a part/portion
meretrix, (L. meretrix) a harlot
merg, (L. merges) a sheaf of corn
merg, (L. mergo) to dip/plunge/immerse
mergus, (L. mergus) a sea-bird, esp. a shearwater or gull
meri -d -s, (Gr. μεριδιον) a small part
meriae, (Gr. μερεια) of the thigh
merico, (Gr. μερικος) particular
merid, (L. meridies) midday/south
meridi, (L. meridies) noon
meridional, (L. meridies) the south
merimna, (Gr. μεριμνα) anxious care/though/solicitude
meringo, (Gr. μεριγξ) a bristle
merintho, (Gr. μηρινθος) a cord/line/string
merism -o -us, (Gr. μερισμος) dividing/division/partition
merist -o, (Gr. μεριστος) divided/separate/individual
merit, (L. meritare) to earn regularly
merluci -us, (NL. merluccius) a kind of hake

mermi -s -th, (Gr. μερμις) a cord
mero -s, (Gr. μηρος) the upper thigh/a ham
-mero, -merous, -mere, -meri, (Gr. μερος/μερις) a part/partion
merop -s, (Gr. μεροψ) the common bee-eater (*Merops apiaster*)
meros/meris, (Gr. μερος/μερις) part/portion/share/section
mers, (L. mersare) to dip in/immerse
merul -a, (L. merula) the European blackbird (*Turdus merula*)/the sea-carp
merus, (Gr. μηρος) the upper thigh
meryc -o, (Gr. μηρυκαζω) chew the cud/ruminate
mes -o, (Gr. μεσος) middle/in the middle
mesar -a -i -um, (Gr. μεσσαριον) a mesentery (membrane to which intestines are
           attached)
mesat, (Gr. μεσσατος) middlemost
mesembri -a, (Gr. μεσημβρια) midday/the south
mesit -es, (Gr. μεσιτης) mediator/umpire/arbitrator
meso, (Gr. μεσος) the middle
mesotoech -o, (Gr. μεσοτοιχος) a dividing wall/party wall
messoro, (Gr. μεσσορος) a boundary-stone
messura, (L. messura) a reaping
mest -o, (Gr. μεστος) full/filled
meta, (Gr. μετα) among/between/with/by means of/change (of place)/after
meta, (L. meta) a boundary/goal/end/post/mark
metab -ol, (Gr. μεταβολη) change/exchange
metalep, (Gr. μεταληψις) participation
metall, (Gr. μεταλλον) mine/quarry/pit/mineral/metal
metalli, (Gr. μεταλλικος) metallic
metallurg, (Gr. μεταλλουργια) working in metal
metastat, (Gr. μεταστασις) removal
metathet, (Gr. μεταθετος) changed
metax -i -y, (Gr. ματαξυ) in the midst/between/intermediate
metax, (Gr. μεταξα) raw silk
metelys, (Gr. μετηλυς) an emigrant
meteor -o, (Gr. μετεωρος) raised off the ground/in mid-air/high in air/buoyed
           up/haughty
-meter, (Gr. μετρον) a measure
meter, (Gr. μητηρ) mother
meth -e, (Gr. μεθη) drunk/strong drink
meth -o -y, (Gr. μεθυ) wine/drink
methecto, (Gr. μεθεκτος) participating/sharing
methetico, (Gr. μεθετικος) relaxing/letting go
method -o, (Gr. μεθοδος) system/method
methys, (Gr. μεθυσμα) an intoxicating drink
metis, (Gr. μητις) wisdom/skill/craft
metoch, (Gr. μετοχη) sharing
metoec, (Gr. μετοικιη) change of abode/migration
metop -i -o, (Gr. μετωπιον) forehead/facade
metoporin, (Gr. μετοπωρινος) autumnal
metr -o, (Gr. μετρον) a measure or rule
metra, (Gr. μητρα) the womb
metre, (Gr. μετρες) measurer
metridio, (Gr. μητριδιος) fruitful/filled with seed
metrio, (Gr. μετρειν) to measure/count/compute
metrio, (Gr. μετριοτης) moderation/middle course
metro, (Gr. μητηρ) mother
metry, (Gr. μετρον) a measure
metus, (L. metus) fear/apprehension

mezo, (Gr. μειζον) greater
mia, (Gr. μει-) smaller
miar -o, (Gr. μιαρος) stained with blood/defiled/polluted
miasm -a -o, (Gr. μιασμα) pollution/stain/defilement
mica -r, (L. mica) a crumb/morsel/grain
micans, (L. micans) shining/twinkling
micell -a, (L. micella) a little crumb
micid, (L. micidus) thin/poor
mico, (L. micare) to vibrate/flicker/twinkle
micr -o, (Gr. μικρος) small/little/petty/trivial/slight
mict -o, (Gr. μικτος) mixed/compound
mictil, (L. mictilis) worthless
micto, (Gr. μικτος) mixed/blended
mictur, (L. micturire) to urinate
micty, (Gr. μυκτηρ) nose
mida -s, (Gr. μιδας) a destructive insect in beans
midemato, (Gr. μειδημα) smile
migma, (Gr. μιγμα) mixture/compound
migr -a, (L. migrare) to transfer/remove/transport/migrate
migratori, (L. migratoria) wandering/migratory
miles, (L. miles) soldier/campaigner/piece on a draughtboard
mili -ar -ol -um, (L. milium) millet
milicho, (Gr. μιλιχος) gentle
milit -ar -i, (L. militaris) of a soldier/of war/military
mill -e -i -o, (L. mille) one thousand
milph -o, (Gr. μιλφος) losing hair
milt -o, (Gr. μιλτος) red earth/red ochre/ruddle
milv -in -us, (L. miluus/milvus) a kite (bird and constellation)/the gurnard (a fish)
mime, (Gr. μιμησις) imitation
mimet -ic, (Gr. μιμητικος) imitative
mimi, (Gr. mimus) a mimic actor
mimic, (Gr. μιμικος) imitative
mimo, (Gr. μιμος) imitator/copyist/actor
mina -c -x, (L. minax) projecting/overhanging/threatening
mina, (L. minari) to threaten/menace
minatio, (L. minatio) a threat/menace
mindax, (Gr. μινδαξ) a Persian incense
minera, (MedL. minera) ore/mine
mini -a -um, (L. minium) red lead/native cinnabar
mini, (L. minimus) least
miniat, (L. miniatus) bright red/vermilion
minim, (L. minumus) smallest/least
minium, (L. minium) native cinnabar/red-lead
minor, (L. minor) jut out/project/overhang/threaten/menace
minor, (L. minor) smaller/lesser
minus, (L. minus) smaller/lesser
minut, (L. minutus) small/little/minute/petty/insignificant
miny -th -s, (Gr. μινυθω) to diminish/lessen
minyorio, (Gr. μινωριος) short-lived
minyr -o, (Gr. μινυρος) complaining in a low tone/whining/whimpering
minys, (Gr. μινυς) little/small
minyth, (Gr. μινυθω) lessen/curtail
mio-, (Gr. μειων) pref. less
mir -a -ab -ac -i, (L. mirus) wonderful/extraordinary/astonishing
miracid, (Gr. μειρακιδιον) little stripling
miraco, (Gr. μειραξ) a young girl/lass
mirand, (L. mirandus) wonderful/strange

mire, (ON. myrr) bog/swamp/deep mud
mirmillo, (L.) a kind of gladiator that used to fight with a Thracian, or a net-fighter, and
        wore a Gallic helmet, with the image of a fish for a crest.
mirus, (L. mirus) wonderful
mis, (Gr. μισεω) hate
misc -o, (Gr. μισχος) stalk of leaves or fruit/husk/shell
misc, (L. miscer) to mix up
misch -o -us, (Gr. μισχος) stalk of leaves or fruit/husk/shell
mise -ll -r, (L. misellus) miserable/wretched
miset(t)ia, (Gr. μισητια) lust/lewdness
miso, (Gr. μισος) hate/hatred
miss -i, (L. missio) sending off/sending away/releasing
missile, (L. missilis) anything cast, hurled or thrown
missus, (L. missus) letting go/sending/throwing/shooting
mist -o, (Gr. μειστος) least
mist -us, (L. mixtus) a mixing
mist, (AS. mist) darkness
mistho, (Gr. μισθος) pay/wages/reward
misticus, (L. misticus) hybrid/mongrel
mit, (L. mittere) to send/let go
mitell -a, (L. mitella) a turban
miter, (L. mitra) a head-dress/turban/cap
mithra, (L. mithrax) a kind of Persian stone
miti, (L. mitis) mild/soft/gentle/ripe
mitig, (L. mitigare) to make mild/make soft/make ripe
mito -s, (Gr. μιτος) a thread/a web
mitr -a -i, (L. mitra) a head band/turban
mitra, (L. mitra) a head-dress/turban/cap
-mitus, (Gr. μιτος) a thread/a web
mitylo, (Gr. μιτυλος) hornless
mitys, (Gr. μιτυς) beeswax
miuro, (Gr. μειουρος) shortened/tapering/mouse-tailed
mix -i -o, (Gr. μιξις) a mixing/mingling
mnem -at -on, (Gr. μνημη) memory
mnester, (Gr. μνηστηρ) wooer/suitor
mni -o -um, (Gr. μνιωδης) mossy
mno, (Gr. μνους/μνοος) fine, soft down
mobil, (L. mobilis) movable
mochl -o -us, (Gr. μοχλος) a lever/bar/crowbar
mocho, (Gr. μωχος) ridicule/mockery
mochth -o -us, (Gr. μοχθος) toil/hardship/distress
moco, (Gr. μωκος) mockery
mod -u, (L. modus) measure
modena, (an Italian city) deep purple
modic, (L. modicus) moderate/limited/not very deep
modiol -us, (L. modulus) a small measure
modul, (L. modulari) to measure regularly/to modulate/to play an instrument
moech -a, (Gr. μοιχος) adulterer/paramour
moell, (Fr. moelle) marrow
moen -i, (L. moenia) walls/fortifications/ramparts/bulwarks
moer -a -o, (Gr. Μοιρα) goddess of fate/portion of land/destiny
moesia, (L. Moesiacus) of Bulgaria and Serbia
mog -i -o, (Gr. μογις/μολις) hardly/scarcely
mogo, (Gr. μογος) trouble/distress/pain
moir -a -o, (Gr. Μοιρα) goddess of fate/portion of land/destiny
mol -i, (Gr. μολις/μογις) hardly/scarcely
mola -r, (L. molere) to grind/mill

mola, (L. molaris) of a block of stone/of a mill stone
mole, (L. moles) a shapeless mass/mass of rock/massive construction
molecul, (L. molecula) a little mass
molen, (L. molere) to grind
molest, (L. molestia) annoyance/affectation
molg -o, (Gr. μολγος) skin/hide
moli, (Gr. μολις/μογις) hardly/scarcely
molin -a, (L. mola) a mill
molit -us, (L. molitus) striven/built
moll -i, (L. mollio) soft/pliable/supple
mollug, (L. mollugo) carpet weed
mollusc, (L. molluscus) soft
molo, (L. molere) to grind (in a mill)
molobro, (Gr. μολοβρος) a greedy fellow/the young of wild swine
moloch, (Hb. Molech) a deity worshipped by sacrifice of the firstborn child
molop -o -us, (Gr. μωλωψ) weal/bruise/ridge/blood-clot
molopast -es, (Gr. μολπαστης) a dancer/minstrel
moloss, (Gr. Μολοσσος) a type of wolf-dog used by shepherds
molp, (Gr. μολπη) a song
molpe, (Gr. μολπη) a dance or rhythmic movement with song
molucrum, (L. molucrum) a broom for sweeping out a mill
moluro, (Gr. μολουρος) a kind of snake
moly -ros -s -x, (Gr. μωλυς) soft/weak/feeble
moly, (Gr. μολυ) a herb with magic properties (? garlic)
molybd -i -o, (Gr. μολιβδος) lead (the metal)
molyn -a, (Gr. μολυνω) stain/sully/defile/debauch
molysm -o, (Gr. μολυσμωδης) tainted/polluted
momentum, (L. momentum) movement/motion/an impulse
momo -s -us, (Gr. μομφη) blame/reproof
mon -a -er -o, (Gr. μονας) solitary/single/a unit
mon, (Gr. μονη) tarrying
mon, (L. mons) mountain
monach, (Gr. μοναχος) single/solitary/unique/a monk
monact, (Gr. μονακτις) with one ray/spine
monarch, (Gr. μοναρχος) a monarch
monas, (Gr. μονας) single/alone
-mone, (Gr. -μονη), quality
monet, (L. moneta) coined metal/money/the mint
-monger, (AS. mangian) trade
moni, (Gr. μονιμος) fixed/stable/steadfast
monil -i, (L. monile) a necklace/collar/string of beads
monimo, (Gr. μονιμος) fixed/stable/steadfast/fixed abode
monio, (Gr. μονιος) of male beasts - solitary/ferocious
monit, (L. monito) reminding/warning
mono, (Gr. μονος) alone/left alone/single
monoto, (Gr. μονοτοκια) one at a time
monstr -a, (L. monstra) show/point out/teach/inform
monstr -a, (L. monstrum) a monster/a wonder/portent
mont -an -i, (L. mons) mountain
mops, (Gr. Μοψος) a celebrated soothsayer
mor -i -us, (L. morus Gr. μορον) a mulberry/blackberry
mor -o, (Gr. μωριων) stupid/foolish
mora -tor, (L. morator) a delayer/retarder
morb -i -os, (L. morbus) disease/sickness/distress
morbill, (Mod.L. morbillus) measles
mord -ac -ax -el -en -ic, (L. mordere) to sting/bite/nip/cut into/take fast hold of
mori -o, (Gr. μοριον) small constituent part/piece/portion

mori, (Gr. μωρια) folly/illicit love
moribund, (L. moribundus) dying/expiring/deadly
moriger, (L. morigerus) complying/obedient/obsequious
morind -a, (L. morus) mulberry/blackberry
morino, (Gr. μορινος) mulberry-coloured
morio, (Gr. μοριος) a narcotic plant used in philtres (love potions)
morion, (Gr. μοριον) a piece/constituent part/portion/section
mormo, (Gr. Μορμω) she-monster/hobgoblin
mormyr -o -us, (Gr. μορμυρος) a sea fish
moro, (Gr. μωρος) stupid/foolish/dull/sluggish
morochto, (Gr. μοροχθος) a kind of pipe-clay
moros, (Gr. μορος) fate/destiny/doom/death
moros, (L. morosus) peevish/fretful/morose
morph -a -o, (Gr. μορφη) form/shape/figure
morph -e -o, (L. Morpheus) god of dreams
morpho, (Gr. μορφωσις) a shaping/semblance/form
morrhu -a, (NL. morrhua) cod
mors, (L. morsus) a bite/biting/eating/seizing
mort -al -i -u, (L. mortalitas) mortality/death/dead
morul -a, (L. morulla) a little mulberry/blackberry
morul -us, (L. morulus) dark coloured/black
-morus, (L. morus) a mulberry/blackberry
mosa, (Gr. Μουσα) Muse
mosch -o -us, (Gr. μοσχος) musk/a calf or young bull/boy/girl/maid
mosquito, (Sp. mosquito) little gnat/fly
moss, (AS. mos) bog
mot -a -i -o, (L. movere) to move
motacill -a, (L. motacilla) a coined word 'little mover' the wagtail (*Motacilla* spp.)
motho -s, (Gr. μοθος) battle-din
motho, (Gr. μοθων) an impudent fellow/a licentious dance
motiv, (L. motivus) moving
motor, (L. motator) mover
mov, (L. movere) to move
mu, (Gr. μυ μ M) twelfth letter of the Greek alphabet
muc -e -i -o -us, (L. mucus) mucus
mucedo, (L. mucedo) mould/mildew
mucil -age, (LL. mucilago) a sticky, gelatinous juice
mucor, (L. mucor) mould/mildew
mucro, (L. mucro) sharp
mucus, (L. mucus) nasal secretion
mugil -i, (L. mugil/mugilis) a fish, perh. the mullet (Mugilidae)
mugitor, (L. mugire) to bellow/roar/bray
mulc, (L. mulceo) stroke/touch lightly/soothe/appease/charm
mulco, (L. mulcare) to thrash/cudgel/handle roughly
mulg, (L. mulgeo) to milk
mulier, (L. mulier) woman/female
mulin, (L. mulinus) of a mule/mulish
mulleol, (L. mulleolus) reddish
mulo, (L. mulus) the mule
muls -i, (L. mulsus) honeyed/sweetened with honey
mult -i, (L. multus) many
multa, (L. multa) penalty/fine
multfar, (L. multifarius) various
multic, (L. multicius) soft
multifid, (L. multifidus) cloven into many parts
multiplico, (L. multiplicatio) increase
multplex, (L. multiplex) having many folds

multus, (L. multus) much/many
mund -an, (L. mundanus) a citizen of the world
mund -i, (L. munditia) cleanness/neatness/elegance
mundus, (L. mundus) the world/earth
muneral, (L. muneralis) of gifts
mungo, (L. mungo) blow the nose
munio, (L. munire) to build a wall/fortify
munus, (L. munus) a gift/duty/service/tax
mur -a -al, (L. murus) a wall
mur -i, (L. muris) a mouse or rat
muraen -a, (L. muraena/murena) the lamprey or murry (Petromyzontidae)
murcid, (L. murcidus, Murcia - goddess of sloth) cowardly/slothful
murex, (L. murex) the shellfish yielding a purple dye/a purple dye
muria, (L. muria) brine/pickle
muric, (L. murica) (as murex)
muricat, (L. muricatus) having a rough, short, hard point
muricul, (L. muriculus) slightly pointed
murin, (L. muris) of a mouse/rat
murrha, (L. murrha) a kind of clay (?fluorspar)
mus -a -o, (Ar.) the banana
mus, (L. mus) a mouse
-mus, (Gr. -μος), ind. an action
musa, (Gr. Μουσα) one of the muses (of fine arts)
musc -a -i -o, (L. musca) a fly/a troublesome person
musc -id -o, (L. muscosus) mossy
muscari, (L. muscarius) of flies/a fly-flap
muscul -o -us, (L. musculus) little mouse/muscle/mussel/a military shed/a pilot-fish
muscus, (L. muscus) moss
-muscus, (L. muscus) moss/musk
museo, (L. musaeus) a muse/poetical/musical/museum
musi, (Gr. μουσα) music/song/one of the nine muses
music -o, (Gr. μουσικος) musical
muss, (L. musso) mutter/murmur/hum (of bees)
must -us, (L. mustus) young/new/fresh
must, (L. mustus) young/new/fresh/new wine
mustel -a -in, (L. mustel(l)a) a weasel (*Mustela* spp.)
musth, (Gr. μυστης) an initiate
mut, (L. mutus) dumb/inarticulate
muta, (L. mutare) to change/move/shift/alter
mutabil, (L. mutabilis) changeable/variable
mute, (L. mutus) silent
muti -c -l, (L. muticus) curtailed
mutil, (L. mutilare) to maim/mutilate/cut off
mutil, (L. mutilus) maimed, mutilated, hence harmless
muto, (L. mutare) to move/shift/change
mutu, (L. mutuus) mutual/reciprocal
muzzle, (OFr. musel) snout/the jaws and face
my -i -a, (Gr. μυια) a fly
my -o -s, (Gr. μυς) a mouse/a muscle
mya -c -x, (Gr. μυαξ) a mussel
myagr -um, (Gr. μυαγρα) a mouse-trap
myaria -n, (Gr. μυς) of muscle
myc -e -et -eto -o, (Gr. μυκης) a mushroom/fungus
mycethmo, (Gr. μυκηθμος) bellowing/roaring
mycho, (Gr. μυχος) innermost part/nook/store chamber/granary
myclo, (Gr. μυκλος) an ass
myct -er -ero -ir, (Gr. μυκτηρ) nostril/nose/trunk

myd -a -ale -o, (Gr. μυδαλεος) wet/dripping/mouldy
myda, (Gr. μυδος) damp/decay/clamminess
mydion, (Gr. μυδιον) a small boat/small forceps
mydo, (Gr. μυδος) dampness/clamminess/decay
mydr -o -us, (Gr. μυδρος) an anvil/red-hot mass of stone or metal
mydriasi -s, (Gr. μυδριασις) dilatation of the pupils
myel -o -us, (Gr. μυελος) marrow/brain/spinal cord/the innermost part
mygal -e, (Gr. μυγαλη) a field mouse
mygmo, (Gr. μυγμος) moaning/whimpering/muttering
myi -a -o, (Gr. μυια) a fly
myl-, (Gr. μυλ-) mill-
mylabr -is, (Gr. μυλαβρις) a cockroach of flour mills and bakehouses
mylacr -is, (Gr. μυλακρις) a millstone
mylio, (Gr. μυλιαω) gnash the teeth
myll -o -us, (Gr. μυλλος) awry/crooked/squint-eyed/a lip/a sea-fish
myllo, (Gr. μυλλον) lip
mylo, (Gr. μυλος) mill/millstone/grinder/molar
mymar, (Gr. μυμαρ/μωμαρ) blame/ridicule/reproach/disgrace
myndo, (Gr. μυνδος) dumb
myo, (Gr. μυς) muscle
myo, (Gr. μυω) close
myodo, (Gr. μυηδης) mouse-like
myop -s, (Gr. μυωψ) short-sighted/a horse-fly/gadfly/goad/spur/incentive
myosot, (Gr. μυοσωτις) mouse-eared/the forgetmenot (*Myosotis* spp.)/madwort
            (*Asperugo procumbens*)/the mouse-ears and chickweeds (various genera)
myox -us, (Gr. μυωξος) the dormouse (*Glis glis* (formerly *Myoxus*))
myr -o -um, (Gr. μυρον) sweet oil/unguent/perfume
myri -a -o, (Gr. μυριος) numberless/countless/infinite
myri -smo -st, (Gr. μυρισμος) anointing
myric -a, (Gr. μυρικη) the tamarisk (*Tamarix* spp.)
myrme -co -x, (Gr. μυρμεξ) an ant
myrmedon, (Gr. μυρμεδον) an ant-nest
myro, (Gr. μυρον) a sweet oil/unguent/perfume
myrsin -a, (Gr. μυρσαινη) the myrtle (*Myrtus communis*)
myrso, (Gr. μυρσος) a basket
myrt -us, (Gr. μυρσαινη) the myrtle (*Myrtus communis*)
mys, (Gr. μυς) mouse/rat/a mussel/a large kind of whale/a muscle/a gag
mysaro, (Gr. μυσαρος) foul/impure/loathsome
mysi -s, (Gr. μυσις) a closing
myso, (Gr. μυσος) uncleanness/defilement/foul/dirty/loathsome
myst -ac -ax, (Gr. μυσταξ) a moustache/the upper lip
myst -eri -i -o, (Gr. μυστηρικος) mystery/secret rite/mystic implements
mystr -i -io -ium -o, (Gr. μυστρον) a spoon/a measure
myth -o -us, (Gr. μυθος) word/speech/thing said/tale/narrative/legend
mytil -o -us, (Gr. μυτιλος) a mussel
myx -a -o, (Gr. μυξα) slime/mucus
myxin -us, (Gr. μυξινος) a slime-fish
myz -o, (Gr. μυζω) to suck in/to mutter

N

nabi -d -s, (L. nabis) a giraffe/camelopard

nabla, (Gr. ναβλα) a ten or twelve stringed harp-like instrument

nac -o, (Gr. νακος) fleece

nacca, (Gr. νακτης) fuller

nacr, (L. nacre) of pearly lustre

nacto, (Gr. νακτος) close pressed/solid

naev -us, (L. naevus) a mole on the body/birthmark

nagma, (Gr. ναγμα) anything piled up

naia -d -s, (Gr. Ναιας) a water nymph

naj -a -, (Skr. naga) a snake

nama -to, (Gr. ναμα) a stream/anything flowing

nan -i -no -o -us, (Gr. νανος) a dwarf

nao, (Gr. ναος) temple/shrine/portable shrine

nap -aea -o, (Gr. ναπαιος) wooded vale/glen/dell

nap -i -us, (L. napus) a kind of turnip

naphth, (Gr. ναφθα) naphtha (a volatile rock oil)

narc -a -o, (Gr. ναρκη) numbness/deadness

nard -o -us, (Gr. ναρδναδος) spikenard (? *Inula conyza*)/oil of spikenard

nari -s, (L. naris) the nostril

naros, (Gr. ναρος) liquid/flowing

narra, (L. narrare) to tell/make known/narrate

narthe -c -x, (Gr. ναρθηξ) a giant fennel (*Peucedanum* sp.)/casket for unguents

nas -i -o -us, (L. nasus) the nose

nasc -en, (L. nascent) being born

nasm -o -us, (Gr. νασμος) flowing/steam/spring

nass -a, (L. nassa) a wicker basket

nast -o, (Gr. ναστος) pressed close/firm/solid

-naste -s -r, (Gr. ναστης/ναστηρ) an inhabitant

nasut, (L. nasutus) large-nosed

nat -a, (L. natare) to swim/float

nat -i -is, (L. natis/nates) buttock/buttocks

nata, (L. nata) birth/born/arise/produced

natan -t, (L. natans) swimming

natic, (MedL. natica) buttock

nato, (L. natare) to swim/float

natri -c -x, (L. natrix) a water snake

natus, (L. natus) birth/born/son

nau -s -si -t -ti, (Gr. ναυς) a ship/a sail

nauc -um, (L. naucum) a trifle/something very small

naucrat, (Gr. ναυκρατης) pilot/master of the sea

naulum, (Gr. ναυλος) fare

naupl, (L. nauplius) a shellfish

naupli -us, (Gr. ναυπλιος) a kind of shell-fish

naus -e -i, (Gr. ναυσια) seasickness/squeamishness

naut -i, (Gr. ναυτης L. nauta) sailor/passenger by sea

nautil -us, (Gr. ναυτιλος) seaman/sailor/a cephalopod mollusc

nav -a -i, (L. navis) a ship/vessel

nave, (AS. nafu) the hub of a wheel

navicul -a, (L. navicula) a little ship/boat

navig -a, (L. navigare) to sail/voyage/proceed/navigate

navis, (Gr. ναυς) a ship/vessel

navus, (L. navus) energetic

nax, (L. naxium) a stone for polishing marble

ne -a -o, (Gr. νεα/νεος) young/youthful/new/fresh

ne, (L. ne/nae Gr. νη) a particle of strong affirmation - yes/truly
ne, (L. ne/nei) a negative participle - not/not even
neal -es, (Gr. νεαλης) newly caught/fresh/not tired
nean -ic, (Gr. νεανικος) youthful/fresh/active/vigorous
near -o, (Gr. νεαρος) youthful/fresh/new
neat, (L. nitidus) shining
nebr -i -o -us, (Gr. νεβρος) a fawn
nebraco, (Gr. νεβραξ) a cockerel
nebul -a -o, (L. nebula) vapour/fog/mist
nec, (L. nec/neque) negative participle - not/not even/and not
necan -t, (L. necare) violent death/killing
necator, (L. necator/necatrix) killer
nechal, (Gr. νηχαλεος = νηκτος) swimming
necop, (L. necopinus) unexpected/careless
necr -o -us, (Gr. νεκρος) corpse/dead
necros -is, (Gr. νεκρωσις) mortification/death
nect -er -o, (Gr. νηκτος) swimming
nect, (L. nectar Gr. νεκταρ) nectar/the drink of the gods
nect, (L. nectere) to tie/fasten together/bind/connect
necto, (Gr. νηκτης) swimmer
nectri, (Gr. νηκτρις) a female swimmer
necy -o -s, (Gr. νεκυς) corpse/spirit of the dead
necydal -us, (Gr. νεκυδαλος) the nympha of the silkworm
nedy -s, (Gr. νηδυς) belly/paunch/stomach
nedym -o, (Gr. νηδυμος) sweet/delightful
neel -y -yx, (Gr. νεηλυς) a newcomer
nefand, (L. nafandus) abominable/criminal
nefrens, (L. nefrens) toothless
nega, (L. negatio) denying
neglect, (L. neglectus) disregard
negr -i, (Sp. negro) black
negret, (Gr. νεγρετος) unwaking
nei, (Gr. νηια) oars
neil -o, (Gr. νειλος) of the river Nile
nel -eo -i, (Gr. νηλης) pitiless/ruthless
nelip -o, (Gr. νελιπους) barefoot/unshod
nem -a -ato -o, (Gr. νημα) thread/yarn/thread of a spider's web
nemerte, (Gr. μημερτης) unerring/infallible
nemesis, (Gr. Νεμεσις) goddess of retributive justice
nemo, (Gr. νεμω) dispense/distribute/graze
nemor -al, (L. nemoralis) of woods or groves
neo -ssi -tt -tti -tto, (Gr. νεοσσια) brood of young birds/nest of young birds/lair/
              beehive
neo, (Gr. νεος) young/youthful/new/fresh
neo, (Gr. νεω) swim/spin/heap/pile up
neo, (Gr. νηος) a temple
neo-, (Gr. νεο-) fresh-/freshly-/new-/newly-
neochm -o, (Gr. νεοχμοω) make innovations/produce a complication
neorio, (Gr. νηοριον) dockyard
neoss, (Gr. νεοσσια) a nest/nest of young birds
neosso, (Gr. νεοσσος) nestling/any young animal
nepa, (L. nepa) scorpion
nepenth -es, (Gr. νηπενθης) free from sorrow/banishing pain and sorrow
nepet -a, (L. nepeta) catnip, a type of mint (*Nepeta cataria*)
neph -el -eli -elo -o -os, (Gr. νεφελη) cloud/mass of clouds
nephali, (Gr. νηφαλιος) sober/without wine

nephr -i -o -us, (Gr. νεφρος) the kidney

nephthy -s, (Gr. Νεφθυς) an Egyptian goddess

nepio, (Gr. νηπιος) infant

nepo -s -t, (L. nepos) a grandson/nephew/descendant/a spendthrift

nepti -s, (L. neptis) a grand-daughter

neptun -us, (L. Neptunus) Neptune, god of the sea

nequit, (L. nequitia) badness/worthlessness/prodigality

nere -i -id -is -t -o, (Gr. Νηρεις) Nereis, a sea-nymph

neri -um, (Gr. νεριον) the oleander (*Nerium oleander*)

nerit -es, (Gr. νηριτης) a sea-snail/sea-mussel

nerithmo, (Gr. νηριθμος) countless/immense

nero, (Gr. ναρος) flowing/liquid/wet

nerter -o, (Gr. νερτερος) lower

nertos, (Gr. νερτος) a vulture

nerv -us, (L. nervus) a nerve/sinew

nesc, (L. nescius) not knowing/ignorant/unaware

-nesia/neso, (Gr. νησος) island

-ness, (AS.) suf. of condition/state/quality

nessa/netta, (Gr. νεσσα/νεττα) duck

nest -i -o, (Gr. νηεστις) fasting/starving

nesti, (Gr. νεστικος) for spinning

nestor, (L. Nestor) Nestor, a mythical hero

nestoris, (Gr. νεστορις) a kind of cup

net, (Gr. νηθω) I spin (weave)

nethis, (Gr. νηθις) spinster

neto, (Gr. νητος) heaped/piled up

netr -o -um, (Gr. νητρον) spindle

nett -a -ion, (Gr. νεττα) a duck

neuma, (Gr. νευμα) nod/sign

neur -a -o, (Gr. νευρα) a sting/cord/sinew

neuro, (Gr. νευρον) sinew/tendon/cord/bow-string

neurode, (Gr. νευρωδης) sinewy/muscular/strong

neust -o, (Gr. ναυστος) swimming (covered in something)/floating

neutr, (L. neuter) neither

nevus, (L. naevus) a birthmark/mole

newt, (AS. efete) a salamander

nex -us, (L. nexus) tying together/entwining

nex, (L. nex/necis) violent death/murder

nexi, (Gr. νεξις) swimming

nexil, (L. nexilis) tied or bound together

nic -o, (Gr. νικη) victory/conquest

nict -o, (L. nictare) to wink

nictitat, (L. nictitatus) winking

nid -i, -us, (L. nidus) a nest

nidor, (L. nidor) vapour/odour/reek

nig -el -er -ra -resc -ri -ro, (L. niger) black/dark coloured

niglaro, (Gr. νιγλαρος) a whistle (the sound)

nigre, (L. nigrescere) to turn black

nihil, (L. nihilum) nothing

nik -o, (Gr. νικη) victory/conquest

nilo -tic, (L. Nilus) the river Nile/a canal/an aqueduct

nimbus, (L. nimbus) a cloud/black rain cloud/cloud mass

nimius, (L. nimbus) too much/excessive

nimma, (Gr. νιμμα) water for washing

nimr, (Hb. Nimrod) valiant/strong/a tyrant/a great hunter

ning, (L. ningues) snow

nioba, (Gr. Νιοβη) daughter of Tantalus

niph -a -o, (Gr. νιφας) snow flake
niphar, (Gr. νιφαργης) snow-white
nipt -o, (Gr. νιπτω) I wash
nipter, (Gr. νιπτη) washing-vessel/basin
nis, (L. nisus) an effort
nitedula, (L. nitedula) a small mouse/dormouse
nitella, (L. nitella) brightness/splendour
nitid, (L. nitidus) bright/brilliant/shining/glittering/elegant/refined/cultivated
nito, (L. niteo) to grow sleek
nitr -a -i -o, (Gr. νιτρον) sodium carbonate/soda
niv -al -e -os, (L. niveus) snowy
niv -i -o, (L. nix/nivis) snow
nivens, (L. nivens) winking
no, (Gr. νωε) we two
nobil, (L. nobilis) celebrated/renowned/well-known
noc -en -i -u, (L. nocere) to hurt/injure/harm
nocaro, (Gr. νωκαρος) sleepy/slothful/dull
noceo, (L. nocere) to hurt/harm
nocheles, (Gr. νωχελης) moving slowly/sluggish
noct -i, (L. nox) night
noctu -a, (L. noctua) an owl
nocturn, (L. nocturnus) of the night
nod -i -o -us, (L. nodus) knot/knob/band/obligation
noe -a, (Gr. νοηω) think/consider/reflect/intend
noema -to, (Gr. νοημα) thought/concept/purpose/idea/design
noetic -o, (Gr. νοητικος) intellectual
noia, (Gr. νοος/νους) the mind/sense/wit
nol -a -i, (LL. nola) a small bell
nolen, (L. nolens) unwilling
nom -en -in, (L. nomen) a name
nom -o, (Gr. νομος) custom/law/song/ode
noma -d, (Gr. νομας) roaming/ranging/wandering/spreading
nomad, (Gr. νομαδικος) nomadic
nome, (Gr. νομευς) a shepherd/herdsman
nomi -co -si -o, (Gr. νομικος) relating to laws/resting on law/forensic
nomo, (Gr. νομος) usage/custom
-nomy, (Gr. -ονομια) the science of/study of
non -a, (L. novem) nine
non, (L. non) not
nonagen, (L. nonaginta) ninety
nonnus, (L. nonnus) a monk
nonus, (L. nonus) ninth
noo -s, (Gr. νοος) the mind/sense/wit
nop -o, (Gr. νωψ) blindness
norm -a, (L. norma) a rule/standard/measure
norop, (Gr. νωροψ) bright/flashing
nosazonto, (Gr. νοσαζω) to be ill/produce sickness
nose -m, (Gr. νοσημα) disease/passion/vice
noso, (Gr. νοσος) disease/sickness/plague
nosphid, (Gr. νοσφιδιος) clandestine/stealthy
nosphist, (Gr. νοσφιστης) embezzler
noss, (Gr. νοσσαξ) chick/cockerel
nost -a -o, (Gr. νοστεω) return/go or come home
not -a -ae -al -o -um, (Gr. νωτον) the back/metaph. any wide surface/any back or ridge
notat, (L. notatus) marked
note -o, (Gr. νοτος) south or south-west/the south wind

noter -o, (Gr. νοτερος) wet/damp/moist

noth -o, (Gr. νοθος) spurious/illegitimate/cross-bred

nothr -o, (Gr. νωθρος) leisurely/gradually/making sluggish

notidan -o, (Gr. νωτιδανος) having a pointed dorsal fin/a type of shark

notio, (Gr. νοτιος) moist/damp/rainy/southerly winds/southern

notor, (L. notus) known

nototh, (Gr. νοτοθεν) from the south

notu, (L. notus) well known

nous, (Gr. νοος) the mind/sense/wit

nov -i -o, (L. novitas) newness/novelty/strangeness

nov -i -o, (L. novus) new/fresh

novaboracens, (L. novaboracum) of New York

novacul, (L. novacula) sharp knife/razor

novem, (L. novem) nine

noverc -a, (L. noverca) a step-mother

nox, (L. noctis) night

noxi -os, (L. noxa) harm/injury/damage

nu, (Gr. νυ ν N) thirteenth letter of the Greek alphabet

nub -a, (L. nubo) marry

nub -e -i, (L. nubes) a cloud/a dense mass

nubilis, (L. nubilis) marriageable

nubilus, (L. nubilus) cloudy/gloomy

nuc -ell -i, (L. nucelus) a nut/the kernel of a nut

nuc, (L. nux) nut

nuch -a, (NL. nucha) nape of the neck

nucle -a -i -o, (L. nucleus) a kernel/a little nut

nud -a -i, (L. nudus) naked/nude

nuga -t, (L. nugatorius) trifling/frivolous/futile

nul, (L. nullum) nothing

nulli, (L. nullus) no/none/not any

numell, (L. numella) shackle/fetter

numen, (L. numen) a nodding with the head

numer, (L. numerus) number

numisma -t, (L. nummus) a coin

nummul -us, (L. nummulus) a little piece of money

nun -ci -ti, (L. nuntis) a messenger/announcer

nuntio, (L. nuntare) to proclaim/call out

nuper, (L. nuperus) recent

nupt -ial, (L. nuptialis) of marriage

nupta, (L. nupta) wife

nut -a -an, (L. nutare) to nod/keep nodding/sway/waver

nutri -c -x, (L. nutrix) nurse/foster-mother

nutri, (L. nutrire) to nourish/feed

-nux, (L. nux) a nut

nyc -t -i -to, (Gr. νυξ) night

nychio, (Gr. νυχιος) nightly

nycter, (Gr. νυκτηρις) a bat

nycti, (Gr. νυκτιος) of the night

nycto, (Gr. νυκτος) by night

nygma -to, (Gr. νυγμα) a puncture wound/sting

-nym, (Gr. ονυμα) name

nymph, (Gr. νυμφη) a bride/young wife/a Nymph/a chrysalis

nymphae -a, (Gr. νυμφαια) a yellow water lily (*Nuphar lutea*)

nyss -o, (Gr. νυσσω/νυττω) prick/stab/pierce

nyss, (Gr. νυσσω) to prick/pierce/puncture/sting/stab

nyss-a, (L. Nyssa) a water nymph/the city where Bacchus was brought up

nyssa, (Gr. νυσσα) a turning post in a race

nysta -gm, (Gr. νυσταγμα) short sleep/drowsiness
nytho, (Gr. νυθος) dumb/dark
nytt -o, (Gr. νυττω/νυσσω) prick/stab/pierce
nyx -eo -is, (Gr. νυξις) pricking/stabbing/stinging
nyx, (Gr. νυξ) night

O

o -o, (Gr. ωον) an egg
o- ob- oc- of- og- op- os-, (L. ob) to/toward/against/opposite/upon/reverse
oa, (Gr. οα) hem/border
oa, (Gr. ωα) sheep-skin
oar, (Gr. οαρ) a consort/mate/wife
oari -o, (Gr. ωαριον) little egg
oaros, (Gr. οαρος) chat/talk/wife
oasis, (Gr. Οασις) a name of towns in the Libyan desert/a fertile place
ob, (L. ob-) to/toward/against/opposite/upon/reverse
obba, (L. obba) beaker/decanter
obdur, (L. obduresco) harden/become hard-hearted
obel -isc, (Gr. οβελος) a pointed square pillar
obelo, (Gr. οβελος) spit/skewer
oberon, (OHG. Oberon) king of the fairies
obes, (L. obesus) fat/plump
obex, (L. obex) an obstacle/barricade/bar/bolt
obfuscat, (L. obfuscare) to darken
obic, (L. obicio) to throw in the way/to hold before as protection or obstacle
obitus, (L. obitus) death/downfall/an approaching/going to
oblat, (L. oblatus) flattened at the poles/spread out
oblativ, (L. oblativus) freely given
oblect -at, (L. oblectator) charmer/delighter
oblido, (L. oblidere) to crush/throttle/squeeze together
oblig, (L. obligare) to tie/bind up/oblige/make liable
obliqu, (L. obliquus) slanting/indirect
obliter-, (L. obliteratus) erased/blotted out
oblivi, (L. oblivio) forgetfulness/oblivion
oblong, (L. oblongus) oblong
obnisus, (L. obnitor) to resist/strive/struggle
obnixus, (L. obnixus) steadfast/firm/resolute
obnoxi, (L. obnoxius) addicted to/guilty of/liable to punishment/indebted/obliged
obnubil, (L. obnubere) to cover
obol -o, (Gr. οβολος) a weight/a small coin
obri -a -o, (Gr. οβρικαλα) the young of animals
obrimo, (Gr. οβριμος) strong/mighty
obrut, (L. obruere) to cover over/bury/collapse
obscur, (L. obscurus) covered/dark/obscure
obses, (L. obses) hostage/pledge/surety
obsit, (L. obsitus) sown/covered/filled
obsole -sc -t, (L. obsolescere) to go out of use/decay/wear out
obstetri -c -x, (L. obstetrix) a midwife
obstip, (L. obstipus) leaning to one side/bent back/bowed down
obstru, (L. obstruere) to build against/to block up/to close off
obtect, (L. obtectus) covered over/concealed
obtur, (L. obturare) to close up/to stop up

obtus, (L. obtusus) blunt/dull/weakened
obumb, (L. obumbrare) to over-shadow
obunc, (L. obuncus) bent in/hooked
obver, (L. obvertere) to turn round
obvol, (L. obvolvere) to wrap around
oc-, (L. ob-) to/toward/against/opposite/upon/reverse
occa, (L. occare) to harrow
occident -al, (L. occidens) the evening/the west
occip -it -ut, (L. occiput) the back of the head
occis, (L. occisus) unfortunate/lost/ruined
occlu -d -s, (L. occludere) to shut in
occulco, (L. occulcare) to trample/tread down
occult, (L. occultare) to hide/conceal
ocean -o, (Gr. ωκεανος) the ocean
oceanit -es, (Gr. ωκεανιτης) an ocean dweller
ocell -us, (L. ocellus) a little eye
och -o -us, (Gr. οχος) a carriage/anything that supports or holds
ochema -to, (Gr. οχημα) a support/stay/chariot/vessel/ship
ochet -o -us, (Gr. οχετος) a water-pipe/conduit/channel/drain
ocheuma, (Gr. οχευμα) an embryo
ocheus, (Gr. οχευς) anything for fastening or holding
ochl -o -us, (Gr. οχλος) crowd/throng/populace/mass/multitude
ochleros, (Gr. οχληρος) troublesome/irksome
ochma, (Gr. οχμα) a tie/band
ochn -a, (Gr. οχνη/ογχνη) the pear tree (*Pirus communis*)
ochos, (Gr. οχος) anything which holds/firm/secure
ochr -o, (Gr. ωχρος) pale/wan/sallow/pale yellow
ochter, (Gr. οχθηρος) hilly
ochth -a -o, (Gr. οχθος) mound/tubercle (on plants)/hill
ochyr -o, (Gr. οχυρος) firm/lasting/stout/strong/secure
ocido, (Gr. ωκις) an earring
ocior, (L. ocior) swifter
-ock, (AS.) dim. suf.
-ocl, (L. oculus) an eye
ocn -o, (Gr. οκνος) hesitation/shrinking
ocnero, (Gr. οκνηρος) timid
ocr -i -io, (Gr. οκρις) a jagged point or prominence/roughness on an edge/rugged
ocre -a, (L. ocrea) a greave (armour for the leg below the knee)
oct -i -o, (Gr. οκτω) eight
ocul -i -o -us, (L. oculus) the eye/bud
ocy, (Gr. ωκυς) quick/swift/fleet
ocymoro, (Gr. ωκυμορος) dying early/short lived
ocypod, (Gr. ωκυπους) swift-footed
od -c -o -us, (Gr. οδος) a way/track/path/road/entrance
oda -c -x, (Gr. οδαξ) by biting with the teeth
-oda, (Gr. οδαξ) biting
odagmo, (Gr. οδαγμος) itching/irritation
ode, (Gr. ωδη) a song/ode/magic song/spell
-odea, (Gr. -οδες), resemblance/fullness
-odes, (Gr. -οδες) suf. ind. likeness/fullness
-odi, (Gr. ωδις) labour (childbirth)/travail/anguish
odi, (L. odi) hate/detest/dislike/be displeased with
odin -o, (Gr. ωδινω) labour pain/any great pain
odium, (L. odiosus) hatred
odo, (Gr. οδος) road/way/channel/travelling
odode, (Gr. οδωδη) smell/scent

-odon -t -to, (Gr. οδων) a tooth/anything pointed or sharp/second vertebra of the neck

odor -i, (L. odor) a smell/odour

odor, (L. odor) a smell

-odous, (Gr. οδους) a tooth/prong/spike

odus, (Gr. οδος) road/way/channel

ody, (Gr. ωδη) a song

odyn -e -ia -o, (Gr. οδυνη) pain (of body or mind)/distress

odyno, (Gr. οδυνημα) pain

odyrtes, (Gr. οδυρτης) a complainer

odysis, (Gr. ωδυσις/ωδυσιη) anger/wrath

oe see also **oi**

oeaco, (Gr. οιαξ) rudder/tiller/helm

oec -i -o -us, (Gr. ιοκος) house/palace/abode (of a deity)

oecen, (Gr. ιοκην) to inhabit/possess/occupy/settle/govern

oeces -is, (Gr. οικησις) the act of dwelling

oecetes, (Gr. οικετης) inhabitant/household slave

oeceto, (Gr. οικετης) dweller/household slave

oecia/oecos, (Gr. οικια/οικος) house/dwelling/household

oecis -e, (Gr. ιοκην) to settle

oecodomo, (Gr. οικοδομος) builder/architect

oecto, (Gr. οικτος) compassion

oecy, (Gr. οικος) house

oed -e -ema, (Gr. οιδημα) a swelling/tumour

oedi, (Gr. οιδι-) swollen

oeg -o, (Gr. οιγω) open

oem -a -o, (Gr. οιμαω) swoop/pounce/dart along

oemo, (Gr. οιμος) way/road/path

oemocto, (Gr. οιμοκτος) pitiable

oen -a, (Gr. οινας) the wild pigeon or rock-dove (*Columba livia*)

oenanth, (Gr. οινανθη) the inflorescence of the grape-vine/a vine/a bird/a salve

oeno, (Gr. οινος) wine

oenothera, (Gr. οινοθερας) a genus of evening primrose (*Oenothera* sp.)

oeo, (Gr. οιος) alone

oeono, (Gr. οιωνος) a large bird/a bird of prey/an omen

oeso, (Gr. οισος) a kind of willow tree

oesophag -i -o, (Gr. οισοφαγος) the gullet

oestr -o -us, (Gr. οιστρος) gadfly/metaph. a sting/goad/anything that torments/a frenzy

oesypo, (Gr. οισυπος/οισυπη) the grease from sheep's wool

oeto, (Gr. οιτος) fate/doom

of-, (L. ob-) to/toward/against/opposite/upon/reverse

officio, (L. officere) to hinder/obstruct/oppose

og-, (L. ob-) to/toward/against/opposite/upon/reverse

ogco, (Gr. ογκος) a barb

ogdo-, (Gr. ογδο-) eight-

ogdoa, (Gr. ογδοας) the number eight

ogdoo, (Gr. ογδοος) eighth

ogmos, (Gr. ογμος) furrow/swathe/row/path/orbit

ogyg, (Gr. Ογυγες) myth. king of Attica, hence generally primeval/primal

oico, (Gr. ιοκος) house/palace/abode (of a deity)

-oid, (Gr. ειδος) shape/form/the like/resemblance

oide -ma, (Gr. οιδημα) a swelling/tumour

-oidea, -oideum, -oideus, (L.) resemblance

-oidea, a recommended but not mandatory suffix used to indicate a superfamily of animals

-oideae, a recommended but not mandatory suffix used to indicate a subfamily of plants

oido, (Gr. οιδημα) a swelling/tumour

oig -o, (Gr. οιγω) open
oik -o -us, (Gr. οικος) a house/a dwelling
oik, (Gr. οικεω) inhabit
ois, (Gr. οις) sheep
oisto, (Gr. οιστος) an arrow
oizyo, (Gr. οιζυς) distress/suffering/misery
ol -o, (Gr. ολος) whole/entire/complete
-ol, chemical suf. ind. an alcohol/an oil/a benzene derivative
-ola, -olum, -olus, (L. -ola) dim. suf.
olax, (L. olacis) odorous
olbi -o, (Gr. ολβιος) happy/blest/blessed
ole -a -astr, (L. oleaster) the wild olive-tree
ole -i -o -um, (L. oleum) olive oil/oil
ole -nt -o, (L. olens/olentis) smelling (either fragrant or stinking)
oleagin, (L. oleaginus) of the olive-tree
olear, (L. olearius) of oil/oily
olecran -o -um, (Gr. ωλεκρανον) the point of the elbow
olen -a -e -i, (Gr. ωλενη) the arm from the elbow downwards/the elbow/mat/mattress
olene, (Gr. ωλενη) the elbow/forearm
olent, (L. olentis) smelling (either fragrant or stinking)
-olenta, -olentum, -olentus, (L.) abundance
oler -i, (L. olus/holus) any culinary vegetable
oles -i, (Gr. ολεσι-) destroying-/slaying-
oleter, (Gr. ολετηρ) destroyer/murderer
olethr -io -o -us, (Gr. ολεθρος) ruin/destruction/death/pest/plague
olfact, (L. olfacere) to smell
olibro, (Gr. ολιβρος) slippery
olid, (L. olidus) smelling/stinking
olig -o, (Gr. ολιγος/ολιος) little/small/few/weak
olisbos, (Gr. ολισβρος) the penis
olisth -em -mo, (Gr. ολισθηρος) slip/fall/slippery/liable to slip
olitor, (L. holitor) a kitchen-gardener
oliv -a -ace, (L. oliva) a olive/olive-green
olla, (L. olla) a jar or pot
ollym, (Gr. ολλυμι) destroy/make an end of/kill
-olo, (Gr. ολος) whole/entire/complete
-ology, (Gr. λογος) discourse/a word/saying/tale/relation/the science of
oloos, (Gr. ολοος) destructive/deadly
olor -i, (L. olor) a swan (*Cygnus olor*)
olos, (Gr. ολος) the ink of the cuttle-fish (*Sepia officianalis*)
olos, (Gr. ολος) whole/entire/complete in all its parts
oloygon, (Gr. ολολυγων) the croaking of a frog
olpi -d -s, (Gr. ολπη) a leathern oil-flask
-olum, (L. -olum) dim. suf.
-olus, (L. -olus) dim. suf.
olynth -us, (Gr. ολυνθος/ολονθος) the wild fig
olyntho, (Gr. ολυνθος) an untimely fig
om -o, (Gr. ωμος) raw/crude/uncooked
om -o, (Gr. ωμος) shoulder plus upper arm
-oma, (Gr. ομα) suf. used in names of tumours
omal -o, (Gr. ομαλος) even/level/equal/average
omas -um, (L. omasum) paunch/tripe
ombr -o -us, (Gr. ομβρος) a rain storm
-ome, (NL) suf. denoting condition/having the nature of
-ome, (Gr. -ομα), condition/having the nature of
omega, (Gr. ωμεγα ω Ω) twenty-fourth (and last) letter of the Greek alphabet

oment -um, (L. omentum) entrails/bowels/fat-skin
omentum, (L. omentum) fat-skin/fat/caul/entrails
omi, (Gr. ωμια) shoulder (of a structure)
omich -m, (Gr. ομειχμα) urine
omicrom, (Gr. ομιχρον ο Ο) fifteenth letter of the Greek alphabet
omilla, (Gr. ωμιλλα) a circle for playing a game
omistes, (Gr. ωμιστης) a porter
-omma -t -to, (Gr. ομματιον) little eye
-omma, (Gr. ομμα) an eye
omni, (L. omnis) all
-omo, (Gr. ωμος) shoulder region/raw/undressed
omorgma, (Gr. ομοργμα) something which is wiped off - a spot
ompha -c -x, (Gr. ομφαξ) an unripe grape/young girl
omphaco, (Gr. ομφαξ) an unripe grape
omphal, (Gr. ομφαλο) navel/umbilicus
omphalo, (Gr. ομφαλος) the navel/umbilical cord
ompheter, (Gr. ομφητηρ) soothsayer
ompne, (Gr. ομπνη) food/bread-corn/sacrificial cakes
onagr -a, (Gr. οναγρα) oleander (*Nerium oleadner*)
onagr -us, (Gr. οναγρος) the wild ass (*Equus hemionus onagar*)
onc -ho -o -us, (Gr. ογκος) hook/barb/bulk/mass/tubercle
oncero, (Gr. ογκηρος) bulky/swollen
onceto, (Gr. ογκηστης) a brayer/ass
onci -a, (Gr. ογκια/ουγκια) a twelfth
onci -o, (Gr. ογκος) hook/barb/bulk/mass/tubercle
onco, (Gr. ογκος) a hook/barb
-one, (Gr. -ωνη) chem. suf./fem. patronymic
oneir -o -od, (Gr. ονειρωδης) dream-like
oner, (L. onerare) to load/freight/burden
onet, (Gr. ονητης) buyer
onias, (Gr. ονιας) a sea-fish
onido, (Gr. ονειδος) blame/reproach/ensure
onir -o, (Gr. ονειρος/ονειρον) a dream/anything unreal
onisc -us, (Gr. ονισκος) a wood louse (Oniscidae)
onisto, (Gr. ονηιστος) most useful
ono, (Gr. ονος) an ass/windlass/upper millstone/beaker/wine cup/spindle
onom -a -at -ato, (Gr. ονομα) a name
onos, (Gr. ονος) an ass/clumsy person
-ont, (Gr. ον) being/existing
-ont, (Gr. οντα) things which actually exist/being/reality
onto, (Gr. ονθος) animal dung
-onto-, (Gr. οντως) real existence
onus -t, (L. onus) load/burden/freight
onych -o, (Gr. ονυξ) a talon/claw/nail/hoof
-onym, (Gr. ονυμα) a name
onyx, (Gr. ονυξ) a talon/claw/nail/hoof/yellowish gem stone
oo-/oon, (Gr. ωον) an egg
oodeo, (Gr. ωοειδης) egg-like/egg-shaped
oophor, (Gr. ωοφορος) bearing eggs/ovary
op -s, (Gr. -ωψ) appearance/aspect/the face/voice
op-, (L. ob-) to/toward/against/opposite/upon/reverse
opac, (L. opacus) shaded/shady/dark/shadowy
opado, (Gr. οπαδος) accompanying/attending
opaeo, (Gr. οπαος) with a hole/with an opening
opal -in -o -us, (Gr. οπαλλιος) opal
ope -o, (Gr. οπη) opening/hole

ope -s, (Gr. οπη) a hole/opening
opera, (L. opus) work
opercul -um, (L. operculum) a lid/a cover
opes, (L. opes) riches/wealth
ophel -ma, (Gr. οφελμα) broom
ophel -o -us, (Gr. ωφελια) aid/succour/help/profit/advantage
ophelo, (Gr. οφελος) useful/helpful
ophi -d -o -s, (Gr. οφις) a serpent/snake
ophileto, (Gr. οφειλετης) debtor
ophio, (Gr. οφιονεος/οφιωδης) snake-like/snakey
ophiur, (Gr. οφιυρ) serpent-tailed
ophry, (Gr. οφρυς) the brow/eyebrow
ophthalm -i -o -us, (Gr. οφθαλμος) the eye
opi -a -o -um, (Gr. οπιον) poppy juice/opium
-opia, (Gr. -οπια) -vision
opic, (L. opicus) rude/stupid/foolish
opidno, (Gr. οπιδνος) dreaded/awful
opifer, (L. opifer) helper
opifex, (L. opifex) a workman/artisan
opilion, (L. opilionis) a shepherd
opimus, (L. opimus) rich/fruitful/fertile
opipes, (Gr. οπιπες) gaper/starer
opisma, (Gr. οπισμα) the milky sap of plants
opiso, (Gr. οπισω) backwards/back
opistho, (Gr. οπισθεν) behind/at the back/yet to come
opl -o, (Gr. οπλον) any tool/implement/weapon
ople, (Gr. οπλη) a hoof
oplit -es, (Gr. οπλιτης) heavily armed/a man-at arms
opo, (Gr. οπος) sap/vegetable juice
opo, (Gr. οψ) the voice
opor, (Gr. οπωρα) the latter part of summer/autumn
opoter -o, (Gr. οποτερος) which of two/either of two
oppid, (L. oppidum) a town
oppil, (L. oppilare) to stop up/close up/block up
oppon, (L. opponere) to place opposite/place before
opposit, (L. oppositio) opposing/opposition
-ops, (Gr. -ωψ) appearance/aspect/the face/voice
ops, (L. ops) power/aid/riches
opsa, (Gr. ωψη) the eye
opsi -o -s, (Gr. οψις) a sight/vision/outward appearance/eyesight
opsi, (Gr. οψι) late
opsio, (Gr. οψιος) late
opso, (Gr. οψον/οψος) prepared food/delicacies/relish
opsum, (Gr. οψον) seasoning/sauce
opt -i -o, (Gr. οπτιλος) the eye/vision
opter, (Gr. οπτηρ) a spy/scout
optes, (Gr. οπτησις) roasting/frying
opti, (L. optio) choice/free choice/option
optico, (Gr. οπτικος) visible/seen
optim, (L. optimus) the best
opul, (L. opulentus) rich/wealthy/powerful/mighty
opus, (L. opus) work/labour
-or, (L.) condition, state
ora, (L. ora) edge/border/rim/boundary/coast line
oral, (LL. oralis) mouth
orama, (Gr. οραμα) that which is seen/visible object/sight/spectacle/dream

orari, (L. orarium) napkin/handkerchief
orari, (L. orarius) coastal
oras -i, (Gr. ορασις) seeing/the act of sight
orbi -s -t, (L. orbis) circle/orbit/eye socket
orbicul, (L. orbiculatus) rounded
orbo, (L. orbare) to bereave
orc, (L. orca) a pot or jar with a large belly
orcham, (Gr. ορχαμος) leader/chief
orches -t, (Gr. ορχηστης) a dancer/pantomimic dancer
orchi -d -do -s, (Gr. ορχιδιον) a little testicle/a plant thus named from the form of its
             roots
orcho, (Gr. ορχις) a testicle
orcho, (Gr. ορχος) a row of vines or fruit trees
orcus, (L. Orcus) the nether world/abode of the dead
ordin, (L. ordinatus) arranged
ordior, (L. ordior) to begin a web
oreades, (Gr. ορειας) a mountain nymph
orect -o, (Gr. ορεκτος) stretched out/longed for/desired
orecto, (Gr. ορεκτος) stretched out
oreg, (Gr. ορεγω) reach/stretch/stretch out/grasp at/yearn for
oreo, (Gr. ορεο-) mountain
oress -i, (Gr. ορεσσι-) mountain-
orestes, (Gr. ορεστης) mountaineer
oreus, (Gr. ορευς) a mule
orex -i, (Gr. ορεξις) longing/yearning after/desire for
orgado, (Gr. οργας) meadow/field
organ -o, (Gr. οργανον L. organum) instrument/tool/organ of sense
orgi, (Gr. οργια) secret rites/secret worship
orgilo, (Gr. οργιλος) inclined to anger/irritable
orgy, (Gr. οργιον) secret rites/secret worship
orgyi -a, (Gr. οργυια) the length of the outstretched arms (about 6 feet or 1 fathom)
orgyia, (Gr. οργυια) the length of the outstretched arms - a fathom
ori-, (Gr. ορει-) mountain-
-oria, -orium, -orius, (L.) capability/a place of work or action or function
oribat, (Gr. ορεοβατης) mountain-ranging
orient -al, (L. oriens) rising of the sun (eastern)
origin, (L. origo) origin/source/beginning
orino, (Gr. ορινω) excite/stir
oriol, (NL. aureolus) little golden
orion, (Gr. οριον) boundary/limit
orion, (Gr. Ωριων L. Orion) a fabled hunter
orism -a, (Gr. ορισμος) boundary/limitation/definition of a thing
-orium, (L. -orium) a place for/a place where
-orius, (L. -orius) pertaining to
orm -o, (Gr. ορμος) cord/chain/necklace/collar
orm, (Gr. ορμαω) to excite/to set in motion/urge on/cheer on
ormeno, (Gr. ορμενος) shoot/sprout/stem/stalk
orn, (L. ornare) to equip/furnish/provide
ornat, (L. ornatus) equip/furnish/provide/adorn/decorate
orneo, (Gr. ορνεον) a bird
orneod, (Gr. ορνεωδης) fickle
orni -s -th -tho, (Gr. ορνις) a bird
oro, (Gr. ορος) a mountain/hill
oropedion, (Gr. οροπεδιον) plateau
oroph -a -o, (Gr. οροφη) house roof/ceiling of a room
orophe, (Gr. οροφη) roof/ceiling

orpe, (Gr. ορπετον) a creeping thing
orpeco, (Gr. ορπεξ) sapling
orphan, (Gr. ορφανος) orphaned/fatherless/neglected
orphe, (Gr. Ορφης) Orpheus
orphn -o, (Gr. ορφναιος) dark/murky
orrh -o -us, (Gr. ορρος) the end of the sacrum/rump
orrho, (Gr. ορος/ορρο-) whey/serum
orrhodia, (Gr. ορρωδια) dread/terror
orsi, (Gr. ορνυμι) stir up/urge on/excite
ort, (L. ortus) origin/birth/source
ortali -d -s, (Gr. ορταλις) a young bird/young animal/chich
orth -o, (Gr. ορθος) straight/right
orthagorisc -us, (Gr. ορθαγορισκος) suckling-pig/a kind of fish
orthes, (Gr. ορθεσιον) upright/rampant
orthrio, (Gr. ορθριος) early/at daybreak/in the morning
ortus, (L. ortus) risen/rising of heavenly bodies/the east
orty -g -x, (Gr. ορτυξ) the quail (*Coturnix coturnix*)
-orum, (L.) of/belonging to/pertaining to
oruss, (Gr. ορυσσω) dig/dig up/gouge/quarry/bury
orych -o, (Gr. ορυχω) dig/dig up/gouge/quarry/bury
oryct -er -o, (Gr. ορυκτος) dug out/quarried/formed by digging
oryct -es, (Gr. ορυκτης) a digger
oryct, (Gr. ορυκτηρ) a tool for digging
oryg, (Gr. ορυξ) a gazelle or antelope/pickaxe or any sharp tool for digging
orymagdo, (Gr. ορυμαγδος) loud noise/a din
oryss, (Gr. ορυσσω) dig/dig up/gouge/quarry/bury
orythmo, (Gr. ωρυθμος) a howling (of dogs)/a roaring (of lions)
oryx, (Gr. ορυξ) a gazelle or antelope/pickaxe or any sharp tool for digging
oryz -a -i -o, (Gr. ορυζα) rice (*Oryza sativa*), both the plant and the grain
oryz, (Gr. οριζω) separate from
-os -a -um -us, (L. -osus -a -um) suf. ind. full of/of full development/abundance
os, (Gr. ος) this/that/he/she/it/which/who
os, (L. os) mouth/face/opening/bone
os-, (L. ob-) to/toward/against/opposite/upon/reverse
-osche -o, (Gr. οσχη) the scrotum
oscho, (Gr. ωσχος) a vine-shoot/a young branch
oscill -a -o, (L. oscillare) to swing
oscin -i, (L. oscen) a bird from whose note auguries were taken (e.g. raven, owl, crow)
oscit, (L. oscitare) to yawn/gape
oscul, (L. osculari) to kiss
oscul, (L. osculum) a little mouth
-ose, (L. -osus) suf. ind. full of/of full development/abundance
-ose, chem. suf. ind. a carbohydrate
-osis, (Gr. -οσις) suf. of condition. Forming verbal nouns of action or condition. Now
        used ad.lib. with Gr. or L. elements e.g. chlorosis, tuberculosis etc.
-osis, (Gr. ωσις) thrusting/pushing
-osity, (L. -ositat-) full of
osm -a -i -o, (Gr. οσμη) a smell/scent/odour
osma, (Gr. οσμη) a smell/scent/odour/perfume
osmo -s -t, (Gr. ωσμος) thrusting/pushing/jostling/struggling/impulse
osmyl -e -os, (Gr. οσμυλη) a strong smelling kind of octopus (Octopoda)
osor, (L. osor) a hater
osphr -a -e -o, (Gr. οσφρααινομαι) smell/catch scent of/get scent of
osphrad, (Gr. οσφραδιον) strong scent/nosegay
osphranto, (Gr. οσφραντος) smellable
osphy -o -s, (Gr. οσφυς) loin/lower part of back

osprio, (Gr. οσπριον) pulse (food)
oss -e -i, (L. osseus) bony
ossa, (Gr. οσσα/οττα) rumour
ossic, (L. ossiculum) a little bone
ost -e -eo -eum, (Gr. οστεον) a bone
ostar, (Gr. οσταριον) a little bone
osti -um, (L. ostium/ostiolum) door/little door
ostinon, (Gr. οστεινος) bone-pipes
ostlingo, (Gr. οστλιγξ) curled hair
ostr -e -ea -i -in, (Gr. οστρειον) an oyster/a purple pigment
ostrac -o -um, (Gr. οστρακον) a tile/potsherd/hard shell as of snails and tortoises
ostrimon, (Gr. οστριμον) byre/stable
ostrinus, (L. ostrinus) purple
ostry -a, (Gr. οστρυα) a hard-wood tree (*Ostrya carpinifolia*)
-osum/-osus, (L. -osus /-osum) suf. ind. full of/of full development/abundance
-osyne, (Gr. -οσυνη), ind. a particular feature or quality
-ot, -ette, -et, (Fr.) dim. suffixes
ot-i -o, (Gr. ωτος) the ear
-ota, -otum, -otus, (L.) resemblance/possession
otar, (Gr. οταριον) a little ear
-otes, (Gr. -οτης) suf. denoting quality
othe -o, (Gr. ωθεω) thrust/push/force back/banish
othni -o, (Gr. οθνειος) strange/foreign/abnormal
othono, (Gr. οθονη) fine linen/sail-cloth/sail
oti -d -s, (Gr. ωτις) the bustard (*Otis* spp.)
otic, (Gr. ωτικος) of or for the ear
otilo, (Gr. ωτειλη) a fresh, open wound
otio -n, (Gr. ωτιον) auricle/little ear/little handle
otios, (L. otiosus) idle/at leisure/quiet/calm/indifferent
otlo, (Gr. οτλος) suffering/distress
-oto, (Gr. -οτο-) combining form of ους the ear
otobos, (Gr. οτοβος) any loud noise/the din of battle
otos, (Gr. ωτος) a horned or eared owl (? *Otus albogularis*)
otrero, (Gr. οτρηρος) nimble/quick/busy
otta, (Gr. οττα/οσσα) rumour
-otus, (L. -otus) suf. ind. having the nature of/pertaining to
ouden, (Gr. ουδεν) nought/zero/none/not once
oul, (Gr. ουλη) a scar
oulo, (Gr. ουλον) the gums
oulo, (Gr. ουλος) whole/entire
oulo, (Gr. ουλος) woolly/of thick, fleecy wool/of twisted and curled plants
our -a, (Gr. ουρα) the tail/rear
ouran -i -o, (Gr. ουρανιος) heavenly/in or of heaven
ouro, (Gr. ουρον) urine
ouro, (Gr. ουρος) a guardian/watcher
ouro, (Gr. ουρος) the wild bull, aurochs (*Bos primigenius*)
ous, (Gr. ους) the ear
-ous, (L. -osus) of the nature of/full of/abounding in/prone to
ousia, (Gr. ουσια) one's essence/substance/property
ov -i -um, (L. ovum) an egg
oval -is, (L. ovatus) oval
ovari -o -um, (L. ovarium) an ovary
ovat, (L. ovatus) egg-shaped
ovi, (L. ovis) sheep
ovin, (L. ovinus) of sheep
ovipar, (L. oviparus) egg-laying

ovis, (L. ovis) a sheep
ovul -um, (L. ovulum) a little egg
ovum, (L. ovum) an egg
ox -a -i -y -ys, (Gr. οξυς) acid/sharp
oxal -is, (Gr. οξαλις) sorrel (*Rumex acetosa*)
oxe -o, (Gr. οξινης) sharp/sour/tart/sour-tempered
oxi -d -s, (Gr. οξυς) sharp/keen/pointed/acid
oxina, (Gr. οξινα) a harrow
oxo, (Gr. οξος) vinegar
oxy -s, (Gr. οξυς) sharp/keen/pointed/acid
oxy, (Fr. oxygéne) acidifying
oxybaphon, (Gr. οξυβαφον) a small saucer
oxyechus, (Gr. οξυηχης) a sharp sound/high-pitched screeching
oxyn, (Gr. οξυνω) to sharpen
oxysm, (Gr. οξυσμα) sharpening
oz -o, (Gr. οζος) bough/branch/twig/offshoot
ozo, (Gr. οζω) a smell (sweet or foul)
ozos, (Gr. οζως) bough/branch/twig/off shoot
ozot -o, (Gr. οζωτος) branching

P

pabul -um, (L. pabulum) food/nourishment/fodder
pach -y, (Gr. παχυς) thick/stout/large
pachn -a -o, (Gr. παχνη) hoar-frost
paci, (L. pax) peace
pact, (L. pactus) fasten/fix/set
paean, (Gr. παιαν) physician/healer/saviour/a choral song
paecto, (Gr. παικτος) played with
paed -a -o, (Gr. παις) a child
paedia, (Gr. παιδεια) teaching/education/training
paedid, (L. paedidus) nasty/filthy/stinky
paegma -to, (Gr. παιγμα) sport/play
paegnio, (Gr. παιγνιον) a plaything/toy/pet
paeminos, (L. paeminosus) uneven/rough
paen, (L. paene) nearly
paepalimo, (Gr. παιπαλιμος) sly/subtle
paepalo, (Gr. παιπαλη) fine flour/meal/pollen
paetus, (L. paetus) squinting
pag -o -us, (Gr. παγος) something firmly fixed or set/rock/crag/frost/evaporite salt
pagan -us, (L. paganus) rural/rustic/a countryman
pageto, (Gr. παγετος) frost
pagi -o -os, (Gr. παγιος) firm/steadfast/solid
pagin -a, (L. pagina) a page of a book
pagis, (Gr. παγις) trap/snare
pagos, (Gr. παγος) something fixed or firmly set/a crag/rock/rocky hill
pagur -o -us, (Gr. παγουρος) a kind of crab
pagus, (L. paugs) village/country district
paid-, (Gr. παιδ-) child-
pal -ae -aeo, (Gr. παλαιος) ancient/aged
pal -i -us, (L. palus) a stake
pal-, (Gr. πας) all/the whole
pala, (L. pala) the bezel of a ring/a spade

palaest, (Gr. παλαιστης) wrestler
palam -a, (Gr. παλαμη) the palm of the hand/the hand
palame, (Gr. παλαμη) palm of the hand/hand
palamed -es, (Gr. Παλαμηδης) an inventor, hence cunning/ingenious
palasia, (L. palasia) the rump of buttocks of an ox
palass -o, (Gr. παλασσω) defile/to be scattered abroad
palasso, (Gr. παλασσο) sprinkle/scatter
palat -i -o -um, (L. palatum) the roof of the mouth/the palate
palat, (L. palatum) the roof of the mouth
palatha, (Gr. παλαθη) a cake of preserved fruit
pale -a, (L. palea) chaff
pale, (Gr. παλη) any fine dust
pale, (Gr. παλη) wrestling/struggling/fight/battle
palea, (L. palea) chaff
palear, (L. palear) the dewlap of an ox
pales, (L. Pales) a tutelary goddess of herds and shepherds
palett -a, (NL. paletta) a little spade
paleum, (Gr. παλευμα) an allurement
pali -n, (Gr. παλιν) again/anew/backwards/reversely
pali, (L. palus) a stake
palinur -us, (Gr. Παλινυρυς) myth. the pilot of Aeneas, who fell into the sea
pall -ens -esc -id -or, (L. pallescere) to grow pale/lose colour
palla -c -x, (Gr. παλλαξ) a youth/a girl
palla, (Gr. παλλα) a ball
palla, (Gr. παλλω) to quiver/sway
pallacido, (Gr. παλλακις) concubine/mistress
palli -at -o -um, (L. pallium) a Greek mantle/a coverlet
pallidu, (L. pallidus) pale/ashen
pallo, (Gr. παλλω) shake/poise/leap
palm -a -i, (L. palma) the palm tree/the palm of the hand
palm -o, (Gr. παλμος) quivering motion/pulsation/throbbing
palmat -i, (L. palmatus) palmate
palme, (Gr. παλμη) a small round shield
palmes, (L. palmes) a young branch or shoot
palor, (L. palor) to wander about/stray
palp -i, (L. palpus) a feeler
palp -o, (L. palpare) to stroke gently/touch softly
palpator, (L. palpator) a flatterer
palpebr -a, (L. palpebrae) the eyelids
palpit, (L. palpitare) to move quickly/tremble/throb
palt -o -um, (Gr. παλτον) missile/dart/projectile
palu -di -str, (L. palus/palustris) marshy/a marsh/a swamp
palus, (L. palus) a stake
palyno, (Gr. παλυνω) sprinkle/strew
pam-, (Gr. παμ-) all/the whole
pampin -us, (L. pampinus) a tendril
pan -i -is, (L. panis) bread
pan, (Gr. Παν) the god of Arcadia
pan-, (Gr. παν-) all/the whole
panaca, (L. panaca) a drinking vessel
panace, (Gr. πανακεια) all-healing/panacea/universal remedy
panct, (L. panctus) fastened
pand, (L. pando) stretch out/extend/spread out/throw open
pand, (L. pandus) bent/curved/crooked
pandem, (Gr. πανδημος) common
pandion, (Gr. Πανδιον) a myth. king of Athens
pando, (L. pandere) to stretch/spread/lay open

pandora, (Gr. Πανδωρα) myth. recipient of presents from the gods
pandura, (Gr. πανδουρα) a three-stringed lute
pandus, (L. pandus) bent/curved/crooked
pango, (L. pangere) to fasten/fix/drive in
panic -um, (L. panicum) a kind of wild millet
panicul -a, (L. paniculus) a tuft
panicum, (L. panicum) a kind of wild millet
panis, (L. panis) bread/loaf
pann -us, (L. pannus) a piece of cloth/garment/a rag
pannicul, (L. panniculus) a little garment
pannos, (L. pannosus) ragged/tattered
pano, (Gr. πανος) a torch
panope, (Gr. Πανοπη) a sea-nymph
panoro, (Gr. πανωρος) produced in every season
pans, (L. pansa) splayed out/broad-footed
pansus, (L. pansus) spread out (to dry)
pant -a -e -i -o, (Gr. παντο-) suf. meaning 'all'
pantele, (Gr. παντελης) complete/entire/absolute
pantex, (L. pantices) bowels
pantoth, (Gr. παντοθεν) from all quarters
panus, (L. panus) an ear of millet
pany, (Gr. πανυ) altogether/very
papas, (Gr. παππας) father
papaver -i, (L. papaver) the poppy
paphlasm, (Gr. παφλασμα) boiling/blustering
papilio -n, (L. papilio) a butterfly
papill -a, (L. papilla) nipple
papp -o -us, (Gr. παππος) grandfather/down (feathers)/down on the seeds of some
              plants
paprax, (Gr. παπραξ) a Thracian lake fish (? perch)
papul -a, (L. papula) a pimple/pustule
papyr -i -us, (L. papyrus) the papyrus rush
par -i, (L. parilis) similar/like/equal
par, (L. parere) to bear/bring forth/produce/lay eggs
par, (L. parvus) little/small
para, (Gr. παρα-) alongside of/beside/near/to/towards/beyond/passing by/together/
              at once
parabola, (Gr. παραβολη) comparison/parallel/allegory
parabolos, (Gr. παραβολος) bold/reckless/deceitful
paradigma, (Gr. παραδειγμα) pattern/model
paradis, (Gr. παραδεισος) an enclosed ground or pleasure garden
paradox -o, (Gr. παραδοξος) incredible/contrary to expectation
paragio, (Gr. παραγειος) pertaining to shallow water
paragogo, (Gr. παραγωγος) misleading/deceitful
paralio, (Gr. παραλιος) by the sea
parallel -i -o, (Gr. παραλληλια) being side-by-side/parallel
paramec, (Gr. παραμηκης) oblong/oval/lengthened/long
paraphron, (Gr. παραφρων) wandering from reason/deranged/senseless
paraplesio, (Gr. παραπλησιος) similar/somewhat like/coming near to
parapod, (Gr. παραποδιος) imminent/at the feet of
parasit -i -o, (Gr. παρασιτος) one who eats at the table of another
parastas, (Gr. παραστας) a square pillar/door post
parat, (Gr. παρατεινω) stretch out along/delay
parat, (L. paratus) preparation/provision
parca, (L. Parca) a goddess of destiny
parci, (L. parcus) sparing/frugal/thrifty/economical
pard -o -us, (Gr. παρδος) leopard

pardaco, (Gr. παρδακος) wet/damp

pardal, (Gr. παρδαλωτος) spotted (like a leopard)

pare, (L. parens) parent

pare, (L. parere) to bring forth/produce/acquire

paredro, (Gr. παρεδρος) sitting beside/near/assessor

parei -a, (Gr. παρειας) the cheek

paren -t, (L. parens) a parent/author

paresi -s, (Gr. παρεσις) letting go/dismissal/paralysis/slackening of strength/neglect

pareuno, (Gr. παρευνος) lying beside/bedfellow

pari -a, (Gr. παρειας) the cheek

parie -s -t, (L. paries) a wall

parili, (L. parilis) equal/like/similar

paritus, (L. paritus) present/visible

parm -a, (L. parma Gr. παρμη) a small, round shield

paro, (Gr. παρων) a small, light ship

parod -o -us, (Gr. παροδος) a way by/passage/entrance

parot -i, (Gr. παρωτις) lobe of the ear/of the hair near the ear

parotid -o, (Gr. παρωτιδος) parotid gland

-parous, (L. parere) to bear/bring forth/produce/lay eggs

-pars, (L. pars) part

parsi, (L. parcus) sparing/frugal/thrifty/economical

part, (L. partire) to divide

parthen -o, (Gr. παρθενος) a maid/maiden/virgin

parti, (L. pars) a part

partim, (L. partim) partly

partit, (L. partio) share out/distribute/divide

partur, (L. parturire) to bring forth/be pregnant with

parv -i, (L. parvitas) smallness/littleness

paryph -a -o, (Gr. παρυφη) a border woven along a robe

pas -i, (Gr. πασι-) pref. with the indication of all-/universal-

pasc -u -uus, (L. pascuus) a pasture/grazing

pasis, (Gr. πασις) acquisition/possession

pasma, (Gr. πασμα) sprinkling

paspal, (Gr. πασπαλη) the finest meal

pass, (L. passus) spread out/dried/having suffered/step/pace

passalo, (Gr. πασσαλος) a peg

passan, (Gr. πασσων) stouter

passer, (L. passer/passeris) a sparrow or other small bird

passi, (L. patior) to suffer/experience/permit/allow

passu, (L. pando) stretch out/extend/spread out

passu, (L. passus) a step/stride/pace

past, (Gr. παστος) sprinkle (with salt)

past, (L. pastus) pasture/feeding

pastill -us, (L. pastillus) a lozenge/a small loaf

pastio -n, (L. pastionis) pasturing/a pasture

pastor -i, (L. pastoris) a shepherd

pat -i, (Gr. πατος) a path/a trodden way/treading

pataec, (Gr. Παταικοι) myth. a dwarfish deity (a figure-head on Phoenician ships)

patag -o -us, (Gr. παταγος) a clatter/clash/crash

patagi -um, (L. patagium) a border/gold edging on a tunic

patasso, (Gr. πατασσω) beat/throb/smite/slaughter

patel, (Gr. πατελις) a limpet

patell -a -i -o, (L. patella) a small pan

paten -s -t, (L. patere) to be open

pater, (L. pater) father

pater, (L. patera) a flat dish

patern, (L. paternus) of a father/of one's ancestors/of one's native country/paternal

patet, (Gr. πατητος) trodden
path -o -y, (Gr. παθη) suffering/misfortune
patho, (Gr. παθος) a suffering/misfortune/feeling
patibul -um, (L. patibulum) a pillory/a fork-shaped yoke
patien -t, (L. patientis) enduring/bearing/suffering
patin -a, (L. patina) a dish
pato, (Gr. πατεω) to trample on
pato, (Gr. πατος) a trodden path/floor/dirt
patr -i -o, (L. pater) father
patr, (Gr. πατηρ) father
patri -a -o, (Gr. πατρη/πατρα) native land/country/habitat
patul, (L. patulus) open/standing open/spreading/extending
-patus, (Gr. πατος) a path/a trodden way/treading
pauci -t, (L. paucitas) scarcity
paucus, (L. paucus) few/little
paul -a, (Gr. παυλα) pause/rest
paul -i -o, (L. paulus) little/small
paur -o -os, (Gr. παυρος) little/brief/few
paus -i, (Gr. παυσις) ceasing
pav -e -i -o, (L. pavere) to quake/tremble/panic
pavicula, (L. pavicula) a rammer
pavid, (L. pavidus) trembling/quaking/fearful
pavo -n, (L. pavo) the peacock (*Pavo cristatus*)
pax, (L. pax) peace
paxill -us, (L. paxillus) a peg
pec -o, (Gr. πεκω) a comb
pec -us, (L. pecus) a single head of cattle/a beast/an animal
pecc, (L. peccare) to make a mistake/to sin
pechy -s, (Gr. πηχυς) the forearm
peco, (Gr. πεσκος) hide/rind/skin
pecor -i, (L. pecoris) cattle/a herd/flock
pect -en -in -o, (L. pecten) comb/crest/reed/rake
pect -o, (Gr. πηκτος) stuck in/fixed/planted/congealed/curdled
pect -or -us, (L. pectus) the chest/breast/heart/soul
pecu -d -s, (L. pecu) sheep/flocks/money
peculat, (L. peculator) defrauder/embezzler
peculiar, (L. peculiaris) one's private property/one's own
pecunia, (L. pecunia) property/wealth/money
ped -a -e -i -o, (L. pes) a foot (human and animal)
ped -a -i -o, (Gr. παιδ-) child-
ped -e, (Gr. πεδη) a fetter/shackle/anklet/bangle
pedal, (L. pedarius) of a foot
pedali -um, (Gr. πηδαλιον) a rudder/steering paddle
pedam, (L. pedamen) stake/prop
pedan -o, (Gr. πεδανος) low-growing/short/light
pedat -i, (L. pedatus) having feet
pede -m -si -t, (Gr. πηδητης) a dancer/leaper
pedema, (Gr. πηδημα) leap/spring/bound
pedetent, (L. pedetentim) step-by-step/proceeding cautiously
pedetic, (Gr. πηδητικος) good at leaping/springing
pedi -o, (Gr. πεδη) a fetter/shackle/anklet/bangle
pedi, (Gr. πεδιας) flat/level/plain
pedi, (Gr. πεδιον) instep/the metatarsus
pedi, (L. pedes) on foot
pedi-, (Gr. παιδ-) child-
-pedia, (Gr. παιδεια) rearing of a child/education
pediaecetes, (Gr. πεδιαικετης) plains-dweller

pedica, (L. pedica) fetter/shackle/anklet/bangle
pedicel, (L. pedicellus) little foot
pedicul -os -us, (L. pediculus) a little louse
pedicul -osus, (L. pediculosus) lousy
pedil -o -us, (Gr. πεδιλον) a sandal/any shoe or boot
pedin -o, (Gr. πεδινος) of the plains
pedino, (Gr. πεδινος/πεδιεινος) flat/level/plain
pedio, (Gr. πεδιον) flat, open country/the metatarsus
pedo -n, (Gr. πηδον) the blade of an oar/an oar
pedo, (Gr. πεδον) ground/soil
pedo, (L. pedere) to break wind
pedum, (L. pedum) a shepherd's crook
peduncul, (LL. pedunculus) small foot
peg -o, (Gr. πηγη) running water (in a stream)/tears/fount/source
pegas -us, (Gr. Πηγασος) a mythical winged horse
pege -o, (Gr. πηγος) well put together/solid/strong
pege-, (Gr. πηγη) metaph. fount/source/origin
pegma -t, (Gr. πηγμα) fixed/fastened/joined/congealed
pego -s, (Gr. πηγος) well put together/solid/strong
pein -a -o, (Gr. πεινα) hunger/famine/longing for
peir -a, (Gr. πειρα) trial/attempt
peira, (Gr. πειρα) sharp point
peith -a, (Gr. πειθω) persuade/mislead/bribe
pejor, (L. peior) comp. of (L.) malus - bad/evil
pel-, (L. per) through/along/over
pelag -i -ic -o -os -us, (Gr. πελαγος) the high or open sea
pelage, (Fr. pelage) fur/coat
pelamo, (Gr. πελανος) any liquid of thick consistency
pelarg -o -us, (Gr. πελαργος) the stork (Ciconia spp.)
pelates, (Gr. πελατης) a neighbour
pelec -an -anus -in, (Gr. πελεκαν) the pelecan (Pelecanus onocrotalus)
pelec -y, (Gr. πελεκυς) an axe
pelecanto, (Gr. πελεκας) a woodpecker
pelecem -a, (Gr. πελεκημα) chips of stone or wood
pelecin, (Gr. πελεκινυς) dovetail (in carpentry)
peleco, (Gr. πηληξ) a helmet
pelecy, (Gr. πελεκυς) two-edged axe/battle axe/image of perseverance
peletho, (Gr. πελεθος) human dung
peli -o, (Gr. πελειος) livid/blueish/leaden-coloured
-pelia, (Gr. πελια) a dove or pigeon
pelichn -a, (Gr. πελιχνα) a bowl
pelico, (Gr. πελλις/πελυξ/πελικη) the pelvis
pelico, (Gr. πηλικος) how large?/how great?/of what age?
pelidn -o, (Gr. πελιδνος) livid/blueish/leaden-coloured
pelino, (Gr. πηλινος) of clay
pell -a -i, (Gr. πελλα) wooden bowl/milk-pail/drinking-cup
pell -is, (L. pellis) skin
pell, (Gr. πελλιον) little cup
pellax, (L. pellax) deceitful/seductive
pellen, (L. pellere) to drive
pellex, (L. paelex) concubine/mistress
pellicle, (L. pellicula) little skin
pello, (Gr. πελλος) dark-coloured/dusky
pello, (L. pellere) to beat/drive/push
pelluc -en -id, (L. pelluceo) shine through/gleam through/be visible/transparent
pelma -to, (Gr. πελμα) sole of foot or shoe/stalk of apples

pelo, (Gr. πηλος) mud/clay/earth

pelo/pello, (Gr. πελος (πελλος) dusky

pelor -o, (Gr. πελοωρος) monstrous/prodigious/huge

pelt -a, (L. pelta Gr. πελτη) a small shield

peltaste, (Gr. πελταστης) a soldier armed with a light shield

pelv -oe -i -io, (L. pelvis) a basin/the pelvis

pely -co -x, (Gr. πελυξ) a wooden bowl/drinking cup/stone

pemph, (Gr. πεμφιξ) drop (of rain)/a cloud

pempheri -s, (Gr. πεμφηρις) a kind of fish

pemphi -g -x, (Gr. πεμφιξ) a drop/cloud/ghost/pustule

pemphre, (Gr. πεμφρηδων) a kind of wasp

pempobolo, (Gr. πεμπωβολον) a five-pronged fork

pempto, (Gr. πεμπτος) sent

pen -e, (L. paena) almost/nearly

pen, (Gr. πηνη) a web/thread

pen, (L. penna) feather

pen-e -ion, (Gr. πηνη) bobbin/spool/the thread on a bobbin

penarius, (L. penarius) a store room

penat, (L. Penates) household deities/home/hearth

pend-an -en -uk, (L. pendere) to hang/float/loiter

pene -s -st -t, (Gr. πενης) day-labourer/poor man

penelope, (Gr. Πηνελοπεια) Penelope, the wife of Ulysses

peneto, (Gr. πενης) a poor man/day-labourer

penetr, (L. penetrare) to pass through/pass into/penetrate

peni -s, (L. penis) a tail/a penis (*Membrum virile*)

penichr -o, (Gr. πενιχρος) poor/needy

penicill -um, (L. penicillus) a painter's brush

penico, (Gr. πηνηκη) false hair/wig

penicul, (L. peniculus) small tail/brush/sponge

penit, (L. penitus) internally/inwardly

penn -a -ati -i, (L. penna) a feather/a flying

penos, (Gr. πηνος) a web

pens -a, (L. pensitare) to weigh out/to weigh carefully/to pay out

pensil, (L. pensilis) hanging down

penta, (Gr. πεντα-) five

pentecost, (Gr. πεντηκοστ) fiftieth

penteteri, (Gr. πεντετηρις) a term of five years

penth -est -o, (Gr. πενθησις) mourning

penula, (L. paenula) mantle/cloak

penult, (L. paenultimus) next to the last

penuri, (L. penuria) lack of the necessities of life/want

penus, (L. penus) provisions/store of food

peo -s, (Gr. πεος) the penis

pep -s -t, (Gr. πεπσις) digestion

pepast, (Gr. πεπειτος) ripen/(of persons) mild

peper -i -o, (Gr. πεπερι) a pepper (*Piper* spp.)

pepiro, (Gr. πεπειρος) ripe

pepl -a -o -um, (Gr. πεπλος) any woven cloth/upper garment/mantle/cloak/robe

pepl -um -us, (Gr. πεπλος) robe/tunic/any woven cloth used as a covering

pepo -n, (Gr. πεπων) a kind of gourd/melon/ripe/cooked by the sun/kind/gentle

peps -s, (Gr. πεπσις) digestion

pept -i -o, (Gr. πεπτω) to digest/soften

pepto, (Gr. πεπτος) cooked

per -a -o, (L. pera Gr. πηρα) a bag/pouch

per -aeo -eio -io, (Gr. περαιος) on the other side/across/beyond

per -o, (Gr. πηροω) mutilate/main/to be defective

per, (L. per) through/by means of
pera, (Gr. περα) more/further/above/higher/beyond
perat, (Gr. περατης) a wanderer/emigrant
peratic, (Gr. περατικος) alien/foreign
perc, (Gr. περκη L. perca) a river-fish
percip, (L. percipere) to feel
percn -o, (Gr. περκνος) dusky/dark in colour
percnoptero, (Gr. περκνοπτερος) a kind of vulture (dusky-winged)
perco, (Gr. περκος) a kind of hawk
percol -a, (L. percolare) to strain (as through a sieve)
percul, (L. perculsus) struck/smitten
percuss, (L. percussus) struck/beaten/shocked
perd -ic -ix, (Gr. περδιξ) a partridge
perd, (L. pedere) to lose/to waste/to squander
perdit, (L. perditus) lost/destroyed/ruined/squandered
pere, (Gr. περαινω) to come to an end
peregrin, (L. peregrinor) to travel in foreign lands/wander/ramble
perenni, (L. perennis) lasting throughout the year
peresus, (L. peresus) consumed/eaten up
perfid, (L. perfidiosus) faithless/treacherous
perfora, (L. perforare) to bore through
perfunct, (L. perfungor) to perform fully/discharge/execute
pergamen -a, (L. pergamena) parchment
pergula, (L. pergula) a projection/balcony/booth/shop/brothel
peri, (Gr. περι) around/about/near
pericul, (L. periculum) danger/trail
perideri -s, (Gr. περιδερις) a necklace
peridi -um, (Gr. πηριδιον) a little pouch
peridin, (Gr. περιδινεω) whirl/wheel around
peridino, (Gr. περιδινος) rover/pirate
peridion, (Gr. περιδιον) a little pouch
periergo, (Gr. περιεργος) talking needless trouble/officious/meddlesome
perimeso, (Gr. περιμεσος) in the middle
perineum, (Gr. περινεος) the space between the pudenda and anus
periosio, (Gr. περιοσιος) immense
peripat -etic, (Gr. περιπατητικος) walking about (esp. while teaching or disputing)
peripher -ia, (Gr. περιφερεια) circumference/curvature/roundness
peripher, (Gr. περιφερης) revolving round
periphor -a, (Gr. περιφορα) carrying round/going round/rotatory motion
periscelis, (Gr. περισκελις) garter/anklet/leg-band
perisso, (Gr. περισσος) odd (of numbers)/strange/unusual
perister -a, (Gr. περιστερα) the common pigeon
peristicto, (Gr. περιστικτος) dappled/branded with
peristole, (Gr. περιστολη) wrapping up (a corpse)/peristaltic action
perito, (Gr. περιτιενω) to stretch around or over
peritone -um, (L. peritoneum) the membrane around the intestines
peritus, (L. peritus) experienced/practised/skilful
perjur, (L. periuro) to swear falsely/a false oath
perl -a, (NL. perla) a kind of insect
perman -en, (L. permaneo) remain/stay/abide
permea, (L. permeo) pass through/traverse
pern -a, (Gr. περνα) a ham
perni -c -ci -x, (L. pernicies) destruction/disaster/ruin
pernic -i, (L. pernicitas) swiftness/agility
-pero -n, (L. peronis) boots of untanned (rawhide) leather
pero, (Gr. πηρα) a bag/pouch

pero, (Gr. πηρος) disabled/helpless/maimed

peron -e -eo -i -o, (Gr. περονη) the fibula/the radius/a linchpin/pin of a brooch/a brooch/buckle

peronat, (L. peronatus) booted

perpero, (Gr. περπερος) braggart/vainglorious

perpet, (L. perpetuus) continuous/constant

persea, (Gr. περσεα/περσια) an Egyptian tree (*Mimusops schimperi*)

persepho, (Gr. Περσεφονη) Persephone, the wife of Hades

persic -a, (L. persicum) a peach

persona -t, (L. persona) a mask/role/character

perspic -at -i, (L. perspicax) sharp-sighted/see through/acute

perth -a -o, (Gr. περθω) waste/ravage/destroy/slay/get by plunder

pertica, (L. pertica) a long pole, esp. for measuring

pertus, (L. pertusus) perforated

perula, (L. perula) little bag/pouch/wallet

perv, (L. pervius) passable

pervicax, (L. pervicax) firm/persistent/stubborn

perysino, (Gr. περυσινος) of last year

-pes, (L. pes) a foot

pesco, (Gr. πεσκος) hide/rind/skin

pess -o, (Gr. πεσσος) an oval-shaped stone/any oval body/bolt of a door

pessim, (L. pessimus) the worst

pesso, (Gr. πεσσω) to digest/soften/ripen

pessul -us, (L. pessulus) a bolt for a door

pessul, (L. pessulus) bolt

pesti -s, (L. pestis) a pest/pestilence/plague/infectious disease

pet -it, (L. petitor) a seeker/one who strives after/a candidate

pet, (L. petere) to seek/aim at/make for

peta -ci -x, (L. petax) catching at/greedy for

petacho, (Gr. πεταχνον) a broad, flat cup

petal -o -um, (Gr. πεταλον) a leaf/crown of leaves/a leaf of metal/spread out/flat

petas -m -ma, (Gr. πετασμα) anything spread out/a carpet

petasus, (Gr. πετασος) a broad-brimmed felt hat

petaur -o -um, (Gr. πετευρον) roosting perch/spar/plank/springboard

petaurist, (Gr. πεταυριστης) tumbler/vaulter

petax, (L. petacis) greedy

petes, (Gr. πετης) a flyer

petig -in -o, (L. petigo) scab/eruption

petil, (L. petilus) thin/slender

petin -o, (Gr. πετομαι) fly (of birds and insects/of a departing spirit/of arrows etc.)

petiol -a -us, (L. petiolus) a little foot/stalk/stem

petit, (L. petitio) seek/ask/lay claim to/aim at

peto, (L. petere) to make for/strive after/attack

petr -a -o, (Gr. πετρα/πετρος) rock/stone

petulc, (L. petulcus) butting with the head/frisky

peuc -a -e -o, (Gr. πευκη) a pine (*Pinus* spp.)

peucedan -um, (Gr. πευκεδανον) hog's fennel or sulphur-wort (*Peucedanum officinale*)

pex -i -is -y, (Gr. πηξις) fixing/coagulation/putting together

pexatus, (L. pexatus) covered with a napped garment (i.e. new)

pexi, (Gr. πεξις) shearing/combing

pexus, (L. pexus) combed/carded

pez -a -i -o, (Gr. πεζις) the foot/end of body/edge/border/round fishing net

pezo, (Gr. πεζος) walking

phabo, (Gr. φαβο-) dove-

phac -a -o -us, (Gr. φακος/φακον) the lentil (*Lens culinaris*)/anything lentil-shaped/a lens

phacel -o -us, (Gr. φακελος) a bundle/faggot

phae -o, (Gr. φαιος) grey/dark-complexioned/dusky/a harsh sound phaecdo, (Gr. φαικας) a white shoe

phaedr -o, (Gr. φαιδρος) bright/beaming/cheerful

phaen -o, (Gr. φαινω) to show/bring to light/make known/make clear/lay bare

phaetho -nt, (Gr. φαεθοντις) shining/of the sun (*Phaethon*)

phag -e -o -ia, (Gr. φαγειν) to eat/devour/consume

-phagous, (Gr. φαγος) -eating

phak -o, (Gr. φακος/φακον) the lentil (*Lens culinaris*)/anything lentil-shaped/a lens

phal -o, (Gr. φαλος) the peak or forepiece of a Homeric helmet

phal -o, (Gr. φαλος) white/stammering/deaf/stupid

phalacr -o, (Gr. φαλακρος) bald-headed

phalaen -a, (Gr. φαλλαινα) a whale/any devouring monster/a moth

phalan -g -ge -go -x, (Gr. φαλαγξ) line of battle/ranks/finger or toe bone

phalangio, (Gr. φαλαγγιον) a kind of venomous spider

phalar -i -is -o, (Gr. φαλαρις) a type of coot (*Phalaropus* spp.)/canary grass (*Phalaris* spp.)

phalar -o, (Gr. φαλαρος) having a white patch/hills patched with snow

phalco-, (Gr. φαλκη) a kind of bat

phaler -a -o, (L. phalerae) ornaments as military decorations/trappings on a horse's head

phall -o -us, (Gr. φαλλος) a symbolic penis

phalo, (Gr. φαλος) bright/shining/white

phan, (Gr. φαινιεν) to appear/to show

phanaeo, (Gr. φαναιος) giving light/bringing light

phane -r -ro, (Gr. φανερος) visible/manifest/openly

phaneros, (Gr. φανερος) visible/evident

phano, (Gr. φανος) light/bright

phantas -ma, (Gr. φαντασμα) apparition/phantom/vision/dream

phantas -mo, (Gr. φαντασμος) mental image/vision

phanto, (Gr. φαντος) visible

phao -s, (Gr. φαος/φως) light/daylight

phao, (Gr. φαος) daylight/light

phaps, (Gr. φαψ/φαβος) a wild pigeon/dove

phar -o, (Gr. φαρος) lighthouse/large piece of cloth/shroud/loose mantle/plough

phar, (Gr. φαρ) spelt/meal

pharan -g -x, (Gr. φαραγξ) cleft/chasm/ravine/gully

pharci -d -s, (Gr. φαρκις) a wrinkle

pharet, (Gr. πηαρετρα) a quiver

pharm -ac -aceu -aco, (Gr. φαρμακον) a drug/a poison

pharso, (Gr. φαρσος) part/portion

pharyn -g -ge -go -x, (Gr. φαρυγξ) the throat/a gulf/cleft/chasm in the earth

phas -ia -is -y, (Gr. φασις) a saying/speech/sentence/affirmation/assertion/accusation information

-phas, (Gr. φαινειν) to show/appearance/aspect

phascol -o, (Gr. φασκωλος) leather bag/pouch

phase, (Gr. φασις) appearance/look/state

phaseol, (Gr. φασηλος) a kind of bean

phasgan -o -um, (Gr. φασγανον) poet. a sword

phasia, (Gr. φασις) utterance/expression/statement/proposition/rumour

phasian -us, (Gr. φασιανος) from the river Phasis (in (what is now) Georgia), the phasian bird or pheasant (*Phasianus* spp.),

-phasis, (Gr. φασις) utterance/expression/statement/proposition/rumour

phasm -a -ato, (Gr. φασμα/φασμιδ) apparition/little monster

phassa, (Gr. φασσα) the ringdove or wood pigeon (*Columba palumbus*)

-phasy, (Gr. φασις) utterance/expression/statement/proposition/rumour

phatn -i -o, (Gr. φατνιον) tooth socket/gum

phatne, (Gr. φατνη) manger/crib

phatos, (Gr. φατος) spoken/may be spoken

phaulo, (Gr. φαυλος) cheap/easy/paltry/ordinary
phausi, (Gr. φαυσις) illumination/lightning
pheg -o -us, (Gr. φεγος) the Valonia oak (*Quercus macrolepis*)
pheid -o -ol, (Gr. φειδος/φιδος) sparing/thrifty
phel -o, (Gr. φηλος) deceitful
phell -o, (Gr. φελλος) the cork oak (*Quercus suber*)/cork
phelli -o, (Gr. φελλευς) stony ground
phem -y, (Gr. φημη/φαμα/φημα) speak/report/prophetic saying/speech
pheme, (Gr. φημη) voice/speech
phen -x, (Gr. φοινιξ) purple/crimson/date palm (*Phoenix dactylifera*)
phen, (Gr. φαινω) to show/bring to light/make known/make clear/lay bare/appear
phenac -o, (Gr. φεναξ) cheat/liar/impostor
phenacist, (Gr. φενακιστης) deceiver/liar/cheat
phene, (Gr. φαινω) make clear/show
phene, (Gr. φηνη) a kind of vulture, perh. the bearded vulture (*Gypaetus barbatus*)
pheng -o, (Gr. φεγγος) light/splendour/lustre
pheni -g -gma, (Gr. φοινιγμα) that which is red
phenico, (Gr. φοινιξ) purple-red/a date palm (*Phoenix dactylifera*)/a fabulous bird
pheno, (Gr. φαινιεν) to appear/to show
pheny, (Gr. φοινιξ) purple/crimson
pheo, (Gr. φαιος) grey/dark-complexioned/dusky
phepsalo, (Gr. φεψαλος) spark/ember
-pher, (Gr. φερειν) to carry/convey/bear
pherb -o, (Gr. φερβο) feed/nourish
pherma, (Gr. φερμα) burden/load/fruit of the womb
pherne, (Gr. φερνη) a portion of a victim reserved for the gods
phernion, (Gr. φερνιον) a fish basket
-phero, (Gr. φερω) to bear/carry
phertato, (Gr. φερτατος) bravest/best
pherto, (Gr. φερτος) endurable
pheug -o, (Gr. φευγο) flee/take flight/avoid/escape
phi, (Gr. φι φ Φ) twenty-first letter of the Greek alphabet
phial, (Gr. φιαλη) bowl/pan/saucer
phiar -o, (Gr. φιαρος) gleaming/shining (of the dawn)/sleek (of a bird)
phibal -i -o, (Gr. φιβαλεως) an early fig/a lean, dried up person
phido, (Gr. φειδος) thrifty/stingy
phil -a -i -o, (Gr. φιλος) loved/beloved/loving
philauto, (Gr. φιλαυτος) loving oneself/selfish
philedon -o, (Gr. φυληδονος) fond of pleasure/wont to bring delight
phileo, (Gr. φιλεω) to love
philio, (Gr. φιλιος) poetical: loving/friendly/fond
phillyr, (Gr. φιλλυρεα/φιλυρεα) the lime tree, the silver lime (*Tilia* spp.)
philo, (Gr. φιλος) loved/beloved/loving
philomel, (Gr. Φιλομελα) daughter of Pandion who changed into a nightingale
philydr -o, (Gr. φιλυδρος) water-loving
philypn -o, (Gr. φιλυπνος) sleep-loving
philyr -a, (Gr. φιλυρα) the lime tree, the silver lime (*Tilia* spp.)
phimo, (Gr. φιμος) a muzzle/nose band/tightening/constriction/gag
phityo, (Gr. φιτυς) begetter/father
phlao, (Gr. φλαω) crush/eat up
phlasco, (Gr. φλασκη) a wine-flask
phlasm, (Gr. φλασμα/θλασμα) bruise
phlaur -o, (Gr. φλαυρος) petty/paltry/trivial/indifferent/bad/plain/shabby
phleb -o, (Gr. φλεψ/φλεβος) vein/artery
phledon, (Gr. φλεδων) babbler/idle talker

phleg -eth -ethon -o, (Gr. φλεγεθω) scorch/burn up/blaze/flare up/blaze forth/shine
phlegm -a -asi -ato, (Gr. φλεγμα) inflammation/heat/angry humour
phlegm, (Gr. φλεγμος) blood
phleo, (Gr. φλεω) teem with abundance/abound/babble
phleps, (Gr. φλεψ) a vein/artery
phlexis, (Gr. φλεξις) an unknown kind of bird
phlia, (Gr. φλια) door post/a support
phlib -o, (Gr. φλιβω/θλιβω) squeeze/chafe
phlips -s, (Gr. φλιψις/θλιψις) pressure/crushing/castration/oppression/affliction
phloe -o, (Gr. φλοιος) smooth or inner bark
phlog -i -mo -o, (Gr. φλογεος) bright as fire/burning/flaming/inflamed/blazing
phlogist -o, (Gr. φλογιστος) burnt up
phlogo -sis, (Gr. φλογωσις) burning/inflammation/warming/heating
phlox, (Gr. φλοξ) a flame/fire (as an element)/blade of a sword
phlyctaen -a -o, (Gr. φλυκταινα) a blister/blood-blister/pustule
phlysi -s, (Gr. φλυσις) a breaking out/an eruption
phlyz, (Gr. φλυζω/φλυω) boil over/bubble up/burst out/babble
phlyzaci, (Gr. φλυζακιον) a small blister
phob -ia -o, (Gr. φοβεω) flee/put to flight
phob -ic, (Gr. φοβος) fear/terror/fright/dread
phoba, (Gr. φοβη) a curl of hair/tuft
phober -o, (Gr. φοβερος) fearful/terrible/formidable
phobetic -o (Gr. φοβητικος) fearful/timid
phobetr -o (Gr. φοβητρον) scarecrow/bugbear/terror
phoc -a (Gr. φωκη) a seal (*Phoca* spp)
phocaen -a (Gr. φοκαινα) a porpoise (*Delphinus* spp.)
phoeb -o (Gr. φοιβος) pure/bright/radiant
phoebe (Gr. Φοιβη) Phoebe, daughter of Uranus and Gaia
phoeni -c -co -x, (Gr. φοινικος) crimson/reddish-purple/date palm (*Phoenix dactylifera*)
phois, (Gr. φωις) a blister on the skin caused by a burn
phola -d -s, (Gr. φωλας) lurking in a hole/full of holes
pholc -o, (Gr. φολκος) bandy-legged/squint eyed
phole -o, (Gr. φωλεος) den/lair
pholi -do -s, (Gr. φολιδοειδης) scaly
pholis, (Gr. φολις) horny scale
phollico, (Gr. φολλιξ) scab/leprous sore
phoma, (NL. phoma) a kind of fungus
phon -a -e -et -i -o, (Gr. φωνη) a sound/tone/the voice
phon, (Gr. φονος) murder/slaughter/homicide
phonaco, (Gr. φοναξ) blood-thirsty
phonema, (Gr. φωνεμη) utterance/the sound made
phono, (Gr. φωνη) sound/voice
phont -es, (Gr. φοντης) murderer/slayer
phor -a -e -i -o, (Gr. φορα-) carrying/bearing/bringing forth/producing
phor, (Gr. φωρ) a thief/a kind of bee (?robber bee)
phora, (Gr. φωρα) a theft
phoras, (Gr. φορας) fruitful/bearing
phorb -a, (Gr. φορβη) food/pasture/fodder/forage
phorbei -a, (Gr. φορβεια/φορβεα) a halter/mouthband/bandage
phorc -o, (Gr. φορκος) grey/white
phoringes, (Gr. φοριγγες) truffles
phorino, (Gr. φορινη) thick skin/hide
phorm -i -o, (Gr. φορμις) small basket
phorm -o, (Gr. φορμος) basket/mat/seaman's cloak/sieve
phorminx, (Gr. φορμιγξ) a kind of cithara or lyre

phormo, (Gr. φορμος) a basket for carrying corn/a plaited mat
-phoro, (Gr. -φορος) carrying/bearing
phortax, (Gr. φορταξ) a porter/carrier/cargo vessel
phortic -o, (Gr. φορτικος) tiresome/coarse/vulgar/common
phortos, (Gr. φορτος) cargo/load/freight
phorycto, (Gr. φορυκτος) stained
phoryto, (Gr. φορυτος) sweepings/rubbish/chaff
phos/phot -a -i -o, (Gr. φως) light
phosson, (Gr. φωσσων) coarse linen/sail
phoster, (Gr. φοστηρ) illuminator/that which gives light
photino, (Gr. φωτεινος) shining/bright/clear/distinct
photinx, (Gr. φωτιγξ) a kind of flute
photo-, (Gr. φωτο-) light
phox -o, (Gr. φοξος) pointed
phoxo, (Gr. φοξος) pointed
phoyx, (Gr. φωυξ/πουξ) a kind of heron
phrac -t, (Gr. φρακτος) fenced/protected
phrade, (Gr. φραδη) knowledge/understanding/warning
phragm -a -it -o, (Gr. φραγμα) fence/palisade/defence/protection
phras -a -e -eo -i, (Gr. φρασις) speech/expression/idiom/phrase
phraster, (Gr. φραστηρ) teller/expounder/guide
phrater -o, (Gr. φρατηρ) brother/clansman
phrax -i, (Gr. φραξις) barricade/fencing in/defensive armour
phreat, (Gr. φρεατια) cistern/tank/opening in a raft
phren -i -ico, (Gr. φρην) the midriff/the heart and parts near the heart/the breast. The
          seat of passion and affections: hence the heart/mind/reason/understanding
phren, (Gr. φρην) midriff
phreoryct -es, (Gr. φρεορυχτης) a digger of wells
phric -o, (Gr. φρικωδης) shivering/causing shuddering or horror/ruffling of a smooth
          surface
phris -o -so, (Gr. φρισσω) rough or uneven on the surface/bristle up/stand on end
phrix -o, (Gr. φριξ) ruffling a smooth surface/a ripple
phrom -ema, (Gr. φρονεω) the mind/spirit
phron, (Gr. φρονεω) to be minded
phron, (Gr. φρονιμευμα) prudent
phron, (Gr. φρονουντας) full-grown
phronim -i -o, (Gr. φρονιμος) sensible/prudent/wise
phrudo, (Gr. φρουδος) fled/departed
phrur -o, (Gr. φουρος) watcher/guard
phryct -o, (Gr. φρυκτος) fire-brand/torch
phryg, (Gr. φρυγω) roast/parch
phrygan -o, (Gr. φρυγανον) a dry stick
phrygio, (Gr. φρυγιος) dry
phryn -a, (Gr. φρυνη) toad
phryn -o, (Gr. φρυνος) a stone
phthalm o, (Gr. οφθαλμος) the eye
phthan, (Gr. φθανω) come first/do something first/act first/overtake
phthar -s -to, (Gr. φθαρτος) transitory/destructible/perishable
phthegma, (Gr. φθεγμα) the sound of a voice/cries of animals
phtheir, (Gr. φθειρ) a louse/a kind of pine seed
phthi -no -si -so, (Gr. φθινας) decaying/waning/wasting away/pining/withering/
          decreasing
phthir -io -o, (Gr. φθειρ) lice
phthoe, (Gr. φθοη) decline
phthois, (Gr. φθοις) a kind of cake

phthon -o, (Gr. φθονος) malice/ill-will

phthong, (Gr. φθογγη) voice/a clear and distinct sound

phthor -a, (Gr. φθορα) destruction/ruin/loss by death

phy -a -o, (Gr. φυη) growth/stature

phyas, (Gr. φυας) shoot/sucker

phyc -o -us, (Gr. φυκος) seaweed/wrack

phycit, (Gr. φυκιτις) a precious stone

phye, (Gr. φυη) bring forth/put forth/produce/beget/engender

phyg -o, (Gr. φυγη) flee/flight/shun/banishment

phyl -et -o -um, (Gr. φυλον) a kind/class/race/people/nation

phyla -ct -cto -xi, (Gr. φυλαξ) a guard/watcher/observer/keeper/chain

phylaco, (Gr. φυλαξ) jester/fool

phyldaro, (Gr. φλυδαρος) soft/flabby

phyll -o -um, (Gr. φυλλον) a leaf

phym -a -to, (Gr. φυμα) a tumour/tubercle/boil/cancer/swelling

phymos, (Gr. φυμος) swollen

phyo, (Gr. φυω) to bring forth/produce/make to grow

phyrto, (Gr. φυρτος) mixed

phys -a -i, (Gr. φυσις) nature/natural origin/natural order/inborn quality/growth

physa, (Gr. φυσα) a pair of bellows/bladder/breath/wind/blast/volcanic crater

physa, (Gr. φυσαω) blow/puff/distend/blow out

physal -i -is, (Gr. φυσαλλις) a bladder/bubble/a kind of pipe (wind instrument)

physal -o -us, (Gr. φυσαλος) a kind of toad said to puff itself up/a kind of poisonous fish
        which puffs itself out (? *Tetrodon*)/a kind of whale (? *Physeter*)

physc -a -o -on, (Gr. φυσκη) the large intestine/a sausage/a blister

physe, (Gr. φυσημα) bubble/bladder/bellows/something produced by blowing

physem, (Gr. φυσημα) blowing/puffing/snorting

physi, (Gr. φυσις) origin/the natural form or constitution/outward form/natural
        place/one's nature

physic, (Gr. φυσικος) physical/natural

physinx, (Gr. φυσιγξ) bladder/bubble/stalk of garlic

physio, (Gr. φυσις) nature

physo, (Gr. φυσω) growth

physo-, (Gr. φυσα) bellows

phyt -o -um, (Gr. φυτον) a plant/tree/fruit tree

-phyta, (L.) suf. used to form the names of plant phyla

phyxelis, (Gr. φυξηλις) cowardly

phyxion, (Gr. φυξιον) refuge/escape

phyzel -o, (Gr. φυζηλος) shy

pi, (Gr. πι π Π) sixteenth letter of the Greek alphabet

pi, (L. pius) pious/dutiful/honest/upright/kind

piacul, (L. piacularis) atoning/expiating

piar -o, (Gr. πιαρος) fat/rich

piar, (Gr. πιαρ) fat/thick juice from trees/cream/richness of soil

pic -a, (L. pica) a jay or magpie

pic -i, (L. picus) woodpecker

picar, (L. pix) of pitch

pice -a, (L. picea) the spruce tree (*Picea* spp.)/pitch

pice, (L. piceus) pitch-black/pitchy

pici, (L. picus) a woodpecker/a griffin

picr -i -o, (Gr. πικραζω) bitter/embitter/irritate

picro, (Gr. πικρος) pointed/sharp/pungent/bitter

pict, (L. picturatus) painted/embroidered

pictus, (L. picus) painted/coloured

pida -c -x, (Gr. πιδαξ) spring/fountain

pieris, (Gr. Πιεριδης) Pierides, the father of the nine muses

pies -m -t, (Gr. πιεσις) squeezing/compression
piesma, (Gr. πιεσμα) something pressed
piesto, (Gr. πιεστηρ) squeezer/compressible
pietas, (L. pietas) sense of duty/piety towards the gods
piezo, (Gr. πιεζω) press tight/squeeze/oppress/distress/press hard
pigeo, (L. pigeo) feel annoyance
piger, (L. piger) slow/lazy/sluggish
pigm, (L. pingere) to paint
pigment -um, (L. pigmentum) a pint/a colour/pigment
pigmy/pygmy, (Gr. πυγμαιος) dwarfish
pign -er -us, (L. pignerare) a pledge/pawn/mortgage
pigo, (Gr. πυγη) the rump/buttocks
pigr, (L. pigratus) slow/indolent/dilatory
pil -a, (L. pila) a ball/a mortar/a pillar
pil -i -us, (L. pilus) a single hair/a trifle
pil, (L. pilus) a single hair
pilat, (L. pilatus) armed with a pilum (heavy javelin)
pile -i -o -us, (L. pilleus) a cap
pileat, (L. pileatus) wearing a cap
pilentum, (L. pilentum) a carriage/coach
pilidi -o -um, (Gr. πιλιδιον) a small felt cap
pill, (L. pilula) little ball
pilo, (Gr. πυλος) anything made of felt
pilos, (L. pilosus) hairy
pilum, (L. pilum) a heavy javelin
-pilus, (L. pilus) hair
pimel -e -o, (Gr. πιμελωδης) fatty
pin -i -us, (L. pineus) pine
pin -o, (Gr. πινος) by foul means/dirt/filth/patina on bronze
pina -c -x, (Gr. πιναξ) board/plank/trencher/platter
pina, (Gr. πιναξ) tablet
pinaleo, (Gr. πειναλεος) hungry
pinar -o, (Gr. πιναρος) dirty/squalid
pine, (L. pineus) pine-cone shaped
pinea, (L. pinea) pine-cone
pinet, (L. pinetum) a pine-wood
pingu -i -op, (L. pinguis) fat/fatness/oily
pinn -a -i, (L. pinna) feather/wing
pinn -a, (L. pinna) a kind of bivalve mollusc
pinn -o, (Gr. πιννα) a pearl
pinnat, (L. pinatus) feathered/winged
pino, (Gr. πινω) drink
pinon, (Gr. πινον) beer
pinos, (Gr. πινος) dirt/filth/patina
pinso, (L. pinsere) to pound/stamp/crush
pinyto, (Gr. πινυτος) prudent/discreet
pio -n, (Gr. πιων) fat/rich milk
pipalis, (Gr. πιπαλις) a kind of lizard
pipatio -n, (L. pipilare) to twitter/chirp
piper -at -i, (L. piper) pepper
piphinx, (Gr. πιφιγξ) a kind of lark
pipi -en, (L. pipulus) a chirping/peeping/whimpering/crying
pipil -o, (L. pipilo) chirp/peep
pipo, (Gr. πιπος) a young bird
pipr -a, (Gr. πιπρα/πιπω) a woodpecker (*Picus* spp.)
pipt -o, (Gr. πιπτω) fall down/cast down/fall up (attack)/fall (in battle)/sink/fall
         short/fail

pir -i -um, (L. pirum) pear
pira, (Gr. πειρα) attempt/experiment
pirat -a -ic, (L. piraticus) a pirate/piratical
pis -i -o -us, (Gr. πισος) peas (*Pisum sativum*)
pis -us, (Gr. πισος) meadows
pisc -i -is, (L. piscis) a fish
piscin -a, (L. piscina) a fish pond/fish tank/reservoir/a swimming bath
piscinari -us, (L. piscinarius) of fish ponds/fond of fish ponds
pisi, (L. pisum) pea (*Pisum sativum*)
pismato, (Gr. πεισματος) a ship's cable/the stalk of the fig
piso, (Gr. πισος) pea (*Pisum sativum*)
piss -a, (Gr. πισσα) raw pitch/a resin
pissocero, (Gr. πισσοκυρος) beeswax
pissod, (Gr. πισσοειδης) pitch-like
pist -i -o, (Gr. πιστευω) trust/put faith in/rely on
pist -o, (Gr. πιστος) liquid/genuine/trusted
pistaci, (Gr. πιστακη) the pistachio tree (*Pistacia vera*)
pistil, (Fr. pistil) the female or seed-bearing part of a flower
pistill -i -um, (L. pistillum) a pestle
pisto, (Gr. πιστος) faithful/genuine
pistor, (L. pistor) a grinder/miller/baker
pistra, (Gr. πιστρα) water-trough for cattle
pisyngo, (Gr. πισυγγος) shoemaker
pisyno, (Gr. πισυνος) relying on/trusting in
pith -o -os -us, (Gr. πιθος) a large wine-jar
pithan -o, (Gr. πιθανος) plausible/persuasive/credible
pithec -o -us, (Gr. πιθηκος) an ape
pithon, (Gr. πιθων) cellar
pitta -a, (Gr. πιττα) raw pitch/a resin
pittaci -on -um, (Gr. πιττακιον) tablet/parchment/label/ticket
pituit -a -ar, (L. pituita) phlegm/a mucous secretion
pity -o -s, (Gr. πιτυο-) pine-
pitylo, (Gr. πιτυλος) the splash of oars/shower/torrent
pityr -o -um, (Gr. πιτυρον) bran/corn husks
pitys, (Gr. πιτυς) pine esp. the Corsican pine (*Pinus nigra*)
pix, (L. pix) pitch
plac, (L. placenta) flat cake
placat, (L. placare) to soothe/calm/quiet
placent -a -i, (L. placenta) a round, flat cake/the placenta
placid, (L. placidus) quiet/still/gentle
placin -o, (Gr. πλακινος) made of marble slabs
placo, (Gr. πλακος/πλαξ) a tablet/plate/anything flat
pladar -o, (Gr. πλαδαρος) damp/moist/flabby/flaccid
plaesio, (Gr. πλαισιον) an oblong body, figure or form/hollow rectangle
plag -a, (L. plagae) a bow/stroke/stripe/wound
plag -a, (L. plagae) a flat surface/district/zone
plag -a, (L. plagae) a net for hunting/snare
plagi -o, (Gr. πλαγιος) sideways/athwart/flanks/sloping/crooked
plagia -r -t, (L. plagiarius) kidnapper
plagu, (L. plagula) curtain
plak, (Gr. πλακας) a floor
plan -i, (L. planus) flat/level
plan -o, (Gr. πλανος) leading astray/deceiving/wandering
planco, (Gr. πλαγγος) a kind of eagle
planct -o, (Gr. πλαγκτος) wandering/drifting
plancus, (L.) flat-footed, also a Roman surname

plane -s -t -tes, (Gr. πλανης) a wanderer/vagabond
plango, (L. plangere) to strike/beat, esp. noisily
plankt -o, (Gr. πλαγκτος) wandering/drifting
plant -a -i, (L. planta) sole of the foot/green twig/cutting/graft
plant -a, (L. plantare) to plant
plas -i, (Gr. πλασις) a moulding
plasm -a -ato -o, (Gr. πλασμα) anything moulded or modelled
plass -o, (Gr. πλασσω) form/mould/shape/fashion
plast -o, (Gr. πλαστος) formed/moulded/modelled/shaped
plastic, (Gr. πλαστικος) pliable
plastr -on, (Fr. plastron) breast plate
plastron, (Gr. πλαστρον) ear-ring
plasty, (Gr. πλαστος) growth/moulding
plat -e -i -y, (Gr. πλατη) a flat or broad object/blade of an oar/shoulder blade
plat-e -i -y, (Gr. πλατυς) flat/wide/broad
plata -c -x, (Gr. πλαταξ) a kind of fish
platagema, (Gr. πλαταγημα) clap/slap
platale -a, (L. platalea) a waterbird/the spoonbill (*Platalea* spp.)
platamon, (Gr. πλαταμων) any broad, flat surface
platan -us, (Gr. πλατανος) the plane tree (*Platanus orientalis*)
platax, (Gr. πλαταξ) a perch-like fish
plathan, (Gr. πλαθανον) a dish/mould for baking bread or cakes
platys, (Gr. πλατυς) broad/wide/flat/level
plaudo, (L. plaudere) to clap the hands/strike
plaus, (L. plausus) the noise made by clapping/applause
plaustrum, (L. plaustrum) wagon/cart
plaut, (L. plautus) flat-footed/broad/flat
plax, (Gr. πλαξ) anything flat and broad (esp. land)
plebe -i, (L. plebeians) the common people
plec -o -t -to, (Gr. πλεκτη) coil/wreath/twisted rope/string/entangling
plect -r -ro -rum, (Gr. πληκτρον) spear-point/plectrum/cock's spur/goad
plect, (L. plectere) to punish with blows
plecto, (Gr. πλεκτος) twisted
plectrum, (Gr. πλεκτρον) a tool for plucking or striking a stringed instrument.
pleg -a -e -i -ia -o, (Gr. πληγη) strike/blow/impact/beat of the pulse
plegan, (Gr. πληγανον) a stick/rod
plegas, (Gr. πληγας) a sickle
-plegia, (Gr. πληγη) a stroke/blow
plegm -a -ato -o, (Gr. πλεγμα) anything twined, twisted of plaited/wicker work
plei -o, (Gr. πλειοαζω) more/excess
pleiades, (Gr. Πλειαδες) the constellation of the seven stars
pleist -o, (Gr. πλειστος) most/very many/greatest/largest
plemno, (Gr. πλεμνη) the nave (hub) of a wheel
plemyris, (Gr. πλημυρις) flood-tide
plen -i, (L. plenus) full of/plump/stout/filled/pregnant/satisfied
pleo-, (Gr. πλεω) to swim/float/sail/go by sea
pleon, (Gr. πλεοναζο) to be more than enough/superfluous/exaggerate
pler -o -om -os, (Gr. πληροω) gorge/satiate/make full or complete/fulfil (destiny)
plere, (Gr. πληρης) full of/infected by/satisfied/satiated
plesi -o, (Gr. πλησιος) near/recent/close/neighbouring
plesmone, (Gr. πλησμονη) satiety/fullness/plenty
pletho -r, (Gr. πληθος) multitude/quantity/number/size/plurality
plethrion, (Gr. πλεθριον) circus/wrestling-ground
plethy -sm -smo, (Gr. πληωυσμος) pluralization/increase/enlargement/spread
pleur -a -i -o -um, (Gr. πλευρα) rib/side/flank
pleuroth -en -o, (Gr. πλευροθεν) from the side

pleust, (Gr. πλευστικος) favourable for sailing/given to seafaring
plex -i -us, (L. plexus) interwoven/braided
plexi -o -s, (Gr. πληξις) a stroke/percussion
plic -o, (L. plicare) to fold/braid
plicat, (L. plicatus) folded
plinth o -us, (Gr. πλινωος) a brick/a stone squared for building
plio, (Gr. πλειον) more
plisto, (Gr. πλειστος) most/greatest/largest
ploc -ar -io -o, (Gr. πλοκη) twining/twisting/weaving/anything twisted or woven
plocam -o, (Gr. πλοκαμος) twist of hair/braid
ploce -i -us, (Gr. πλοκευς) a weaver/braider
ploco, (Gr. πλοκος) a lock of hair/braid/curl/wreath
plodo, (L. pluado) clap/strike
ploeo, (Gr. πλοιον) a floating vessel
ploiari -um, (Gr. πλοιαριον) a small floating vessel/skiff/boat/a type of woman's shoe
ploim, (Gr. πλωιμος) fit for sailing/seaworthy
plor -an, (L. ploratus) wailing/lamenting/crying
plot -er, (Gr. πλωτηρ) a sailor/seaman/swimmer
plot -i -o, (Gr. πλωτος) floating/swimming (of fish and water birds)/navigable
ploto, (Gr. πλωτος) floating
plum -a -e -i, (L. pluma) feather/down
plum -e -eus, (L. plumbeus) lead/leaden/dull/stupid/oppressive
plumbago, (L. plumbeus) of lead/lead-like
plur -i, (L. plurimus) more/much/many/several
plus, (L. plus) more
plusi -a -o, (Gr. πλουσιος) rich/wealthy/abundant
plut -o, (Gr. πλουτος) riches/wealth
plut -us, (L. pluteus) shed/shelter/parapet/shelf
pluto, (Gr. πλουτος) wealth/riches
pluto, (L. Pluto Gr. Πλουτων) Pluto, god of the nether world
pluvi -us, (L. pluvius) rain/rainy/rain-bringing/a rainbow
ply -no -si -to, (Gr. πλυνος) washtub/basin
plynteri -o, (Gr. πλυντηριος) washing/for washing
plysi -s, (Gr. πλυσις) a washing
plysma, (Gr. πλυσμα) dish-water
pne -o -u -um -us, (Gr. πνεω) to breathe/blow/send forth an odour/exhale/pant/gasp
pneuma -ti -to, (Gr. πνευμα) air/wind
pneumat -o, (Gr. πνευματοω) inflate/blow up/breath of life/vapour
pneumo -n -no, (Gr. πνευμον) the lungs
pneus -i -is -o, (Gr. πνευσις) blowing/breathing
pnicto, (Gr. πνικτος) strangled/suffocated
pnig -o, (Gr. πνιγος) choke/stifle/throttle/strangle
pnigali, (Gr. πνιγαλιων) nightmare
pnigeus, (Gr. πνιγευς) damper/extinguisher/cover for a stove
pnigma, (Gr. πηιγμα) choking/stifling
pno -i, (Gr. πνον) breathing/blowing
pnyx, (Gr. πνυξ) a place for public gathering
pampa, (Gr. πομπη) a solemn procession
po -a -e -o, (Gr. ποα) grass/a grassy place
poc -o -us, (Gr. ποκος) fleece
poca -do -s, (Gr. ποκας) wool/hair
pocill, (L. pocillum) a little drinking cup
pocul, (L. poculum) a drinking cup/goblet
pod -a -o -i -y, (Gr. ποδ-) foot
pod, (Gr. ποδεων) a narrow end/neck
podabr -o, (Gr. ποδαβρος) tender-footed

podarg -o, (Gr. ποδαργος) swift-footed/white-footed
podex, (L. podex) rump/anus
podi -um, (Gr. ποδιον) a foot
podic -i, (L. podicis) the anus/fundament
poecil -i -o, (Gr. ποικιλος) diversified/various/variegated
poemeno, (Gr. ποιμην) shepherd
-poeus, (Gr. ποιος) of a give nature, kind, quality
pogo -n -ni -no, (Gr. πωγων) a beard
poie -sis, (Gr. ποιησις) making/forming/creating
poiet, (Gr. ποιητοκος) productive
poikilo, (Gr. ποικιλος) diversified/changeable/various/intricate/complex
poimen -o, (Gr. ποιμην) a herdsman/shepherd
pol, (Gr. πολος) a pole /pivot/axis
pol, (L. polus) pole
polar -i, (L. polaris) of the pole/polarity
polem -i -o, (Gr. πολεμος) war/battle/fight
polenta, (L. polenta) pearl-barley
polesis, (Gr. πολησις) movement
poli -a -o, (Gr. πολιος) grey/grizzled/hoary/venerable
poli -s, (Gr. πολις) a city/community of citizens
polimen, (L. polimen) brightness
polios, (Gr. πολιος) grey/grizzled/grisly
polis, (Gr. πολις) city
polist -es, (Gr. πολιστης) a founder of a city
polit, (Gr. πολιτης) citizen
polit, (L. politus) polished/refined/accomplished
polium, (Gr. πολιον) an aromatic plant
poll -en -in, (L. pollen) fine flour/meal
poll -ex -ic, (L. pollex) the thumb/the big toe
poll, (L. polleo) to be strong/mighty/powerful/able
pollac -i, (Gr. πολλακις) many times/often/mostly
pollache, (Gr. πολλαχη) in many places/in divers manners
pollinct, (L. pollinctor) undertaker
pollosto, (Gr. πολλοστος) smallest/least
pollut, (L. polutus) defiled/polluted/unchaste
polo, (Gr. πολο) an axis of the celestial sphere/poles-star/orbit of a star/head dress
polo, (Gr. πωλος) a foal/any young animal/young girl/maiden
polphos, (Gr. πολφος) a kind of farinaceous food
poltos, (Gr. πολτος) porridge
polus, (L. polus) pivot/axis
poly, (Gr. πολυς) much/many/very/often
polybor -o, (Gr. πολυβορος) voracious/greedy
polychrom, (Gr. πολυχρωματος) variegated
polyclad, (Gr. πολυκλαδης) with many branches
polydactyl, (Gr. πολυδακτυλος) many toed
polymer, (Gr. πολυμερης) of many parts
polymorph, (Gr. πολυμορφος) multiform
polyp -i -o, (Gr. πολυπους) many-footed
polyphem -us, (Gr. πολυφημια) far-spread fame/a one-eyed giant
polypodi, (Gr. πολυποδια) having many feet
pom -o -um, (L. pomum) apple
poma -to, (Gr. πωμα) a lid/cover/drink/drinking cup
pomph -o -us, (Gr. πομφος) a blister
pompholy -g -go -x, (Gr. πομφολυξ) bubble/boss of a shield
pompil -us, (Gr. πομπιλος) a fish which follows ships (*Gasterosteus ductor*)
pompo, (Gr. πομπος) conductor/escort/guide

pomum, (L. pomum) an apple/a fruit of any kind
pon -o -us, (Gr. πονος) work hard/toil/task/pain
ponder, (L. ponderosus) heavy/weighty
poner -i -o, (Gr. πονηρος) oppressed/in sorry plight/worthless/knavish. base/cowardly
poner, (Gr. πονηρος) oppressed by toils
pons, (L. pons) a bridge
pont -o, (Gr. ποντος) the open sea
ponti, (L. ponticulus) a little bridge
poo, (Gr. ποη-) grass/a grassy place
popina, (L. popina) a cook-house/eating-house
popl -es -it, (L. poples) the ham/knee
poples, (L. poples) the knee/the back part of the knee
popul -es, (L. populus) people
por -o, (Gr. πωρος) a friable stone/a kind of marble/a chalk-stone
por -us, (Gr. πορος L. porus) a passage/a way through/a hole
porc -i -us, (L. porcus) a pig
porca, (L. porca) the ridge between two furrows
porcell -i -us, (L. porcella) a little sow - (L. porcellus) a little pig
porcin, (L. porcinus) of a pig/pork
pordon, (Gr. πορδη) a stinker (as a nickname)
porist -o, (Gr. ποριζω) furnish/provide
porn -o, (Gr. πορνη) harlot/prostitute
poro, (Gr. πωροω/πωρος) petrify/unite fractured bones by a callus/metaph.
           blindness/obtuseness
poroma, (Gr. πωρωμα) a callus
poros, (Gr. πορος) ford/ferry/narrow part of the sea/bridge/passage through/
           opening/duct
porp -a, (Gr. πορπη) pin/buckle/brooch/clasp
porpa -c -x, (Gr. πορπαξ) ring, loop or handle of a shield
porphyr -io -o, (Gr. πορφυπα) purple
porrect, (L. porrectus) stretched outwards and forward
porrho, (Gr. προσω) forwards/onwards
porrigo, (L. porrigo) dandruff
port -a -i, (L. porta) gate/door
port -i -un -us, (L. portus) harbour/port/haven
port, (L. portare) to carry
portaco, (Gr. πορταξ/πορτις) a calf
porth -e -o, (Gr. πορθεω) destroy/ravage/plunder
porthmi -d -s, (Gr. πορθμος) strait/narrow/place crossed by a ferry
portio, (L. portio) part of a whole/a section/division
portis, (Gr. πορτις) poet. calf/young heifer
portus, (L. portus) a harbour/haven
porus, (Gr. πορος) hole/passage
pos -is, (Gr. ποσις) drink/drinking/husband/spouse
pos -o, (Gr. ποσος) how many?/how far?/how long?/how much?
poseidon, (Gr. Ποσειδων) Poseidon, a god of the sea
posit, (L. positum) lay/place/put/store/deposit/invest
post -er -ero -ic, (L. posterior) later/following after/next
post, (L. post) behind/backwards/after/later
posth -i -o, (Gr. ποσθη) membrum virile/foreskin
postul, (L. postulatio) claim/demand/complaint
pot -a -i -o, (Gr. ποτης) a drink
potaeno, (Gr. ποταινιος) fresh/new/unexpected
potam -o -us, (Gr. ποταμος) a river/stream
potano, (Gr. ποτανος) flying/winged
potass -i, (L. potassium) potash, potassium
poten -t, (L. potens) powerful

poter -i -io -ium, (Gr. ποτηριον) a drinking-cup/wine-cup

potero, (Gr. ποτερως) in which of two ways?/either

potes, (Gr. ποτης) a drinker/tippler

poth -o -us, (Gr. ποθος) longing/yearning/regret/desire/love

pothos, (NL. pothos) a type of arum (*Pothos loureiri*)

potis, (L. potis) able/capable

potitor, (L. potitor) master

potmo, (Gr. ποτμος) lot/destiny/luck

potnia, (Gr. ποτνια) mistress/queen

poto, (L. potos) drink

-pous, (Gr. -πους) foot

pra -o, (Gr. πραος) mild/soft/gentle

pract, (L. practicus Gr. πρακτικος) do/act

prae, (L. prae) before/infront/very

praecia, (L. praeco) public crier/herald

praeco -c -x, (L. praecox) early mature/before the time

praedium, (L. praedium) farm/landed estate/manor

praenum, (L. praenum) a hatchel (an instrument for combing flax)

praesep, (L. praesaepium) enclosure/crib/mange/stall/hive/haunt/lodging

praeter, (L. praeter) beyond/past/beside/contrary to

praeust, (L. praeustus) burnt at the end or tip/frost-bitten

pragma -to, (Gr. πραγμα) deed/act/occurrence/matter/thing of consequence

pran -is, (Gr. πρανης) lie face down/falling forwards

praniz, (Gr. πρανιζ) capsize

praos, (Gr. πραος) mild/soft/gentle

pras -eo -in -um, (Gr. πρασινος) leek-green/light-green

prason, (Gr. πρασον) leek (*Allium porrum*)

prat -i -um, (L. pratium) a meadow

pratens, (L. pratensis) of a meadow/found in meadows

prav, (L. pravus) crooked/irregular/deformed

prax is, (Gr. πραξις) doing/transaction/business/action/exercise

pre, (L. prae) before

preca, (L. precatio) a begging/request/prayer

precator, (L. precator) one who prays

preco -ci -x, (L. praecox) early mature/before the time

preda, (L. praeda) booty/plunder/spoils of war/prey

predat, (L. praedator) plunderer/hunter

predi -um, (L. praedium) farm/landed estate

prefect, (L. prefectus) chief/overseer

pregnan -t, (L. praegnans) pregnant/full of

prehen, (L. prehendere) to seize

premn -o -um, (Gr. πρεμνον) stem or trunk of a tree

pren -es -o, (Gr. πρηνης) drooping/bent forward

preniz, (Gr. πρηνιζ) capsize

prenunt, (L. praenuntius) harbinger/omen/sign/token

prep -o, (Gr. πρεπω) conspicuous/distinguished/resemble

prepes, (L. praepes) rapidly flying/fleet/swift

prepon, (Gr. πρεπων) a sea fish

prept -o, (Gr. πρεπτος) distinguished/renowned

preputium, (L. praeputium) foreskin

presag, (L. praesagire) a foreboding

presby -s -t, (Gr. πρεσβυς) old man/elders/ambassador

press, (L. pressare) to press

pressus, (L. pressus) subdued/measured/compressed/concise

prester, (Gr. πρηστηρ) hurricane/pair of bellows/a kind of serpent

presul, (L. presul) public dancer

preter, (L. praeter) beyond/past/beside/contrary to

pretho, (Gr. πρηθω) swell/blowup/swell out by blowing

pretium, (L. pretium) worth/value/price/money/pay

pretor, (L. praetor) leader/chief/magistrate

prex, (L. prex) request/entreaty/prayer

pri, (Gr. πρινος) metaph. tough

priap -us, (Gr. Πριαπος) the god of reproduction

prick, (AS. prica) point/puncture

prim -a -i, (L. primus) first

prima, (L. primaria) distinguished

prima, (L. primas) one of the first

primi, (L. primitus) first

primord, (L. primordium) beginning

primul -us, (L. primulus) the primrose (*Primulus* spp.)

prin -o -us, (Gr. πρινος) the holm oak (*Quercus ilex*)

princip -ali, (L. principalis) first/original/chief

prino, (Gr. πρινος) the evergreen oak (*Quercus ilex*)

prion -o, (Gr. πριων) a saw

prior, (L. prior) earlier/former

pris, (Gr. πρισις) sawing

prisc, (L. priscus) ancient/antique/old fashioned/venerable

prisma -t -o, (Gr. πρισμα) a thing sawn/sawdust

prist -i -io -o, (Gr. πριστις) the saw-fish (*Pristis* spp.)/ship of war/stone mason's
       implement

pristin, (L. pristinus) former/previous/earlier/old fashioned

pristis, (Gr. πριστις) a sawfish/a war ship/a stone mason's tool

pristo, (Gr. πριστης) a sawyer

prius, (L. prior) earlier/former

priv -a -i, (L. privus) one each/single/one's own

privo, (L. privare) to rob/deprive of/to free from

pro, (Gr. προ-) pref. ind. before/in front of

pro, (Gr. προς) from/from the side of

pro, (L. pro) before/in front of/in place of/like

proales, (Gr. προαλης) sloping/heedless/rash

prob, (L. probatio) a trial/proving/examination/proof/demonstration

probat-, (Gr. προβαταγριον) wild sheep

proble -s -t, (Gr. προβλης) thrown forward/jutting out/projecting/headland/obstacle

probol -o -us, (Gr. προβολος) anything that projects/a jutting rock/obstacle/defense/
       bulwark/shield/guardian/hunting spear/missile

probosc -i, (Gr. προβοσκις) means of providing food/elephant's trunk/fly's proboscis/
       decapod's tentacles

probus, (L. probus) good/excellent/morally good

proca, (Gr. προκα) forthwith/straightway

procax, (L. procax) bold/forward/impudent

procell -a, (L. procella) violent wind/storm

procer, (L. procer) leader/chief/noble

procer, (L. procerus) tall/long/upraised

process, (L. processus) advance/progress

prochny, (Gr. προχνυ) kneeling or crouching

procidu, (L. prociduus) fallen down/prostrate

proclivis, (L. proclivis) sloping/going downwards/inclined forwards

procne, (L. Procne/Progne Gr. Προκνη) myth. daughter of Pandion - changed into a
       swallow

proco, (Gr. προξ/προκος) the roe deer (*Cervus capreolus*)

proct -o -us, (Gr. πρωκτος) the anus/hinder parts/rump

procumben, (L. procumbere) to lean or bend forward/fall down/sink down

prodig, (L. prodigus) profuse/extravagant

prodigios, (L. prodigious) unnatural/strange/wonderful

prodot -o, (Gr. προδοτεον) betray/abandon

prodox, (Gr. προδοξος) judging hastily

prodrom -us, (Gr. προδρομος) running before/a forerunner

proece, (Gr. προιξ) gift/present/dowry

proelium, (L. proeliuj) a battle/fight

proeo, (Gr. προιος) early/early morning

profane, (L. profanus) outside the temple

profund, (L. profundus) deep

profusus, (L. profusus) lavish/extravagant

progano, (Gr. προγανοω) comfort beforehand

progeny, (L. progenies) descent/lineage/offspring

progn -e, (L. Progne/Procne Gr. Προκνη) myth. daughter of Pandion - changed into a
swallow

prognosis, (Gr. προγνωσις) forecast

proio, (Gr. προιος) early/early morning

projic, (L. projiciens) projecting

prol -i, (L. proles) offspring

prol, (L. proles) offspring/youth

prolatus, (L. prolatare) to extend/elongate

prolep -sis -t, (Gr. προληψις) anticipation/preconception/taking beforehand

proletar, (L. proletarius) a citizen of the lowest class

prolix, (L. prolixus) stretched out

prolobos, (Gr. προλοβος) the crop of birds

promach -o -us, (Gr. προμαχιζω) fight in front as a champion

prometh -ea, (Gr. πορμηθεια) foresight/forethought

prominen -t, (L. prominens) jutting out/projecting

promotus, (L. promotus) advanced/pushed forward

pron -us, (L. pronare) to bend forward

prono, (Gr. πρωνος) headland/promontory

pronomo, (Gr. προνομος) gazing forward

pronuba, (L. pronuba) a matron who attended a bride at a Roman wedding

propaga, (L. propagare) to spread/propagate/extend/enlarge/prolong

prope, (L. prope) near

propinqu, (L. propinquo/propinquus) come near/draw near/hasten on/neighbouring/
nearby

propior -i, (L. propior) nearer

propolis, (L. propolis) bee-glue

propri, (L. proprius) special/one's own

pror -a, (Gr. πρωρα) prow of a ship

prors, (L. prorsus) forwards/straight-forward

pros -o, (Gr. προσω) forward/onwards/in front/far off

prosat, (L. prosator) ancestor

prosbato, (Gr. προσβατος) accessible

proscenium, (L. proscaenium) the stage

prosenes, (Gr. προσηνης) gentle/smooth/mild

proserp, (L. Proserpina Gr. Περσεφονη) Proserpina, the wife of Pluto and queen of hades

prosilo, (Gr. προσειλος) towards the sun/sunny/warm

prositos, (Gr. προσιτος) approachable/accessible

proso, (Gr. προσω) forward/onward

prosod, (Gr. προσοδος) advanced

prosodia, (Gr. προσωδια) song/tone/accent

prosodo, (Gr. προσοδος) approach/advance/onset/attack

prosop -o -um, (Gr. προσωπον) the countenance/face

prosphor -o, (Gr. προσφορος) serviceable/suitable/fitting

prostat -o, (Gr. πορστατης) one who stands before and protects/chief/the prostate gland

prostat, (L. prostatus) projecting

prosteth, (Gr. προστηθιον) a girdle/breast ornament of horses

prosth -en -o, (Gr. προσθεν) before/infront/formerly
prosthe -c -m, (Gr. προσθηκη) an addition/appendage/supplement/aid/assistance
prostrat, (L. prostratus) down flat/laid low
prot -e -o, (Gr. πρωτειον) to be the first/chief rank/excel/primary
proteles, (Gr. προτελης) sacrifice offered before marriage
protelum, (L. protelum) a team of draught-oxen
proten, (L. protenus/protinus) forward/further/further on
protensus, (L. protensus) stretched out
protero, (Gr. προτερος) in front/former/earlier
protervus, (L. protervus) bold/impudent/shameless
proteus, (Gr. Πρωτευς) myth. a sea-god who can assume various forms
prothet, (Gr. προθεω) run before
protisto, (Gr. προτιστος) the very first/principal/primal
proto, (Gr. πρωτος) first/foremost/front/original
provid, (L. providus) foreseeing/providing/cautious
proxim, (L. proximus) nearest/next
pruin -a -o, (L. pruina) hoar-frost/winter/snow
prun -us, (L. prunus) a plum tree
pruri -t, (L. prurire) to itch
prymn -o -us, (Gr. πρυμνος) lower part/hind-most/end-most
prymna, (Gr. πρυμνα) the stern of a ship
prytanis, (Gr. πρυτανις) a chief magistrate
psaca -d -s, (Gr. ψακας) a drop of rain/small drop
psaenythio, (Gr. ψαινυθιος) false/vain
psaer -o, (Gr. ψαιρω) touch lightly/graze/brush/quiver/flutter
psagan, (Gr. ψαγδαν) an Egyptian unguent
psal -i -id -o, (Gr. ψαλιδιον) a pair of scissors
psalion, (Gr. ψαλιον/ψαλλιον) a curb-chain (part of a bridle)
psalist -o, (Gr. ψαλιστος) clipped
psallo, (Gr. ψαλλω) pull/twitch/pluck (a musical instrument)
psalm -a -i -o, (Gr. ψαλμα) tune played on a stringed instrument
psalo, (Gr. ψαλις) a pair of scissors
psalter, (Gr. ψαλτηριον) a stringed instrument resembling a dulcimer/book of psalms
psamm -o -us, (Gr. ψαμμος) sand
psapharo, (Gr. ψαφαρος) easily powdered/crumbling/friable
psar -o, (Gr. ψαρος) speckled like a starling (ψαρ)/dappled
psathy -o, (Gr. ψαθυρος) friable/crumbling
psecado, (Gr. ψεκας) a bit/crumb/small drop
psecs, (Gr. ψηξις) rubbing down/currying
psecto, (Gr. ψεκτης) a censurer/a faultfinder
psectr -a -o, (Gr. ψηκτρα) a curry-comb for horses/a scraper
psedn -o, (Gr. ψεδνος) thin/spare/scanty/bare/naked/bald-headed
psegma -to, (Gr. ψηγμα) shavings/scrapings/chippings
pselaph -etos, (Gr. ψηλαφαω) to grope around (like a blind man)/feel/touch/handle/ stroke
pselli -o -um, (Gr. ψελλιον/ψελιον) an armlet/anklet
psellism, (Gr. ψελλισμος) stammering/indistinctness
psen, (Gr. ψεν) a gall-insect (Cynips psenes) of the wild fig and male palm
pseph -i, (Gr. ψηφις) a small pebble/gem/amulet
pseph -o, (Gr. ψεφος) darkness
psephen -o, (Gr. ψεφηνος) dark/obscure
psesto, (Gr. ψεστος) scraped/rubbed
psett -a, (Gr. ψηττα) a kind of flat fish, prob. the turbot (Rhombus maximus)
pseud -o, (Gr. ψευδης) false/lying/untrue
psi, (Gr. ψι ψ Ψ) the twenty-third letter of the Greek alphabet
psiado, (Gr. ψιας) a drop

psiathos, (Gr. ψιαθος) a rush mat/rush basket
psicho, (Gr. ψιξ) bit/crumb/morsel
psilo, (Gr. ψιλος) bare (of land)/smooth/stripped of hair or feathers/uncovered
psilo, (Gr. ψιλοω) strip bare/strip/rob/deprive/unarmed/defenceless
psimythion, (Gr. ψιμυθιον) white lead
psinathos, (Gr. ψιναθος) a wild goat
psithyr -o, (Gr. ψιθυρος) whispering/slandering/twittering of birds
psitt -ac -acus, (L. psittacus) a parrot (Psittacidae)
psoa, (Gr. ψοα) muscles of the loins
psoc, (Gr. ψωχω) to rub to a powder
psogo, (Gr. ψογος) blame/censure
psol -o, (Gr. ψολος) smoke/soot
psom -o -us, (Gr. ψωμος) a morsel/a bit
psoph -o -us, (Gr. ψοφος) a noise; as of a trumpet, insects, a clash
psor -a -i -o, (Gr. ψωρα) itch/mange/scurvy
psorale -o, (Gr. ψωραλεος) itchy/scabby/mangy
psych -e -i -o, (Gr. ψυχη) breath of life/spirit/soul/butterfly/moth/a maiden beloved by
            Cupid (Eros) and made immortal by Jupiter (Zeus)
psych -o, (Gr. ψυχος) cold
psychro, (Gr. ψυχρος) cold/ineffectual/vain/lifeless
psycto, (Gr. ψυκτος) cool
psydra -c -x, (Gr. ψυδρακιον) a pimple/blister
psydro, (Gr. ψυδρος) false/lying/untrue
psygm -a -ato -o, (Gr. ψυγμα) anything that cools (lotion/medicine/breath/fan)
psylla, (Gr. ψυλλα) a flea/louse/a venomous spider
psyllo, (Gr. ψυλλος) a sea-flea
psyro, (Gr. ψυρος) an unknown fish
psytton, (Gr. ψυττον) spittle
ptacismo, (Gr. πτακισμος) shyness/timidity
ptaer, (Gr. πταιρω) sneeze
ptaesmato, (Gr. πταισμα) mistake/false step/stumble
ptarm -ic -o, (Gr. πταρμικος) causing to sneeze
ptelas, (Gr. πτελας) a wild boar
ptele -a -o, (Gr. πτελεα) the wych elm (*Ulmus glabra*)
pten -o, (Gr. πτηνος) winged/feathered/flying/swift-footed
pter -o -um, (Gr. πτερον) a feather/wing/fin
pteri -do -s, (Gr. πτερις) the male fern (*Dryopteris felix-mas*)
pterna, (Gr. πτερνη) heel/heel bone/hoof
pternis, (Gr. πτερνις) the bottom of a dish/a kind of hawk
pternix, (Gr. πτερνιξ) the stem of a plant
ptero, (Gr. πτερον) feather/wing/fin
pterot, (Gr. πτερωτος) winged/feathered
ptery -g -go -x, (Gr. πτερυξ) a wing/feather/fin
pterygi, (Gr. πτερυγιον) a little wing or fin
pteryl -a, (Mod.L. pteryla) a wing/feather
ptes i io, (Gr. πτησις) flight
ptexis, (Gr. πτηξις) terror
ptil -o -um, (Gr. πτιλον) a feather/plumage/wing/the plume of a helmet
ptilin -um, (Mod.L. ptilin) a wing-like membrane
ptin, (Mod.L. ptin) feathered
ptis, (Gr. πτισσω) winnow grain/peel
ptisane, (Gr. πτισανη) hulled barley/barley gruel
pto -s -t, (Gr. πτωσις) a fall/falling
ptocho, (Gr. πτωχος) poor/a beggar/poorly/scantily
ptolemo, (Gr. πτολεμος) war
ptoma -to, (Gr. πτωμα) a fall/misfortune/calamity/fallen body/corpse

ptorth -o -us, (Gr. πτορθος) young branch/shoot/sapling
ptot, (Gr. πτωτος) apt to fall/fallen
ptox, (Gr. πτωξ) a cowering animal, i.e. hare
ptux -i, (Gr. πτυξ) fold/layers (of muscle)/folds (of hills and valleys)/leaves of a folding
          door
pty -ch -ct -g -gm, (Gr. πτυκτος) folded/capable of being folded/doubled up
ptya -l -li -lo, (Gr. πτυαλον) saliva/spittle/spit
ptyas, (Gr. πτυας) a spitter/a kind of asp
ptych -a, (Gr. πτυχη) a fold/layer/plate/wrinkles
ptych -o, (Gr. πτυχωδης) in layers
ptyct -o, (Gr. πτυκτος) folded/doubled up
ptyg -m -ma -mat -o, (Gr. πτυγμα) fold/anything folded
ptyngo, (Gr. πτυγξ) an eagle owl
ptyon -o, (Gr. πτυον) a winnowing fan/a fan
ptysma -to, (Gr. πτυσμα) spittle/sputum
ptyss -o, (Gr. πτυσσω) fold/double up/fold up
ptyux, (Gr. πτυξ) fold/layer/plate
pub -i -io, (L. pubes) the region of the pubes
puber, (L. pubes) mature/adult/the pubes
pubesc, (L. pubescere) to become mature/downy
pud -en -i -ic, (L. pudere) to be ashamed/bashful
pudend -um, (L. pudendum) the external female genitals/shameful
puell -a, (L. puella) a girl/maiden/young wife
puer, (L. puer) a child/a male child/boy/lad
pueril, (L. puerilis) childish/silly
puerper -i, (L. puerperium) childbirth/labour
pugil -i, (L. pugilis) a boxer
pugillus, (L. pugillus) a handful
pugio -n, (L. pugio) a dagger/dirk
pugn -a -ac -ax, (L. pugna) a fight/a battle/a battle line
pugn -o -us, (L. pugnus) the fist
pul -ex -ic, (L. pulex) a flea
pulch -ell -er -r, (L. puchellus) very pretty/fair/lovely
pull -us, (L. pullus) a young animal/chick
pull -us, (L. pullus) dark-coloured/blackish/greyish-black/sad/gloomy
pullari -us, (L. pullarius) the feed of sacred chickens
pullat, (L. pullatus) clothed in dirty or black clothes
pullul -a, (L. pullulare) to shoot up/sprout up/luxuriate
pulmo -n -no, (L. pulmones) lungs
pulp -a, (L. pulposus) fleshy
pulpit, (L. pulpitum) a platform
puls -a -i -ilo -o, (L. pulsus) a beating/striking/blow/push/drive/influence/impulse
puls, (L. pultis) porridge/pottage
pult -i, (L. pultis) a porridge of flour, pulses etc.
pult, (L. pultare) to knock/beat/strike
pulv -er -is, (L. pulvis) powder/dust
pulverul, (L. pulverulentus) dusty
pulvi -n, (L. pulvinus) pillow/cushion/seat of honour
pulvill, (L. pulvillus) a small pillow
pum -ex -ic, (L. pumex) pumice-stone/any soft, porous stone
pumil -io -o, (L. pumilio) a dwarf
punct -i, (L. punctum) a spot/point/prick/sting
punct, (L. pungere) to prick/stab/puncture/penetrate
punctat, (L. punctatus) marked with pricks or punctures
pung -en, (L. pungere) to penetrate/prick/stab puncture
pungen, (L. pungens) sharp/acrid/piercing/biting
puni -t, (L. punitor) a punisher/avenger

punic -a, (L. punica) the pomegranate (*Punica granatum*)
punic, (L. puniceus) purple/red
pup -a -i, (L. pupa) a little girl/a doll
pupill -a -i, (L. pupilla) an orphan girl/ward/minor/the pupil of the eye
puppis, (L.) the poop/stern of a ship
pupul, (L. pupula) the pupil of the eye/the whole eye
pupus, (L. pupus) a boy/child
pur -i -o, (L. purus) pure/clean/simple/plain
purg -a, (L. purgare) to cleanse/clear/purge/defend/justify
purpur -e, (L. purpurea) purple
-pus, (Gr. -πους) -foot
-pus, (L. puris) corrupt matter/bitterness/gaul/venom
pusill, (L. pusillus) very small/tiny/puny
pusillanim, (L. pusillanimis) faint-hearted/mean-spirited
pusio, (L. pusio) a little boy
pusiola, (L. pusiola) a little girl
pustul -a, (L. pustula) a blister/pimple
put-a, (L. putare) to prune/to clear up/to settle
putam -en -in, (L. putamen) a cutting/pairing/shred/shell
puteus, (L. puteus) well/cistern/pit
putidus, (L. putidus) stinking/fetid/putrid
putill -us, (L. putillus) a child/a boy
putor, (L. putor) a stench/stink
putr -e -i, (L. putridus) rotten/decayed
putus, (L. putus) pure/unmixed/unadulterated
py -e -o, (Gr. πυος) discharge from a sore/pus
pycn -o, (Gr. πυκνος) dense/thick/solid/constricted
pyct -es, (Gr. πυκτευτης) a boxer
pyctido, (Gr. πυκτις) perhaps a badger (*Meles meles*) or beaver (*Castor fiber*)
pyel -o -us, (Gr. πυελος) a trough/bathing tub/vat/infundibulum of the brain
pyelis, (Gr. πυελις) a socket/setting
pyg -a, (Gr. πυγη) the rump/buttocks
pygarg -us, (L. pygargus) a kind of antelope (perh. *Damaliscus pygargus*)/a kind of eagle
          (perh. *Circus pygargus*)/a kind of water-bird (perh *Cinclus cinclus*)
pygidi, (Gr. πυγιδιον) a thin, narrow rump
pygio, (Gr. πυγ-) metaph. of fat
pygm, (Gr. Πυγμαιοι) the Pygmies. a fabulous race of dwarfs on the upper Nile
pygm, (Gr. πυγμη) a fist/boxing/a fight/the distance from the elbow to the knuckles
pygo, (Gr. πυγη) rump/buttocks
pyl -a -e -o, (Gr. πυλη/πυλος) a gate/entrance/inlet
pylor -o -us, (Gr. πυλωρος) gate keeper
pymato, (Gr. πυματος) hindmost/last
pyndaco, (Gr. πυνδαξ) the bottom of a jar, cup or other vessel
pyon, (Gr. πυον) pus
pyos, (Gr. πυος) the first milk after parturition
pyosis, (Gr. πυοποιος) pus formation
pyr -i -o, (Gr. πυρο-) fire
pyr -i -um -us, (L. pyrum) a pear
pyr -o -um, (Gr. πυρος) wheat (*Triticum vulgare*)
pyrali -d -s, (Gr. πυραλις) an insect said to live in fire
pyramid -a, (L. pyramis Gr. πυραμις) a pyramid/the pyramid as a geometrical figure
pyrausta, (Gr. πυραυστης) a moth that gets singed in the candle flame
pyrdalon, (Gr. πυρδαλον) firewood/brushwood
pyren -o, (Gr. πυρην) a fruit stone
pyret -i -o, (Gr. πυρετος) burning heat/fiery heat/fever
pyrexi, (Gr. πυρεξις) fever/fire
pyrg -o -us, (Gr. πυργος) a tower

pyria, (Gr. πυρια) a vapour bath
pyrin -o, (Gr. πυρινος) of wheat/wheaten/of fire/fiery
pyrites, (Gr. πυριτης) a mineral that strikes fire
pyro-, (Gr. πυρο-) fire
pyrochro, (Gr. πυροχρους) fire-coloured
pyros, (Gr. πυρος) wheat (*Triticum*)/grain
pyrrh -o, (Gr. πυρροχροος) red-coloured/reddish
pyrrhic, (Gr. πυρριχη) a war dance/strange contortions
pyrro-, (Gr. πυρρο-) red
pyrsos, (Gr. πυρσος) fire/torch/beacon
pysma, (Gr. πυσμα) question
pysto, (Gr. πυστος) learned
pythagoras, (Gr. Πυθαγορας) Pythagoras, a celebrated Greek mathematician
pythedon, (Gr. πυθεδων) putrefaction
pythmeno, (Gr. πυθμην) base/foundation/bottom/stock
pytho, (Gr. πυθω) cause to rot
python -i -o, (Gr. πυθον) myth. serpent slain by Apollo
pytine, (Gr. πυτινη) a flask covered with plaited osier
pytinos, (Gr. πυτινος) a kind of fish
pyx, (Gr. πυξ/πυγη) the rump
pyxi -d -s, (Gr. πυξις) a box/a box of box-wood

Q

quad, (L. quattuor) four
quadr, (L. quadrans) fourth part
quadragesim, (L. quadragesimus) the fortieth
quadrant, (L. quadrans) fourth part
quadrat, (L. quadratus) squared
quadri, (L. quatuor) four
quadrus, (L. quadrus) square
quaestor, (L. quaestor) a roman magistrate
quali, (L. qualis) what sort of/what kind of
qualum, (L. qualum) a wicker basket/hamper
quant, (L. quantus) how much/how great/at whatever price, at any cost
quart -i -o, (L. quartus) a fourth
quasi, (L. quasi) as if/almost/nearly
quass -at, (L. quassare) to shale violently/to shatter
quass -us, (L. quassus) shaken/broken/shattered
quatern, (L. quaterni) four each/by fours
quatr -i, (L. quatuor) four
quer -e -i, (L. querela) complaining/complaint
querc -i -us, (L. querceus) an oak tree (*Quercus* spp.)
quern, (L. querneus) of the oak tree
querquer, (L. querquerus) shivering
questu -s, (L. questus) a complaint/lament/of the nightingale's song
-quetrus, (L. -quetrus) suf. meaning angled, cornered, sided
quie -sc -t, (L. quiescere) to become still/quiet/resting
quin -a -i -qu, (L. quinque) five
quint -i -o, (L. quintus) fifth
quiris, (L. quiris) spear
quirit, (L. quiritare) cry out/shriek/wail
quis, (L. quis) what?/who?

quisquil, (L. quisquiliae) refuse/sweepings/rubbish
quitus, (L. quitus) enabled/strong
quondam, (L. quondam) formerly/once/sometimes
quot, (L. quot) how many?
quotidian, (L. quotidianus) daily

R

(see also rh)

rabi -d -ies -os, (L. rabidus) raving mad/savage/raging
rabul, (L. rabula) a bawling advocate/pettifogger
racem -i -o -us, (L. racemus) a cluster
rachi -a -o -s, (Gr. ραχις) the backbone/anything ridged like the backbone/ridge of a hill
rachi -a, (Gr. ραχια) a rocky shore/flood tide
radi -a -at -o, (L. radius) radius/ray/spoke/staff/rod
radian, (L. radiatus) shining/beaming/rayed
radic -a -i -l -ul, (L. radix) a root/foundation/basis/origin
radio, (L. radiolus) feeble sunbeam/ray
radix, (L. radix) a root
rado, (L. radere) to scratch/scrape/smooth
radul -a, (L. radula) a little scraper
rai -a, (L. raia) a flatfish/skate (*Raja* spp.)
rall -i -us, (L. rallus) thin/a rail
rall -um, (L. rallum) a kind of scraper
ram -ex -ic, (L. ramex) a rupture/the blood vessels of the lungs
ram -i -o -us, (L. ramus) a bough/branch/twig/branch of a stag's antlers
rament, (L. ramentum) shavings/splinters/chips
ramex, (L. ramex) a hernia/rupture
rampan, (Fr. ramper - to crawl) creeping/climbing
rampho, (Gr. ραμφος) beak
ramul, (L. ramulus) a twig
ramus, (L. ramus) bough/branch/antler
ran -a, (L. rana) a frog
ranc -en id, (L. rancidus) stinking/rank/disgusting/offensive
rangifer, (NL. rangifer) the reindeer or caribou (*Rangifer tarandus*)
ranuncl -us, (L. ranunculus) a little frog/a tadpole/the buttercup
rapa -c -x, (L. rapax) seizing/grasping/snatching/greedy
raph -a, (Gr. ραφη) a seam/suture
raphan -is, (Gr. ραφανις) a radish
raphan -o -us, (Gr. ραφανος) a cabbage
raphi -d -o, (Gr. ραφιδο-) a needle-
rapid, (L. rapidus) tearing/seizing/impetuous/swift
rapin, (L. rapina) robbery/pillage/plundering
rapt -i -o, (Gr. ραπτος) stitched/patched/sewn together
rapt -or -u, (L. rapere) to seize/snatch/tear away/plunder
rar -e -i -us, (L. rarus) scanty/infrequent/rare
rasi -l, (L. rasilis) scraped/polished/having a smooth surface
rasor, (L. rasor) a scraper
rast, (L. rastellus) a rake
rastr -at -i, (L. rastrum) an instrument for scraping/a toothed hoe
rati -o -on, (L. ratio) calculation/computation/rate/proportion
rati -s -t, (L. ratis) a raft/flat-bottomed boat
ratus, (L. ratus) calculated/fixed/settled
rauc, (L. raucus) hoarse/harsh-sounding

rav -i -id -us, (L. ravus) greyish-yellow/grey
re, (L. re-) pref. again/back/against
reburr, (L. reburrus) one with bristling hair
recens, (L. recens) new/fresh/young
recept, (L. recipere) to receive
receptac, (L. receptaculum) reservoir
recess, (L. recessus) receding/retreat/a place of retreat
recidiv -us, (L. recidivus) returning/repeated/relapse/recoil/fall back upon
recipi, (L. recipere) to take back/regain/receive/accept
reciproco, (L. reciprocus) moving backwards and forwards
recit, (L. recito) reading aloud/reading publicly
reclinat, (L. reclinis) leaning backwards/reclining
reclus, (L. reclusus) separated/removed/shut up
recondit, (L. reconditus) put away/concealed/reserved/mysterious
rect -i -o, (L. rectum) straight/the rectum
rect, (L. rector) a ruler/governor/director/guide
rect, (L. rectus) straight/upright/correct
recula, (L. recula) a little thing
recumben, (L. recumbere) to lie back/recline/sink down/fall down
red, (L. re-) pref. again/back/against
redact, (L. redactus) edited/reduced
redditus, (L. redditus) returned/given back
redivivus, (L. redivivus) living again/revived
redol, (L. redolere) to emit an odour/to smell of
reduct, (L. reductus) reduced
redunc, (L. reduncus) bent or curved backwards
redund, (L. redundare) to overflow/stream over/to be in excess
reduvi -a, (L. reduvia) a hangnail/whitlow
refertus, (L. refertus) crammed/stuffed full
reflex, (L. reflexus) bent or turned back
refract, (L. refractarius) stubborn/contentious
refug, (L. refugere) to flee away
reg -al -i, (L. regalis) royal
reg, (L. regula) rule
regelo, (L. regelare) to thaw/warm
regim -en -in, (L. regimen) directing/guiding/controlling
regin -a, (L. regina) a queen
regma -to, (Gr. ρηγμα) breakage/fracture/laceration/rupture/rent/tear
regn, (L. regnare) to exercise royal authority/reign
regress, (L. regressus) returned
regula -ri -t, (L. regula) a straight length/a plank/a ruler/pattern/model
regulus, (L. regulus) a petty king/a prince
relect, (L. relectus) gathered/recollected
relict, (L. relictus) abandoned/left behind
rem -ex -ig, (L. remex) a rower
rem -i -us, (L. remus) an oar
remedi, (L. remedium) a means of healing/a cure/medicine
remig, (L. remigium) the oars
remiges, (L. remiges) a crew
remigo, (L. remigare) to row
reminisc, (L. reminiscor) to recollect/remember/call to mind
remis, (L. remissus) slack/relaxed
remor -a, (L. remora) delay/hindrance
remulc -um, (L. remulcum) a tow-rope/towing cable
remus, (L. remus) an oar
ren -a -cul -i -o, (L. renes) kidneys
reniten, (L. renitor) to oppose/withstand/resist
renod, (L. renodis) unbound/loose

repag, (L. repagula) the bars fastening a door
repand, (L. repandus) bent backwards/turned up
repens, (L. repens) sudden/unexpected
repeti, (L. repetere) to seek again/return/renew/begin again
repigrat, (L. repigratus) retarded/slow
repl -um, (L. replum) a bolt for closing folding doors
replet, (L. repletus) filled up
replic, (L. replicare) to fold back
replum, (L. reoplum) a bolt for closing folding doors
repres, (L. repressus) restrained
rept -a -il, (L. reptare) to creep/crawl
reptil -i, (L. reptilis) creeping/crawling
repudio, (L. repudare) to cast off/reject/divorce
repug, (L. repugnare) to fight against
res, (L. res) a thing/object/matter/affair/circumstance
resect, (L. resecare) to cut back/cut short
resero, (L. reserare) to unlock/unbolt/open
reserv, (L. reservare) to keep back
reses, (L. reses) sitting/staying/inactive
resid -en, (L. residuus) remaining/left behind/abide/stay/outstanding
resid -i, (L. residis) staying/inactive
residu, (L. residuus) residue
resil, (L. resilire) to leap back
resimus, (L. resimus) turned up/bent backward
resin -a -i, (L. resina) resin
respir, (L. respirare) breath/blow back
resplenden, (L. resplendere) to glitter back/gleam again
restan, (L. restare) to stand still/stay behind/remain/to be left over/to survive
resti -s, (L. restis) a rope/cord
restor, (L. restauro) repair/renew/restore/rebuild
resupin, (L. resupinus) bent backwards/on one's back
resuscita, (L. resuscitare) to revive/resuscitate
ret -e -i -in, (L. rete) a net/network
retiari -us, (L. retiarius) a fighter with a net
reticen, (L. reticentia) keeping silent/a sudden pause
reticul -ari, (L. reticulum) a little net/a net-bag/a hair-net
retin -a -i -o, (Gr. ρητινη) pine resin
retin -a -i -o, (Mod.L. retina) the retina of the eye/a net
retinacul -um, (L. retinaculum) a tether/a holdfast
retr -o, (L. retro) backwards/back/behind/formerly
retrors, (L. retrorsus) turned or bent backwards
retus, (L. retusum) blunt
reveh, (L. revehens) carrying back
revela, (L. revelare) to unveil/uncover/lay bare
rever, (L. reversio) turning back
revolut, (L. revolvere) to roll back
rex, (L. rex) king/ruler/prince
rh (see also r)
rhabd -o -us, (Gr. ραβδος) a rod/wand/stick/switch
rhabdo, (Gr. ραβδωτος) striped/streaked
rhac -o -us, (Gr. ρακος) ragged/tattered garment/strip of cloth/rag/lint
rhachi -a -o -s, (Gr. ραχις) the backbone/anything ridged like the backbone/ridge of a
           hill
rhachi -a, (Gr. ραχια) a rocky shore/flood tide
rhachist -o, (Gr. ραχιστος) cut up/cleft
rhacho, (Gr. ραχος) thorn hedge/briar/palisade/wattle fence
rhacho, (Gr. ραχοω) covered with wattle-work
rhaco-, (Gr. ρακιον) rag/remnant

rhadico, (Gr. ραδιξ) branch/palm frond

rhadin -o, (Gr. ραδινος) slander/taper/slender

rhadio, (Gr. ραδιος) easy/ready/adaptable/light

rhadion, (Gr. ραδιον) a type of easy-shoe

rhaeb -o, (Gr. ραιβος) crooked/bent (esp. of bandy legs)

rhaestero, (Gr. ραιστηρ) a smasher/hammer

rhag, (Gr. ραξ) a grape/a venomous kind of spider/finger tips

rhaga -do, (Gr. ραγας) a rent/chink/fissure/crevice

rhagi -o -um, (Gr. ραγιον) a poisonous spider

-rhagia, (Gr. -ραγια) a breaking out

rhago, (Gr. ραξ) grape/berry/a venomous spider/the finger tips

rhamma, (Gr. ραμμα) anything sewn/seam/thread

rhamn -o -us, (Gr. ραμνος) a name for various prickly shrubs (e.g. buck thorn – *Rhamnus catharticus*)

rhamph -id -is -o, (Gr. ραμφος) a crooked beak/hooked beak/a hook/hooked knife

rhamphest, (Gr. ραμφηστης) probably a pike (*Esox lucius*)

rhani -d -s, (Gr. ρανις) a drop/spot

rhanto, (Gr. ραντος) sprinkled/speckled/spotted

rhaph -a -o, (Gr. ραφη) a seam/suture

rhaphan -is, (Gr. ραφανις) a radish

rhaphan -o -us, (Gr. ραφανος) a cabbage

rhaphi -d -o -s, (Gr. ραφιδο-) a needle

rhapi -do -s, (Gr. ραπιδος) a rod/stick/needle

rhapisma, (Gr. ραπισμα) a blow with palm of the hand/slap

rhapto, (Gr. ραπτος) stitched/sewn/patched

rhasma, (Gr. ρασμα) a shower/sprinkling

rhatane, (Gr. ρατανav) ladle/stirrer

rhathymo, (Gr. ραθυμος) light hearted/frivolous

rhax, (Gr. ραξ) a grape/a berry

rhe -a, (NL. rhea) an ostrich-like bird (*Rhea americana*)

rhe -um, (Mod.L. rheum) rhubarb (*Rheum* spp.)

rheb -o, (Gr. ραιβος) crooked/bent

rhect -i, (Gr. ρεκτικος) fit to burst/causing abscesses to break

rhectero, (Gr. ρεκτηρ) a worker/doer

rhecto, (Gr. ρηκτος) breakable/brittle/penetrable

rheda, (Gr. ρεδα L. raeda/rheda) a four-wheeled wagon

rheg -ma, (Gr. ρεγμα) breakage/fracture/laceration/rupture/rent/tear

rhegeus, (Gr. ρεγευς) a dyer

rhegma, (Gr. ρεγμα) something dyed

rhegma, (Gr. ρηγμα) break/fracture/tear

rhegmin, (Gr. ρηγμιν/ρεγμις) a line of breakers/surf

rhegno, (Gr. ρηγνυμι) rend/tear

rhegos, (Gr. ρηγος) a blanket/rug

rheithr -o -um, (Gr. ρειθρον) river/stream/channel

rhema -to, (Gr. ρεμα) a word/saying

rhembo, (Gr. ρεμβος) wandering/roving

rhen, (Gr. ρην) sheep/lamb

rhenco, (Gr. ρεγκος/ρεγχη) snoring/stenorous breathing

rheo, (Gr. ρεω) flow/run/stream/gush

rheos, (Gr. ρεος) stream/current

rhest -o, (Gr. ραιστηρ) destroyer/smasher

rhet -i -or, (Gr. ρητορεια) oratory/set speech

rhetho, (Gr. ρεθος) a limb

rhetin -a -i -o, (Gr. ρητινη) pine resin

rhetor, (Gr. ρετωρ) orator

rheum -a -ato -i -o, (Gr. ρευμα) that which flows/current/stream/lava/flood of men
rhex -a -i -is -s, (Gr. ρηξις) breaking/bursting/rent/cleft
rhicno, (Gr. ρικνος) shrivelled/wrinkled
rhig -o, (Gr. ριγος) frost/cold
rhimma, (Gr. ριμμα) throw/cast
rhimpha, (Gr. ριμφα) swiftly
rhin -a, (Gr. ρινη) a rasp/file/a shark with a rough skin
rhin -o, (Gr. ρινες) the nostrils/nose
rhino, (Gr. ρινος) skin/hide/ox-hide shield
rhion, (Gr. ριον) any jutting part of a mountain/headland/peak
rhipi -do -s, (Gr. ριπιδιον/ριπις) small bellows/a fan
rhipo, (Gr. ριψ) wickerwork/plaited work
rhipt -o, (Gr. ριπτος) thrown/cast/hurled/thrown down
rhis, (Gr. ρις) nose/snout/brow of hill
rhisco, (Gr. ρισκος) box/chest/coffer
rhithro, (Gr. ρειθρον) a stream/something which flows
rhiz -a -o, (Gr. ριζα) a root
rho, (Gr. ρω ρ P) seventeenth letter of the Greek alphabet
rhochmos, (Gr. ρωχμος) cleft
rhochthos, (Gr. ροχθος) roaring, as of the sea
rhod -o -um, (Gr. ροδον) rose/red
rhodane, (Gr. ροδανη) a spun thread
rhodano, (Gr. ροδανος) flickering/wavering
rhoe, (Gr. ροη) a stream/river/a flowing
rhoea -d -s, (Gr. ροιας) the corn poppy (*Papaver rhoeas*)
rhoec -o, (Gr. ροικος) crooked
rhoec -o, (Gr. ροικος) flabby
rhoezo, (Gr. ροιζος) the whistling or whizzing of an arrow
rhoga -d -s, (Gr. ρωγας) ragged/cloven/cleft
rhogo, (Gr. ροξ) cleft/break/breach
rhomaleo, (Gr. ρωμαλεος) able-bodied/strong/robust
rhomb -o -us, (Gr. ρομβος) a lozenge/rhomb
rhomphaeo, (Gr. ρομφαια) a Thracian sword (large and broad)
rhomphus, (Gr. ρομφος) shoemaker's waxed thread
rhonch -o, (Gr. ρογχαλιζω) snore
rhonco, (Gr. ρεγκος/ρεγχη) snoring/stenorous breathing
rhop -i -o -s, (Gr. ρωπιον) bush/twig/bough/brush wood
rhop -o, (Gr. ροπη) turn of the scale/balancing/make-weight/decisive moment
rhopal -o -us, (Gr. ροπαλον) a club/cudgel
rhope, (Gr. ροπη) fall of the scale pan/decisive moment/weight
rhoph, (Gr. ροφεω) to swallow/gulp down/drain dry/empty
rhophema, (Gr. ροφημα) thick gruel/porridge
rhopo, (Gr. ρωπος) petty wares
rhops, (Gr. ρωψ) bushes/brush wood
rhopt -o, (Gr. ροφητικος) absorbing/drawing in
rhoptr -o -um, (Gr. ροπτρον) a door knocker/club/kettle-drum
rhoro, (Gr. ρωος) strong/mighty
rhothon, (Gr. ρωθων) nose/nostrils
rhothos, (Gr. ροθος) a rushing noise/roar of waves/dashing noise
rhya -co -x, (Gr. ρυαξ) a rushing stream
rhydon, (Gr. ρυδον) abundantly
rhyma -to, (Gr. ρυμα) anything that flows/that which is drawn/a towing line/a
            defence/a protection
rhymb -o -us, (Gr. ρυμβος) a whirling/a top
rhymo, (Gr. ρυμος) the pole of a chariot/trail of a shooting star

rhynch -o -us, (Gr. ρυγχος) a snout/muzzle/beak

rhyndaco, (Gr. ρυνδακη/ρυντακης) probably a bird of paradise (Paradisaeidae)

rhyo, (Gr. ρυω) a stream

rhyp -ar -i -o, (Gr. ρυπαρια) dirt/filth/sordidness

rhypt, (Gr. ρυπτω) cleanse/wash

rhyptico, (Gr. ρυπτικος) cleaning

rhysi -s, (Gr. ρυσις) deliverance (from death)

rhysi -s, (Gr. ρυσις) flow/course of a river

rhyss -o, (Gr. ρυσος/ρυσσος) wrinkled/shrivelled

rhyter, (Gr. ρυτηρ) strap/rein/trace

rhythm -o, (Gr. ρυθμος) rhythm/measured motion

rhyti -do -s, (Gr. ρυτιδοω) make wrinkled/shrivel up/be wrinkled

rhytism -a, (Gr. ρυτισμα) darn/patch

rhytium, (Gr. ρυτιον) a drinking horn

rhytos, (Gr. ρυτος) flowing/fluid/liquid

rhyz -o, (Gr. ρυζεω) growl/snarl (as an angry dog)

ribes, (Ar. ribas) an acid-flavoured berry

ribo-, chemical affix derived from transposition of the letters in *arabinose*

rica, (L. rica) veil

rice, (Gr. ορυζα) rice (*Oryza sativa*)

ricin -us, (L. ricinús) castor oil/the castor oil plant (*Ricinus communis*)/a kind of tick

ricin, (L. ricinum) small veil

rict, (L. rictus) the mouth aperture

rid -e -en, (L. ridere) to laugh

ridibund, (L. ridibundus) prone to laughter/laughter

ridica, (L. ridica) a prop/stake

ridicul, (L. ridicularis) laughable/droll

rig -esc -id -or, (L. rigor) stiffness/rigidity/hardness

rigator, (L. rigator) waterer

rigid, (L. rigidus) stiff/hard/inflexible

rim -a -o, (L. rima) a crack/cleft/fissure

-rima, -rimum, -rimus, (L.) super. suf.

ring -en, (L. ringor) to show the teeth/to snarl/growl/be angry

rino, (Gr. ρινο-) nose-/-nosed

rio, (Sp. rio) river

rip -a -ar -i, (L. ripa) river bank/sea shore

rip -ido -is, (Gr. ριπιδιον/ριπις) small bellows/a fan

ris -or, (L. risus) laughter

riscus, (L. riscus Gr. ρισκος) trunk/chest

risibili, (L. risibilis) causing laughter/capable of laughter

ritu, (L. ritus) a rite/a ceremony

riv -os -ul, (L. rivulus) a small brook/rivulet

rixa, (L. rixa) quarrel/brawl/strife/scuffle

rob -or -ust, (L. robur/robus) hardness/strength/firmness/oaken/oak-wood

rod -en, (L. rodere) to gnaw

rodo, (Gr. ροδον) a rose/red

roga, (L. rogatio) a question/entreaty/request

rogo, (L. rogare) to ask/inquire/question

rogus, (L. rogus) funeral pile

romale -o, (Gr. ρομαλον) club/cudgel/war-club/mace/membrum virile

ror, (L. ros) dew

ros -a, (L. rosa) a rose

ros-a-o, (L. roseus) rose-coloured/rosey

roscid, (L. roscidus) dewy/moistened

rosi, (L. rodere) gnaw/nibble at/corrode/consume

rosor, (L. rosor) a gnawer/nibbler

rostell -um, (L. rostellum) a little beak

rostr -um, (L. rostrum) a beak/snout (that which gnaws)/ship's prow

rota -li -t, (L. rota) a wheel

rotat, (L. rotatore) rotator

rotund, (L. rotundus) round/circular/spherical (occasionally)

rub -e -i -us, (L. rubus) a bramble bush/a blackberry

rub, (L. ruber) red

rube -d -din -o -r -scen, (L. rubens) red/ruddy/reddened/grow red

rubell, (L. rubellus) reddish

rubeta, (L. rubeta) a type of toad (*Rana rubeta*) found in bramble bushes/bramble thickets

rubi -d -g, (L. rubigo) rust

rubicund, (L. rubicundus) very red

rubid, (L. rubidus) reddish

rubigin, (L. rubigo/robigo) rusty

rubrica, (L. rubrica) red earth, esp. red ochre

rubus, (L. rubus) bramble/blackberry/raspberry

ruct -o, (L. ructus) a belch

rud -eri -us, (L. rudus/rodus) debris

ruden, (L. rudere) to cry out/bellow/roar/bray

rudens, (L. rudens) rope/line/cord/halyard/sheet

rudero, (L. rudero) pave with crushed stones or rubbish

rudi -s, (L. rudis) uncultivated/raw/rough/unrefined/ignorant

rudor, (L. rudere) to bray/creek/rattle

rudus, (L. rudus) crushed stone/rubbish/debris

ruf -esc -i, (L. rufus) reddish/ruddy

rug -a -os -ul, (L. ruga) a wrinkle (on the face - as in age/anger/sadness, etc.)

ruidus, (L. ruidus) rough

rum -en -in, (L. rumen) the throat

rum -ex -ic, (L. rumex) sorrel (*Rumex* spp.)

ruminat, (L. ruminare) to chew the cud

rumor, (L. rumor) a report/rumour/common talk/hearsay/popular opinion

rump, (L. rumpere) to break/shatter/burst open

run -a -i, (L. runa) a missile/dart/javelin

runcat, (L. runcator) a weeder

runcin -a, (L. runcina) a carpenter's plane (formerly taken to mean a saw)

runco, (L. runcare) to weed/thin out

rup -es -estr -i, (L. rupes) a rock/cliff

rup -i -ia -o, (Gr. ρυπαρος) filthy/dirty/sordid/mean

rupex, (L. rupex) an uncultivated man/boor

rupina, (L. rupina) a rocky chasm

rupt, (L. ruptor) a breaker/violator

ruptur, (L. ruptura) fracture/break

rur -a -i, (L. ruris) the country/a farm/estate

rural, (L. ruralis) of the countryside

rursus, (L. rursus) turned back/backwards/on the other hand

rusc -um, (L. ruscum) butcher's broom (*Ruscus aculeatus*)

russ, (L. russus) reddish/red/russet

rustic, (L. rusticanus) of or in the country

rut -a, (L. ruta) rue (a herb)/bitterness/unpleasantness

rutabul, (L. rutabulum) a fire-shovel

ruti, (Gr. ρυτις) a wrinkle/pucker

rutil, (L. rutilus) red-auburn

rutilo, (L. rutilare) to shine with a reddish gleam

rutr -um, (L. rutrum) a spade/shovel

rynch -o -us, (Gr. ρυγχος) a snout/muzzle/beak

S

sa -o, (Gr. σωζω/σαω) save from death/preserve/heal/recover
sab -ell -ellum, (L. sabellum) little sand
sab -ell -ul -urr, (L. sabulum) coarse sand/gravel
sab -ul -um, (L. sabulum) sand/gravel
sabaco, (Gr. σαβακος) feeble/effeminate
saban, (Gr. σαβανον) linen cloth/towel
sabaten, (L. sabatenum) a kind of slipper
sabyttos, (Gr. σαβυττος) the female pudenda (pudenda muliebria)
sac -o -us, (Gr. σακος) a shield/defence
sac, (L. sacer) sacred
sacc -i -o, -us, (Gr. σακκος L. saccus) a sack/bag/sackcloth
sacchar, (L. saccharum) sugar
sacell, (L. sacellum) small shrine/chapel
sacer, (L. sacer) sacred/holy/consecrate
sacerdo -t, (L. sacerdos) a priest/priestess
sacr -a -i, (L. sacrum) sacred/holy thing/temple
sacr -o -um, (NL. sacrum) the sacrum
sacri -b -pt, (L. scribere) to engrave with a sharp pointed tool, hence - to write
sacroma, (Gr. σαρκωμα) tumour/cancer
sact -o, (Gr. σακτος) crammed/stuffed
saeno, (Gr. σαινω) wag the tail/fawn upon
saenur -id, (Gr. σαινουρις) wagging the tail (as of a dog)
saep -es -i, (L. saepes) a fence/hedge
saev, (L. saevus) raging/fierce/furious/violent
saffr, (ME. saffran) yellow
sag -o, (Gr. σαγος) a coarse cloak/plaid/soldier's cloak/horse-cloth
saga -c -x, (L. sagacitas) keenness/acuteness/shrewdness
sagana, (L. sagana) fortune teller
sagar -i, (Gr. σαγαρις) a type of sword used by the Scythian tribes
sagax, (L. sagax) having keen senses/mentally acute/shrewd/clever
sage, (Gr. σαγη) a pack/baggage/harness/equipment/furniture
sagen -a, (Gr. σαγηνη) a large drag-net for taking fish (seine)
sagi -do -s, (Gr. σαγις) a wallet/pouch
sagitt -a, (L. sagitta) an arrow
sagma, (Gr. σαγμα) a covering/clothing/large cloak/covering of a shield/pack-saddle
sagum, (L. sagum) cloak/mantle made of coarse wool
sagus, (L. sagus) prophetic/soothsaying
sal -i, (L. sal) salt
sal -o, (Gr. σαλος) a tossing motion (as of an earthquake)/rolling swell (as of the sea)/
    restlessness/open roads
sal -o, (Gr. σαλος) silly/imbecile
sala -ci -x, (L. salax) lustful/lecherous
salaco, (Gr. σαλακων) braggart/pretentious person
salamandr -a, (Gr. σαλαμανδρα) a salamander
salambe, (Gr. σαλαμβη) vent/chimney/door
salang, (Gr. σαλαγεω) to overload
salari, (L. salarius) of salt
salebr -a -os, (L. salebra) a jolting - hence a rough patch of road/roughness/ruggedness
salen, (Gr. σαλευω) to be unstable
sali -ci -x, (L. salix) a willow (*Salix* spp.)
sali, (L. salio) spring/leap/jump/bound
salien -t, (L. saliens) leaping
salin, (L. salinae) salt works/brine pits
salinum, (L. salinum) saltcellar

salio, (L. salire) to leap/jump/bound/dance
saliv -a, (L. saliva) spittle
salix, (L. salix) a willow (*Salix* spp.)
salmo -n, (L. salmo) the trout (*Salmo trutta*) or salmon (*Salmo salar*)
salos, (Gr. σαλος) a shaking/a tossing motion
salos, (Gr. σαλος) silly/imbecile
salp -a -i, (L. salpa) a kind of stock-fish
salpin -ct -g -go -x, (Gr. σαλπιγξ) a war-trumpet
sals, (L. salsus) salted/salty
salt -a -i, (L. saltare) to leap/dance
saltator, (L. saltator) a dancer
saltu -s, (L. saltus) a forest/mountain pasture/dale/ravine/glade
salu -bri -ti, (L. salubris) healthful/healthy/wholesome
salum, (L. salum) the open sea
salus, (L. salus) health/soundness
salv -a, (L. salvus) safe/unhurt/well/sound
salvi -a, (L. salvia) sage (*Salvia* spp.)
salvus, (L. salvus) safe/unhurt
samar -a, (L. samara) an elm seed (*Ulmus* spp.)/any dry, indehiscent, winged fruit
samardac, (Gr. σαμαρδακος) a buffoon
sambuc -a, (L. sambuca) a type of harp
sambuc -us, (L. sambucus) the elder (*Sambucus* spp)
sana -b -t, (L. sanare) to heal/cure/restore to health
sanct -i, (L. sanctus) consecrated/holy/hallowed
sandal -o -um, (Gr. σανδαλιον) a sandal/a flat fish
sandapila, (L. sandapila) a bier for the lower classes
sandix, (Gr. σανδυξ) vermilion
sangui -ni -s, (L. sanguis) blood
sanguisuga, (L. sanguisuga) a bloodsucker
sani -do -s, (Gr. σανις) a board/plank/timber
sanicul -a, (NL. sanicula) a genus of the carrot family (*Sanicula europea* - Umbelliferae)
sanid, (Gr. σανιδιον) small splint
sanies, (L. sanies) bloody matter/pus/venom/poison
sanit -a, (L. sanitas) health/soundness/sanity
sannio, (L. sannio) one who makes faces/grimacer/buffoon
santal -um, (NL. sandalum/santalum) the sandalwood tree (*Santalum album*)
sao, (Gr. σαος/σως) safe and sound/alive and well/safe/whole
sap, (L. sapere) to be wise
saperd -es, (Gr. σαπερδης) a salted fish, prob. the Nile perch (*Lates niloticus*)
saph -en -o, (Gr. σαφης) distinct/clear/plain
sapid, (L. sapere) to taste/to have taste/to discern/be wise/think
sapien -s -t, (L. sapiens) wise/sensible/thinking
sapinda, (NL. sapindus) the soapberry (*Sapindus* spp.)
sapo -ni, (L. sapo/saponis) soap
sapor -i, (L. sapor) taste/sense of taste/flavouring
sapphir -o, (Gr. σαπφειρος) lapis lazuli/the sapphire
sapr -o, (Gr. σαπρος) rotten/putrid/diseased
sarabo, (Gr. σαραβος) female pudenda
sarc -i -o, (Gr. σαρξ) flesh
sarcas -m, (LL. sarcasmos) speak bitterly/sneer/tear flesh/gnash the teeth
sarcin -a, (L. sarcina) a bundle/pack/portable luggage
sarcin, (L. sarcina) package
sarcio, (L. sarcire) to sew/patch/mend
sarco-, (Gr. σαρκο-) fleshy
sarcod, (Gr. σαρκωδης) fleshy
sarcolip -es, (Gr. σαρκολιπης) forsaken by flesh/with little flesh
sarcul, (L. sarculum) a light hoe

sard -a, (Gr. σαρδινη) the sardine or pilchard (*Sardina pilchardus*)

sardon, (Gr. σαρδων) a kind of rope

sargane, (Gr. σαργανη) wickerwork

sargass -o, (Pg. sargasso) gulfweed (a type of seaweed)

sarginos, (Gr. σαργινος) a gar (Lepisosteidae)

sargos, (Gr. σαργος) a sea-fish (*Sargus rondeletii*)

sarisa, (Gr. σαρισα/σαρισσα) a long lance used by the Macedonians

sarma, (Gr. σαρμα) a chasm in the earth

sarment -um, (L. sarmentum) twigs/small branches/brushwood

sarment, (L. sarmentum) twig/brush

sarmos, (Gr. σαρμος) a heap of earth or sand

saron -to, (Gr. σαρον) a broom/sweepings/refuse/rubbish

saronis, (Gr. σαρωνις) an old, hollow oak

sarp -t, (L. sarptus) trim/prune

sarracum, (L. sarracum/serracum) a kind of wagon

sarri, (L. sarrio) hoe/cultivate

sartago, (L. sartago) a frying pan

sartori -us, (L. sartor) a patch/botch/a patcher/a tailor

sarum, (Gr. σαρον) a broom/sweepings/refuse/rubbish

sarx, (Gr. σαρξ) flesh (animal or fruit)/of the flesh

satan, (Gr. Σαταν) the devil/adversary/opponent

satell -es -it, (L. satelles) an attendant/guard/escort

sathe, (Gr. σαθη) penis (membrum virile)

satherion, (Gr. σαθεριον) probably a kind of beaver

sathr -o, (Gr. σαθρος) unsound/weakened/cracked

sathrax, (Gr. σαθραξ) louse

sathros, (Gr. σαθρος) decayed/rotten/unsound

satiat, (L. satias) sufficiency

satine, (Gr. σατινη) a chariot

sativus, (L. sativus) cultivated

satrapa, (Gr. σατραπης) regional governor/viceroy

satur -a, (L. satur) full

saturn, (L. Saturnus) Saturn, a god of agriculture

satyr, (Gr. σατυρος L. satyrus) a satyr (a woodland deity)

sauci, (L. saucio) wound/hurt

saucr -o, (Gr. σαυκρος = αβρος) dainty/delicate/pretty/soft/graceful/splendid/
        luxurious

saulo, (Gr. σαυλος) waddling/swaying

saunion, (Gr. σαυνιον) a javelin/membrum virile

saur -o -us, (Gr. σαυρος) a lizard

sauroter, (Gr. σαυρωτηρ) a ferule or spike at the butt end of a spear

savanna/savannah (Sp. zavana) a meadow

sax -i -o -um, (L. saxum) a rock/large stone

saxatil, (L. saxatilis) frequenting rocks/found among rocks

sbest -os, (Gr. σβεσις) quenching/putting out

scab-er -r, (L. scaber) scabby/mangy/rough/scurfy

scabel-um, (L. scabellum) a small stool/footstool

scabi -es, (L. scabies) an itch/mange/roughness

scabios, (L. scabiosus) scabby/mangy/rough/mouldy

scabr -i, (L. scabra) scabby/rough

scae -o, (Gr. σκαιος) on the left/western/unlucky/ill-omened/awkward/clumsy/
        stupid

scaer -o, (Gr. σκαιρω) skip/dance/frisk (as of calves)

scaevus, (Gr. σκαιος) left/towards the left/west

scal -a -ari -i, (L. scalas) a ladder/stairs/staircase

scalen -e -o, (Gr. σκαληνος) unequal/rough/uneven

scali -d -s, (Gr. σκαλις) a hoe/shovel

scali, (Gr. σκαλεια) hoeing

scalidris, (Gr. σκαλιδρις) a speckled shore bird, ? redshank (*Scolopax rusticola*)

scalm -o -us, (Gr. σκαλμος) an oar-pin/row-lock

scalmo, (Gr. σκαλμη) knife/sword

scalop -o -s, (Gr. σκαλοψ/σκαλωψ) a mole rat

scalp, (L. scalpo) crave/scrape/scratch

scalpr -i -um, (L. scalprum) chisel/pen-knife

scalpt, (L. scalptum) carved/scarped/scratched

scamb -o, (Gr. σκαμβος) crooked/bent

scamill -us, (L. scamillus) a little bench/little stool

scammato, (Gr. σκαμμα) something dug/trench/pit

scamn -o -um, (L. scamnum) a bench/stool

scan -d -s -sor, (L. scandere) to climb

scan -i -o -us, (Gr. σκανος/σκηνος) the body (as temple of the soul)/a corpse

scandix, (Gr. σκανδιξ) the wild chervil (*Anthriscus sylvestris*)

scando, (L. scandere) to climb

scap -us, (Gr. σκαπος) a stalk/staff

scap -us, (L. scapus) stem of a plant/weaver's beam

scapan -e -i -o, (Gr. σκαπανη) spade/mattock/any digging tool

scapan, (Gr. σκαπανη) a spade/mattock/digging tool

scaph -i -o, (Gr. σκαφη) trough/tub/basin/bowl/skiff/digging/delving

scaph, (Gr. σκαφευς) digger/delver

scaphio, (Gr. σκαφιδιον) small boat

scapl, (L. scalpellum) small knife

scapt -es -o, (Gr. σκαπτω) dig/delve/cultivate

scapul -a, (L. scapula) a shoulder blade

scapus, (Gr. σκαπος) a stem/staff

scar -us, (Gr. σκαρος) the parrotfish (*Scarus cretensis*)

scarabae -i -us, (L. scarabaeus) a kind of beetle

scardamycto, (Gr. σκαρδαμυκτης) blinker/winker

scari -d -s, (Gr. σκαρις = ασκαρις) a worm in the intestines

scarifico, (L. scarifare) to scratch up/scarify

scart, (Gr. σκαιρτης) nimble/quick

scat -o, (Gr. σκατος [σκωρ]) dung/ordure

scatula, (Mod.L. scatula) a kind of pill box

scaturgio, (L. scaturrgio) a bubbling spring

scaumo, (Gr. σκαυμος) limping/halting

scaur, (Gr. σκαυρος) having large or swollen ankles

scedasto, (Gr. σκεδαστος) scatterable

scel -i -id -is -o -us, (Gr. σκελος) the leg

sceler, (L. scelero) wicked/profane/impious/wretched/tiresome

sceleto, (Gr. σκελετος) dried up/withered

sceli -do -s, (Gr. σκελις/σχελις) a leg/rib of beef

scelio -n, (L. scelion) rascal/scoundrel

sceliphro, (Gr. σκελιφρος) dry-looking/lean/thin

scello, (Gr. σκελλος) bowlegged/crook-legged

scelo, (Gr. σκελος) leg

scelus, (L. scelus) evil deed/crime

scen -a -o, (Gr. σκην-) tent/stage/metaph. hidden

scene, (Gr. σκηνη) tent/booth/stage/decorative setting

scepano, (Gr. σκεπανον) a covering

sceps, (Gr. σκεψις) examination/consideration

sceptic -o, (Gr. σκεπτικος) thoughtful/reflective

scepto, (Gr. σκηπτος) thunderbolt/hurricane

sceptr -um, (L. sceptrum) a sceptre/royal staff/wand/baton scerbolo, (Gr. σκερβολλω) scolding/abusive

sceu -o -us, (Gr. σκευος) any implement/any vessel/a thing

schadon -o, (Gr. σχαδων) a bee or wasp larva/breeding cell/honey cell/honey comb

schalidoma, (Gr. σχαλιδωμα) a forked prop

sched -o, (Gr. σχεδη) leaf/page/strip of papyrus

schedo, (Gr. σχεδον) near

schelis, (Gr. σχελις) a rib of beef

schema -t -to, (Gr. σχημα) form/shape/figure

scher -o, (Gr. σχερος) one after another/uninterruptedly

sches -is, (Gr. σχεσις) state/condition/nature/quality

schid -i -ium -o, (Gr. σχιζα) a splinter/lath

schism -a -at -o, (Gr. σχισμα) cleft (as of hooves)/division/rent (in a garment)

schist -o, (Gr. σχιστος) cloven/divided/split

schiz -o, (Gr. σχιζειν) to split/cleave

schiza, (Gr. σχιζα) a splinter or chip of wood

schoen -i, (Gr. σχοινις) rope/cord

schoen -o, (Gr. σχοινος) a rush/reed/an aromatic reed/rush-bed/a (Persian) land-
         measure

schola, (Gr. σχολη) leisure/rest/ease

schola, (L. schola) a school/sect/learned leisure

schyr, (Gr. σχυρ) a hedgehog (*Erinaceus europaeus*)

sci -a -o, (Gr. σκιη) a shadow/shade

sciad -i, (Gr. σκιαδειον) sunshade/parasol/umbel

sciar -o, (Gr. σκιερος) shady/dark coloured/faint

sciasma -to, (Gr. σκιασμα) a shadow

sciatic, (LL. sciaticus) of the hip joint

scien -s -t, (L. scientia) knowledge/skill

scier -o, (Gr. σκιερος) shady/dark coloured/faint

scilla (squilla), (L. scilla/squilla) a sea-leek (*Scilla* spp.)/a small lobster, perh. a crayfish

scimpodium, (Gr. σκιμποδιον) a low bed/couch

scinaco, (Gr. σκιναξ) quick/nimble

scinc -i -us, (Gr. σκιγκος/σκιγγος) a skink

scindapho, (Gr. σκινδαφος) a vixen (*Vulpes vulpes vulpes*)

scindo, (L. scissus) cut/cleave

scintho, (Gr. σκινθος) diving

scintill, (L. scintillare) to sparkle/glitter

scintilla, (L. skintilla) spark/glimmer

scio, (Gr. σκιο-) a shadow/shadowy

scion, (Fr. scion) branch/shoot

scirp -us, (L. scirpus/sirpus) a bulrush

scirrh -o -us, (Gr. σκιρρος/σκιρος) hardened swelling or tumour/hard land (perh. chalk)

scirt -et -o, (Gr. σκιρτητης) a leaper

sciss -i, (L. scissilis) cleavable

scissur -a, (L. scissura) a splitting/separating/parting

sciur o -us, (L. sciurus Gr. σκιουρος) a squirrel (*Sciurus* spp.)

scler -o, (Gr. σκληρος) hard/dry

scobi -s, (L. scobiculum) sawdust

scobin -a, (L. scobina) a file/rasp

scol -o -us, (Gr. σκολως) pointed stake/thorn/prickle/evil/ruin

scol, (Gr. σκολιος) curved

scole -c -x, (Gr. σκωληξ) a worm

scoli -o, (Gr. σκολιος) curved/bent/winding/crooked/unjust

scolop -o -s, (Gr. σκολοψ) anything pointed/thorn

scolopa -c -x, (Gr. σκολοπαξ) a snipe (*Scolopax* spp.)

scolopendr -a, (Gr. σκολοπενδρα) a centipede (*Scolopendra* spp.)/the hart's tongue fern
         (*Asplenium scolopendrium*)

scolyt -i, (Gr. σκολυτι) clip/shorten
scomb -er -r, (L. scomber) the mackerel (*Scomber* spp.)
scop -a, (L. scopa) a broom/twigs/brush
scop -e -o, (Gr. σκοπη) a watch-tower
scop -i -o, (Gr. σκοπια) lookout/watch-tower/hill top/peak
scop, (Gr. σκοπεω) look/view/regard/consider
scopae -o -us, (Gr. σκωπαιος) a dwarf
scopel -o -us, (Gr. σκοπελος) a lookout place/high peak/headland/watch tower
scops, (Gr. σκωψ) a small owl/the little horned owl (?*Otus* spp.)
scopt, (Gr. σκωπω) mock/jeer/scoff at
scopul -a, (L. scopula) a small broom
scopul -us, (L. scopulus) a rock/crag/cliff/a rock in the sea
scopus, (L. scopus) a mark at which to shoot
scopy, (Gr. σκοπη) lookout place/watchtower
scor -a -ia, (Gr. σκωρια) dross of metal/slag
scorbut -us, (Mod.L. scorbutus) scurvy
scord -o -um, (Gr. σκορδιον) garlic germander (*Allium* spp.)
scordal, (L. scordalus) quarreller/brawler/wrangler
scorod -um, (Gr. σκοροδον) garlic (*Allium sativum*)
scorpaen -a, (Gr. σκορπαινα) a fish with a poisonous sting
scorpi -o -us, (Gr. σκορπιος) scorpion
scorpio -n, (L. scorpius) a scorpion/a military engine for throwing missiles
scortator, (L. scortator) whoremonger
scortum, (L. scortum) skin/hide/prostitute
scoto -ia -o -us, (Gr. σκοτος) darkness/gloom
screa -t, (L. screatus) clearing the throat/hawking
script, (L. scriptum) writing
scrob -i -is, (L. scrobis) a ditch/a trench
scrofa, (L. scrofa) breeding sow
scroful -ari, (L. scrofula) a small breeding-sow/a glandular swelling (like piglets)
scrot -um, (L. scrotum) a pouch/the pouch containing the testicles
scrup -e -os -ul -us, (L. scrupus) a rough or sharp stone
scrut -at, (L. scrutator) one who searches/an investigator
scrutum, (L. scrutum) rubbish
sculpt, (L. sculpere) to carve
scurra, (L. scurra) jester/buffoon/dandy
scut -i -um, (L. scutum) an oblong shield
scutell -a, (L. scutella) a flat dish/saucer
scutell -um, (L. scutellum) small shield
scuti, (L. scutica) a whip
scutula, (L. scutula) a roller/cylinder
scutum, (L. scutum) shield
scybal -o -um, (Gr. σκυβαλον) dung/excrement/refuse/offal
scydmaen, (Gr. σκυδμαινω) angry
scyla -co -x, (Gr. σκυλαξ) a young dog/puppy/a cub
scylio, (Gr. σκυλιον) a dogfish
scyll, (Gr. σκυλλω) tear/rend apart/maltreat/molest
scyllar -us, (Gr. σκυλλαρος/κυλλαρος) a hermit crab (*Pagurus* spp.)
scylmo, (Gr. σκυλμος) a tearing/rending/plucking
scylo, (Gr. σκυλον) booty pulled from a slain enemy
scylo, (Gr. σκυλος) an animal skin
scymn -o -us, (Gr. σκυμνος) a cub/a whelp, especially a lion's whelp
scyph -o -us, (L. scyphus) drinking-cup
scyr -o, (Gr. σκυρος) stone chippings
scyt -i, (Gr. σκυτη) part of the neck
scyt -o, (Gr. σκυτος) skin/hide/tanned hide/leather thong/whip
scytal -a -i -o, (Gr. σκυταλη) staff/cudgel/club/dispatch/message

scythi, (Gr. σκυθισμος) shaving the head/scalping
scythr -o, (Gr. σκυθρος) angry/sullen
scytod, (Gr. σκυτωδης) like leather
scyzo, (Gr. σκυζα) lust
seb -i -um, (L. sebum) tallow/grease
sebas -m -t, (Gr. σεβαστος) venerable/reverend/august
sebenion, (Gr. σεβενιον) the sheath of the palm flower
sec -o, (Gr. σεκος) an enclosure/pen/shrine
sec, (L. secare) to cut
secern, (L. secernere) to separate
seclu -d -s, (L. secludo) shut off/confine/hidden
secotero, (Gr. σεκωτηρ) the beam of a balance
secret, (L. secretus) separated/set apart/secret
secta, (L. secta) way of life
secti, (L. sectio) a cutting/a lot at an auction
sectil, (L. sectilis) cut
sector, (L. sector) cutter
secula, (L. secula) sickle
seculum, (L. saeculum) the period of one human generation
secund, (L. secundus) second/next
secur -i -is, (L. securis) an axe/hatchet
secutor, (L. secutor) a gladiator/follower/pursuer
sed -ent -i, (L. sedere) to sit/sitting
sedat, (L. sedatio) soothing/calming
sedentarius, (L. sedentarius) sitting
sedit, (L. seditio) going apart/civil or military revolt
seduc, (L. seductio) leading aside
sedul, (L. sedulus) busy/diligent/assiduous/officious
sege -s -t, (L. seges) a corn field/a crop/field/ground/soil
segestr -e -i, (Gr. σεγεστρον) a blanket/covering/wrapping
segm -ent, (L. segmentum) a piece cut off/cutting/shred
segn -i, (L. segnis) slow/slothful/tardy/sluggish
segreg, (L. segregare) separate from the flock/set apart
sei -o, (Gr. σειω) shake/move to and fro/agitate/disturb
seir -i, (Gr. σειριαω) hot/scorching
seir -o, (Gr. σειρα) cord/rope/band
seism -o -us, (Gr. σεισμος) shaking/shock/earthquake
sejug -i, (L. seiugis) a six-horse chariot
sejunct, (L. seiunctio) separation
seko, (Gr. σεκος) an enclosure/pen/shrine
sela -sm, (Gr. σελασμα) shining
selach -o -us, (Gr. σελαχος) a shark
selago, (L. selago) a kind of clubmoss (Pteridophyta)
selas, (Gr. σελας) light/flash/meteor
selates, (Gr. σελατης) a snail
select, (L. selectio) choice
selen -e -i, (Gr. σεληνη) the moon
seleni, (NL. selenium) selenium
seleucido, (Gr. σελευλις) a kind of woman's shoe/a drinking cup/a bird
seli -d -do -s, (Gr. σελις) a cross beam/column/plank/a leaf of papyrus
selin -um, (Gr. σελινον) celery (*Apium graveolens*)
sell -a -i, (Gr. σελλα) saddle/seat
sem -en -in, (L. semen) a seed
sema -t -o, (Gr. σημα) a sign/mark/token/signal
semae -o, (Gr. σημεια) military standard
semant -o, (Gr. σημαντος) marked
semasi, (Gr. σημασια) an indication/the giving of a signal or command

semat -i -o, (Gr. σηματιον) little mark, sign, token

seme, (L. semel) once/first

semeio -t, (Gr. σεμειωτος) signified/inferred from a sign

semi, (Gr. σημιεοω) to mark

semi, (L. semi-) half

semin/semen, (L. semen) seed/sperm

semio, (Gr. σημειον) sign/signal/flag

semita, (L. semita) narrow way/footpath

semn -o, (Gr. σεμνος) revered/holy/august

semotus, (L. semotus) distant/removed

semper, (L. semper) always/on each occasion

semyda, (Gr. σημυδα) probably the Judas tree (*Cercis siliquastrum*)

sen -ex -i, (L. senex) old/aged/an old person

sen -i, (L. seni) six at a time/six each

senari, (L. senarius) composed of six

senect, (L. senectus) old/aged

senesc, (L. senescere) to grow old/to loose power/to wane

senex, (L. senex) old

seni, (L. senilis) an old person

senicul -us, (L. seniculus) an old man

senil -i, (L. senilis) senile/of old people

sens, (L. sensilis) sensitive/with feelings

sens, (L. sensus) sense

sensor, (L. sensorium) an organ of sense

sent -i, (L. sentio) feel/experience/feel the force of

senti -s, (L. sentis) a thorn bush/briar

sentina, (L. sentina) bilge water

seorsus, (L. seorsum) apart/separately

sepedo, (Gr. σηπεδων) decay/putrefaction/rottenness/mortification

sepi, (L. saepes) a hedge/fence

sepi, (L. saepire) to hedge in/enclose/fence in

sepia, (Gr. σηπια) a cuttlefish (*Sepia*)/squid/ink

sepicula, (L. sepicula) small hedge/small fence

sepiment, (L. sepimentum) fence/hedge

sepion, (Gr. σηπιον) the internal shell (pro-ostracum) of a squid

seps -i -is, (Gr. σεψις) fermentation/putrefaction/decay

seps, (Gr. σηψ) a putrefying sore/a serpent (whose bite causes intense thirst)/a lizard

sept -em -en, (L. septem) seven

sept -i -o -um, (L. saeptum) partition/barrier/enclosure/fence/hedge

sept -i -o, (Gr. σηπτικος) putrefactive/septic

septen -ari, (L. septenarius) containing seven

septendecim, (L. septendecim) seventeen

septentrion -al, (L. septemtrionalis) northern

septim -us, (L. septimus) seventh

septuagesi, (L. septuagesimus) seventieth

septuagint, (L. septuaginta) seventy

sepulcrum, (L. sepulcrum) grave/tomb

sequa -c -x, (L. sequax) following/attending

sequen, (LL. sequentia) sequence

sequest -er -r, (L. sequester) a depository/an agent/a mediator

ser -i -o -um, (L. serum) whey/serum/watery part of fluids

ser -o -otin, (L. sero) late/acting late/too late

sera, (L. sera) a movable bar for fastening doors

seran -g -x, (Gr. σραγξ) a cave hollowed out by water/lion's den

serapi -ado -as, (Gr. Σαραπις) an orchid/an Egyptian god/a white Persian robe with purple stripes

seren, (L. sereno) make clear/serene/bright

seri -do -s, (Gr. σερις) endive or chicory (*Chicorium endivia* or *C. intybus*)
seri, (L. serere) to put in a row/to join together
seria, (L. seria) a large, earthen jar for wine or oil
seric -a -ar -e -o, (Gr. σηρικος) silk/silken
seric, (LL. Sericus) Chinese/silken
serili, (L. serilium) rope/cordage
serius, (L. serius) grave/earnest
sermo -n, (L. sermonis) talk/discourse/conversation
sero, (L. sertus) join/knit/connect
serotinus, (L. serotinus) happening late
serp, (L. serpens) a creeping animal/serpent
serpent -ar -i, (L. serpentis) a creeping animal/serpent
serph -o -us, (Gr. σερφος) a small winged insect
serpul -a -o, (L. serpula) a little snake
serr -a -at -i, (L. serra) a saw
serraculum, (L. serraculum) a rudder
serrat, (L. serratus) toothed like a saw
sert -a, (L. serta) a garland/wreath
sert, (L. sertum) connected/joined/put in a row/linked
serus, (L. serus) late
serv -a -i -us, (L. servus) a slave/subject
ses -i, (Gr. σης) a moth
sesam -e, (Gr. σεσαμη) sesame (*Sesamum indicum*)
sesel -i, (Gr. σεσελις) several types of shrub
sesi, (Gr. σεσις) sifting
sesqui, (L. sesqui) one and a half
sess, (L. sedere) to sit
sessil, (L. sessilis) sitting on/sedentary/of plants - low/dwarf
sest, (Gr. σησις) sifting
sestr -o -um, (Gr. σηστρον) a sieve
set -a -i, (L. seta) a bristle
set -o, (Gr. σης) a moth/bookworm
setanios, (Gr. σητανειος) this year's
seth -o -us, (Gr. σηθω) sieve/sift
sever, (L. severus) harsh/rigorous
sex -a, (L. sex) six
sexagesim, (L. sexagesimus) sixtieth
sexagint, (L. sexaginta) sixty
sext, (L. sextus) sixth
sexu, (L. sexus) sex
-ship, (AS. -scipe), state, office, art
si -o, (Gr. σειω) move to and fro/shake
siag -on, (Gr. σιαγων) the jaw-bone/jaw/cheek
sial -i -o, (Gr. σιαλον) saliva/spittle
sial -o, (Gr. σιαλος) a fat hog/fat/grease
siali -s, (Gr. σιαλις) a kind of bird
-sialum, (Gr. σιαλον) saliva
sib, (OE. sibling) relative
sibil, (L. sibila) hissing
sibyl, (Gr. Σιβυλλα) a female soothsayer
sibyn -e -o, (Gr. σιβυνη) a hunting spear/spear/pike
sica, (L. sica) a dagger/dirk/poniard
sicari -us, (Gr. σικαριος) an assassin/murderer
sicc, (L. siccus) dry
sicilis, (L. sicilis) sickle
sicinis, (Gr. σικιννις) a satyric dance
siclus, (Gr. σικλος) a shekel

sicul, (L. sicula) little dagger

sicy -o -us, (Gr. σικυος) a cucumber (*Cucumis sativus*)

sid -a, (Gr. σιδη) the pomegranate tree (*Punica* spp.) and fruit/a type of water plant

sid -eri -us, (L. sidereus) starry/of the stars

sider -a -o -us, (Gr. σιδηρος) iron

sidere, (L. sidereus) starry

sido, (L. sidere) to sit down/settle/alight

sig -a -an -o, (Gr. σιγας) silent/silence

sigal, (Gr. σιγαλεος) silent/still

sigaloma, (Gr. σιγαλωμα) a tool for smoothing or polishing

sigalos/sigelos, (Gr. σιγαλος) mute/silent

sigill -a -o, (L. sigilla) small figures/images/a seal

siglos, (Gr. σιγλος) a shekel/earring

sigm -a -ato -o, (Gr. σιγμα) s-shaped

sigma, (Gr. σιγμα σ ς Σ) the eighteenth letter of the Greek alphabet

sigmo, (Gr. σιγμος) the hissing of a tortoise

sign -i -um, (L. signum) sign/mark/token

sigo, (Gr. σιγη) silence

sigras, (Gr. σιγρας) a wild fig

sigyno, (Gr. σιγυνες) a spear

sil -o, (L. silus) flat-nosed/snub-nosed/pug-nosed

sil, (L. sil) a kind of yellow earth/yellow ochre

silanus, (Gr. σιληνος) a fountain or jet of water

silen -t, (L. silentium) silence/stillness/quietness

silenus, (Gr. Σειλννος) a bearded, bald, woodland deity

silex, (L. silex) flint/any hard stone/crag/rock/cliff

silic -i, (L. silicis) flint

silic, (L. silex) flint

siliqu -a, (L. siliqua) a pod/husk/shell

sillo, (Gr. σιλλος) squint-eyed/satirical poem/satire

silph -a, (Gr. σιλφη) cockroach/bookworm

silphi -um, (Gr. σιλφιον) laserwort (*Ferula* sp.), a medicinal and food plant

silub -o -um, (Gr. σιλλυβος) a type of thistle (*Silybum* sp.)

silur, (L. Silures) a tribe of South Wales

silur, (L. silurus) a type of river fish

silus, (L. silus) pug-nosed

silv -a -at -estr -i, (L. Silvanus) a god of the woods/woods/trees

silvi, (L. silvi-) forest-

silyb -o -um, (Gr. σιλλυβος) a type of thistle (*Silybum* spp.)

sim -o, (Gr. σιμος) snub-nosed/flat-nosed

simbl -o -us, (Gr. σιμβλος) bee-hive/any store or hoard

simi -a -us, (L. simias) an ape/monkey

simil, (L. similis) similar/like

simoma, (Gr. σιμωμα) anything turned up/upturned ship's bow

simpl -ex -ic -ici, (L. simplici-) simple

simpul, (L. simpulum) small ladle

simpuvium, (L. simpuvium) a kind of bowl

simul, (L. simul) at once/together/at the same time

simula, (L. simulare) to simulate/make a copy

simus, (Gr. σιμος) flat-nosed

sin -a -o, (Gr. Σιναι) Chinese

sin -a, (Gr. σινας) destructive

sinamor, (Gr. σιναμωρος) hurtful/mischievous

sinapi -s, (L. sinapis) mustard

sincer, (L. sincerus) pure/unmixed/genuine

sincip -it -ut, (L. sinciput) the forehead

sindon, (Gr. σινδονη) muslin

sindron, (Gr. σινδρων) mischievous
sinens, (NL. sinensis) of China
singul -ar, (L. singularis) separate/solitary/alone/individual
sini -o -um, (Gr. σινιον) a sieve
sinido, (Gr. σινις) ravager/plunderer/destroyer
sinis, (L. sinister) left
sinist -er -r, (L. sinister) left/on the left/wrong/perverse/unfavourable
sino, (Gr. σινος) harm/hurt/damage
sintor, (Gr. σιντωρ) ravenous/tearing
sinu -a -o -s, (L. sinus) curve/fold/a bay/gulf/a hollow
sio, (Gr. σειω) shake/move to and fro
-sion, (L.) suf. meaning act of, process of, having the nature of
siopelo, (Gr. σιωπηλος) silent
sipal -o, (Gr. σιπαλος) ugly/purblind
siparium, (L. siparium) a theatre curtain/sun blind
siphl -o, (Gr. σιφλος) crippled/maimed/mad
siphn -e, (Gr. σιφνευς = ασπαλαξ) the blind rat (*Spalax typhlus*)
siphn -o, (Gr. σιφνος = σιφλος) crippled/maimed/mad
sipho -n -no, (Gr. σιφων) a reed/straw/any tube
siphunc, (L. siphunculus) little tube
sipya/sipydnos, (Gr. σιπυη/συπιδνος) a meal-tub
sircul, (L. sircula) a kind of grape
siren, (Gr. Ζειρην) a fabulous monster/a deceitful woman/a bewitching woman
sirius, (Gr. Σειριος) the dog-star
-sis, (Gr. -σις) suf. ind. the act of/the process of/an action of a general or abstract nature
sismos, (Gr. σισμος) a hissing
sistr -um, (L. sistrum) a type of rattle (used in the worship of Isis)
sisymbr -i -ium -o, (Gr. σισυμβριον) bergamont or water mint (*Mentha aquatica*)/water-
cress (*Nasturtium officionale*)
sisyr -a -o, (Gr. σισυρα) a goat's-hair cloak
sit -i -io -o -us, (Gr. σιτος) food/wheat/corn/grain/flour/bread
sit -u -us, (L. situs) a layout/site/position/place
sitis, (L. sitis) thirst/dryness
sitt -a, (Gr. σιττη) a nuthatch (*Sitta europaea*)
sittybus, (L. sittybus) a strip of parchment
situla, (L. situla) a bucket or urn for drawing water or drawing lots
sixis, (Gr. σιξις) a hissing
sk see also sc
skat, (Gr. σκατος) dung
skelet -o, (Gr. σκελετος) hardened/dried up/withered
skelo, (Gr. σκελος) the leg
skeptic -o, (Gr. σκεπτικος) thoughtful/reflective
skia, (Gr. σκιη) a shadow/shade/dark colour
skler -o, (Gr. σκληρος) hard/stiff/harsh/bitter
skolio, (Gr. σκολιος) curved/bent/winding/twisted/crooked
skoto, (Gr. σκοτος) darkness/gloom
smaragd -o, (Gr. σμαραγδος) name of several green stones, including emerald
smari -s, (Gr. σμαρις) a small sea-fish (*Smaris vulgaris*)
smectic, (Gr. σμηκτικος) cleansing
smegma -to, (Gr. σμηγμα = σμημα) soap/unguent
smenos, (Gr. σμηνος) beehive/swarm of bees
smerdal -eo, (Gr. σμερδαλεος) terrible
smeringo, (Gr. σμεριγξ) a bristle
smerinth -o -us, (Gr. σμηρινθος) a cord/line/string
smicro, (Gr. σμικρος) Ionic for *micros* - little
smil -a -o, (Gr. σμιλη) a carving knife

smila -c -x, (Gr. σμιλαξ) the holm-oak (*Quercus ilex*)/yew (*Taxus baccata*)/kidney bean (*Phaseolus vulgaris*)/various bindweeds (*Calystegis/Convolvulus* spp.)

sminth -us, (Gr. σμινθος) field mouse

sminye, (Gr. σμινυη) a two-pronged hoe

smodi -c -ng -x, (Gr. σμοδιξ) weal/swollen bruise

sobar -o, (Gr. σοβαρος) rushing/violent/swaggering/pompous

sobe, (Gr. σοβη) a horse's tail

sobetes, (Gr. σοβητης) a frightener

sobol -es -i, (L. soboles = suboles) a sprout/shoot/sucker

sobrin -us, (L. sobrina/sobrinus) a female cousin/male cousin

soc -a -o -us, (L. socius) companion/ally

soccus, (L. soccus) a low-heeled, light shoe

soci, (L. sociare) to unite

socius, (L. socius) a companion/associate

soco, (Gr. σωκος) the stout one/the strong one

socors, (L. socors) weak minded/stupid/silly

sodal -i -is, (L. sodalis) a member of an association/secret society/a companion

sol -a, (L. sol) the sun

sol -i -o, (L. solitarius) alone/solitary/lonely

sol -um, (L. solum) the lowest part or bottom/foundation/floor

-sol, (L. solutus) dissolved

solan -a -um, (L. solanum) a nightshade (*Solanum* spp.)

solar -i, (L. solaris) of the sun

sole -a, (L. solea) a sandal/a fetter/a fish (the sole - *Solea* Spp.)

solen -i -o, (Gr. σωληv) a channel/gutter/pipe

solic, (L. solictio) disturb/temp

solid, (L. solidus) solid/firm/dense

solit, (L. solitus) customary/habitual

solitari, (L. solitarius) alone/solitary/lonely

solium, (L. solium) royal seat/throne

soller, (L. sollers) skilled/clever/adroit

sollus, (L. sollus) entire/complete

solo, (L. solo) alone/solitary

solon, (Gr. Σολων) a celebrated Athenian legislator

solor, (L. solor) comfort/soothe

solos, (Gr. σολος) a mass of iron

solox, (L. solox) coarse/rough/bristly

solpug, (L. solpuga) a kind of venomous spider (or ant)

solu, (L. solus) alone/only/sole

solu, (L. solutus) loosened/unbound/free/dissolved

solum, (L. solum) the bottom of any thing/ground/floor/earth

solv -o, (L. solvere) to loosen/untie/release/dissolve

-som, -some, (AS. -sum), like/full of/having the quality of

soma -t -o, (Gr. σωμα) the body

somch -us, (Gr. σονχος) the sow-thistle (*Sonchus* spp.)

somn -i --ium -us, (L. somnus) sleep/slumber

somph -o, (Gr. σομφος) spongy/porous

son -a -it -o, (L. sonitus) a sound/noise/thunder

sonor -o, (L. sonor) a sound/noise/din

sontic, (L. sonticus) serious/dangerous

soph -o, (Gr. σοφος) skilled in many crafts or arts/wise/learned/prudent

sophistic, (Gr. σοφιστικος) artful/contrived

sophron -o, (Gr. σωφρων) of sound mind/discreet

-sophy, (Gr. σοφια) wisdom/skill

sopor -i, (L. sopor) deep sleep/laziness/inactivity

sor -i -o -us, (Gr. σορος) a vessel for holding human remains (cinerary urn)

-sor, (L.) suf. ind. agent

sorac, (Gr. σωρακος) basket/hamper
sorb -a -us, (L. sorbus) the service-tree (*Sorbus* spp.)
sorb, (L. sorbere) to suck in/drink down/swallow
sord -id, (L. sordidus) dirty/filthy/shabby
sorex, (L. sorex) a shrew (Soricidae)
soric, (L. soricinus) of a shrew
soror -i, (L. soror) a sister
soros, (Gr. σορος) coffin/cinerary urn
sorpt, (L. sorbere) to suck in/drink down/swallow
sort -i, (L. sortis) a lot/fate/prophecy/fortune/destiny
sor -o -us, (L. soros Gr. σωρος) heap/mound/quantity
sos -i, (Gr. σως) safe and sound/alive and well/sure/certain
sospes, (L. sospes) saving/delivering
sostr -o, (Gr. σωστρα) a reward for saving one's life/physician's fee/thank-offering
sot -er -eri, (Gr. σωτηρ) saviour/deliverer
soucho, (Gr. σουχος) name of the crocodile in Egypt
soz -o, (Gr. σωζω) saved/preserved/kept alive
spad, (Gr. σπαδιζω) strip off
spadi -c -x, (Gr. σπαδιξ) a palm frond/palm-coloured/lyre-like stringed instrument
spadice, (NL. spadiceus) bright brown
spado -n, (Gr. σπαδος) a eunuch/a castrated individual
spala -ci -co -x, (Gr. σπαλαξ) a mole rat (*Spalax typhlus*)
span -o, (Gr. σπανος) rare/uncommon/lacking
spara -ct -gm -ss -xi, (Gr. σπαραγμα) piece torn off/shred/fragment
sparass -o, (Gr. σπαρασσω) tear/rend/pull to pieces/retch/convulse
sparg, (Gr. σπαργαω) swell/full to bursting/ripe
sparg, (L. spargere) to strew/sprinkle/scatter
spargan, (Gr. σπαργανον) the bur reed (*Sparganium* spp.)/swaddling clothes/swathing
spargos, (Gr. σπαργωσις) distension/swelling
spars, (L. sparsus) spread out/scattered/speckled/spotted
spart -e -i -o, (Gr. σπαρτη/σπαρτον) a rope/cable/measuring cord
spart -o, (Gr. σπαρτος) sown/cultivated/grow from seed
spasm -a -at -o -us, (Gr. σπασμος) tension/convulsion/spasm/fit/violent agitation (as of
            the sea)
spaso, (Gr. σπαω) to pluck off/tear/drag away
spastic, (Gr. σπαστικος) drawing in/absorbing
spat, (L. spatium) space
spatal, (Gr. σπαταλιον) bracelet
spatalos, (Gr. σπαταλος) wanton/lascivious
spatang -es, (Gr. σπαταγγης) a sea urchin (*Spatangus* spp.)
spath -a -i -o, (Gr. σπαθη) any broad blade
spati -um, (L. spatium) a space/extent/room/interval
spatil -a -o, (Gr. σπατιλη) thin excrement (as in diarrhoea)
spatul -a, (L. spathula) a small spoon/a two-edged sword lacking a point
spe -o, (Gr. σπεος) cavern/grotto
spec, (L. speculum) mirror
speci, (L. specere) look at
specie, (L. species) particular kind
specios, (L. speciosus) beautiful/splendid/handsome
spect, (L. specto) observe/watch/contemplate
spectabili, (L. spectabilis) visible/notable/remarkable
spectr -o, (L. spectrum) image/apparition
specu -s, (L. specus) a cave/hole/hollow
specul -a, (L. specula) a watch tower/look-out
specula -t, (L. speculator) a spy/scout/observer/investigator
speculum, (L. speculum) a mirror/image/copy
specus, (L. specus) cave/den

speir -o, (Gr. σπειρα) anything twisted or wound/coils of a serpent/rope/cord
speir -o, (Gr. σπειρω) sow/scatter/disperse/engender/beget
speirem, (Gr. σπειρημα) a fold/coil/spire
spel -ae -ea -eo -o, (Gr. σπηλαιον) cave/grotto/pit
spelt, (AS. spelt) a kind of wheat
speos, (Gr. σπεος) cavern/grotto
spep, (Gr. σηψις) putrefaction
sperat, (L. speratus) expected
sperchnos, (Gr. σπερχνος) hasty/hurried
sperg, (L. spergere) to strew
sperm -a -at -ato -i -o, (Gr. σπερμα) a seed
spernax, (L. spernax) despising/contemptuous
spes, (L. spes) expectation
speudo, (Gr. σπευδω) hasten/quicken
sphacel -o -us, (Gr. σφακελος) gangrene/mortification
sphaco, (Gr. σφακος) sage (*Salvia* spp.)/a kind of lichen found on oaks
sphacto, (Gr. σφακτος) slain
sphadasm -o -us, (Gr. σφαδασμος) spasm/convulsion
sphere -a -i -o, (Gr. σαφαρι) a sphere/ball/globe
sphag -e, (Gr. σφαγευς) butcher/slayer/cut-throat
sphag -i, (Gr. σφαγη) the throat
sphagi, (Gr. σφαγιον) victim/offering/sacrifice
sphagido, (Gr. σφαγις) a sacrificial knife
sphagn -um, (Gr. σφαγνος) a kind of moss (*Sphagnum* spp.)
sphago, (Gr. σφαξ) throat
sphaler -o, (Gr. σφαλερος) slippery/perilous/tottering/reeling
sphallo, (Gr. σφαλλος) a round, metal plate for throwing
sphalma, (Gr. σφαλμα) a false step/stumble
spharag -o, (Gr. σφαραγος) noisy/spluttering
sphe -ci -x, (Gr. σφηξ) a wasp (Vespidae)
spheag-, (Gr. σφραγις) a seal
sphedan -o, (Gr. σφεδανος) vehement/violent/eagerly
sphelas, (Gr. σφελας) a footstool/pedestal
sphen -a -o, (Gr. σφην) a wedge
sphendone, (Gr. σφενδονη) a sling (used as a bandage)
spher -a -o, (Gr. σφαιρα) a ball/sphere/globe
sphigm -o, (Gr. σφυγμος) the pulse/beating of the heart
sphin -ct -g -x, (Gr. σφιγκτηρ) tight band/that which binds tight
sphing -o, (Gr. σφιγγω) to draw tight/bind tight/squeeze/throttle
sphing, (Gr. Σφιγξ) the Sphinx
sphingia, (Gr. σφιγγια) greed
sphingion, (Gr. σφιγγιον) a bracelet/necklace
sphodr -o, (Gr. σφοδρος) vehement/violent/excessive
sphondylo, (Gr. σφονδυλος) vertebra
sphrag -i -is, (Gr. σφραγις) a seal/signet/gem for a ring
sphrig -o, (Gr. σφριγος) full strength
sphygm, (Gr. σφυγμος) the pulse/beating of the heart
sphyr -o, (Gr. σφυρα) a hammer/mallet
sphyr -o, (Gr. σφυρον) the ankle/foothills of a mountain range
sphyraena, (Gr. σφυραινα) a pike-like fish
spic -a -ul, (L. spica) spike/an ear of corn
spicul, (L. spiculum) small spike/dart/sting/sharp point
spiegel, (Ger. speigel) a mirror
spil -o -os -us, (Gr. σπιλος) spot/fleck/blemish/stain/cliff/rock
spilas, (Gr. σπιλας) a rock over which the sea dashes/slab/storm/squall
spilo, (Gr. σπιλος) rock/cliff

spin -a, (L. spina) thorn/spine
spinos, (L. spinosus) thorny/obscure
spinter, (L. spinter) a kind of bracelet
spinthar -i -is, (Gr. σπινθαρις) a spark
spinther -o, (Gr. σπινθηρ) a spark
spio, (L. Speio) a sea nymph
spion, (L. spionia) a kind of grapevine
spir -a, (L. spira Gr. σπειρα) a coil/anything coiled
spirac -l -ul -ulum, (L. spiraculum) an air hole
spirat, (L. spiratus) breath
-spire, (L. spirare) breathe
spirem -a -at, (Gr. σπειρημα) coil/convolution/twisted thread/rolled bandage
spiro, (L. spirare) to breathe/blow/breathe out/exhale
spiss -a -at -i, (L. spissus) close/dense/thick/tardy/difficult
spitham, (Gr. σπιθαμη) a hand's span
spiz -a, (Gr. σπιζα) a chaffinch (*Fringilla* spp.)
spizias, (Gr. σπιζιας) a sparrow hawk (*Accipiter* spp.)
splanch -i -o -um, (Gr. σπλαγχνα) the viscera/inward parts/entrails
splen -i -ico -o, (Gr. σπλην) the spleen
splen, (L. splenium Gr. σπλενιον) patch
spod -i -o, (Gr. σποδος) wood ashes/embers/dust/oxide
spolia -t, (L. spolium) booty/plunder
sponda, (L. sponda) bedstead/bed
sponde, (Gr. σπονδη) drink-offering/libation
spondeo, (L. spondeo) promise/pledge
spondyl -o, (Gr. σφονδυλος) a vertebra
spong -i -ia -io -o, (L. spongia Gr. σπογγιη/σφογγια) a sponge
sponsa, (L. sponsa) a bride
spor -a -i -o, (Gr. σπορος) a seed/produce/a crop/a sowing
sporad -o, (Gr. σποραδην) scattered
sporid, (Gr. σποριδιον) little seed
sporta, (L. sporta) basket/hamper
spret, (L. spretus) despised/scorned
spuda -st, (Gr. σπουδη) haste/speed/zeal/effort/esteem/regard
spudo, (Gr. σπουδη) zeal/exertion
spui, (L. spui) spit out
spum -a, (L. spuma) foam/froth/scum
spurc, (L. spurcus) dirty/filthy/unclean/impure
spuri, (L. spurius) illegitimate/false
sput -um, (L. sputum) spittle
spyr -id -o, (Gr. σπυρις) a large basket
spyras, (Gr. σπυρας/σφυρας) a ball of dung
sqalor, (L. squalor) roughness/stiffness
squal -us, (L. squalus) a dog fish (*Squalus* spp.)
squal, (L. squaleo) to be rough
squalid, (L. squalidus) rough/stiff/squalid/dirty
squam -a -at -i -o, (L. squama) a fish scale
squamo, (L. squamosus) of the nature of a scale
squarros, (LL. squarrosus) scurfy/scaly/rough
squatina, (L. squatina) a skate
squilla (scilla), (L. squilla/scilla) a sea-leek (*Scilla* spp.)/a small lobster, perh. a crayfish
stabil -i, (L. stabilis) firm
stach -ys, (Gr. σταχυς) an ear of corn
stact -o, (Gr. στακτος) oozing out in drops/trickling/distilling
staeto, (Gr. σταιτος) dough
stag -eto -ma -mat -mo, (Gr. σταγμα) that which drips/honey/aromatic oil/perfume
stagn -a -i -um, (L. stagnum) standing water/pool/pond/marsh

stal, (L. stare) to stand

stala -ct -gm -gma, (Gr. σταλαγμα) that which drops/a drop/dropping/dripping

stalico, (Gr. σταλιξ) a stake to which nets are fastened

stalsis, (Gr. σταλσις) a constriction/staunching/checking

stalt, (Gr. σταλτεον) one must constrict/staunch/check

stam -en -in, (L. stamen) an upright thread (warp)/anything standing upright/a stamen

stamn -o, (Gr. σταμνος) a wine jar

stann -i -um, (L. stannum) an alloy of silver and lead/tin

stape -di -s, (L. stapes) a stirrup/the stapes (a bone of the inner ear)

staphi -s, (Gr. σταφις) a raisin

staphyl -a -o, (Gr. σταφυλη) a bunch of grapes/a cluster

staphylin -us, (Gr. σταφυλινος) the wild and domestic carrot (*Daucus* spp.)/a beetle, prob. *Meloe* spp.

stas -i -is, (Gr. στασις) placing/setting/standing

stat -i -o, (Gr. στατικος) causing to stand

stat -o, (Gr. στατος) stationary/standing

stater, (Gr. στατηρ) a weight/a coin

stath, (Gr. σταθμος) standing place/dwelling/resting station

stathme, (Gr. σταθμη) a carpenter's rule/line

stathmo, (Gr. σταθμος) stall/stable/abode/post

static -e -o, (Gr. στατη/στατκη) an astringent herb (thrift - *Armeria* spp.)

stato, (Gr. στατος) fixed/placed/standing

statumen, (L. statumen) support/prop

staur -o -us, (Gr. σταυρος) an upright stake/a pale/a cross (for crucifixion)

staxi -s, (Gr. σταξις) a dropping

stea -r -t -to, (Gr. στεαρ) suet/hard fat/tallow

steg -an -ano -no -o, (Gr. στεγη/στεγα) a roof/covered place/ship's deck/tent

stegano, (Gr. στεγανος) covered

stegn, (Gr. στεγνος) watertight/a covered dwelling

stego, (Gr. στεγη) roof/ceiling/roofed place

steir -a, (Gr. στειρα) forepart of a ship's keel, continuing into the stem or cutwater

steir -o, (Gr. στειρος) of females - sterile/barren

stel -a -id -o, (Gr. στηλωμα) a block of stone/pillar/monument

stele -o, (Gr. στελεος) a haft/shaft/handle

stelgi -do -s, (Gr. στελγις/στλεγγις) a scraper used in washing/bathing

stelis, (Gr. στελις) a kind of mistletoe (*Viscum* sp.)

stell -a -i -o, (L. stella) a star

stellio, (L. stellio) a spotted lizard

stello, (Gr. στελλω) arrange/array/dispatch

stelm -a, (Gr. στελμα/στεμμα) wreath/garland/chaplet

stem -a -o, (Gr. στημα) a stamen

stemma -to, (Gr. στεμμα) wreath/garland

sten -o, (Gr. στενος) narrow/the narrows/straits

stenagma, (Gr. στεναγμα) sigh/groan/moan

stenos, (Gr. στενος) narrow

stentor, (Gr. Στεντωρ) A Greek famous for his loud voice/a loud voice/trumpet

stenygro, (Gr. στενυγρος) narrow pass/straight

steph -ano -anus -o, (Gr. στεφανος) a crown/wreath/something which surrounds or encompasses

sterc -o -or -us, (L. stercus) dung/manure

sterctico, (Gr. στερκτικος) affection

stere -o -ic, (Gr. στερεος) solid/firm/stiff/stark

steres -is, (Gr. στερεσις) deprivation/loss/confiscation/negation

stergema, (Gr. στεργημα) a love charm

stericto, (Gr. στηρικτος) fixed/firmly set

sterigma -to, (Gr. στηριγμα) support/foundation

steril -i, (L. sterilis) unfruitful/barren/sterile

steringo, (Gr. στεριγξ) support/prop

steriph -o, (Gr. στεριφος) firm/solid/barren/unfruitful

stern -o -um, (Gr. στερνον L. sternum) the breast/chest/sternum

sternax, (L. sternax) that throws the rider/throwing to the ground

sternu -t, (L. sternuere) to sneeze/of a light - to crackle or splutter

stero, (Gr. στεαρ) suet/hard fat

sterop, (Gr. στεροπη) poet. flash of lightning

sterpho, (Gr. στερφος) hide/skin

sterquil, (L. sterquilinum) a dung heap/dung pit

sterr -ho -o, (Gr. στερρος) stiff/firm/solid/hard/rugged

stert, (L. stertere) to snore

steth -o -us, (Gr. στηθος) the breast/chest

sthen -ar -o -us, (Gr. σθενος) strength/might/prowess

stia, (Gr. στια) pebble/small stone

stib -a, (Gr. στιβη) hoar frost/rime

stib -i, (L. stibium Gr. στιβι) antimony

stib -o -us, (Gr. στιβος) a trodden track/path/footstep

stibado, (Gr. στιβας) bed/mattress

stich -o -us, (Gr. στιχος) a row/line/rank

stichari -um, (Gr. στιχαριον) a variegated tunic

stict -o, (Gr. στικτος) pricked/tattooed/spotted/dappled/punctured

stigeus, (Gr. στιγευς) tattooer

stigm -a -at -ato -o, (Gr. στιγμη) a mark/spot/stud/brand/pricking

stil -a, (Gr. στιλη) a drop/little bit/a moment

stil -us, (L. stilus) a stake/pale/a writing implement

stilb, (Gr. στιλβω) glitter/gleam/twinkle/shine/be bright

stilba, (Gr. στιλβη) a lamp/mirror

still -a -ic, (L. stilla) a drop

stilpn -o -os, (Gr. στιλπνος) gleaming/glittering

stilus, (L. stilus) a stake/a pen for writing on waxen tablets

stimul -a -us, (L. stimulus) a goad/sting/torment

stinct, (L. stinctus) quenched

stinct, (L. stinguere) to prick

stino, (Gr. στεινος) confined/narrow/close

stipat -io -ni -us, (L. stipare) to crowd/press closely together/surround

stipator, (L. stipator) an attendant/follower

stipes, (L. stipes) stalk/tree trunk/log/stump/branch/club

stiphr -o, (Gr. στιφρος) firm/solid/stout

stipi -ti, (L. stipitis) stalk/tree trunk/log/stump/branch/club

stipt -o, (Gr. στιπτος) trodden down/crammed/packed/tough/sturdy

stipule, (L. stipula) little stalk

stiri -a, (L. stiria) an icicle

stiro, (Gr. στειρος) sterile/barren

stirp -i -s, (L. stirps) the stock or stem of a tree - with the roots

stiva, (L. stiva) a plough handle

stixi -s, (Gr. στιξις) a spot or mark

stiz -o, (Gr. στιζω) a tattoo/identity mark

stlengido, (Gr. στλεγγις) a scraper

stoa, (Gr. στοα/στοια) a cloister/roofed colonnade/gallery/storehouse/magazine

stocho, (Gr. στοχος) aim at/shoot at/guess/pillar of brick

stoichi -o, (Gr. στοιειωδης) elementary/of the nature of an element

stol -a -o, (L. stola) a long outer garment/robe worn by musicians

stolid, (L. stolidus) stupid/dull/foolish/obtuse

stolido, (Gr. στολιδωδες) full of folds

stolis, (Gr. στολις) a leather jerkin

stolmus, (Gr. στολμος) raiment
stolo -n -ni, (L. stolon) a shoot/twig
stolos, (Gr. στολος) journey/voyage
stom -a -ato -o, (Gr. στομα) the mouth
stomach -i -o -us, (Gr. στομαχος) the throat/gullet/stomach
stomachos, (L. stomachosus) peevish/irritable
stomb -o, (Gr. στομβος) deep-voiced/deep-roaring
stomot, (Gr. στομωτος) hardened
stomph -ac-o, (Gr. στομφαξ) a ranter
stomphos, (Gr. στομφος) bombastic/lofty phrases
stomyl -o, (Gr. στωμυλλω) to be talkative/chatter/babble
stonos, (Gr. στονος) sighing/groaning
stony -cho -x, (Gr. στονυξ) a sharp point/of a boar's tusk/of a fish's barb
storea, (L. storea) a rush mat
storthy -a -o -ng, (Gr. στορθυγξ) point/spike/tyne of a deer's antler/boar's tusk/spike of
          land
strab -i -ism -o, (Gr. στραβος) squinting
strabelo, (Gr. στραβηλος) a kind of snail or shellfish/wild olive
stragul -um, (L. stragulus) a covering/carpet
stram -en -in -ine, (L. stramentum) straw/litter
stran -g -x, (Gr. στραγξ) trickle/drop
strang -o, (Gr. στραγγος) twisted/crooked/complicated/irregular/shameless
strangale, (Gr. στραγγαλη) a halter/choke
strangalis, (Gr. στραγγαλις) a knot
strangos, (Gr. στραγγος) twisted/crooked/complicated/irregular
strangulat, (L. strangulatus) choked/strangled
strat -age -eg, (Gr. στρατεγις) of the general
strat -i -um, (L. stratum) a layer/a covering/a bed covering/saddle-cloth/pavement
strat -io -o, (Gr. στρατειος) a warrior, particularly Zeus
stratos, (Gr. στρατος) army
strebl -o -os, (Gr. στρεβλη) twisted cords/instrument of torture
strebula, (L. strebula) the flesh around the haunches
stremma -to, (Gr. στρεμμα) twist/roll/wrench/sprain
stren -o, (Gr. στρηνης) harsh/rough - especially of sounds/insolence/arrogance
strena, (L. strena) a favourable sign/omen
strene, (Gr. στρηνης) rough/harsh
strenu, (L. strenuus) active/vigorous/brisk/prompt
streper, (L. strepere) to make a loud noise/clatter/creak/rattle/clash
streph -o, (Gr. στρεφω) turn about/twist/plait/wheel around/torture
strepit -an, (L. strepitans) noisy
strepsi -s, (Gr. στρεψις) turning round/deceit/twisted
strept -o -os, (Gr. στρεπτος) easily twisted/pliant
stria -t, (L. stria) a groove/furrow/channel
strict, (L. strictus) drawn together/bound/tight/rigid/severe/strict
strid -en -or -ul, (L. stridere) to make a harsh noise/to creak/grate/hiss
strig -a, (L. striga) ridge/furrow
strig -i -o, (Gr. στριξ L. strix) a screech owl (Strigidae)
strigat, (L. striga) a row of grain/a bristle
strigil -is, (L. strigilis) a scraper used in washing/bathing
strigos, (L. strigosus) thin/lean/dry/meagre
stringen, (L. stringere) to bind/fold tightly /compress
striol -a, (L. striola) small channel/small furrow
striphno, (Gr. στριπηνος) firm/hard/solid
strix, (L. strix Gr. στριξ) a screech owl (Strigidae)
strob -o, (Gr. στροβιλη) something twisted like a pine cone
strob -o, (Gr. στροβος) whirling around

strobil -o -us, (Gr. στροβιλος) spinning-top/whirlwind/cyclone/whirling dance/pine cone

stroma -t -to, (Gr. στρωμα) anything laid out for lying or sitting on/bedding/bed/horse-cloth

stromat -o, (Gr. στρωματευς) patchwork quilt

stromb -i -uli -us, (L. strombos) a spiral shell/a top

strongyl -o, (Gr. στρογγυλω) round off/well rounded

stroph -i -io -o, (Gr. στροφος) a twisted band, rope or cord/swaddling band/woman's girdle

strophe, (Gr. στροφη) a turning point

strophinx, (Gr. στροφιγξ) axle/pivot

strophis, (Gr. στροφις) a twister/rogue/slippery fellow

stroppus, (L. stroppus) a strap/thong

stroter, (Gr. στρωτηρ) a crossbeam

stroto -s, (Gr. στρωτος) spread/laid/covered

stru, (L. struere) to flow

struct, (L. structura) building/arrangement

strum -a -o, (L. struma) a scrofulous tumour

struthio -n, (L. struthionis Gr. στρουθιον) the ostrich (*Struthio camelus*)

strutho, (Gr. στρουθος) the sparrow (*Passer* spp.)

strychn -o -us, (Gr. στρυχνον/στρυχνος) sleepy nightshade (*Withania somnifera*)/the winter cherry (*Physalis alkekengi*)/hound's berry or black nightshade (*Solanum nigrum*)/thorn apple (*Datura stramonium*)

stryphn -o, (Gr. στρυφνος) sour/harsh/astringent/austere/stiff/rigid

stud -en, (L. studere) to be eager/be earnest/take pains

stult -i, (L. stultitia) foolishness/folly/silliness

stup -a -o, (L. stupa/stuppa) oakum (the coarse part of flax)

stup -e -id, (L. stupiditas) dullness/senselessness

stupro, (L. stuprare) ravish/defile/pollute

sturio -n, (LL. sterio) a sturgeon (*Acipenser sturio*)

sturn -i -us, (L. sturnus) a starling (Sturnidae)

styg -ano -er -et -no -o, (Gr. Στυγιος) Stygian - of the nether world/hateful/abominable

styl -o -us, (Gr. στυλος L. stylus) a pillar/post/pricker/a pointed instrument

stym -a, (Gr. στυμα) stiff/erect/priapism

stymphalis, (Gr. Στυμφαλις) myth. a man-eating bird in Arcadia

styp -h -t, (Gr. στυπτικος) astringent

styp -o -us, (Gr. στυπος) stem/stump/block

styphel -o, (Gr. στυφελος) hard/rough/astringent/sour/harsh/severe

styphl -o, (Gr. στυφλος) hard/rough/astringent/sour/harsh/severe

stypos, (Gr. στυπος) stem/stump

styr -ac -az -o, (Gr. στυραξ) a spike at the lower end of a spear-shaft/a gum-producing tree (*Styrax officionale*)

styx, (Gr. Στυξ) a river in the nether world

suas, (L. suasor) an advisor/recommender

sub -ex -ic, (L. subicio) throw up from below/build under

sub, (L. sub) under/underneath/close under

subatus, (L. subatus) estrual/being in heat, esp. of swine

subdolus, (L. subdolus) somewhat crafty

suber -i, (L. suber) the cork oak (*Quercus suber*)

suber, (L. suber) cork

subex, (L. subex) basal layer

subis, (L. subis) an unidentified bird

sublatus, (L. sublatus) raised aloft

sublestus, (L. sublestus) slight/trifling

sublica, (L. sublica) palisade

sublim, (L. sublimis) high/raised/lifted up/elevated/lofty

subnuba, (L. subnuba) rival

subruf -i, (L. subrufus) reddish/buff
subsessa, (L. subsessa) ambush
subter, (L. subter) beneath/below
subtilis, (L. subtilis) finely woven/thin/fine/slender
subucula, (L. subucula) shirt
subul -a, (L. subula) a shoemaker's awl
subulcus, (L. subulcus) swineherd
subulo, (L. subulo) a flute player
succ -us, (L. succus/sucus) juice/sap/a draught/potion
succis, (L. succisus) abruptly broken off/cut across from below/trimmed
succuba, (L. succuba) a female demon
succuss, (L. succussus) tossed up/flung/shaken
such -i -o -us, (Gr. σουχος) the name of the crocodile in Egypt
sucr -o, (Fr. sucre) sugar
suct -or, (L. suctum) suck/sucker
sucula, (L. sucula) piglet
sud -a -or -ori, (L. sudor) sweat/perspiration
sudi -s, (L. sudis) a stake/spike/point
suecic, (L. suecicus) Swedish
suf, (L. sufficio) put under/imbue/stain/steep/suffuse
sufflat, (L. sufflare) to blow up/inflate
suffrag -in -o, (L. suffrago) the ham on the hind leg of a quadruped
suffrag, (L. suffragor) support/approve/vote in favour of
suffult, (L. suffultus) propped up
sug -o, (L. sugere) to suck
suggrund, (L. suggrunda) the eaves of a house
sui, (L. suis) a pig (*Sus* sp.)
sulc -a -i -us, (L. sulcus) a furrow/groove/ditch/trench
sulf -o, (L. sulfer/sulphur/sulpur) sulfur/sulphur
sulph -o, (L. sulfer/sulphur/sulpur) sulfur/sulphur
sum-, (L. sub-) under
sumen, (L. sumen) breast/sow's udder
summ -a, (L. summus) highest/topmost
super, (L. super) over/above
superstes, (L. superstes) bystander/witness
supin, (L. supinus) bent backwards
supplic, (L. supplicare) to kneel/beseech/entreat/pray to the gods
suppra, (L. suppurare) to form pus/suppurate
supra, (L. supra) above/over/on the top
sur, (Fr. sur) over/on/above
sura, (L. sura) the lower part of the leg (calf)
surcul -us, (L. surculus) a young shoot/sprout/twig/sucker
surd -it, (L. surditas) deafness
surg, (L. surgo) rise/get up/stand up
surgeon, (Gr. χειρουργος) working with the hand
surgo, (L. surrectus) rise
surrogat, (L. surrogatus) substituted
sursum, (L. sursum) upwards/on high
surus, (L. Surus) a celebrated elephant in the Carthaginian army
sus, (L. suis) a pig (*Sus* spp.)
suscept, (L. susceptio) an undertaking
suscip, (L. suscipere) to take up/catch up/support/raise
suscito, (L. suscitare) to raise/arouse/stir up
susurr, (L. susurro) murmur/mutter/whisper/hum - of bees
sutil, (L. sutilis) stitched together/fastened together
sutor, (L. sutor) a cobbler
sutur -a, (L. sutura) a seam/suture
sy -g -l -m -n -s, (Gr. συμ-/συν-) pref. together/jointly/similarly/alike

syaco, (Gr. συαξ) a kind of fish

syaena, (Gr. συαινα) a sow

syba -co -x, (Gr. συβαξ) swinish/hog-like

sybari, (Gr. Συβαρις) myth. voluptuousness/luxury

sybot, (Gr. συβοτης) a swineherd

syc -a -i -o -um, (Gr. συκον) a fig (*Ficus* sp.)

sycamin -o -us, (Gr. συκαμινος) the mulberry tree (*Morus* spp.)

sychn -o -os, (Gr. συχνος) many/much/great/often/long/long time

sychneon, (Gr. συχνεων) thicket

syg/syl, (Gr. συγ-/συλ-) pref. together/jointly/similarly

syl, (Gr. συν-) with/together with/including/at the same time

syletes, (Gr. συλητης) robber

syllab, (Gr. συλλαβη) grip/hold/that which holds (or is held) together

sylleg -o, (Gr. συλλεγω) bring together/collect/gather/assemble

sylleps -s, (Gr. συλληψις) taking together/inclusion/seizing/conception/pregnancy

sylleptor, (Gr. συλλεπτωρ) partner/assistant

syllexis, (Gr. συλλεξις) contribution/selection by lot

sylli, (L. syllis) an annelid worm (*Syllis* spp.)

syllog -i -o, (Gr. συλλογη) gathering/collecting/raising/aggregation

sylph, (Gr. συλφη) a fairy-like spirit of the air

sylv -a -at -estr -i, (L. sylva) a wood/forest/plantation/grove/park

sym-, (Gr. συμ-) with/together with/including/at the same time

symbio, (Gr. συμβιος) living together

symbion, (Gr. συμβιωναι) to live with

symbiot, (Gr. συμβιωτης) companion

symmetr, (Gr. συμμετρια) symmetry/suitable relation/convenient size

symp -y, (Gr. συμπυκνοω) press close together/make compact/condense

sympher -o, (Gr. συμφερω) gather/collect/be useful/fitting/assist

symphora, (Gr. συμφορα) bringing together

symphy -o -so, (Gr. συμφυω) grow together/unite

symphysis, (Gr. συμφυσις) junction/seam

symplect, (Gr. συμπλεκτος) entwined

symploc -o, (Gr. συμπλοκη) intertwining/interweaving/complication/combination/ embrace/sexual intercourse

symptom -a -ato -o, (Gr. συμπτωμα) a chance occurrence/mishap/attribute

symptosi -s, (Gr. συμπτοσις) falling together/collapsing/meeting/meeting point

syn, (Gr. συν) with/together with/including/at the same time

-syna, (Gr. -συνη) suf. ind. condition/state/quality

synap -s -sis -t, (Gr. συναπτος) joined together/fastened/tied/a union

synapho, (Gr. συναφης) united

synapto, (Gr. συναπτος) joined together/linked together/united

synbas, (Gr. συμβασις) agreement

synchis, (Gr. συγχις) a shoe/sock

synclydo, (Gr. συγκλυς) mixed/promiscuous

syncop, (Gr. συγκοπη) cutting up into small pieces/cutting short

synd, (Gr. συνδεσις) binding together

syndesm -o -us, (Gr. συνδεσμος) that which binds together/ligament

synech -i -o, (Gr. συνεχω) hold together/keep together/confine/secure

synerg, (Gr. συνεργος) working together/accomplice

synesi -s, (Gr. συνεσις) uniting/union/sagacity/conscience/decision

syneth, (Gr. συνηθης) well-suited

syneto, (Gr. συνετος) intelligent/sagacious/wise

syniz, (Gr. συνιζησις) collapse

synoch -o, (Gr. συνοχος) joined together/in accord with

synoeco, (Gr. συνοικος) living in the same house/associated with

synoria, (Gr. συνορια) borderland
syntegma, (Gr. συντηγμα) a waste product
synthes -is, (Gr. συνθεσις) a putting together
syntresis, (Gr. συντρησις) a connection by a channel, passage or strait
synul -o, (Gr. συνουλοω) cause scar formation
synyphe, (Gr. συνυφη) a web/a construction
syphar -o, (Gr. συφαρ) a piece of old or wrinkled skin/slough/skin of milk
syphax, (Gr. συφαξ) sweet new wine
syphil -i -o, (Mod.L. syphilis) syphilis
syr, (Gr. συρ-) with/together with/including/at the same time
syrig -m, (Gr. συριγμα) the sound of a pipe/whistling
syrin -g -go -x, (Gr. συριγξ) a shepherd's pipe
syrizo, (Gr. συριζω) pipe/whistle/hiss
syrm -a -ato -o, (Gr. συρμα) anything trailed or dragged/sweepings/refuse/litter
syrma, (Gr. συρμα) a robe with a train/anything trailed or dragged along
syro, (Gr. συρω) drag/draw/sweep/trail
syrph -a -ac -ax -et, (Gr. συρφετος) anything dragged or swept together/sweepings/
          refuse/mixed crowd/rabble
syrph -o -us, (Gr. συρφος) a gnat
syrrho, (Gr. συρροος) flowing together
syrtes, (Gr. συρτης) cord/rein
syrti -do -s, (Gr. Συρτις) the Syrtis, two large shallow gulfs on the coast of Lybia, hence –
          sand banks
syrtos, (Gr. συρτος) washed along by a stream
sys, (Gr. συν-) with/together with/including/at the same time
sysci -o, (Gr. συσκιος) shaded/thickly shaded
syspasto, (Gr. συσπαστος) capable of being drawn together
systatic, (Gr. συστατικος) for putting together/acomponent/consolidating/
          confirmatory/introductory
systell, (Gr. συστελλω) draw together/contract
systema -t -to, (Gr. συστημα) a composite whole/assembly/system
systenos, (Gr. συστενος) tapering to a point
systol -o, (Gr. συστολη) a contraction/a drawing together
systom -o, (Gr. συστομος) with a narrow mouth/mouth to mouth
systremma, (Gr. συστρεμμα) anything aggregated or twisted together
systroph, (Gr. συστροφη) twisting together/turning round/gathering/condensation/
          aggregate
syzyg -o, (Gr. συζιγιος) united/paired/yoked

T

-ta, -tum, -tus, (L.) past participle suf.
tab -e -id, (L. tabeo) waste away/be consumed/to drip
tab -l -ul -ula, (L. tabula) a flat board/plank/table
taban -us, (L. tabanus) a horse-fly/gad-fly (Tabanidae)
tabe -s -t, (L. tabes) wasting away/decay/melting
tabel, (L. tabella) tablet/small flat board
tabern, (L. taberna) a booth/hut/cottage/hovel/shop
tabid, (L. tabidus) melting/wasting away/dissolving/decaying
tabul -a, (L. tabula) a flat board/plank/table
tacero, (Gr. τακερος) melting/tender/dissolving
tach -eo, (Gr. ταχα) quickly/presently

tach -in -inos -y, (Gr. ταχυς) quick/swift/fast/fleet
tach -o, (Gr. ταχος) speed
tacit, (L. tacitus) silent/without words/mute/quiet
tact -i, (L. tactio) a touching/sense of touch
tactic, (Gr. τακτικη) ordered/arrangement/tactics
taedios, (L. taedium) disgust/weariness/boredom
taeni -a -o, (Gr. ταινια L. taenia) a ribbon
tagax, (L. tagax) light fingered/thievish
tagenias, (Gr. ταγηνιας) a pancake
tagenon, (Gr. ταγενον) a frying pan/saucepan
tagma -to, (Gr. ταγμα) a division, brigade of soldiers/order/rank/status
tagos, (Gr. ταγος) commander/ruler/chief
tal -ari -i -o -us, (L. talua) the ankle/ankle bone/heel
tala -n, (Gr. ταλας) suffering/wretched/sorry
talaepor -i, (Gr. ταλαιπωρος) suffering/distressed/miserable
talant -o -um, (Gr. ταλαντον) a balance/a pair of scales
talaris, (L. talaris) of the ankle
talaros, (Gr. ταλαρος) a basket
talasios, (Gr. ταλασιος) of wool spinning
talea, (L. talea) a slender staff/rod/stick/cutting/set/layer
talent, (Gr. ταλαντον) an ancient weight and sum of money
talipes, (L. talipes) clubfoot
talis, (L. talis) of such a kind
talitrum, (L. talitrum) a rap with the knuckles
talla, (L. talla) an onion skin
talp, (L. talpa) a mole (*Talpa* spp.)
talpon, (L. talpona) a kind of grape vine
talus, (L. talus) the ankle/ankle bone/heel
tamia -s, (Gr. ταμιας) distributor/dispenser/steward/paymaster
tamia, (Gr. ταμια) housekeeper/housewife
tana -o, (Gr. ταναος) outstretched/tall/taper
tang -i -o, (L. tangere) to touch/reach/strike/push/hit/move/affect
tangen, (L. tangens) touching
tango, (Gr. ταγγος) rancid
tantus, (L. tantus) of such a size (large or small)
tany -o, (Gr. τανυω) stretch/strain/stretch out/lay out
tao -n -s, (Gr. ταος) the peacock (*Pavo cristatus*)
tape -s -to, (Gr. ταπης) a carpet/rug
tapein-o, (Gr. ταπεινος) low/low-lying/humbled/downcast
taph -o -r, (Gr. ταφος) funeral rites/grave/tomb/astonishment
taphr -o -us, (Gr. ταφρος) ditch/trench
tapin -o, (Gr. ταπεινος) low/low-lying/humbled/downcast
tarac -h -t, (Gr. ταραχη) disorder/disturbance/upheaval/tumult
taragma -to, (Gr. ταραγμα) disturbance/trouble
tarandus, (Gr. ταρανδος) reindeer (*Rangifer tarandus*), or maybe elk (*Alces alces*)
taraxi -s, (Gr. ταραξις) confusion/a disorder of the bowels/an irritation of the eye
tarb -o, (Gr. ταρβος) alarm/terror/awe/reverence
tarbale, (Gr. ταρβαλεος) fearful/terrible
tard -i, (L. tardus) slow
tarichos, (Gr. ταριχος) an embalmed body/pickled meat
tarpe, (Gr. ταρπη) a large wicker basket
tarph -i -o, (Gr. ταρφος) a thicket
tarphy, (Gr. ταρφυς) thick/close/often
tarquinius, (L. tarquinius) proud/haughty
tarrhos, (Gr. ταρρος) cheese crate/basket/crate

tars -o -us, (Gr. ταρσος) any broad flat surface/a crate/flat basket/mat of reeds/palm of hand/sole of foot/an oar blade

tars, (LL. tarsus) ankle joint

tas -eo -i, (Gr. τασις) stretching/tension

tass, (Gr. τασσω) draw up in order of battle/form/array/marshal/post/station

tat, (Gr. τατικος) stretched/exerting tension

tata, (L. tata) daddy

-tatos, (Gr. -τατος) a super. suf.

tau, (Gr. ταυ τ T) nineteenth letter of the Greek alphabet

taur -us, (L. taurus) a bull

taut -o, (Gr. ταυτος) identical

tax -eo -i -is -o, (Gr. ταξις) an arranging/arrangement/assessment (of tribute)/an order/rank/class

tax -o -u, (Gr. ταξος) the yew tree (*Taxus baccata*)

tax -o -us, (NL. taxus) the American badger (*Taxidea taxus*)

taxill, (L. taxillus) a little ankle

tebenn -a, (Gr. τηβεννα) a toga

tec -o, (Gr. τηκω) melt/dissolve/waste away

tecedono, (Gr. τηκεδων) melting (of snow)/wasting away

techn -i -o, (Gr. τεχνικος) artistic/skilful

tecmarto, (Gr. τεκμαρτος) a fixed mark/boundary/goal

tecmerio, (Gr. τεκμηριον) a sure sign/positive proof

tecn -o -um, (Gr. τεκνον) a child

tect -i -o, (L. tectum) a roof/ceiling/cover/shelter/dwelling

tect -o, (Gr. τεκτων) builder/carpenter/any craftsman

tect -o, (Gr. τηκτος) melted/molten/soluble

tector -i, (L. tectoriolum) plaster/stucco

tectum, (L. tectum) roof

tedi, (L. taedium) weariness/boredom

teg -o -us, (Gr. τεγος) roof/any covered hall or chamber/brothel

teg, (L. tegere) to cover/to shield/to conceal

tegm -en -in, (L. tegmen) a cover/covering

tegos, (Gr. τεγος) roof

tegul -a, (L. tegula) a roofing tile

tegul -um, (L. tegulum) covering

tegument -um, (L. tegimentum) a cover

teich -o -us, (Gr. τειχος) a wall/city wall/temple wall/fortification/castle

tein -o, (Gr. τεινω) stretch/extend/pull tight

-teira, -ter, -tes, -tis, -tor, -tria, -tris, (Gr.) suffixes ind. agent/doer

tekn -o -um, (Gr. τεκνον) a child

tel -a -i, (L. tela) something woven/a web/a design

tel -eo -o, (Gr. τελεος/τελειος) complete/perfect/entire/full grown/an end

telamon, (Gr. τελαμων) a broad strap/belt

telchin, (Gr. τελχινια) a spiteful person/backbiter

tele, (Gr. τηλε) far off/at a distance/far from

teleos/teleios, (Gr. τελεος/τελειος) having reached its end/finished/complete/perfect

telephanes, (Gr. τηλεφανης) conspicuous/visible from a distance

telesma, (Gr. τελεσμα) payment

teleta, (Gr. τελετη) initiation

teleuto, (Gr. τελευτη) completion/accomplishment

telisto, (Gr. τηλιστος) farthest

tellin -a, (Gr. τελλινη) a small bivalve mollusc

tello, (Gr. τελλω) to accomplish/make to arise

tellu -r -ri -s, (L. tellus/telluris) the earth

telma -to, (Gr. τελμα) pond/marsh/swamp

telo -s, (Gr. τελος) the completion/end/fulfilment

telotero, (Gr. τηλοτερος) farther

telson, (Gr. τελσον) a boundary/headland

telum, (L. telum) dart/javelin/spear/missile

temacho, (Gr. τεμαχος) a slice

temen -us, (Gr. τεμενος) a piece land

temer, (L. temere) by chance/blindly/accidentally/casually

temet -um, (L. temetum) any intoxicating drink

temn -a -o, (Gr. τεμνω) to hew/cut/maim

temnibil, (L. temnibilis) despicable/hateful

temo, (L. temo) the pole or beam of a wagon/a wagon

temper, (L. tempero) to observe limits/be moderate/to control

templ -um, (L. templum) any open space/a sanctuary/shrine

tempor -a -o, (L. temporalis) temporary/lasting for a time

tempor, (L. tempora) the temples (of head)

tempus, (L. tempus) time

temulent-, (L. temulentus) drunken/intoxicated

ten -a, (L. tenere) to hold fast

ten -d -s -t, (L. tendere) to stretch/stretch out/extend/spread/strive

ten -s -t, (L. tendo) stretched/extended/spread out

tena -ci -x, (L. tenax) holding fast/gripping/clinging/firm/steady/obstinate

tenac, (L. tenax) griping

tenag -o -us, (Gr. τεναγος) shoal-water/shallows/lagoon

tenan, (L. tenax) holding fast/gripping/clinging/firm/steady/obstinate

tendo, (L. tendere) to stretch/stretch out/extend

tendon, (L. tendon) tendon

tenebric, (L. tenebricus) dark/gloomy

tener, (L. tener) tender/delicate/soft

tenesm -us, (Gr. τεινεσμος) a vain endeavour to evacuate/a straining

teni -a -o, (Gr. ταινια) a band/ribbon

tenon -t -to, (Gr. τενων) sinew/tendon

tensio, (L. tensio) stretching

tensus, (L. tensus) stretched/extended

tent, (L. tentare) to feel

tenta, (L. tentantum) to handle/touch/feel a thing

tentacul -i -um, (LL. tentaculum) a feeler/holdfast

tentamen, (L. tentamen) trial/test/attempt

tenthes, (Gr. τενθης) a gourmand

tenthred -in -o, (Gr. τενθρηδων) a kind of wasp that makes its nest in the earth
        (Tenthredinidae)

tentig in -o, (L. tentiginis/tentigo) tension/lust

tentori -um, (L. tentorium) a tent

tentus, (L. tentus) holding

tenu -i -is, (L. tenuis) thin/fine/slight/slender

tep -id -or, (L. tepidus) lukewarm/tepid

tephr -a, (Gr. τεφρα/τεφρη) ashes (as of a funeral)

tephr -o, (Gr. τεφρος) ash-coloured

tephras, (Gr. τεφρας) ash-coloured/a cicada (Cicadellidae)

tephritis, (L. tephritis) an ash-coloured precious stone

ter, (L. ter) three times

-ter, -tes, -tis, -tor, -tria, -tris, -teira, (Gr.) suf. ind. agent/means/doer

tera -s, (Gr. τερας) a sign/wonder/marvel/portent/monster/monstrosity

teram -no -o, (Gr. τεραμων) becoming soft (by boiling)

teramn -o -us, (Gr. τεραμνον) a chamber/house

terasti, (Gr. τεραστιος) monstrous/prodigious/portentous

terato, (Gr. τερας) monster/sign/marvel/wonder

teratogen, (Gr. τερατογονια) favouring the birth of monsters

terchno, (Gr. τερχνος) twig/young shoot

tere -n -no, (Gr. τερενος) soft/tender/delicate
tere -o, (Gr. τερεω) bore through/pierce
tere -o, (Gr. τηρεω) watch over/guard/observe/notice
tere -s -t, (L. teres) rounded/polished/smooth/refined/elegant
terebinth -us, (Gr. τερεβινθος) the turpentine (terebinth) tree (*Pistacia* spp.)
terebr -a, (L. terebra) bore through/pierce/a boring tool/wheedle/coax
tered -o, (Gr. τερηδων) wood-worm/a worm in the bowls
teretico, (Gr. τερετικος) watchful/observant
teretr -o, (Gr. τερετρον) a borer/gimlet
terg -i -um, (L. tergum) the back/rear
tergen, (L. tergens) cleansing
-terium, (Gr. -τηριον) instrument/organ/thing used
term -es -it, (L. termes) a wood-worm
term -in, (L. terminus) limit/boundary/end
terma -t, (Gr. τερμα) end/boundary/limit
termin -a -us, (L. terminus) limit/boundary/end
tern -ari, (L. terni) three in a group/three at a time
terph -o -us, (Gr. τερφος) a skin/shell
terpn -o, (Gr. τερπνος) delightful/pleasant
terps -i, (Gr. τερψις) enjoyment/delight
terr -a, (L. terra) earth/land/ground/region
terr -i, (L. terror) fright/fear/terror/alarm/dread
terrestr, (L. terrestris) of the earth/terrestrial
ters, (L. tersus) clean/neat/free from mistakes
terthreus, (Gr. τερθρευς) a quibbler
terthrios, (Gr. τερθριος) rope or brace at the end of a sail yard
terti, (L. tertius) the third
-tes, -tis, -tor, -tria, -tris, -teira, -ter, (Gr.) suffixes ind. agent/doer
tescum, (L. tesqua) wastes/deserts
tessar, (Gr. τεσσαρα-) four-/square
tesselat, (L. tessellatus) set with small cubes/mosaic/chequered
test -a, (L. testa) a shell/a tile/brick/a covering
testac -e, (L. testaceus) having a shell
testi-s, (L. testis) a witness/eye-witness/spectator
testicul, (L. testiculus) a testicle/of the testes
testis, (L. testis) a testicle
testud -in -o, (L. testudo) a tortoise/tortoise-shell/a curved string-instrument/an arch/a
            vault
tetan -o -us, (Gr. τετανος) stretched/rigid/straightened/convulsive tension
tetart -o, (Gr. τεταρτος) fourth/fourthly/fourfold
teter, (L. taeter) foul/hideous/offensive
tethe, (Gr. τηθη) grandmother/nurse
tethea, (L. tethea) a kind of sponge
tethys, (Gr. Τηθυς) a sea-goddess, wife of Oceanus
tetr -a, (Gr. τετρας) four
tetra -c -x, (Gr. τετραξ) a type of pheasant
tetrapla, (Gr. τετραπλη) in a fourfold manner/fourfold
tetraplo, (Gr. τετραπλοος) a fourfold portion
tetri -g -x, (Gr. τετριξ) a kind of bird, perh. pipit (*Anthus campestris*)
tetric, (L. tetricus) harsh/gloomy/severe/forbidding
tetti -g -x, (Gr. τεττιξ) a cicada (*Cicada* spp.) or allied insect
teuch -o -us, (Gr. τευχος) tool/implement of war/armour/case/vessel
teusio, (Gr. τηυσιος) vain/futile/idle
teuthi -do -s, (Gr. τευθις) a squid (*Loligo vulgaris*)
teutl -o -um, (Gr. τευτλον) sea beet (*Beta maritima*)
texi, (Gr. τεξις) child-bearing
text -i, (L. textilis) woven/textile

thacemato, (Gr. θακημα) a sitting/seat

thair -o -us, (Gr. θαιρος) a door hinge/an axle

thal -o -us, (Gr. θαλλος) young shoot/young branch/child

thalam -i -o -us, (Gr. θαλαμος) an inner room/chamber

thalass -a -i -o, (Gr. θαλασσα) the sea/sea water/salt water

thaler -o, (Gr. θαλερος) stout/sturdy/buxom/blooming/fresh

thalia, (Gr. θαλια) abundance/good cheer

thall -o -us, (Gr. θαλλος) young shoot/young branch/child

thalo, (Gr. θαλος) a young shoot/twig

thalp -o, (Gr. θαλπος) warmth/heat/summer heat

thalycr -o, (Gr. θαλυκρος) hot/glowing

thamb -o -us, (Gr. θαμβος) amazement

thamino, (Gr. θαμινος) crowded/close set

thamn -o -us, (Gr. θαμνος) a bush/shrub

thana -s -to -tus, (Gr. θανατος) death

thapsia, (Gr. θαψια) a poisonous plant - deadly carrot (*Thapsia garganica*)

thapsin, (Gr. θαψινος) yellow/yellow-coloured/sallow

thapt -o, (Gr. θαπτω) honour with funereal rites

tharso, (Gr. θαρσος) courage/boldness

thasso/thatto, (Gr. θασσω) sit/sit idle

thauma -si -st -to, (Gr. θαυμα) wonder/marvel/honour/admire/worship

the -a, (Gr. θεα) seeing/looking at/aspect/view

the -i -o, (Gr. θεω) behold!

the -i, (Gr. θειον) the divinity

the -o, (Gr. θεω) run/run over/shine/gleam

thea, (L. thea) tea

theaphion, (Gr. θεαφιον) sulphur

theat -r, (Gr. θεατρον) theatre/audience

thec -a -o, (Gr. θηκη) a case/box/chest/cup

thect -o, (Gr. θηκτος) sharpened/whetted

theg -o, (Gr. θεγω) sharpen/whet/excite

thei -o, (Gr. θειον) brimstone

theic, (Gr. θειναι) to settle

thel -a, (Gr. θηλη) nipple/teat

thel -y, (Gr. θηλυς) female/of females/soft/gentle

thelasm -o, (Gr. θηλασμος) suckling

thelax, (Gr. θηλαξ) suckle

thelic -o, (Gr. θηλυκος) woman-like/feminine

thelx -i, (Gr. θελξις) an enchanting/bewitching

thema -t, (Gr. θεμα) something paced or laid down/a deposit/a pile/a theme/ proposition/premise

themeli -a, (Gr. θεμειλια/θεμεθλα) a foundations/roots

themis, (Gr. θεμις) customary laws/ordinances/judgements

themon, (Gr. θημων) heap

thenar -o, (Gr. θεναρ) the palm of the hand

theo, (Gr. θεος) god

theorema -to, (Gr. θεωρεημα) sight/spectacle/festival/speculation/theorum/ investigation

ther -es, (Gr. θηραω) I hunt

ther -i -io -ium, (Gr. θηριον) a wild beast/beat of prey/a fabulous monster

ther -o, (Gr. θερος) summer/summer fruits/harvest/crop

ther -o, (Gr. θερω) heat/make hot/become hot

thera -to, (Gr. θηρα/θηρη) hunting/the chase/eager pursuit/prey/game

therap -eu -o -y, (Gr. θεραπεια) healing/attendance/tending

theri -a -d -o, (Gr. θηρ) a wild beast/beat of prey/a fabulous monster

theri, (Gr. θηριον) a little animal

therismo, (Gr. θερισμος) mowing/reaping/harvest

theriz, (Gr. θεριζω) reap

therm -o, (Gr. θερμος) warm/heat/feverish heat/hot-headed

thermastr -is, (Gr. θερμαστρις) tongs/pincers/pliers

thermos, (Gr. θερμος) a type of lupine (*Lupinus albus*)

theros, (Gr. θερος) summer

thesaur -i -o, (Gr. θησαυρος) store/treasure/strongroom/magazine

thesis, (Gr. θεσις) arranging

thesm -o -us, (Gr. θεσμος) a law/ordinance/rule

thespesio, (Gr. θεσπεσιος) divine

thet, (Gr. θετεια) hired service/servility

thet, (Gr. θετος) placed/set/having position/adopted

theta, (Gr. θητα τ Τ) eighth letter of the Greek alphabet

thetis, (L. Thetis) a sea-nymph, wife of Peleus, mother of Achilles

theto, (Gr. θετος) adopted

theurg, (Gr. θεουργια) sorcery/divine work

thias -o -us, (Gr. θιασος) bacchic revel/rout/company/troop

thibe, (Gr. θιβη) basket/ark

thigm -a -ato -o, (Gr. θιγημα) a touch

thin -o, (Gr. θινωδης) sandy beach/sandy

thio, (Gr. θειον) sulphur

thixis, (Gr. θιξις) touching

thladias, (Gr. θλαδιας) eunuch

thlas -t, (Gr. θλαστος) crushed/compressed/bruised

thlib -o, (Gr. θλιβω) compress/reduce/press

thlips -i, (Gr. θλιψις) pressure/oppression/affliction/crushing/castration

thneto, (Gr. θνητος) mortal

tho -o, (Gr. θοος) quick/nimble/pointed/sharp

thoe, (Gr. θωη) penalty

thoeno, (Gr. θοινη) meal/feast

thol -o -us, (Gr. θολος) dome/mud/dirt

tholer -o, (Gr. θολερος) muddy/foul/turbid/troubled by madness or passion

tholia, (Gr. θολια) a conical hat with a broad rim/parasol

tholos, (Gr. θολος) mud/dirt

tholus, (Gr. θολος) a rounded building with as conical roof

thomi -ng -nx -s, (Gr. θομιγξ) cord/string/bow-string/fishing line

thomi -s, (Gr. θομιζω) whip/scourge

thomis, (Gr. θωμιξω) cord/bind

thomos, (Gr. θωμος) heap

thoos, (Gr. θοως) quick/nimble/swift

thops, (Gr. θωψ) flatterer

thor -ect -ecto -ict -icto, (Gr. θωρηκτης) armed with a breastplate

thor -o, (Gr. θουρος) rushing/impetuous

thora -co -x, (Gr. θωραξ L. thorax) breastplate/cuirass/chest

thoros, (Gr. θορος) male seed/semen

thoryb -o -us, (Gr. θορυβος) noise/uproar/clamour

thos, (Gr. θως) the golden jackal (*Canis aureus*)

thoysmo, (Gr. θωυσσω) barking/baying/cry aloud/shout

thran -i -o, (Gr. θρανις) a swordfish

thran -i -o, (Gr. θρανος) bench/form/wooden beam

thras -y, (Gr. θρασυς) bold/over bold/rash/audacious/arrogant/insolent

thrass -o, (Gr. θρασσω) trouble/disquiet/disturb/destroy

thraulo, (Gr. θραυλος) brittle

thraupalos, (Gr. θραυπαλος) a shrub (*Ephedra campulopoda*)

thraupi -s, (Gr. θραυπις) a small bird
thraust -o, (Gr. θραυστος) frangible/brittle/broken/crushed
thremma -to, (Gr. θρεμμα) a nursling
thren -o, (Gr. θρενος) dirge/lament/complaint
threps -i -o, (Gr. θρεψις) nourishing
thrept, (Gr. θρεπτεος) fed/nurtured
threski, (Gr. θρησκος) religious
thri -c -x, (Gr. θριξ) hair/wool
thriambos, (Gr. θριαμβος) triumph
thrida -c -x, (Gr. θριδαξ) lettuce
thrina -c -x, (Gr. θριναξ) a trident/three-pronged fork
thrinc -o -us, (Gr. θρινκος) eaves/cornice/coping
thrion, (Gr. θριον) a fig-leaf
thrip -i -o -s, (Gr. θριψ) a wood-worm/skinflint/miser
thrip, (Gr. θριψ) a wood worm
thrix, (Gr. θριξ) hair
thromb -o -us, (Gr. θρομβος) a lump/clot/blood clot/curd
throsc -o, (Gr. θρωσκω) leap/spring/leap upon/assault/attack/rush/dart
throsis, (Gr. θρωσις) cord/line
thry -o -on, (Gr. θρυον) a rush/reed
thryligma, (Gr. θρυλιγμα) fragment
thrylos, (Gr. θρυλος) the noise of many voices/mummer
thrymma, (Gr. θρυμμα) a bit broken off/piece
thryon, (Gr. θρυον) reed/rush
thrypsi -s -t, (Gr. θυρψις) fragmentation/dispersion/softness/weakness/daintiness
thuja, (Gr. θυια) a resinous sweetly-scented tree - arbour vitae (*Thuja* spp.)
thunn -us, (L. thunnus) a tunny fish
thur -a, (Gr. θυρη) a door
thur -i, (L. tureus) incense
thur -id -o, (Gr. θουρος) rushing/impetuous
thur, (Gr. θυρις) small plate
thura, (Gr. θυρα/θυρη) door/gate/entrance
thyell -a -o, (Gr. θυελλα) a hurricane/squall
thyestes, (Gr. θυεστης) pestle
thygater, (Gr. θυγατηρ) daughter
thyio, (Gr. θυεια) mortar
thylac -o, (Gr. θυλακος/θυλαξ) pouch/sac
thym -o -us, (Gr. θυμος) soul/spirit/life/mind as seat of thought/heart as seat of
            emotions/desire/temper/courage/anger
thymall -us, (Gr. θυμαλλος) a type of fish
thymel, (Gr. θυμελη) hearth/altar/platform/stage
thymele, (Gr. θυμελη) an alter/place for sacrifice/hearth
thymiama, (Gr. θυμιαμα) incense/stuff used for embalming
thymos, (Gr. θυμος) mind/soul/spirit/temper
thynn-us, (Gr. θυννος) a tunny fish
thyo, (Gr. θυω) a sacrifice/slay a sacrifice/tear into pieces
thyo, (Gr. θυω) rage/seethe/storm
thyr -a -a -o, (Gr. θυριον) a little door/wicket
thyr -eo, (Gr. θυρεος) an oblong shield
thyr, (Gr. θυρις) a small plate
thyri, (Gr. θυρις) a little window
thyrs -o, (Gr. θυρσος) a wand wreathed in ivy
thysan -o -us, (Gr. θυσανος) a tassel/fringe
thysio, (Gr. θυσια) rite/sacrifice
-tia, (L.) suf. den. condition/pertaining to
tiar -a -o, (Gr. τιαρα) a Persian head-dress

tibi -a -o, (L. tibia) the shin bone

tibic -en -in, (L. tibicen) a flute player/a pillar/prop

-tic (tein), (Gr. τικ (τειν)) suf. to bear young/lay eggs/hatch

-tic, (L.) suf. belonging to

-tica, -ticum, -ticus, (L.) belonging to (generally referring to habitats)

tich -o, (Gr. τειχιον/τειχος) a wall

tid, (AS. tid) time

tigill -um, (L. tigillum) a small beam

tign -um, (L. tignum) a wooden beam/timber

tigri -n, (L. tigris) a tiger/a river in Asia

tilia, (L. tilia) the lime tree/linden tree (Tilia spp.)

till -o, (Gr. τιλλω) to pull/pluck/tear

tilma, (Gr. τιλμα) anything pulled, plucked or shredded

tilos, (Gr. τιλος) shred/fibre

tilt -o, (Gr. τιλτος) plucked/gathered

tim -a -o, (Gr. τιμαω) honour/reverence/reward

tim -id, (L. timidus) fearful/timid/faint-hearted

tim -or, (L. timor) fear/dread

timi -o, (Gr. τιμιος) valued/worthy/costly/honourable

timor, (Gr. τιμωρια) retribution/vengeance/succour

tin -o, (Gr. τεινω) stretch/pull tight/strain/spread/extend/lengthen/aim at exert oneself

tinagma -to, (Gr. τιναγμα) a shake/quake

tinct, (L. tingere) to dye/moisten

tine -a -i, (L. tinea) a moth

tingabarino, (Gr. τιγγαβαρινος) vermilion

tinn -it -ul, (L. tinnitus) a ringing/tinkling/jingling

tino, (Gr. τινω) repay (a debt)/take vengeance

tintinn, (L. tintinno) ring/jingle/tinkle

tintinnabul -um, (L. tintinnabulum) a bell

-tion, (L.) suf. den. act/process/result/state of

tiph -a -i, (Gr. τιφη) a type of beetle

tiph -o, (Gr. τιφος) standing water/marsh/pond

tiphi -o, (Gr. τιφιος) from the marsh

tiphys, (Gr. τυφυς) nightmare

tipula, (L. tippula) a water spider/water fly

tiro, (L. tiro) recruit

-tis, -tor, -tria, -tris, -teira, -ter, -tes, (Gr.) suffixes ind. agent/doer

titan -o, (Gr. Τιταν) myth. one of the gods/gigantic

titan -o, (Gr. τιτανος) a white earth prob. gypsum or lime

tithasos, (Gr. τιθασος) tamed/domesticated

tithen, (Gr. τιθηνη) a nurse

tithymal -us, (Gr. τιθυμαλλος) a spurge (Euphorbia peplus)

titill -a, (L. titillo) tickle

titth -o -us, (Gr. τιτθος) a woman's breast/nurser

titub -a, (L. titubo) totter/stagger/stammer/falter/hesitate

titulus, (L. titulus) inscription/label/title

tityr -us, (Gr. τιτυρος) a short-tailed ape/a kind of pheasant/a reed or pipe

tla -s, (Gr. τλαω) suffer/endure/dare/venture

tmema -to, (Gr. τμημα) a section/piece

tmesi -s, (Gr. τμησις) cutting/ravaging

toc -o -us, (Gr. τοκος) childbirth/parturition/delivery/offspring

toecho, (Gr. τοιχος) the wall of a house/side of a ship

toga, (L. toga) a covering/a robe/a prostitute

toich -o, (Gr. τοιχος) wall of a house or enclosure/side of a ship

tok -o -us, (Gr. τοκος) childbirth/parturition/delivery/offspring

toler -a, (L. tolerare) to bear/endure

tolleno, (L. tolleno) a swing-beam

tolm -a -ero, (Gr. τολμα) courage/hardihood/recklessness/dare/endure
tolutar, (L. tolutarius) trotting
tolyp -a, (Gr. τολυπη) ball of wool ready for spinning/globular cake
tom -e -i -o -y, (Gr. τομη) a cut/stroke/wound/a cutting
-tom, (Gr. τεμνω) to hew
tomar, (Gr. τομαριον) small volume
toment -os -um, (L. tomentum) the stuffing in a pillow/dense hair
toment, (L. tomentum) the stuffing of a pillow
tomi -d -s, (Gr. τομις) knife
tomo, (Gr. τομος) a piece cut off/a slice
ton -o, (Gr. τονος) tension/that which strains and tightens a thing
tone, (Gr. τονος) sound/pitch
tonos, (Gr. τονος) a stretching/tightening
tons -or -ur, (L. tonsor) a barber/hair-cutter
tonsa, (L. tonsa) an oar
tonsill -a, (L. tonsillae) the tonsils
tonsor, (L. tonsor) a barber
tonu, (L. tonus) tension/brace
top -o -us -y, (Gr. τοπος) a place/spot
toph -us, (L. tophus/tofus) a porous stone
tor -o -us, (Gr. τορος) piercing/a borer/a drill
tor -o -us, (L. torosus) muscular/brawny
-tor, -tria, -tris, -teira, -ter, -tes, -tis, (Gr.) suffixes ind. agent/doer
torcul -a, (L. torcular) a wine or oil press
toretos, (Gr. τορητος) liable to be pierced/vulnerable
toreuma -to, (Gr. τορευμα) an embossed work/carving
toreus -i, (Gr. τορευς) a boring tool
torgos, (Gr. τοργος) a vulture
torm -o -us, (Gr. τορμος) a hole or socket/peg/pivot
torment, (L. tormentum) an instrument for twisting, winding/a missile/instrument of
              torture
tormos, (Gr. τορμος) a hole/socket
torn -eu -o, (Gr. τορνευω) work with a lathe/turn
toros, (Gr. τορος) piercing
torosus, (L. torosus) muscular/bulging/lusty
torp -e -ed -es -id -or, (L. topor) numbness/sluggishness/mental dullness
torqu -e -i, (L. torqueo) twist/wind/wrench
torquat, (L. torquatus) collared/wearing a necklace
torqui -s, (L. torquis/torques) a twisted necklace or collar/wreath/ring
torr -e -i, (L. torreo) burn/parch/dry up with heat
torren, (L. torrens) burning/hot/parched/rushing/seething/a torrent
torrid, (L. torridus) parched/burnt/dry
tors -i -o, (L. torsi) twist/wind/wrench
tort -i, (L. tortrix) twisted
tortil, (L. tortilis) twisted
tortri -c -x, (L. tortor) a tormentor/torturer
tortu, (L. tortus) winding/twisting
torul -i -us, (L. torulus) a tuft of hair
torus, (L. torus) any round swelling/a muscle/a mattress/mound
torv -i, (L. torvus) savage/grim/fierce
toryn -a -i -o, (Gr. τορυνη) ladle/stirrer
tosa-, (Gr. τοσα-) so many/so very/so much
tostus, (L. tostus) burned/parched
tot -a -i, (L. totus) all/whole
tothastes, (Gr. τωθαστης) scoffer
totietas, (L. totietas) the whole
tox -o -um, (Gr. τοξον) a bow/curved support/cradle

toxe -us, (Gr. τοξευς) a bowman

toxeuma -to, (Gr. τοξευμα) an arrow

toxic -um, (L. toxicum Gr. τοξικον) a poison/arrow poison

toxo, (Gr. τοξον) a bow (of an archer)

-tra, -tron, -tros, -trum, -trus, (Gr. -τρα/-τρον/-τρος) a tool/ means of doing something

trab -i -s, (L. trabs) a beam of wood/tree trunk/roof

trabe -a, (L. trabae) a state robe (worn by kings and knights)

trabec, (L. trabecula) little beam

trabeculat, (L. trabeculatus) marked with crossbars

trach -i,-y, (Gr. τραχυς) rough

trache -a -i -o, (L. trachia) windpipe

trachel -o, (Gr. τραχηλος) the neck/throat

trachy -s -te, (Gr. τραχυτης) roughness/ruggedness/harshness

tract, (L. tractus) region

tract, (L. trahere) to draw/drag

tradit, (L. traditio) a surrender

trag -ed -i, (Gr. τραγωδεω) a tragedy

trag -i -o -us, (Gr. τραγος) a part of the ear/male goat

tragan, (Gr. τραγανον) cartilage/gristle

tragema, (Gr. τραγημα) dried fruits

tragopan, (Gr. τραγοπαν) a fabulous (Ethiopian) bird

tragula, (L. tragula) a type of javelin

tragus, (Gr. τραγος) a he-goat

trah -a, (L. trahere) to drag/draw/pull

trahax, (L. trahax) greedy/grasping

tram -a -o, (L. trama) cross woven/the woof in weaving

tram -es -it, (L. trames) by-way/foot-path

trampis, (Gr. ταμπις) a ship

tran -es -i, (Gr. τρανης) clear/distinct

tran -s, (L. trans) over/across/on or to the other side

tranos, (Gr. τρανης) clear/distinct

transenna, (L. transenna) lattice work/a net for catching birds/a trap

transtrum, (L. transtrum) a cross beam

transvers -o, (L. transversus) transverse/oblique

trapez -a -i -o, (Gr. τραπεζα) a table/counter/any flat surface

traphe -c -x, (Gr. τραφηξ) a baker's board/oar handle

trapher -o, (Gr. τραφερος) well-fed/fat

trasia, (Gr. τρασια) a drying place for corn/kiln

traul -o, (Gr. τραυλος) lisping/stammering/twittering

trauma -to, (Gr. τραυμα) wound/hurt/damage/heavy blow/defeat

trebax, (L. trebacis) experienced

trech -o, (Gr. τρεχω) run/move quickly/run over

trechn -o -us, (Gr. τρεχνος) twig/young shoot/young tree

trem -e -o -or -ul, (L. tremo) tremble/quake

trema -to, (Gr. τρημα) a hole

trep -o, (Gr. τρεπω) to turn

trepan -i -o, (Gr. τρυπανον) a borer/auger/surgical instrument (trepan)

treph -i -o, (Gr. τρεφειν) to nourish/feed/make grow

trepid, (L. trepidus) agitated/anxious/restless/disturbed

trepo, (Gr. τρεπω) turn/alter/turn away/put to flight

trept -o, (Gr. τρεπτος) liable to be turned or changed

trero -no, (Gr. τρερων) timorous/shy

tresi -s, (Gr. τρησις) perforation/orifice/boring through

tret -o, (Gr. τρητος) perforated/bored/pierced through

tri, (Gr. τρι- L. tri-) three-

tri, (L. tres) three

tria -do -s, (Gr. τριας LL. trias) three/a triad
-tria, -tris, -teira, -ter, -tes, -tis, -tor, (Gr.) suffixes ind. agent/doer
triaconta, (Gr. τριακοντα) thirty
triaen -a, (Gr. τριαινα) a trident
trib -o, (Gr. τριβω) rub/thresh/knead
tribel -o, (Gr. τριβηλες) three-pointed
triben, (Gr. τριβην) tripod
tribo, (Gr. τριβαια) mortar
tribol -o, (Gr. τριβολος) three-pronged
tribon, (Gr. τριβων) a threadbare cloak
tribos, (Gr. τριβος) a worn path/rubbing/attrition
tribul -us, (L. tribulus) a thorny plant
tribul, (L. tribulum) a threshing flail
tribune, (L. tribune) chieftain
trica, (L. tricae) trifles/nonsense/vexations
tricesim, (L. tricesimus/tricensimus/trigesimus) thirtieth
trich -o, (Gr. θριχο-) hair
tricha -do -s, (Gr. τριχας) the song thrush (*Turdus philomelos*)
trichila, (L. trichila) arbour/summerhouse
trichin -o, (Gr. τριχινος) of hair/hairy
tricho, (Gr. τριχος) hair
trichod -o, (Gr. τριχωδης) like hair
trico, (Gr. τριχος) hair
tridens, (L. tridens) a fork with three tines/having three prongs
trien -t, (L. triens) one third/a third part
trifax, (L. trifaux) having three throats
trifid, (L. trifidus) split into three parts
trigesim, (L. trigesimus/tricesimus/tricensimus) thirtieth
triginta, (L. triginta) thirty
trigl -a, (Gr. τριγλη) the red mullet (*Mullus surmuletus*)
trigmos, (Gr. τριγμος) a strident sound/shrill cry
trigon -o, (Gr. τριγωνος) three-cornered/triangular
trime -no, (Gr. τριμηνος) of three months
trime -str, (L. trimestris) of three months
trimma -to, (Gr. τριμμα) that which is rubbed/a practised knave
trimma, (Gr. τριμμα) anything rubbed/a practised knave
tring -a, (Gr. τρυγγας) a sandpiper (*Tringa* spp.)
trinus, (L. trinus) in groups of three/three each
trio -no, (L. triones) a ploughing oxen
tripan, (Gr. τρυπανον) a borer/auger/surgical instrument (trepan)
tripl -i -o, (Gr. τριπλοος L. triplex) triple/threefold
triplar, (L. triplaris) threefold
triplex, (L. triplex) threefold
trips -i, (Gr. τριψις) rubbing/friction
tript -o, (Gr. τριπτος) rubbed/pounded
tripter, (Gr. τριπτηρ) a pestle
triquetr, (L. triquetrus) triangular/three cornered
-tris, -teira, -ter, -tes, -tis, -tor, -tria, (Gr.) suffixes ind. agent/doer
trism -o -us, (Gr. τρισμος/τριγμος) a shrill cry/scream
triss -o, (Gr. τρισσος) threefold
trist -i, (L. tristis) sad/sorrowful/gloomy/forbidding
trit, (L. tritus) rubbed/much trodden/frequented/practised
tritic -um, (L. triticum) wheat (*Triticum vulgare*)
trito, (Gr. τριτος) third/the third
triton, (Gr. Τριτων) a sea god (son of Poseidon and Amphitrite)
tritur -a, (L. tritura) rub together/thresh/grind

trivi, (L. trivium) a three-way cross roads

trix, (Gr. θριξ) hair/wool

-trix, (L. -trix) the agent of an action

trix-, (Gr. τριξ) three-

troch -o -us, (Gr. τροχος) anything round or circular that runs around

trochado, (Gr. τροχας) a light shoe for running

trochanter, (Gr. τροχαντηρ) a runner/the 'ball' of the hip joint

trochil, (Gr. τροχιλος) a plover (*Charadrius* spp.)/wren (*Troglodytes* spp.)/a pulley in
            block and tackle

trochl, (L. trochlea) a pulley

trochle -a, (Gr. τροχιλεια) block and tackle equipment/roller of a windlass

trocho, (Gr. τροχος) a wheel/potters wheel/hoop

troct -es -o, (Gr. τρωκτης) gnawer/nibbler

trog, (Gr. τρωξ) gnawer

trogl -e -o, (Gr. τρωγλη) a hole/mouse hole/cave

trogo, (Gr. τρωγω) gnaw/nibble/munch

trom -o -us, (Gr. τρομος) trembling/quaking/quivering

troma, (Gr. τρωμα) a wound

trombid, (NL. trombid) a little timid one

-tron, (Gr. -τρον) suf. den. tool, instrument

tron, (L. trutina) a pair of scales

trop -ae -e -o, (Gr. τροπη) a turn/turning round/a change

trop -ic, (Gr. τροπος) suf. turning/direction

tropalis, (Gr. τροπαλις) bundle/bunch

tropeco, (Gr. τροπηξ) the handle of an oar/an oar

troph -i -o, (Gr. τροφη) nourishment/food/maintenance

tropi -d -do -o -s, (Gr. τροπις) ship's keel

tropic -a -o, (Gr. τροπικος) of the tropics

tropism, (Gr. τροπος) suf. turning

tropo, (Gr. τροπος) turn/direction/way/manner/fashion/guise

trosis, (Gr. τρωσις) wounding/an injury

trotos, (Gr. τρωτος) vulnerable

trox, (Gr. τρωξ) a gnawer/a weevil

troxalis, (Gr. τρωξαλις) a grasshopper/cricket

troxan, (Gr. τρωξανον) a twig

truc -i -ido, (L. trucido) cut to pieces/slaughter/massacre

truch -ero -o, (Gr. τρυχηρος) ragged/tattered/worn out/tormenting

truculent, (L. truculentus) rough/ferocious/savage/cruel

trud -i -is, (L. trudis) a pointed staff/stake

trud, (L. trudo) push/press/thrust/urge/force

trulla, (L. trulla) a ladle

trulleum, (L. trulleum) a basin

-trum, (Gr. -τρον) suf. den. tool, instrument

trunic -a -at -us, (L. truncus) maimed/lopped/cut short/trunk/stem/blockhead

trup, (Gr. τρυπαω) bore/pierce through

trupa, (Gr. τρυπα/η) a hole

trus, (L. trusi) push/press/thrust/urge/force

trutina, (L. trutina) a balance/pair of scales

trutt -a, (L. trutta) trout (*Salmo trutta*)

trux, (L. trux) rough/savage/fierce/grim

try, (L. tres) three/three times

trybli -o -um, (Gr. τρυβλιον) a cup/bowl

trych -o, (Gr. τρυχω) wear out/waste/consume

trychero, (Gr. τρυχηρος) ragged/tattered/worn out

trychin -o, (Gr. τρυχινος) ragged

trychn -o -us, (Gr. τρυχνον/τρυχνος) sleepy nightshade (*Withania somnifera*)/the winter cherry (*Physalis alkekengi*)/hound's berry or black nightshade (*Solanum nigrum*)/thorn apple (*Datura stramonium*)

trygeto, (Gr. τρυγητος) gathering of fruits/harvest

trygo -n -no, (L. trygonus/trygon Gr. τρυγων) the sting-ray (Dasyatidae)

trym -a -o, (Gr. τρυμη) a hole

tryo, (Gr. τρυω) wear out/distress

tryos, (Gr. τρυος) distress/labour/toil

tryp -a -ano, (Gr. τρυπανον) borer/auger/hole

tryp -s -t, (Gr. τριψις) friction/rubbing

trypet, (Gr. τρυπητης) borer

tryphe, (Gr. τρυφη) softness/delicacy/daintiness

tryphos, (Gr. τρυφος) something broken off/piece/morsel/lump

trysi, (Gr. τρυσις) wearing out

trysmo, (Gr. τρυσμος) gurgling

tryss -o, (Gr. τρυσσον) dainty

tryx, (Gr. τρυξ) new wine/raw wine

tub -a, (L. tuba) a war trumpet

tub -i -us, (L. tubus) a pipe/tube

tuber -i, (L. tuber) swelling/protuberance/hump/knob

tubercul -um, (L. tuberculum) a small swelling/small knob

tubul -i -us, (L. tubulus) a little tube/little pipe

-tude, (L. -tudo) suf. ind. state/condition/pertaining to

tudes, (L. tudes) hammer/mallet

tugurium, (L. tugurium) a peasant's hut

tuit, (L. tuitio) protecting/preserving

tum-e -esc, (L. tumesco) begin to swell/swell with anger/swell with excitement

tumba, (L. tumba) a sepulchral mound/tomb

tumid, (L. tumidus) swollen/puffed up/pompous

tumor -i, (L. tumor) a swelling/protuberance

tumul -us, (L. tumulus) a hill/hillock/sepulchral mound

tumul, (L. tumulus) mound/barrow/hillock

tund, (L. tundo) beat/thump/strike repeatedly

tungsten, (Sw.) *tung,* heavy; *sten,* stone

tunic -a, (L. tunica) coating/covering/jacket

tupi -d -s, (Gr. τυπας) mallet/hammer

turb -a, (L. turba) tumult/uproar/commotion/mob/swarm

turbell -a, (L. turbellae) tumult/bustle/disorder/little crowd

turbid, (L. turbidus) confused/disordered/unquiet/wild

turbin, (L. turbineus) shaped like a top

turbo, (L. turbo) whorl/eddy/storm/commotion

turbulen -t, (L. turbulentus) disturbed/confused/restless/stormy

turd -i -us, (L. turdus) a thrush (*Turdus* spp.)/a kind of fish

turg -id, (L. turgidus) swollen/bombastic

turma, (L. turma) a troop of cavalry containing thirty men

turp -i, (L. turpis) ugly/foul/unsightly/deformed

turr -i -is, (L. turris) a tower/a dove cote

tus, (L. tus/turis) incense

-tus, (L.) suf. having the nature of/pertaining to/provided with

tuss -i, (L. tussis) a cough

tusus, (L. tusus) struck/beaten

tut -am -or, (L. tutamen) a defence/protection/safe guard

tutus, (L. tutus) watched over/safe/secure

tw -i -y, (AS. twi) two/double

tych -ae -e -ero -o, (Gr. τυχη) chance/fortune

tyco, (Gr. τυκος) a mason's hammer/mason's pick

tycto, (Gr. τυκτος) finished/wrought/complete

tyl -a -ar -o -us, (Gr. τυλος) callus/lump/knob/swelling
tylot -o, (Gr. τυλος) knobbed/knotted
tymb -o -us, (Gr. τυμβος) sepulchral mound/cairn/tomb
tymma -to, (Gr. τυμμα) a blow/wound
tympan -i -o -um, (Gr. τυμπανον) drum/kettle-drum
tympan, (L. tympani) tambourine
tyntlo, (Gr. τυντλος) mud
typ -i -o, (Gr. τυπος) blow/strike/impression (of a seal)/a type/pattern/model
typ, (L. typus) image/impression
typado, (Gr. τυπας) hammer/mallet
typh -a, (Gr. τυφη) reed mace, a plant used for stuffing beds (*Typha angustifolia*)
typh -o -us, (Gr. τυφω) smoke/smoulder
typhl -o, (Gr. τυφλος) blind/blind-ended
typhon, (Gr. τυφων) whirlwind/tempest
typis, (Gr. τυπις) a hammer
typot -o, (Gr. τυπωτος) fashioned/moulded
typt -o, (Gr. τυπτω) beat/strike/smite
tyr -eum -o, (Gr. τυρευμα) cheese/something curdled
tyrann -o -us, (L. tyrannus) a monarch/tyrant/master
tyrb -a, (Gr. τυρβη) disorder/confusion/tumult
tyrba, (Gr. τυρβη) disorder/confusion
tyrbastes, (Gr. τυρβαστης) agitator
tyros, (Gr. τυρος) cheese
tyrris/tyrsis, (Gr. τυρρις/τυρσις) a tower/bastion
tyto -n, (Gr. τυτω) a night owl (*Tyto* spp.)
tytthos, (Gr. τυτθος) little/small/young
tyxis, (Gr. τυξις) artifice

U

-ua, -uum, -uus, (L.) possibility/result of an action
uber, (L. uber) a udder/breast/abundance/fertility
ubiqu -it, (L. ubique) everywhere
-uchus, (NL. -uchus) suf. ind. hold/bear
ud -am -en, (Gr. ουδαμος) no-one/none
ud -o, (Gr. ουδος) threshold/entrance
ud -o, (L. udus) wet/moist
udaeo, (Gr. ουδαιος) on the ground/under the earth
udamino, (Gr. ουδαμινος) good for nothing
ude -o, (Gr. ουδεος) ground/surface of the earth
udeter -o, (Gr. ουδετερος) neither/neutral
udo, (Gr. ουδων) a kind of felt shoe
udus, (L. udus) wet/moist
-ugo, (L. -ugo) resemblance,/connection/property possessed (a common botanical suffix)
ul -a -e -i, (Gr. ουλη) a scar/wound scarred over
ul -o, (Gr. ουλος) destructive/baneful/cruel
ul -o, (Gr. ουλος) woolly (of thick, fleecy wool)/curly/compact/concise
ul -o, (Gr. ουλω) healthful/sound
-ul/-ula/-ule/-uline/-ulum/-ulus (L.) dim. suf.
ulamo, (Gr. ουλαμος) a crowd of warriors
ulc -er -us, (L. ulcus) an ulcer/a sore
-ulenta, -ulentum, -ulentus, (L.) abundance

uli -o, (Gr. ουλιος) deadly

ulig -in -o, (L. uliginosus) wetness/moisture

-ulis, (L.) pertaining to/having the nature/quality/condition of

-ulla, -ullum, -ullus, (L.) dim, suf.

ullus, (L. ullus) anyone/anything

-um, (L.) neuter termination for many adjectives

-um, (L.) of/belonging to/pertaining to

ulm -us, (L. ulmus) the elm tree (*Ulmus* spp.)

ulna, (L. ulna) the elbow/the ulna

-uncula, -unculum, -unculus, (L.) dim. suf.

-und, (L.) having the quality of

-undus, (L.) increased quality/aptitude/tendency towards

ulo, (Gr. ουλον) the gum

-ulous, (L. -ulosus/-ulus) adj. suf., full of

ultim, (L. ultimus) most distant/extreme/last

ultr -a -o, (L. ultra) beyond/on the far side/more than

ultrone, (L. ultro) voluntarily

ultus, (L. ultus) avenged/punished

ulul -a, (L. ulula) a screech owl/hoot

-unus, (L.) belonging to/pertaining to/one who

ulva, (L. ulva) sedge

umbel -a -i, (L. umbella) an umbrella/parasol

umbilic -us, (L. umbilicus) navel

umbo -n, (L. umbo) shield boss/projecting knob

umbr -a -i, (L. umbra) shade/shadow/ghost

umbros, (L. umbrosus) shady

umor (humor), (L.) moisture fluid

un -a -i, (L. unicus) only one/uncommon/sole/single /unique

un-, (AS. un) prefix of negation, not/back /off

unc -in -inus -us, (L. uncus) a hook/hooked/curved

uncia, (L. uncia) a twelfth

uncinat, (L. uncinatus) hooked/bearing hooks/hook-like

unct, (L. unctito) anoint

-uncul -a -um -us, (L.) dim. suf.

uncul, (L. unculus) little hook

uncus, (L. uncus) hooked (aduncus - bent inwards)

und -a -i, (L. unda) a wave/water in motion

undo, (L. undosus) billowy

undulat, (L. undulare) waved/wavy

-undus, (L. undus) suf. den. continuance/augmentation

ungi -s, (L. unguis) finger nail/claw/hoof

ungu -en in, (L. unguen) an ointment

ungul -a, (L. ungula) hoof/claw/talon

uni, (L. unus) one

unicus, (L. unicus) only/sole/singular

unio -n, (L. unio) a single large pearl

unus, (L. unus) one/the whole

-unus, (L.) suf. pertaining to

uper, (Gr. υπερ-) (in a general sense) from above/over/excessive

upsilon, (Gr. υψιλον υ Y) twentieth letter of the Greek alphabet

upti -o, (Gr. υπτιος) bent back/laid back/with the underside uppermost

upup -a -i, (L. upupa) the hoopoe (*Upupa epops*)

ur -a -o, (Gr. ουρα) the tail

ur, (Ger. ur-) earliest/original/primitive

-ura, (L.) result of an action

urach -o -us, (Gr. ουραχος) foetal urinary canal/apex of the heart/the point of a drill or borer

urae -o, (Gr. ουραιος) the tail/hindmost part

urag -i, (Gr. ουραγια) rearguard/the rear

urani -o, (Gr. ουρανιος) heavenly/dwelling in heaven

uranisc -o -us, (Gr. ουρανισκος) a little heaven/roof of the mouth

urano, (Gr. ουρανος) the vault of the heavens/sky/roof of the mouth/the god of heaven

urb -an -i -s, (L. urbanus) a city/walled town/of a city

urce -ol -us, (L. urceolus) small pitcher

ure, (Gr. ουρον L. urina) urine/tail

ured -in -o, (L. uredo) a blight of plants

uren, (L. urens) burning/stinging

ureo, (Gr. ουρεω) urine/urea/pass water

ureter -o, (Gr. ουρητηρ) the urethra

urethr -a -o, (Gr. ουρηθρα) the urethra/sewage tank

urg -y, (Gr. ουργ/εργ) work

-urge, -urgo, -urgy, (Gr. -ουργος) suf. den. work

uri, (Gr. ουρον L. urina) urine/tail

urigo, (L. urigo) lustful/heat/desire

urin -a, (L. urina) urine

urin -o, (L. urinor) dive

urinator, (L. urinator) a diver

urio, (Gr. ουριος) with a fair wind/a prosperous voyage/successful

urn, (L. urna) a pitcher

uro, (Gr. ουρα) the tail

urs -a, (L. ursa) a female bear

ursus, (L. ursus) a bear (*Ursus* spp.)

urtic -a, (L. urtica) the nettle (*Urtica dioica*)/a sea-nettle/lustful/desire

urtica, (L. urtica) the nettle (*Urtica dioica*)

urus, (L. urus) the extinct wild ox (aurochs - *Bos urus* or *Bos primigenius*)

-us, -a, -um, (L.) respectively: masculine, feminine, neuter terminations of many adjectives

-us, (Gr. -ος), of/pertaining to/belonging to

usio, (Gr. ουσια) one's property/one's substance

usitat, (L. usitatus) common/customary/usual

ust -ici -ul -ulat, (L. ustulo) burnt/scorched/singed/browned

ustilag -in -o, (LL. ustilago) smut/a thistle

ustricula, (L. ustricula) hair curler

ustulat, (L. ustulatus) scorched brown

-uta, -utum, -utus, (L.) possession

uter -i -o -us, (L. uterus) the womb/the uterus

uter, (L. uter) which of the two?/one or the other

utesi, (Gr. ουτησις) wounding

uthato, (Gr. ουθαρ) udder/breast/the most fertile land

utidano, (Gr. ουτιδανος) worthless

util, (L. utilis) useful/fit/serviceable/beneficial

utri -c -cul, (L. uter) leather bottle/leather bag

-utus, (L. utus) having the nature of/pertaining to/provided with

-uum, (L.) of/belonging to/pertaining to

uv -a -i, (L. uva) a grape/a berry

uvid, (L. uvidus) damp/moist/wet/drunken

uvul, (LL. uvula) little grape/the fleshy lobe of the soft palate

uxor -i, (L. uxor) a wife/spouse/a man's cloak

V

vac -a -u, (L. vacuus) empty/free
vacca, (L. vacca) cow
vaccin -i -o, (L. vaccinus) vaccine (from *virus vaccinus* - cowpox)
vacerra, (L. vacerra) log/post
vacill -a, (L. vacillo) waver/totter/reel/stagger/wave to and fro
vacu, (L. vacuus) empty/void/exempt
vad -o -um, (L. vadum) a ford/a shallow
vadi, (L. vadimonium) bail/security
vado, (L. vadere) to hasten/rush
vafer, (L. vafer) artful/subtle/sly/crafty
vag -a -an -us, (L. vagus) wandering/indefinite
vagabund, (L. vagabundus) roaming
vagin -a -o, (L. vagina) a sheath
vagit, (L. vagio) cry/whimper/bleat
vague, (L. vagus) wandering/roaming/roving
val, (L. valare) to fortify
valen -t, (L. valere) to be strong/vigorous/healthy
valen, (L. valentia) strength
valeria, (L. valeria) a kind of eagle
valetud -in -o, (L. valetudo) state of health (good or bad)
valg, (L. valgus) bow-legged/wry-mouth
valid -us, (L. validus) strong/powerful/stout/muscular
vall, (L. vallum) a palisade/rampart/valley
vallat-, (L. valatus) surrounded by a rampart
valv -a, (L. valvae) folding doors
valva, (L. valva) a fold
van -i, (L. vanitas) emptiness/worthlessness/unreality/untruth/vanity
vang, (L. vanga) a mattock
vannus, (L. vannus) a winnowing fan
vanus, (L. vanus) empty/void
vapid, (L. vapidus) spiritless/spoiled/flat
vapor, (L. vapor) steam
vappo, (L. vappo) a moth
vapul, (L. vapulare) to be flogged/whipped/beaten
var, (L. varus) crooked/bent/diverse/different/knock-kneed
vara, (L. vara) a trestle
varan -i, (Ar. waran) a monitor lizard (*Varanus* spp.)
vari -a -o, (L. varius) diverse/manifold/variegated
vari -c -x, (L. varix) a varicose vein
varic, (L. varix) dilatation
variegat, (L. variegatus) of different sorts/of different colours
variet, (L. varietas) variety/difference
variol, (LL. variola) smallpox/spotted
varix, (L. varix) a dilated, twisted (varicose) vein
varus, (L. varus) blotch/pimple
vas -a -o, (L. vasa) a vessel/duct/receptacle
vascul -a -um, (L. vasculum) a small vessel
vass, (LL. vassus) a servant
vast, (L. vastitas) waste/emptiness/desolation/huge
vates, (L. vates) prophet/soothsayer/seer
vati, (L. vates) prophet/soothsayer/seer
vaticin, (L. vaticinium) a prophecy
vatius, (L. vatius) bent outward/bow-legged
vatrax, (L. vatrax) with crooked feet/club-footed
ve-, (L.) pref. ind. without, intensive

vecors, (L. vecors/vaecors) senseless/foolish
vect, (L. vectare) to carry/convey
vectis, (L. vectis) a lever/crow-bar//the Isle of Wight
veget, (L. vegetus) lively/vigorous/fresh
vehemen, (L. vehemens) violent/furious/impetuous
vehicul -um, (L. vehiculum) a vehicle/conveyance
vel -a -i -um, (L. velum) covering/sail/awning
vel -es -it, (L. velitare) to skirmish/wrangle/dispute
vela, (L. velarium) an awning
velamen, (L. velamentum) a covering/garment/veil
vell -eri -os -us, (L. vellus) shorn wool/fleece
vellic -a, (L. vellico) pluck/twitch/taunt/criticise
vellus, (L. vellus) fleece/pelt
velo -ci -x, (L. velox) swift/rapid/fleet
velo, (L. velare) to cover/conceal
velocit, (L. velocitas) rapidity
velum, (L. velum) veil/covering/sail/awning
velutin, (NL. velutinus) velvety
ven -a -o, (L. vena) a vein
ven -i -o -um, (L. venenum) poison/drug/love-potion
venabul, (L. venabulum) a hunting spear
venat, (L. venatio) the chase/hunting/a game
venator, (L. venator) a hunter
venen -um, (L. venenum) poison
vener -a -ea, (L. venereus) of Venus
vener -a, (L. venerabilis) venerable/reverend
venet, (L. venetus) sea-coloured/blue
veni -a, (L. venia) grace/favour/indulgence
venos, (L. venosus) with many veins/veiny
vent -er -r -ro, (L. venter) the belly/stomach/womb/a curve/protuberance
vent -i -o -us, (L. ventus) wind
vent, (L. venter) belly
ventos, (L. ventosus) windy/full of wind
ventricul, (L. ventriculus) a small cavity/the belly
venus, (L. Venus) goddess of love/charm/loveliness/attraction
venust, (L. venustus) charming/lovely/graceful
ver -a -ac -i, (L. verax) truthful
ver -us, (L. verus) genuine/true/real
ver, (L. ver) spring time
veratr -um, (L. veratrum) a hellebore (*Veratrum* spp.)
verb -i -o -um, (L. verbum) a word
verben -a, (L. verbenae) sacred boughs of olive, laurel. etc.
verber, (L. verber) a whip/scourge/blow/strike/flogging
verd -an -i ur, (Fr. vert) green
vereor, (L. vereor) fear/respect
veret -ill -r, (L. veretillum) the private parts/sex organs
vergo, (L. vergere) to bend/to be inclined
veri, (L. veritas) truth/reality
vericul, (L. vericulum) a small javelin
verm -i -is, (L. vermis) worm
vermilion, (OFr. vermeil) bright red
vern -a, (L. vernalis) of the spring
vernacul -um, (L. vernaculus) native/a domestic/buffoon/jester
vernil, (L. vernilis) servile/slavish
vernix, (LL. vernix) varnish
verpa, (L. verpa) the penis
verres, (L. verres) a boar
verricul -um, (L. verriculum) a drag net

verro, (L. verrere) sweep/clear away
verruc -a, (L. verruca) a wart
vers -a, (L. verto) turn/turn around/alter/change/overthrow
vers -o, (L. verso) turn about often/turn hither and thither/twist round
versat, (L. versatilis) turning round/revolving
versi, (L. versus) turning
versicolor, (L. versicolor) changing colour
versus, (L. versus) towards/a furrow/row/line/line of poetry
versut, (L. versutus) dextrous/adroit/cunning/crafty/sly
vert -a, (L. vertere) to turn/change
vert -ex -ic, (L. vertex) a top/a whirl/the crown of the head/the apex
verteb, (L. vertebratus) jointed
vertebr -a -o, (L. vertebra) a joint, especially of the back bone
vertex, (L. vertex) the crown of the head/top/summit
vertex, (L. vortex) a whirl/eddy
vertical, (L. vertcalis) directly overhead
verticill -a -us, (L. verticillus) a whorl
vertig -in -o, (L. vertigo) a turning round/whirling round/giddiness
verto, (L. vertere) to turn/turn round
veru, (L. verus) true/genuine
verutus, (L. verutus) armed with a javelin
vervact, (L. vervactum) a fallow field
vervex, (L. vervex) a stupid fellow/a wether
vesan, (L. vesania) madness/insanity
vescor, (L. vescori) eat/feed on
vescus, (L. vescus) weak/poor/thin/little
vesic -a -o, (L. vesica) a bladder
vesicul -a -o, (L. vesicula) a little bladder
vesp -a, (L. vespa) a wasp
vesper -i -tin, (L. vespertinus) of the evening/western
vespertilio -n, (L. vespertilionis) a bat (Vespertilionidae - evening bats)
vest -i -is, (L. vestis) a garment/coat
vest, (L. vestis) a covering/garment/clothing
vesta, (L. Vespa) the goddess of the hearth
vestibul -um, (L. vestibulum) a porch/entrance court
vestig -i -ium, (L. vestigium) a trace/a footstep
vetera -n, (L. veteranus) old (esp. of soldiers)
veterin, (L. veterinus) a beast of burden/draught-animals
veto, (L. vetare) to forbid/prohibit
vetul -a -o -us, (L. vetulus) an old person
vex, (OFr. vexer) annoy/harass
vexan, (L. vexare) to shake/toss/jostle/harass/annoy/molest
vexill -um, (L. vexillum) a banner/standard/a troop
via, (L. via) a road/street/way/method
vib -ex -ic, (L. vibix) a weal/mark of a blow
vibia, (L. vibia) plank/cross piece
vibr -a -i -o, (L. vibrare) to quiver/shake/vibrate/tremble
vibrissa, (L. vibrissae) the hairs of the nostrils
viburn -um, (L. viburnum) the wayfaring tree (*Viburnum* spp.)
vicari, (L. vicarius) deputy/substitute
vice, (L. vicis) in place of/interchange
vicen, (L. viceni) twenty at a time/twenty each
vicia, (L. vicia) a vetch
vicin -i, (L. vicinia) neighbourhood/vicinity/near
vict, (L. victor) conqueror
victu, (L. victus) living/way of living/support/nourishment/food
vidu -i, (L. viduitas) widowhood
viet, (L. vietus) shrivelled/shrunken/withered

vigesim, (L. vigesimus/vicesimus) the twentieth

vigil -i, (L. vigil) awake/watchful

vigint, (L. viginta) twenty

vigor, (L. vigor) force/energy/vigour

vili, (L. vilis) cheap/worth little

vill -i -us, (L. villus) shaggy hair

villos, (L. villosus) hairy/shaggy

vim -en -in, (L. vimen) an osier/twig/basket made of twigs

vin -a -e -o -um, (L. vinum) wine

vinace, (L. vinaceus) belonging to wine or grape

vinc, (L. vincio) bind/tie round/put in bonds/surround/restrain/confine

vinc, (L. vinco) conquer/subdue/vanquish

vincul -um, (L. vinculum) bond/chain/fetter

vind -ex -ic, (L. vindex) an avenger/defender/claimant

vinnul, (L. vinnulus) sweet/charming/pleasant

vinos, (L. vinosus) full of wine/fond of wine

viol -a -en, (L. violens) vehement/violent/furious

viola -ce, (L. viola) a violet (*Viola* spp.)/the colour violet

violat, (L. violatio) injury/violation/profanation

viper -a -i, (L. vipera) a snake/a viper

vir, (L. vir) a man/grown man/husband/soldier/a 'he-man'

virago, (L. virago) a female warrior

vire -ns, (L. virens) green/vigorous/fresh

vireo, (L. vireo) a bird

vireo, (L. vireo) to be vigorous/healthy/fresh/youthful

virescens, (L. virescens) to become green

virg -a, (L. virga) green twig/rod/magic wand

virgo, (L. virgo) a virgin

viria, (L. viria) a bracelet

virid -is, (L. viridis) green (in all shades)

viril, (L. virilis) manly/virile

viro, (L. virosus) stinking/fetid

virtu, (L. virtus) manliness/manly excellence/goodness/virtue

virul, (L. virulentus) poisonous

virus, (L. virus) poison/slime/bitter taste

vis -a -i -u, (L. visio) a seeing/view/appearance/notion/idea

vis, (L. visio) sight

vis, (L. vis) force/power/strength

viscer -a -o, (L. viscera) the bowels/entrails/internal organs

viscos, (LL. viscosus) glutinous/sticky

viscul, (L. viscum) mistletoe/birdlime (made from mistletoe berries)

viscus, (L. viscus) the flesh of the body/an internal organ

visi, (L. visio) look/see

vit -a -al, (L. vita) life

vit -i -is, (L. vitis) a vine/centurion's staff

vitell -i -o -us, (L. vitellus) yolk

viti -um, (L. vitium) fault/defect/blemish

vitil, (L. vitilis) interwoven

vitr -e -i -oo, (L. vitrum) glass/glassy

vitta -t, (L. vitta) a ribbon/band/fillet

vitul -a -i, (L. vitula) a calf/heifer

vituper -a -o, (L. vituperare) to blame/scold/censure

viv -a -i, (L. vivus/vivos) alive/living/life-like

viva -c -x, (L. vivax) long-lived/tenacious/enduring/brisk/lively/vigorous

viverr -a, (L. viverra) a ferret (Viverridae)

vivid, (L. vividus) animated

vivipar, (L. viviparous) bearing active, live, offspring

vix, (L. vix) with difficulty/with effort

voc -a -i, (L. vocalis) speaking/singing/uttering sounds
voc -o, (L. vocare) to call/summon/urge
vocal, (L. vocalis) vocal
vocifer, (L. vociferor) to cry aloud/shout/vociferate
vola, (L. vola) the hollow of the hand
volan, (L. volans) flying
volat -il, (L. volatilis) having wings/swift/rapid/fleeting
volat, (L. volatus) a flying/flight
volit -a, (L. volito) fly about/flutter/flit
volsella, (L. volsella) a pair of tweezers/pincers
volt, (It. volta) time
volubil, (L. volubilis) rolling/revolving/twisting round/rapid/fluent
volucr, (L. volucer) winged/flying/fleet/rapid/swift
volum -en -in, (L. volumen) anything rolled/a wreath/whirl/fold
volunt, (L. voluntas) wish/will/inclination
volupt, (L. voluptas) pleasure/delight/enjoyment
volut -a, (L. voluto) roll around/tumble about
volut, (L. voluta) rolled
volv, (L. volva) any covering/husk/womb
volv, (L. volvere) to roll/wind/turn round/twist round
vomer -i, (L. vomer) a ploughshare
vomi, (L. vomitio) vomiting/throwing up
vomic, (L. vomica) an ulcer/sore/boil
vor-a, (L. vorare) to devour/destroy
vora -c -x, (L. vorax) gluttonous/voracious
vorago, (L. vorago) abyss/chasm/pit
vort -ex -ic, (L. vortex/vertex) whirlpool/eddy/whirlwind
vox, (L. vox) a voice/cry/call
vulcan, (L. Vulcanus/Volcanus) the god of fire/fire
vulga -r -ris -t, (L. vulgatus) common/generally accessible/commonly known
vuln -er -us, (L. vulnero/volnero) wound/injure
vulp -es -i, (L. vuples/volpes) a fox (*Vuples* spp.)/often an emblem of cunning, slyness
vulsus, (L. vulsus) plucked/shorn
vultur, (L. vultur/voltur) a vulture/a rapacious man
vulv -a -o, (L. vulva/volva) any covering/husk/shell

W

(No Entries)

X

xandaros, (Gr. ξανδαρος) a fabulous sea monster of the Atlantic
xani -o -um, (Gr. ξανιον) a card for combing wool
xanth -o, (Gr. ξανθος) yellow (of various shades)
xasma, (Gr. ξασμα) carded wool
xen -i -o -us, (Gr. ξενος) friend/guest/stranger/host
xen -o -us, (Gr. ξενος) stranger/wanderer/refugee/guest-friend
xenago, (Gr. ξεναγος) commander of mercenary troops
xenia, (Gr. ξενιος) hospitable

xenic, (Gr. ξενικος) foreign/strange
xenis -m, (Gr. ξενισις) entertainment (of a guest)
xenium, (Gr. ξενιον) a gift for a guest
xenodochium, (Gr. ξενοδοχειον) inn/lodge
xer -o, (Gr. ξηρος) dry/withered
xes -i -m, (Gr. ξεσις) planing/something smooth or carved/shavings filings
xest -o, (Gr. ξεστος) hewn/shaved/planed
xi, (Gr. ξι ξ Ξ) fourteenth letter of the Greek alphabet
xiph -i -o -us, (Gr. ξιφος) a sword/sword-shaped bone in cuttlefish
xiphid, (Gr. ξιφιδιον) dagger
xoan -o, (Gr. ξοανον) a carved image (in wood)
xunon, (Gr. ξυνων) companionship/partnership
xusilos, (Gr. ξυσιλος) shaven/smooth
xuth -o, (Gr. ξουθος) golden-yellow/nimble/chirruping
xyalbion, (Gr. ξυλαβιον) fire-tongs
xyel -a -o, (Gr. ξυηλη) a curved knife used in shaping a javelin
xyl -o -umo, (Gr. ξυλον) cut wood/timber
xyleus, (Gr. ξυλευς) a wood cutter
xylinum, (Gr. ξυλινον) cotton
xyloch -o -us, (Gr. ξυλοχος) thicket/copse
xylod, (Gr. ξυλωδης) woody/hard as wood
xyn -o -os, (Gr. ξυνος) common/public/general
xyr -o -um, (Gr. ξυρον) a razor
xyri -d -s, (Gr. ξυρις/ξιρις) a iris (*Iris foetidissima*)
xysma -to, (Gr. ξυσμα) filings/shavings
xyst -er -o -r, (Gr. ξυστηρ) scrapper
xyst -on, (Gr. ξυστον) shaft/pole/spear-shaft/spear/lance
xysticus, (Gr. ξυστικος) of scrapping or polishing
xystis, (Gr. ξυστις) a robe of rich and soft material
xystr -a, (Gr. ξυστρα) scrapper used in bathing
xystus, (Gr. ξυστος) a covered colonnade/portico/gallery

Y

(see also hy)

-ygium, (Gr. -υγιον) dim. suf
-yl, (Gr. υλη) material
ymen -o, (Gr. υμην) thin skin/membrane/capsule of plants/parchment/Hymen (Υμην) the god of marriages
yper, (Gr. υπερ-) (in a general sense) from above/over/excessive
ypn -o, (Gr. υπνος) sleep (in a general sense) from under/below/not quite like
yponom, (Gr. υπονομος) undermined/underground/mine/waterpipe/conduit
ypsil -i -o, (Gr. Y - υψιλον) Y-shaped
ypsilon, (Gr. υ Y) twentieth letter of the Greek alphabet

Z

za, (Gr. ζα-) intensifying prefix

zabr -o, (Gr. ζαβορος/ζαβρος) gluttonous

zachol, (Gr. ζαχολος/ζακοτος) very angry

zal -e -o, (Gr. ζαλη) squall/storm/driving rain

zalmos, (Gr. ζαλμος) a skin

zamen, (Gr. ζαμενης) very strong/mighty/raging

zamia, (Gr. ζημια) loss/damage

zancl -o -um, (Gr. ζαγκλον) a reaping-hook/sickle

ze -a, (Gr. ζεια) one-seeded wheat (*Triticum monococcum*)/rice-wheat

ze -i -us, (L. zeus) a type of fish (*Zeus faber*)

zeal, (Gr. ζηλος) enthusiasm

zelo, (Gr. ζηλος) emulation/jealousy/eager rivalry

zem -a, (Gr. ζεμα) fermentation/boiling/a decoction

zemi -a, (Gr. ζημια/ζαμια) loss/damage/penalty/fine

zen, (Gr. ζηνη) a goldfinch

zeo, (Gr. ζεω) boil/seethe/ferment/bubble up

zephyr -o -us, (Gr. ζεφυρος) the west wind

zest -o, (Gr. ζεστος) boiled/seethed/hot

zeta, (Gr. ζητα ζ Z) sixth letter of the Greek alphabet

zete, (Gr. ζητεω) seek/search/inquire/investigate

zetetes, (Gr. ζετετης) a seeker/searcher

zeuct -o, (Gr. ζευκτος) yoked/harnessed/joined in pairs/joined

zeug -o, (Gr. ζευγος) a yoke/a pair or couple of anything joined

zeugl -o, (Gr. ζευγλη) a loop attached to a yoke

zeugma -to, (Gr. ζευγμα) something used for joining/a bond/band

zeus, (Gr. Ζευς/Ζηυς) chief of the gods

zeuxi -s, (Gr. ζευξις) a yoking/bridging

zignis, (Gr. ζιγνις) a kind of lizard

zinc -o, (Gr. ζινκ) zinc

zingiberi -s, (Gr. ζιγγιβερις) ginger (prob.)

ziro, (Gr. ζειρα) a wide garment/robe

zizani -um, (Gr. ζιζανιον) a weed that grows in wheat

zizyph -um, (Gr. ζιζυφον) the jujube tree (*Zizyphus jujuba*)

zo -a -i -o -on, (Gr. ζωη) life/living/way of life

-zoa, (Gr. ζωον) a living being/an animal

zoarc, (Gr. ζωαρκης) life supporting

zoarion, (Gr. ζωαριον) a little animal (in general)

zodar, (Gr. ζωδαριον) little animal

zodi, (Gr. ζωδιον) a small sculptured figure/a sign of the zodiac

zodiac, (Gr. ζωδιακος) of animals/the zodiac

zoe, (Gr. ζωη) life

zogrion, (Gr. ζογρειον) menagerie/cage/fish pond

zoi, (Gr. ζωικος) animal/of animals

zom -o -us, (Gr. ζωμος) soup/sauce/a fat or greasy fellow

zoma, (Gr. ζωμα) a loin cloth/girdle

zomerysis, (Gr. ζομηρυσις) a soup ladle

zon -a -i, (Gr. ζωνη) a belt/girdle/zone

zoo -n, (Gr. ζωον) an animal/living being

zoph -er -ero -o, (Gr. ζοφερος) dusky/gloomy/misty

zopyron, (Gr. ζωπυρον) a spark/a hot coal

zoro -s, (Gr. ζωρος) pure/sheer

zorr -o, (Sp. zorra) a fox

zos -m -mer -ter, (Gr. ζωστηρ) a belt/girdle/warrior's belt/anything like a girdle

zotheca, (Gr. ζωθηκη) small room/dormitorium/niche in the wall

zoyphion, (Gr. ζωυφιον) little animal

zyg -o -on -os -us, (Gr. ζυγον/ζυγος) a yoke/cross bar/bolt

zygaen -a, (Gr. ζυγαινα) the hammer-headed shark (*Sphyrna zygaena*)

zygastron, (Gr. ζυγαστρον) chest/box

zygoma, (Gr. ζυγωμα) bar/bolt/cross-rod

zygot, (Gr. ζυγωτος) harnessed/yoked

zyl -o, (Gr. ξυλον) cut wood/timber

zym -a -o, (Gr. ζυμη) leaven/ferment/yeast/corruption/falsehood

zyth -us, (Gr. ζυθος) a type of Egyptian beer

GEOGRAPHICAL NAMES

Adjectival forms of some common place names. Alternative names are in parenthesis and Latin names are in brackets at the end of each entry.

The names of regions and countries as used by earlier authors will not necessarily apply to the same regions and countries today. Sometimes they were vaguely applied and often regional boundaries have changed, especially in the last half of the twentieth century. For example, Canada in the Linnaean sense does not correspond to the modern Dominion of Canada but to a region of north-eastern America, partly in Canada but mostly in the United States, roughly from Philadelphia north to Québec and west to Lake Ontario and the Niagara Falls. Many places and regions in Europe have also changed, especially following the break up of the Soviet Union.

abbatiscellanus	Appenzell, N.E. Switzerland [Abbatis Cella]
acadiensis	Nova Scotia, Canada [Acadia/Accadia]
achaius	Akhaia, Peloponnisos, Greece [Achaia]
aegyptiacus	Egypt (i.e. the Nile valley between 24° 3′ E and 31° 37′ N [Aegyptus]
aequatorialis	Ecuador [Aequatoria]
aetensis	Mt. Etna, Sicily [Aetna]
aethiopicus	Africa, commonly South Africa but in classical usage Africa south of Lybia and Egypt; hence Abyssinia [Aethiopia]
aetolicus	Aitolia, mid. Greece [Aetolia]
afer, africanus	Africa
afghanicus	Afghanistan [Afghania/Affghania]
aleppicus (chalepensis, halepensis)	Alep (Haleb), N. Syria [Aleppo]
alexandrinus	Alexandria, Egypt [Alexandria]
algarvicus	Algarve, Portugal [Algarbia]
allobrogicus	Savoy (Savoie), France [Allobrogicae Alps]
alpinus	European Alps [Alpes]
alsaticus	Alsace (Elass), France [Alsatia]
altdorfiensis	Altdorf, Germany [Altdorffium]
altorfinus	Altdorf, Germany [Altorfia]
amboinensis, amboinicus	Ambon, Moluccas, Indonesia [Amboina, Ambona],
amstelodamensis	Amsterdam, Netherlands [Amstelodamum]
anatolicus	Turkey [Anatolia, Natolia]
ancyrensis	Ankara, Turkey [Ancyra]
andegavensis	Angers, France [Andegavum]
anglicus	East England [Anglia]
antillanus	West Indies [Antillae, India Occidentalis]
apenninus	the Apennines, Italy [Apennius]
aplestris	European Alps [Alpes]
arabicus	Arabia [Arabia]
arcadiensis	Arkadhia, Peloponnisos, Greece [Arcadia]
argoviensis	Aargau (Argovie), Switzerland [Argovia]
arvonicus, arvoniensis	Caernarvonshire, N. Wales, Britain [Arvonia]
atrebatensis	Arras, N. France [Atrebatum]
atropatanus	Azerbaijan, N.W. Iran [Atropatene]
atticus	Attili. S. Greece [Attica]
aurelianensis	Orléans, N. France [Aurelia, Aurelianum]
australiensis	Australia [Australia, Nova Hollandia]
austriacus	Austria (Österreich), [Austria]
baeticus	Andalucia, S. Spain [Baetica]
bahusiensis	Bohuslän, S. Sweden [Bahusia]
balearicus	Balearic Islands, Spain [Balaeres]

banaticus	Banat, former Austro-Hungarian crownland approx. 20° - 23° E., 45° - 46° N. Romania [Banatus]
barcinensis	Barcelona, N.E. Spain [Barcino]
basiliensis	Basel (Bâle), N. Switzerland [Basilea, Basilia]
batavus	Dutch Netherlands [Batavia]
bathoniensis	Bath, S.W. England [Bathonia]
batrianus	N.E. Afghanistan [Bactria]
bavaricus	Bavaria (Bayern), Germany [Bavaria]
belgicus	Netherlands, i.e. the Dutch Netherlands [Belgium Confederatum; Belgium Foederatum) and modern Belgium [Belgium Austriacum; Belgia; Brabantia et Flandria]
benghalensis	Bengal, India and Pakistan [Benghala]
berolinensis	Berlin, Germany [Berolinum]
berytensis, berytheus	Beirut, Lebanon [Berytus]
berytius	Berit Dagi (Berytdagh), Central Turkey [Berytus]
bipontinus	Zweibrücken, Germany [Bipontium]
bithynicus, bithynus	N.W. Turkey [Bithynia]
blesensis	Blois, N. France [Blesae]
boeoticus	Voiotia, mid-Greece [Boeotia]
boloniensis	Boulogne, N.E. France [Bolonia]
bonariensis	Buenos Aries, Argentina [Bonaria, Bonaeropolis]
bonnensis	Bonn, Germany [Bonna]
bononiensis	Bologna, N. Italy [Bononia]
borbonicus	Réunion, Mascarenes, Indian Ocean [Borbonia Insula]
borysthenicus	the river Dnieper, Russia, Belorussia (Belarus) and the Ukraine [Borysthenes]
bottnicus	Gulf of Bothnia, Scandanavia [Bottnicus Sinus]
brasiliensis	Brazil [Brasilia]
britannicus	Britain [Britannia]
brunsvicensis	Brunswick (Braunschweig), Germany [Brunsviga, Brunswiga]
burdigalensis	Bordeaux, S.W. France [Burdigala]
burmanicus	Myanmar (formerly Burma), [Burma, Birmania]
byzantinus, constantinopolitanus	Istanbul, Turkey [Byzantium,Constantinopolis]
cadmicus	Babadag, S.W. Turkey [Cadmus]
caffer	S. Africa [Caffraria]
cairicus, kahiricus	Cairo, Egypt [Cairum, Cairus]
calabricus	Calabria, S. Italy [Calabria]
caledonicus, scoticus	Scotland [Caledonial, Scotia]
calpensis, gibraltaricus	Gibralter, S. Spain [Calpe]
cambrensis, cambricus	Wales, [Cambria, Cambro-britannia, Wallia]
campechianus	Campeche, S.E. Mexico [Campechia]
camschatcensis	Kamchatka, Siberia [Camschatca]
canariensis	Gran Canaria or the Canary Islands [Fortunatae Insulae, Insulae Canarienses]
cantabricus	Cantabrica, N. Spain [Cantabria]
cantabrigiensis	Cambridge, England [Cantabrigia]
cantianus	Kent, S.E. England [Cantia, Cantium]
capensis	Cape of Good Hope, S. Africa [Caput Bonae Spei, Cap.B.Spei]
caribaeus	Lesser Antilles, W. Indies [Caribaeae, Caribae Insulae]
caricus	a region of S.W. Asia Minor [Caria]

carinthiacus	Carithia (Kärnten), S. Austria [Carinthia]
carniolicus	Carniola, a former Austrian crownland, now part of Slovenia [Carniola]
carolinus, carolinensis, carolinianus	Carolina, U.S.A. [Carolina]
carolsruanus, caroliquietanus	Karlsruhe, Germany [Carolsruha]
carpathicus, carpaticus	The Carpathians, E, Europe [Carpathus Mons]
carpetanus	Cordillera mountain range, central Spain [Carpetani Montes]
carthaginensis	Cartagena, N. Columbia [Carthagena]
cashemirianus, cashmerianus	Kashmir [Cashmiria]
caspicus, caspius	Caspian Sea [Mare Caspium)
cassubicus	the region around Gdansk (Danzig), Poland [Cassubia]
castellanus	Castile (Castilla), Spain [Castella]
castulonensis, cazorlensis	Sierra de Cazorla, Andalucia, S. Spain [Castulonensis, Saltus]
catalaunicus	Catalonia (Cataluña), N.E. Spain [Catalaunia]
cathayanus, chinensis, sinensis	China [Sina]
caucasicus	The Caucasus mountains, between the Black Sea and the Caspian Sea [Caucasia]
ceylanicus, zeylanicus, taprobanicus	Sri Lanka (formerly Ceylon) [Ceylona, Zeylona, Taprobane]
chalepensis (aleppicus, halepensis)	Alep (Haleb), N. Syria [Aleppo]
chersonensis, tauricus	the Crimea (Krym), Ukraine [Chersonesus Taurica, Tauria]
chinensis, cathayanus, sinensis	China [Sina]
cilicius	A region of S. Turkey, north of the Gulf of Iskenderun [Cilicia]
conimbricensis	Coimbra, Portugal [Conimbrica]
constantinopolitanus, byzantinus	Istanbul, Turkey [Constantinopolis, Byzantium]
cornubiensis	Cornwall, S.W. England [Cornubia]
corsicus	Corsica (Corse), France [Corsica]
creticus, cretensis	Crete, Greece [Creta]
curassavicus	Curaçao, Caribbean Sea [Curassao]
cyprius (veneris)	Cyprus, E. Mediterranean Sea [Cyprus]
dalecarlicus	Dalarna, mid. Sweden [Dalecarlia]
danicus	Denmark [Dania]
danubialis	the river Danube (Donau), central Europe [Danubius]
dauricus, dahuricus, davuricus	a region of S.E. Siberia [Dauria, Dahuria, Davuria)]
delphinensis	Dauphiné, E. France [Delphinatus]
dyrrhachinus	Durazzo (Durres), Albania [Dyrrachium]
eboracensis	York, N. England [Eboracum]
ebudicus (hebridensis)	The Hebrides, off the coast of W. Scotland [EbudaeInsulae]
edinensis	Edinburgh, Scotland [Edinum, Edinburgum]
emodensis (himalaicus, himalayensis)	The Himalaya, of which the Greeks knew only the western region [Emodus, Emodi Montes]
etruscus	Tuscany (Toscana), N. Italy [Etruria, Hetruria]
europaeus	Europe [Europa]
exoniensis	Exeter, S.W. England [Exonia]
eystettensis	Eichstätt, Bavaria (Bayern), Germany [Eystettum,Eustadium]
faeroensis	The Faeroes (Faeröerne) [Faeroenses Insulae]
falklandicus (maclovianus)	Falkland Islands, S. Atlantic [Maclovianae Insulae]

fennicus	Finland (Suomi) [Fennia, Fenningia, Finnia,Finlandia]
florentinus	Florence (Firenze), Italy [Florentia]
fluminensis	Rio de Janeiro, E. Brazil [Flumen Januarii, Sebastianopolis]
formosanus, taiwanensis	Taiwan (formerly Formosa) [Formosa]
fuegianus	Tierra del Fuego, Chile and Argentina [Fuegia,Terra Ignis]
gaditanus	Cadiz, S. Spain [Gades]
gaetulicus	Sahara, N. Africa [Gaetulia]
galaticus	A region of central Asia Minor [Galatia]. Now in central Turkey
gallicus	France (Gallia)
gandavensis	Gent (Gand), Belgium [Gandavum]
garganicus	Monte Gargano, Italy [Garganus Mons]
gedanensis	Gdansk (Danzig), Poland [Gedanum, Dantiscum]
gelricus	Gelderland, Netherlands [Gelria, Geldria]
genevensis, genavensis	Geneva (Genève), Switzerland [Geneva, Augusta Allobrogum, Colonia Allobrogum]
genuensis (januensis)	Genoa (Genova), Italy [Genua, Janua Ligurum]
germanicus	Germany [Germania]
gibraltaricus, calpensis	Gibralter, S. Spain [Calpe]
gissensis	Giessen, central Germany [Gissa]
gorgoneus	Cape Verde Islands, Atlantic Ocean [Gorgades, Insulae Capitis Viridis]
gotoburgensis, gothoburgensis	Gothenburg (Göteborg), S. Sweden [Gotoburgum]
gottingensis	Göttingen, central Germany [Gottinga, Goettinga]
graecus (hellenicus)	Greece [Graecia]
gratianopolitanus	Grenoble, S.E. France [Gratianopolis]
groelandicus	Greenland [Groelandia]
groningensis	Groningen, Netherlands [Groninga]
gryphicus	Greifswald, Germany [Gryphiswaldia, Gryphia]
guadalupensis	Guadeloupe, W. Indies [Gaudalupa Insula]
guineensis	Guinea, W. Africa [Guinea]
hafniensis	Copenhagen (København), Denmark [Hafnia, Havnia]
halepensis (aleppicus, chalepensis)	Alep (Haleb), N. Syria [Aleppo]
hannoveranus	Hannover, central Germany [Hannovera]
hebridensis (ebudicus)	The Hebrides, off the coast of W. Scotland [Ebudae Insulae]
heirosolymitanus	Jerusalem, Palestine, Israel [Heirosolyma]
hellenicus (graecus)	Greece [Graecia]
helveticus	Switzerland [Helvatia]
hercynicus	Harz region, central Germany [Hercynia, Harcynia]
hibernicus (irensis, iricus)	Ireland [Hibernia, Irlandia]
himalaicus, himalayensis (emodensis)	The Himalaya, of which the Greeks knew only the western region [Emodus, Emodi Montes]
hispalensis	Sevilla, S. Spain [Hispalis]
hispanicus	Spain [Hispania]
hollandicus	Holland/Netherlands [Hollandia]
holmensis	Stockholm, S. Sweden [Holmia, Stockholmia]
holsaticus	Holstein, Germany [Holsatia]
hungaricus (pannonicus)	Hungary [Ungaria, Ungaria, Pannonia]

hydaspidis	the river Jhelum, W. Himalaya, Pakistan [Hydaspes]
hyrcanus	N. Persia bordering the Caspian Sea [Hyrcania]
ibericus	Iberian Peninsula, i.e. Spain and Portugal (Iberia)
illyricus	the east coast of the Adriatic sea from Trieste (Slovenia) to Albania [Illyria, Illyrium]
ilvensis	Elba, Italy [Ilva]
indicus	India [India]
ingricus	the St. Petersburg region of Russia [Ingria]
insubricus	the regions of Lago Maggiore, Lago di Lugano and Lago di Como, N. Italy and S. Switzerland [Insubria]
irensis, iricus (hibernicus)	Ireland [Hibernia, Irlandia]
isauricus	a region of S. Turkey [Isauria]
iscanus	a region of S.W. England [Isca]
islandicus	Iceland [Islandia]
jacobaeus	St. Jago (S. Iago), Cape Verde Islands [Sancti Jacobi Insula]
jamaicensis	Jamaica, West Indies [Jamaica]
januensis (genuensis)	Genoa (Genova), Italy [Genua, Janua Ligurum]
japonicus (nipponicus)	Japan [Japonia]
javanicus	Java, Indonesia [Java, Indonesia]
jenensis	Jens, Germany [Jena]
jurassicus	Jura, a region of S.E. France and N.W. Switzerland [Jura]
juressi	Serra do Gerez, Portugal [Juressus Mons]
kahiricus, cairicus	Cairo, Egypt [Cairus, Cairum]
kurdicus	Kurdistan, S.E. Turkey and N. Iraq [Kurdistania]
laconicus	Lakonia, Peloponnisos, Greece [Laconia]
lapponicus	Lapland, N. Scandinavia [Lapponia]
laurentianus	Gulf of St. Lawrence, Canada [Laurentianus Sinus]
legionensis	León, N.W. Spain [Legio]
leopolitanus	Lvov, Ukraine [Leopolis, Lemberga]
leydensis	Leiden, Netherlands [Lugdunum Batavorum, Leyda]
libanensis	Mt. Liban near Santiago de Cuba, Cuba [Libanus Mons]
libanoticus	Lebanon mountain range [Libanus Mons]
liburnicus	a region of the east Croatian Istrian coast [Liburnia]
libycus	Libya, N. Africa [Libya]
ligusticus	Liguria, N. Italy [Ligura]
lipsiensis	Leipzig, Germany [Lipsia]
lisbonensis	Lisbon, Portugal [Lisbona]
londinensis	London, England [Londinum]
luceburgensis	Luxembourg (Lützelburg) [Luxemburgum, Luciliburgum]
ludovicianus, louisianus	Louisiana (former Louisiana Territory), U.S.A. [Ludovicia]
lugdunensis	Lyon, S. France [Lugdunum]
lundensis	Lund, S. Sweden [Lunda, Londinum Gothorum]
lusitanicus	Portugal [Lusitania, Portugallia]
lycaonicus	a region of central Turkey [Lycaonia]
lycius	a region of S.W. Turkey [Lycia]

lydius	a region of western Asia Minor [Lydia]
macedonicus	Macedonia, Balkan Peninsula between 20°-24° E and 40°-42° N. [Macedonia]
maclovianus (falklandicus)	Falkland Islands, S. Atlantic [Maclovianae Insulae]
macloviensis	Saint-Malo, N.W. France [Maclovium Aletae]
maderaspatanus	the Madras region of S. India [Maderaspata]
maderensis	Madeira [Madera]
magellanicus	the Strait of Magellan, Chile [Magellanicum Fretum, Magellani Fretum]
malabaricus	Malabar, S.W. India [Malabara]
mancuniensis	Manchester, England [Mancunium]
marianus (marilandicus)	Maryland U.S.A. [Marilandia]
marmaricus	a coastal region of Libya and Egypt between Derna and El Alamein [Marmarica]
maroccanus	Morocco [Maroccanum Regnum]
martabanicus	Martaban district of S. Burma (Myanmar) [Martabania]
martinicensis	Martinique, West Indies [Martinica]
massanensis	Messina, Sicily [Messana]
massilianus, massiliensis	Marseille, S. France [Massilia]
matritensis	Madrid, Spain [Matritum, Madritum]
mauritanicus	Mauritania, N.W. Africa [Mauritania]
mechlinensis	Mechelen (Malines), Belgium [Machlinium, Mechlinia]
mediterraneus	Mediterranean Sea [Mare Mediterraneum]
megalopolitanus	Mecklenburg, Germany [Megalopolis]
melitensis	Malta [Melita]
messeniensis	Messinia, S. Greece [Messenia]
mexicanus	Mexico [Nova Hispania]
moesiacus	a region of the mid. Balkan Peninsula (Bulgaria and Serbia) [Moesia]
moldavicus	a region between Romania and the Ukraine at approximately 26°-29° E. and 46°-48° N. [Moldavia]
moluccanus, moluccensis	Moluccas (Amboina, Ceram), Indonesia [Moluccae]
monacensis	Munich (München), Germany [Monachum, Monachium]
monensis	Anglesey, N. Wales, also Isle of Man, Britain [Mona]
monspeliensis, monspeliacus, monspessulanus	Montpellier, S. France [Monspelium, Monspessulus]
mosquensis	Moscow (Moskva), Russia [Mosqua]
murcicus	Murcia, S. Spain [Murcicum Regnum]
mysicus	a region of N.W. Turkey [Mysia]
narbonensis	southern France around Narbonne; in Roman times all of southern France [Gallia Narbonensis]
neapolitanus	Naples (Napoli), Italy [Neapolis]
neocomensis	Neuchâtel, Switzerland [neocomum]
nepalensis, napaulensis	Nepal [Nepalia]
nerlandicus	Netherlands [Nerlandia]
nicaeensis	Nice, France [Nicaea Maritima]
nipponicus (japonicus)	Japan [Japonia]
noricus	eastern Alps, Austria [Noricae Alpes]
norimbergensis	Nuremburg (Nürnberg), Germany [Norimberga]

norvegicus	Norway [Norvegia]
norvicensis	Norwich, E. England
noveboracensis	New York, U.S.A. [Noveboracum]
nubicus	Nubia, Sudan (or N.E. Africa in general [Nubia]
numidicus	N.E. Algeria [Numidia]
occitanicus	Languedoc, S. France [Occitania]
oelandicus	the island of Öland, S. Sweden [Oelandia]
olbius	Hyères, S. France [Olbia Galloprovinciae]
olympicus	applied to many high mountains in Greece, Asia Minor and the U.S.A. [Olympus]
orcadensis	Orkney, Scotland [Orcades]
orubicus	the island of Aruba, Caribbean [Oruba]
oscensis	Huesca, N. Spain [Osca]
osloensis	Oslo, S. Norway [Christiana]
oxoniensis	Oxford, England [Oxonia]
palatinus	Palatinate (Pfalz), Germany [Palatinatus]
palestinus, palaestinus	Palestine [Palestina, Palaestina]
pamphylicus	a region of S.W. Asia Minor [Pamphylia]. Now the southern coast of Turkey
pannonicus (hungaricus)	Hungary [Pannonia, Hungaria, Ungaria]
panormitanus	Palermo, Sicily [Panormus, Panormum]
paphlagonicus	a region of northern Turkey [Paphlagonia]
parisiensis, lutetianus	Paris, France [Parisii, Lutetia, Parisiorum]
patavinus	Padua (Padova), N. Italy [Patavium]
pedemontanus	Piedmont, N. Italy [Pedemnotium]
peloponnesiacus	Peloponnisos, S, Greece [Peloponnesus]
pensylvanicus	Pennsylvania, U.S.A. [Pensylvania]
persepolitanus	Persepolis, S. Iran [Persepolis]
persicus, iranicus	Iran (Persia) [Persia]
peruvianus	Peru [Peruvia]
petropolitanus	St Petersburg (Lenningrad), Russia [Petropolils]
philippensis. philippinensis	Philippines [Philippinae]
phrygius	a region of W. Turkey [Phrygia]
pisidicus	a region of S.W. Turkey [Pisidia]
podolicus	Podolia, S.W. Ukraine [Podolia]
polonicus	Poland [Polonia]
ponticus	a region of N.E. Asia Minor (Pontus)
portuensis	Porto, Portugal [Portus Lusitaniae, Portus Calensis]
praensis	Prague (Praha), Czech Republic [Praga]
praetutianus	Abruzzi region, central Italy [Praetutianus Ager]
proponticus	Sea of Marmara, Turkey [Propontis]
provincialis	Provence, S. France [Galloprovincia, Provincia]
pyrenaicus, pyrenaeus	Pyrenees, France and Spain [Pyrenaei Montes]
ratisbonensis	Regensburg, Germany [Ratisbona]
regiomontanus	Kaliningrad (formerly Königsberg), Russia [Regiomontum]
rhaeticus	the Alps of E. Switzerland and W. Austria [Rhaeticae Alpes]
rhenanus	the river Rhine [Rhenus]
rhodius	Rhodes (Rodhos), Greece [Rhodus]
romanicus	Romania [Romania]
romanus	Rome (Roma), Italy [Roma]
rossicusa, russicus	Russia (former U.S.S.R.)
rothomagensis	Rouen, N. France [Rothomagus]

rumelicus	a division of the former Ottoman Empire consisting of S. Bulgaria, Greek Thrace and Turkish Thrace [Rumelia]
ruscinonensis	Perpignan, S.W. France [Ruscino]
ruthenicus	southern European former U.S.S.R. [Ruthenia]
sabaudus	Savoy (Savoie), E. France [Sabauda]
sabbatius	Savona, N. Italy [Sabbatia]
salamanticus, salamanticensis	Salamanca, N. Spain [Salamantica]
salisburgensis	Salzburg, Austria [Salsburgum]
salomonensis	Solomon Islands, Pacific Ocean (Salomonae Insulae]
sardensis	Sart, W. Turkey [Sardes]
sardicus	Sar Planina (Shardagh, Sar Mountains), S. Serbia, N. Macedonia, N.E, Albania.
sardous	Sardinina (Sardegna), Italy [Sardinia]
sarisberiensis	Salisbury, England [Sarisberia], also applied to plants of Salisbury (now Harare), Rhodesia (now Zimbabwe)
sarmaticus	eastern Europe [Sarmatia]
sarniensis	Guernsey, Channel Islands, Britain [Sarnia]
saxonicus	Saxony (Sachsen), Germany [Saxonia]
scandicus, scandinavicus	Scandinavia [Scandia, Scandinavia]
scilloniensis	Isles of Scilly, S.W. England [Scillonia]
scoticus, caledonicus	Scotland [Scotia, Caledonial]
senegambicus	a region of W. Africa comprising Senegal, The Gambia, Guinea-Bissau, Guinea [Senegambia]
senensis	Siena, N. Italy [Sena]
sibiricus	Siberia [Sibiria]
siculus	Sciliy [Sicilia]
sinaiticus, sinaicus	Sinia peninsula, Egypt [Sinai]
sinensis, chinensis, cathayanus	China [Sina]
sipyleus	Sipuli Dag, a mountain near Manisa, W. Turkey [Sipylus Mons]
sitchensis	Sitka, Alaska [Sitcha]
smyrnaeus	Izmir, W. Turkey [Smyrna]
sogdianus	a region of central Asia between the rivers Amu Darya and Syr Darya [Sogdiana]
songaricus	Dzungaria, Sinkiang, Central Asia [Songaria, Sungaria, Soongaria]
sonticus	the river Isonzo, N. Italy [Sontius Fluvius]
sponhemicus	Sponheim, Germany
stiriacus	Steiermark, Austria [Stiria]
sudeticus	the Sudeten mountains (Sudety) N.W. Czech republic and S.W. Poland
suecicus	Sweden [Seucia, Svecia]
surinamensis	Surinam, S. America [Surinama]
surrejanus	Surrey, S. England [Surrejanus Comitatus]
susianus	Shush, S.W. Iran [Susa]
syriacus	Syria [Syria]
taiwanensis, formosanus	Taiwan (formerly Formosa) [Formosa]
tamesis	the river Thames, S. England [Tamesis]
tanaicensis	the river Don, Russia [Tanais]
taprobanicus, ceylanicus, zeylanicus	Sri Lanka (formerly Ceylon) [Taprobane, Ceylona, Zeylona]
tataricus	a region of central Asia and European Russia, east of the river Don (Russia) [Tataria]. Little Tatary is the Black Sea region, east of the river Dnieper.

tauricus, chersonensis	the Crimea (Krym), Ukraine [Tauria, Chersonesus Taurica]
tergestinus	Trieste, N. Italy [Tergeste]
thessalus	Thessalia, N. Greece [Thessalia]
thracicus	Thrace, central Balkan Peninsula, Turkey [Thracia]
thuringiacus	Thurgingia (Thüringen), central Germany [Thuringia, Turingia]
tingitanus	Tangier, N.W. Africa [Tingitana]
tirolensis, tyrolensis	the Tyrol, S. Austria and N. Italy [Tiroloa]
toletanus	Toledo, central Spain [Toletum]
tornacensis	Tournai, Belgium [Tornacum]
transwallianus	Pembroke, Wales [Transwallia]
trapezuntinus	Trebizond (Trabzon), N.E. Turkey [Trapezus]
trinitatensis, trinitensis	Trinidad, West Indies [Trinitatis Insula, Trinitatum]
tubingensis	Tübingen, Germany [Tubinga]
turcicus	Turkey [Turcia]
turicensis	Zürich, N. Switzerland [Tigurum, Turicum Helvetiorum]
turkestanicus	Türkistan, Kazakhstan [Turkestania]
turolensis	Teruel, E. Spain [Turolum, Terulium]
ucrtanicus	Ukraine [Ucrania]
uplandicus	Upland, S. Sweden [Uplandia]
upsaliensis	Uppsala, S. Sweden [Upsala]
valdensis	the canton of Vaud, W. Switzerland [Valdia, Valdensis Pagus]
valentius	Valencia, E. Spain [Valentia]
varsaviensis, warsaviensis	Warsaw (Warszawa), Poland [Varsavia, Varsovia, Warsavia]
vectensis	Isle of Wight, S. England [Vectis Insula]
veneris (cyprius)	Cyprus, E. Mediterranean Sea [Cyprus]
venetus	the Veneto region of N. Italy [Venetia]
verbanensis	Lago Maggiore, N. Italy and Switzerland [Verbanus Lacus]
viennensis	Vienne, S.W. France [Vienna Allobrogum]
vindobonensis	Vienna (Wein), Austria [Vindobona, Vienna Austriae]
warsaviensis, varsaviensis	Warsaw (Warszawa), Poland [Warsavia, Varsavia, Varsovia]
zetlandicus	Shetland Isles, Britain [Zetlandia]
zeylanicus, ceylanicus, taprobanicus	Sri Lanka (formerly Ceylon) Zeylona, Ceylona,Taprobane]

SOME COMMON TERMS FOR ANIMALS, PLANTS, STRUCTURES, ACTIVITIES AND HABITATS

animal	zoo- -zoon (Gr. ζωον)
ankle	tars- tarsi- -tarsus (L. tarsus)
anus	ano- -anus; (L. anus); procto- -proctus (Gr. πρωκτος)
arm	branchi- -brachium (Gr. βραχιων)
back	dors- dorsi- -dorsum (L. dorsum); noto- -notus (Gr. νωτον); tergi- -tergum (L. tergum)
bark	-cortex cortici- (L. cortex); phloeo- -phloeus (Gr. φλοιος)
beak	rostr- -rostrum (L. rostrum); rhyncho- -rhynchus (Gr. ρυγχος)
belly	-venter ventr- ventro- (L. venter); -gaster gastro- (Gr. γαστηρ)
berry	acini- -acinus (L. acinus); -bacca bacci- (L. baca/bacca); cocco- -coccus (Gr. κοκκος)
bird	avi -avis (L. avis); ornitho -ornis (Gr. ορνις)
bladder	asco- -ascus (Gr. ασκος); cysto- -cystis (Gr. κυστις); -physa physo- (Gr. φυσαλλις); -vesica vesico- (L. vesica)
blood	sangui- sanguini- -sanguis (L. sanguis); -haema haemato- haem- (Gr. αιμα)
body	corporo- -corpus; (L. corpora); -soma somat- (Gr. σωμα)
bone	-os ossi- (L. os); osteo- -osteum (Gr.οστεον)
border	chilo- -chilus; (Gr. χειλος); craspedo- -craspedum (Gr. κρασπεδον)
brain	cereb- cerebr- cerebrum; (L. cerebrum); encephalo- -encephalus (Gr. εγκεφαλος)
bramble	bato- -batus; (Gr. βατος); rube- rubi- rubus (L. rubus)
branch	ram- rami- ramo- -ramus; (L. ramus); clado- -cladus (Gr. κλαδος)
breast	pector- -pectus; (L. pectus); stern- sterni- -sternum (L. sternum)
breathe	pneumato- pneumo- (Gr. πνευματοω)
bristle	-seta seti- (L. seta)
bud	gemm- -gemma (L. gemma)
carry	fer- (L. ferre); phoro- (Gr. φορος)
cartilage	chondro- chondrus (Gr. χονδρος)
cat	feli- -felis (L. felis); aeluro- -aelurus (Gr. αιλουρος)
caterpillar	-eruca eruci- (L. eruca); campa- campo- (Gr. καμπη)
cave	antro- (L. antrum Gr. αντρον); caverni- (L. caverna); spel- speleo- (Gr. σπηλαιον); troglo-(Gr. τρωγλη)
cell	-cella celli- (L. cella); cyto- -cytus (Gr. κυτος)
cheek	bucc- -bucca (L. bucca); gen- -gena geno- (L. gena)
chest	stetho- -stethus (Gr. στηθος)
claw	chel- -chela chelo- (Gr. χηλη); onycho- -onyx (Gr. ονυξ); ungui-. unguis- (L. unguis)
cow	-bos -bov- (L. bos); boo- -bus (Gr. βους)
creep	rept- reptili- (L. reptilis); erpet- (Gr. ερπετον)
crest	crist- -crista (L. crista); lopho- -lophus (Gr. λοφος)
crown	coron- -corona (L. corona); stephano- -stephanus (Gr. στεφανος)
cut	sect- (L. secare); tom- (Gr. τομη)
dance	choreo- (Gr. χορευω)
depths	batho- bathy- (Gr. βαθυς); bentho- (Gr. βενθος); bysso- (Gr. βυσσος); bytho (Gr. βυθιος)
digit	digiti- digitus (L. digitus); dactylo- -dactylus (Gr. δακτυλος)

dog	cani- -canis (L. canis); cyno- -cyon (Gr. κυων)
dry	xero- (Gr. ξηρος)
dry	arid- (L. aridus); azo- (Gr. αζω)
dung	copro- (Gr. κοπρος); scato- (Gr. σκατος); spatilo- (Gr. σπατιλη)
dung	sterco- (L. stercus); bolito- (Gr. βολιτον)
dwell	col- coli- (L. colere); -ecetes -etes (Gr. οικησις); -estr (L. -estris)
ear	auri- -auris (L. auris); otido- oto- -ous (Gr. ωτος)
earth	chamae- (Gr. χαμαι-); chthono- (Gr. χθων); geo (Gr. γεω-)
eat	phago- (Gr. φαγος); tropho- (Gr. τροφη); vor- vora- (L. vorare)
egg	ovi- -ovum (L. ovum); oo- -oum (Gr. ωον)
eye	oculi- -oculus (L. oculus); -omma ommato- (Gr. ομμα); ophthalmo- ophthalmus (Gr. οφθαλμος); opo- -ops opto- (Gr. ωψη)
eyelash	blepharis blepharo- (Gr. βλεφαρις)
eyelid	cili-, -cilium (L. cilium)
face	faci- -facies (L. facies); -ops (Gr. οψ)
feather	-pinna pinni- (L. pinna); plum- -pluma plumi- (L. pluma); -pteryla pterylo- (Gr. πτερυξ); ptilo- -ptilum (Gr. πτιλον)
fern	pterido- -pteris (Gr. πτερις)
field	agri- agro- (L. agri Gr. αγρος); arv- arvens- (L. arvus); camp- campestr- (L. campester); prati- prati- (L. pratium)
fish	pisci -piscis (L. piscis); ichthyo -ichthys (Gr. ιχθυς)
flesh	carni- -caro (L. carno); sarco- -sarx (Gr. σαρκο)
flower	-flora flori- (L. flora); -anthemum antho- -anthus (Gr. ανθεμις/ανθος)
fly	musci -musca (L. musca); myi- -myia (Gr. μυια)
foot	pedi- -pes (L. pedes); podo- -pus (Gr. ποδ-/πους)
forehead	-frons fronto- (L. frons); metopo- -metopus -metopius (Gr. μετωπιον)
frog/toad	batracho -batrachus (Gr. βατραχος); -rana rani- (L. rana); -phyrna phyrno- (Gr. φρυνη)
fruit	carp- carpo- -carpus (Gr. καρπος); fructi -fructus (L. fructus); pomo- -pomus (L. pomum)
fungus	fungi- -fungus (L. fungus); -myces myceto- myco- (Gr. μυκης)
gill	branch- -branchium; brancho- (Gr. βραγχος)
gland	glandi- -glans (L. glans); -aden adeno- (Gr. αδην)
grain	-chondruim chondro- (Gr. χονδρος)
grass	-gramen gramini- (L. gramen); grani- -granum (L. granum); -poa poo- (Gr. ποα)
groin	-inguen inguini- (L. inguen)
habit	etho- -ethus (Gr. εθος); habit- (L. habitus)
hair	capill- -capillus (L. capillus); -chaeta chaeto- (Gr. χαιτη); crini- crinis (L. crinis); pil- pili- -pilus (L. pilus); -thrix tricho- (Gr. θριξ)
hand	mani- manu- -manus (L. manus); -chir chiro- (Gr. χειρ)
head	capit- capiti- -caput (L. caput); -cephala cephalo- (Gr. κεφαλη)
heart	-cor cordi- (L. cor); cardi- -cardia (Gr. καρδια)
heel	calcan- calcane- -calcaneum (L. calcaneum); talari- tali- -talus (L. talua)
horn	corn- -cornus (L. cornu); -cera cerato- (Gr. κερας)
horse	equi -equus (L. equus); hippo -hippus (Gr. ιππος)
house	eco- (Gr. οικος)

insect	insecti- (L. insectum); entomo- (Gr. εντομον)
island	insul- insular- (L. insula); neso- (Gr. νησος)
jaw	genyo- -genys (Gr. γενυς); gnatho- -gnathus (Gr. γναθος); maxill- -maxilla (L. maxilla)
joint	articuli- articulus -artus (L. articulus); arthro- arthru (Gr. αρθρον)
jump/leap	salt- (L. saltare); salien- (L. saliens); scirto- (Gr. σκιρτητης)
kidney	ren- -ren -reni (L. renes) ; nephro- -nephrus (Gr. νεφρος)
knee	genu- -genu (L. genu) ; -gonatium gonato- (Gr. γονατιον); gony- gonyo- -gonys (Gr. γονυ)
knuckle	condylo- -condylus (Gr. κονδυλος)
lake	lacustr- (L. lacustrus); limno- (Gr. λιμνη)
leaf	foli- -folium (L. folium); phyllo- -phyllum (Gr. φυλλον)
leech	hirudini- -hirudo (L. hirudo); -bdella bdello- (Gr. βδελλη)
leg	crur- -crus (L. crus); cnemi- -cnemis (Gr. κνημη/κνημις) ; -scelis scelo- scelido- (Gr. σκελος)
light	luci- (L. lucis); photo- (Gr. φως)
lip	labi- labio- -labium labr- (L. labia); chilo- -chilus (Gr. χειλος)
liver	jecori- -jecur (L. hepar); -hepar hepato- (Gr. ηπαρ)
lizard	-lacerta lacerti- (L. lacerta); sauro- -saurus (Gr. σαυρος)
love	philo- (Gr. φιλος); ama- (L. amo)
lungs	pulmo- -pulmo pulmono- (L. pulmones); -pneuma pneumo- (Gr. πνευμον)
man	homini- -homo (L. hominis); anthropo- -anthropus (Gr. ανθρωπος)
marsh	helo- heleo- helod- (Gr. ελειος); limno- (Gr. λιμνη)
marsh	paludi (L. palus/palustris); eleo- elo- (Gr. ελεο-)
membrane	chorio- -chorium (Gr. χοριον); -hymen hymeno- (Gr. υμην); membran- -membrana (L. membrana); meningo- -meninx (Gr. μενιγξ)
moss	bryo- -bryum (Gr. βρυον)
mossy	mnio- -mnium (Gr. μνιωδης)
motion	moti (L. movere); cine- cinemato- cinet- (Gr. κινησις)
mountain	alpestr- alpin- (L. Alpes); mont- montan- (L. mons); oreo- (Gr. ορεο-)
mouse	muri- -mus (L. muris); myo- -mys (Gr. μυς)
mouth	ora- ori- -os (L. oralis); -stoma stomata- (Gr. στομα)
mucus/slime	blenno- -blennus (Gr. βλεννυς); myxa- myxo- (Gr. μυξα)
mud	borboro- (Gr. βορβοριζω); limi- (L. limosus); lut- (L. lutum); pelo- (Gr. πηλος)
muscle	myo- -mys (Gr. μυς)
neck	-auchen aucheno- (Gr. αυχην); -dera dero- (Gr. δειρη); trachelo- -trachelus (Gr. τραχηλος)
neck	cervic- -cervix (L. cervix); coll- -collum (L. collum)
noisy	garrul- (L. garrulus); spharago- (Gr. σφαραγος); stombo- (Gr. στομβος); vocifer (L. vociferor)
nose	nasi- -nasus (L. nasus); rhino- -rhis (Gr. ρινο)
nut	nuci- -nux (L. nux); caryo- -caryum (Gr. καρυον)
pig	sui- -sus (L. suis); hyo- -hys (Gr. υος)
place	topo- (Gr. τοπος)
plant	phyto- -phytum (Gr. φυτον)
pond	stagni- (L. stagnum); telmato- (Gr. τελμα)
quick	aeolo- aeluro- (Gr. αιολος)
reed	arundi- -arundo (L. harundo); calamo- calamu- (L. calamus); donaci- -donax (Gr. δοναξ)
reptile	herpeto- (Gr. ερπετον)

rib	cost- -costa costi- (L. costa); scelido- -scelis (Gr. σκελις)
river	amni- (L. amnis); flumini- (L. flumen); fluvia- fluviatil- (L. fluvius); potamo- (Gr. ποταμος)
root	radici- -radix (L. radix); -rhiza rhizo- (Gr. ριζα)
rump	clun- cluni- (L. clunis); gluteo- -gluteus (Gr. γλουτος); -pyga pygo- (Gr. πυγη)
run	cursor (L. cursor); dromo (Gr. δρομας)
sand	areni- (L. harena); ammo- (Gr. αμμος); psammo- (Gr. ψαμμος)
scale	squam- -squama squami- (L. squama); lepido- -lepis (Gr. λεπις)
sea	enalio- (Gr. εναλιος); halio- (Gr. αλιος); marin- maritim- (L. maritimus); oceano- (Gr. ωκεανος); pelag- pelago- (Gr. πελαγος); thalasso (Gr. θαλασσα)
seed	blasto- -blastus (Gr. βλαστος); -semen semini- (L. semen); -sperma spermato- (Gr. σπερμα); -spora sporo- (Gr. σπορος)
shade	umbri- (L. umbra); scio- (Gr. σκιο-)
shell	concha- concho- (Gr. κογχη); ostraco- -ostracum (Gr. οστρακον)
shellfish/shell	-concha (L. concha); -concha concho- (Gr. κογχη)
shore	litori- (L. litus); aegialo- (Gr. αιγιαλος)
shoulder	omo- -omus (Gr. ωμος)
shrub	thamno- thamnus (Gr. θαμνος)
sing	acheto- (Gr. αχετας/ηχετης)
skin	-byrsa byrso- (Gr. βυρσα); chorio- -chorium (Gr. χοριον); cutan- cuti- -cutis (L. cutis); derm- -derma dermo- dermato- (Gr. δερμα); scyto- -scytus (Gr. σκυτος)
skull	cranio- -cranium (Gr. κρανιον)
sleep	dorm- (L. dormire); hypno- (Gr. υπνος); somni- (L. somnus); sopor- (L. sopor)
slow	tardi- (L. tardus); brady- (Gr. βραδυς)
snake	aspidi- -aspis (L. aspis); -coluber colubri- (L. coluber); ophio- -ophis (Gr. οφις)
snow	chiono- (Gr. χιων); nipho- (Gr. νιφας); nival- (L. nix/nivis)
sound	-phona phono- (Gr. φωνη)
sperm	-semen semin- (L. semen); -sperma spermato- (Gr. σπερμα)
spider	aranei- -aranea (L. aranea); -arachna arachno- (Gr. αραχης)
spine	-acantha acantho- (Gr. ακανθα); rhachi- -rhachis (Gr. ραχις); -spina spini- (L. spina)
stalk/stem	cauli- -caulis (L. caulis); caulo- -caulus (Gr. καυλος); petiol- -petiolus (L. petiolus); -stipes stipit- (L. stipes)
suture	rhapha- rhapho- (Gr. ραφη)
swift	celeri- (L. celer); citi- (L. citatus); tachy- (Gr. ταχυς); veloci- (L. velox)
swim	nata- natant- (L. natans); necto- (Gr. νηκτος)
swim	pleo- (Gr. πλεω)
tail	caud- -cauda (L. cauda); cerco- -cercus (Gr. κερκος); -ura uro- (Gr. ουρα)
thicket	dumi- (L. dumetum); lochmo- (Gr. λοχμη); thamno- (Gr. θαμνος); xylocho- (Gr. ξυλοχος)
thigh	femor- -femur (L. femur); mero- -merus (Gr. μηρος)
thorax	thoraco- -thorax (Gr. θωραξ)
thorn/prickle	-acantha acantho- (Gr. ακανθα)
throat	gula- -gula (L. gula); guttur- -guttur (L. guttur); laemo- -laemus (Gr. λαιμος); pharyngo- -pharynx (Gr. φαρυγξ); trachelo- -trachelus (Gr. τραχηλος)

tissue	tel- -tela teli- (L. tela); histo- -histus (Gr. ιστος)
tongue	-glossa glosso- (Gr. γλοσσα); -glotta glotto- (Gr. γλοττα); -lingu- -lingua (L. lingua)
tooth	-dens dent- denti- (L. dens); odonto- -odous -odos (Gr. οδων/οδους)
tree	arbor- -arbor arbore- (L. arbor); dendro- -dendron -dendrum (Gr. δενδρον)
turn	trop- tropi- tropido (Gr. τροπη)
turtle/tortoise	chelono- -chelys (Gr. χελωνη); emydo -emys (Gr. εμυς); testudini -testudo (L. testudo);
vein	ven- -vena veni- (L. vena); phlebo- phleps (Gr. φλεψ)
vine	viti- -vitis (L. vitis); ampelo- -ampelus (Gr. αμπελος)
walk	ambulat- (L. ambulare); baeno- (Gr. βαινειν); bat- -bates Gr. βατες); gressor- (L. gressus)
wander	peregrin (L. peregrinor); vag- vagan- (L. vagus)
water	aquao- aquat- (L. aqua); hydro- (Gr. υδωρ); hygro- (Gr. υγρος)
wheat	tritici- -triticum (L. triticum); pyro- -pyrum (Gr. πυρος)
windpipe	trache- -trachea (L. trachia); broncho- -bronchus (Gr. βρογχος)
wing	ala- -ala ali- (L. ala); ptero- -pterum (Gr. πτερον); pterygo- -pteryx (Gr. πτερυξ)
woods	sylvestr- sylvi- (L. Silvanus); drymo- (Gr. δρυμος)
worm	vermi -vermis (L. vermis); -helmins helmintho- (Gr. ελμινθ)
wrist	carpo- -carpus (L. carpus)

SHAPES

angled	anguli- (L. angulus); gonio- (Gr. γονια)
bent	ancylo- (Gr. αγκυλος); campto- (Gr. καμπτιεν); campylo- (Gr. καμπυλη); cypho- (Gr. κυφος)
blunt	ambly- (Gr. αμβλυς); obtus- (L. obtusus); retus- (L. retusum)
closed	arcan (L. arcanus); clisto- cleiosto- (Gr. κλειστος); clus- clusus (L. clusus)
clubbed	clavat- (L. clava); rhopalo- (Gr. ροπαλον)
crescent-shaped	lunula- lunuli- (L. lunatus); menisco- (Gr. μηνισκος)
crooked	ancylo- (Gr. αγκυλος); corono- (Gr. κορονος); rhaebo- (Gr. ραιβος); scolio- (Gr. σκολιος)
curled	bostrycho- (Gr. βοστρυχος); crispi- (L. crispus)
curved	cyrto- (Gr. κυρτος); gampso- (Gr. γαμψος); toxo- (Gr. τοξον)
cylindrical	cylind- cylindro- (L. cylindrus)
egg-shaped	oodeo- (Gr. ωοειδης); ovat- (L. ovatus)
flat	aplanat- (NL. applanatus); plani- (L. planus); platy- (Gr. πλατη)
forked	dicho- (Gr. διχα); dicro- (Gr. δικροος)
forked	forficat- (L. forficatus); furc- (L. furca)
form	-form (L. forma); morpho- (Gr. μορφη); schemato- (Gr. σχημα)
hollow	alveo- (L. alveolus); cavi- (L. cavus); coelo- (Gr. κοιλος)
hooked	ancistr- (Gr. αγκιστρον); ancylo- (Gr. αγκυλος); grypo- (Gr. γρυπος); hamat- (L. hamus); onco- (Gr. ογκος)
horned	cerato- (Gr. κερας); cornut- (L. cornu)
keeled	carinat- (L. carina)
lobed	lobat- lobi- (NL. lobatus); lobo- (Gr. λοβος)

narrow	angusti- (L. angustus); steno- (Gr. στενος)
open	aperi- (L. apertus); chaeno- (Gr. χαινω); oego- (Gr. οιγω)
pointed	acuminat- (L. acuminatus); muricat- (L. muricatus)
ragged	charcharo- (Gr. καρχαρος); pannos- (L. pannosus); rhago- (Gr. ραγας)
round	circuli- (L. circulus); cyclo- (Gr. κυκλος); gyro- (Gr. γυρος); rotundi- (L. rotundus); strongylo- (Gr. στρογγυλω)
sharp	acri- (L. acri-); acuti- (L. acutus); oxy- (Gr. οξυς)
slanting	declivi- (L. declivis); dochmo- (Gr. δοχμιος); epiphoro- (Gr. επιφορος); lechrio- (Gr. λεχριος); loxo- (Gr. λοξος); obliqu- (L. obliquus); oxy- (Gr. οξυς); plagio- (Gr. πλαγιος)
slender	gracil- (L. gracilis); lepto- (Gr. λεπτος); tenui- (L. tenuis)
spherical	glob- globo- globus (L. globus); sphaero- (Gr. σφαιρα)
spiral	helico- (Gr. ελιξ); spirali- (L. spira); strombi- (L. strombos)
split	dicho- (Gr. διχα); dicrano- (Gr. δικρανον); schisto- schizo- (Gr. σχιστος)
square	quadrat- (L. quadratus); tessar- (Gr. τεσσαρα-)
steep	ananto- (Gr. αναντα); ardu- (L. arduus)
straight	euthy- (Gr. ευθυς); ortho- (Gr. ορθος); recti- (L. rectum)
thick	crassi- (L. crassus); hadro- (Gr. αδρος); pachy- (Gr. παχυς); pycno- (Gr. πυκνος)
torn	laci- lacid- lacist- (Gr. λακις); rhago- (Gr. ραγας)
triangular	delt- (Gr. δελτα); trigono- (Gr. τριγωνος)
twisted	ileo- (Gr. ειλεω); plecto- (Gr. πλεκτος); strepto- (Gr. στρεψις); strobilo- strobo- (Gr. στροβιλος)
twisted	plecto- (Gr. πλεκτος); stropho- (Gr. στροφος)
wavy	cladar- cladaro- (Gr. κλαδαρος); undulat- (L. undulare)
wide	eury- (Gr. ευρυς); lati- (L. lati-); platy- (Gr. πλατυς)

SIZES

dwarf	nano- (Gr. νανος); pulmili- (L. pumilio)
equal	equi- (L. aequus); iso- (Gr. ισος); pari- (L. parilis)
gigantic	colosso- (Gr. κολοσσιαιος); giganto- (Gr. gigas); ingenti- (L. ingens); peloro- (Gr. πελοωρος); titano- (Gr. Τιταν)
heavy	baro- bary- (Gr. βαρος); gravi- (L. gravis)
large	grandi- (L. grandis); macro- (Gr. μακρος); magni- (L. magnus); mega- megalo- (Gr. μεγας)
largest	maxim- (L. maximus); megisto- (Gr. μεγιστο-)
less than	meio- mio- (Gr. μειον/μειων); sub- (L. sub)
light	elaphro- (Gr. ελαφρος); levi- (L. levigare)
long	dolicho- (Gr. δολιχος); longi- (L. longus); meco- (Gr. μηκος)
longest	mecisto- (Gr. μηκιστος)
short	brachy- (Gr. βραχυς); brevi- (L. brevis); curti- (L. curtus)
shortest	elach- elachist- elachy- (Gr. ελαχιστος)
small	baeo- (Gr. βαιος); micro- (Gr. μικρος); minut- (L. minutus); parvi- (L. parvitas); pauro- (Gr. παυρος); pusill- , (L. pusillus)
smallest	elachisto- (Gr. ελαχιστος); minim- (L. minumus)
tall	aep- aepy- (Gr. αιπος); alti- (L. altus); procer- proceri- (L. procerus)
tallest	mecist- mecisto- (Gr. μηκιστος)
unequal	aniso- (Gr. ανισος); anomal- anomalo- (Gr. ανωμαλος); impar impari- (L. impar); scalen- scalene- scaleno-

COLOURS

Whites

alb-, albi-, leuco-,	a general white
niphar-, nive-,	snow-white, purest white
argo-, candid-,	slightly less pure than snow-white
eborin-, eburn-,	ivory-white; a cream-coloured white tending to yellow
galacto-, lact-,	milk-white; a dull white with a hint of blue
calcar-, cretac-, gyps-,	chalk-white; a very dull white with a hint of grey
argent-, argyr-, aygro-,	a silvery white tending to bluish grey
albid-,	whitish
albescens,	turning white
dealbatus,	whitened

Greys

ciner-, tephro-, spodo-,	ash-grey; intermediate between pure white and pure black
tephra-	ash-coloured
cinera-, phorco-	ash-greyish, as above but whiter
gris-,	pearl-grey; pure grey with a hint of blue
livid-, schistac-,	slate-grey; a pure grey with a strong element of blue
ferreus,	iron-grey, as slate-grey with a weak metallic lustre
plumb-, plumbe-, molybdo-	lead-grey, as slate-grey with a metallic lustre
fumeus, fumosus	smoky-grey, with a brown tint
murinus,	mousy-grey, with a red tint
canus, incanus, polio-,	hoary greyish-white
canescens,	rather hoary, stronger than hoary
ravid-	greyish
ravus	greyish-yellow

Yellows

citrin-, citro-,	lemon-coloured, pure yellow
luteus, xantho-,	yellow of various shades
icter-,	yellowish, jaundiced yellow
flav-, lute-, luteol-, lurid-,	a pure, pale yellow
gilv-/gilb-	pale yellow
thapsino-,	sallow-yellow; very pale yellow
sulphur-,	sulphur-coloured; a pale, bright yellow with a mixture of white
stramini-,	straw-coloured, dull yellow mixed with white
alut-,	leather-yellow, a whitish yellow
cerin-, cere-,	wax-coloured, a dull yellow with a soft tinge of reddish-brown
melichro-,	honey-coloured
ochro-,	ochre; yellow with a tinge of brown
ochroleucus,	whitish-ochre; as above tinged with white
vitellin-,	dull yellow with a hint of red
aur-, aurat-, aure-,	golden-yellow, pure, bright yellow
chryso-,	gold, golden-yellow
lut-, xantho-,	orange-yellow, mid orange-yellow
croc-,	saffron; a deep yellow with a strong element of red and a hint of brown

helvo-,	greyish-yellow with a hint of brown
testac-,	a brownish-yellow like unglazed earthenware
fulvi-, cneco-,	tawny; dull yellow with tinges of grey and brown
xutho-	yellowish-brown
electric-, succin-,	amber; a deep yellow with a tinge of red

Oranges

aurantiac-, aurant-,	orange; yellow with a strong element of red
croc-,	rich-orange
armeniac-,	apricot; yellow with a definite mixture of red
cirrho-,	tawny-orange

Reds

kermesin-, punic-,	carmine, the purest red
phoenico-, punic-,	crimson; a pure red with carmine and scarlet
erythro-, erysi-, pyrrho-,	pure red
rubi-, rubr-,	pure red
rhodo-, rose-,	rosy; pale pure red
carn-, incarnat-	fleshy-red; paler than rosy
byrrh, flamme-, ign-, pyrrho-,	flame-red; a very lively scarlet, fiery red
rutilan-, rutil-,	reddish with a metallic lustre
cinnabarin-,	cinnabar; scarlet with a tinge of orange
coccin-,	scarlet; pure carmine with a hint of yellow
miniat-, vermiculat-, sandix,	vermilion; scarlet with a strong yellow component
tingabarino	vermilion
laterit-,	brick-red; a dull red with a tinge of grey
cupr-, rubigin-, haemat-,	a brownish-red
sanguin-, xerampelin-,	a dull red tending to brownish black
cupr-,	coppery; a brownish-red with a metallic lustre
rufi-,	ruddy; a general red, somewhat ambiguous
subrufus,	reddish/buff
russ	reddish/russet
rubigo-,	rusty red
rubid-	reddish
ferrugin-,	rust-coloured/dusky
daphoeno-,	bloody, blood coloured
haemo-, haemato-, sanguini-,	blood-red
mulleol,	reddish

Greens

smaragdinus, prasinus,	grass-green/emerald-green; a clear, pure green
chloro-, virid-,	green; a clear green but less bright than grass-green
virens, verd-,	green; a clear green but less bright than grass-green
prasinus,	leek-green, bright green
aeruginos-,	verdigris-green; a deep green with a tinge of blue
glauc-, thalassi-,	sea-green; a dull green tending to greyish blue
aquamarinus,	sea greenish-blue; a dull green tending to blue
venetus,	deep sea-green; a dark green tending to dark grey
flavovirens,	yellowish-green; green with a strong yellow component
galb-	greenish-yellow
elaio-, olivaceus,	olive-green; green with a strong brown component
atrovirens,	deep green; green tending to black

Browns

aer-, chalco-,	bronze
aene-,	brassy
fusc-, phaeo-,	brown tinged greyish or blackish
brunne-,	a pure dull brown, a deep brown
umbrin-,	umber; a pure dull brown
badi-, castane-,	chestnut-brown; a dull brown tinged with red
fulv-	reddish-brown
spadic-,	a bright brown
ferrugin-,	rusty-brown; a light brown with a tinge of red
cinnamom,	cinnamon; a bright brown with slight tinges of yellow and red
porphyr-,	brown mixed with red
rufus,	as previous, but redder
glandac-,	as previous but yellower
hepatic-,	liver-coloured; a dull brown with a tinge of yellow
fuligi-,	sooty-brown; a dirty brown tending to black
lurid-,	a dirty-brown, rather clouded

Blues, Violets and Purples

caerule-, cyano-,	a light dull blue/sky-blue
cyaneus, cyano-	Prussian-blue; a clear bright blue
azur-,	sky-blue/azure; a light blue
venet-	sea-blue
caes-,	lavender-coloured; a pale blue with a tinge of grey
indigo,	indigo; a very deep blue
violace-, ianthin-, iodo-, iono-,	violet; a pure blue tinged with red
lilacin-,	lilac; a pale violet tinged with white
caesi-, livid-,	a mid blue tinged with mid grey
blatt-, porphyro-, purpur-,	purple: a dull red with a dash of blue
ostrin-,	purple
halurgo,	sea-purple/purple
morino	mulberry-coloured

Blacks

pelidno	a leaden-blueish colour
melan-,	pure black
nigr-, nigri-,	black with a hint of grey
atr -, atri-,	blackness
anthraco-, carb-,	coal-black; black tending to blue
coracin-, pullus,	raven-black; a lustrous black
piceus,	pitch-black; a black tending to brown
memnon-,	brown-black; almost as pitch-back
morul-,	dark coloured/black
pello	dark-coloured/dusky

TEXTURES

bare	gymno- (Gr. γυμνος); nudi- (L. nudus); psilo- (Gr. ψιλος)
bearded	barbat- (L. barba); crinit- (L. crinis); pogono- (Gr. πωγων)
downy	pappo- (Gr. παππος); pubesc- (L. pubescere)
flexible	campto- (Gr. καμπτιεν); lygero- (Gr. λυγερος)
inflexible	astrepto- (Gr. αστρεπτος); rigid- (L. rigidus)
furrowed	aulaco- (Gr. αυλαξ); glypho- glypto- (Gr. γλυφα); striat- (L. stria); strigat- (L. striga); sulcat- (L. sulcus)
hairy	dasy- (Gr. δασυς); hirsut- (L. hirsutus); lasio- (L. λασιος); trichodo- (Gr. τριχος); villos- (L. villosus)
hard	duri- (L. dura); sclero (L. σκληρος)
networked	arcy- (Gr. αρκυς); reti- retin- (L. retina)
punctured	punctat- (L. punctatus); sticto- (Gr. στικτος)
rough	asper- aspr- (L. aspera); scabr- (L. scabra); trach- trachin- tracho- trachy- (Gr. τραχυς)
smooth	aphelo- (Gr. αφελης); glabr- (L. glaber); leio- (Gr. λειος); lisso- (Gr. λισσος)
soft	malaco- (Gr. μαλακος); molli- (L. mollio)
spiny	acantho- (Gr. ακανθα); echino- (Gr. εχινος); spini- (L. spina)
woolly	lachno- (Gr. λαχνος); lani- (L. lana); mallo- (Gr. μαλλος)
wrinkled	caperat- (L. caperare); corrugat- (L. corrugare); rhysso- (Gr. ρυσος/ρυσσος); rugos- (L. ruga)

PATTERNS

a band/banded	fasciat- (L. fasciatus); tenia- teniao- (Gr. ταινια)
checkered	tesselat- (L. tessellatus)
dappled	bali- balio- (Gr. βαλιος); peristicto- (Gr. περιστικτος); stict- sticto- (Gr. στικτος)
speckled	psaro- (Gr. ψαρος)
a spot/spotted	balio- (Gr. βαλιος); celido- (Gr. κηλις); ephel- ephelis- (Gr. εφηλις); gutt- gutta- (L. gutta); maculat- (L. macula); stigmato- (Gr. στιγμη); punctat (L. punctatus); rhanid- rhanis- (Gr. ρανις); stixi- (Gr. στιξις)
streaked	plagat- (L. plaga); rhabdo- (Gr. ραβδωτος)
stripe/striped	clav- (L. clavus); plag- plaga- (L. plagae); rhabdo- (Gr. ραβδωτος); vittat- (L. vitta)
variegated	daedal- (L. daedalus); poecil- poecili- poecilo (Gr. ποικιλος); polychrome- (Gr. πολυχρωματος); vari- varia- vario- (L. varius)

NUMBERS

They were no cyphers (characters 0-9) in Ancient Greek, instead the alphabet was used such that a given character had a corresponding number. For example, the Alpha character (α) also stood for the number 1.
This alphabetic system was used for ordinal as well as cardinal numerals, for dates, lengths of time, money, distances, and as numeral adjectives (first, second, etc.).

In the following list the character corresponding to the number is noted in brackets [ ].

Latin	English	Greek
quart- (quartus)	quarter	tetar- (τεταρτος)
tert- (tertius)	third	trito- (τριτος)
semi- (semis)	half	hemi- (ημι)
demi- (dimidium)	half	
uni- (unus)	one	eis (εις μια εν) [α]
di- duo-(duo)	two	duo- (δυο) [β]
tri- (tres tria)	three	tri- (τρεις τρια) [γ]
quad- (quattour)	four	tetra- (τετρας τεσσαρες) [δ]
quinqu- (quinque)	five	penta- (πεντε) [ε]
sex (sex)	six	hex (εξ) [ς]
sept- (septem)	seven	hept- (επτα) [ζ]
oct- (octo)	eight	oct- (οκτω) [η]
nov- (novem)	nine	enne (εννεα) [θ]
dec- (decem)	ten	dec- (δεκα) [ι]
undeci- (undecim)	eleven	hendec- (ενδεκα) [ια]
duodeci- (duodecim)	twelve	dodec- (δωδεκα) [ιβ]
tredeci- (tredecim)	thirteen	(τρεισκαιδεκα) [ιγ]
(quartuordecim)	fourteen	(τεσσαρεσκαιδεκα) [ιδ]
(quindecim)	fifteen	(πεντεκαιδεκα) [ιε]
(sedecim)	sixteen	(εκκαιδεκα) [ις]
(septemdecim)	seventeen	(επτακαιδεκα) [ιζ]
(odeviginti)	eighteen	(οκτωκαιδεκα) [ιη]
(undeviginti)	ninteen	(εννεακαιδεκα) [ιθ]
vigint- (viginta)	twenty	icos- (εικοσι) [κ]
trigent- (trigenta)	thirty	(τριακοντα) [λ]
(quadraginta)	forty	(τεσσαρακοντα) [μ]
(quinquaginta)	fifty	(πεντηκοντα) [ν]
(sexaginta)	sixty	(εξηκοντα) [ξ]
(septuaginta)	seventy	(εβδομηκοντα) [ο]
(octoginta)	eighty	(ογδοηκοντα) [π]
(nonaginta)	ninety	(ενενηκοντα) [ϙ] (koppa)
cent- (centum)	hundred	heca- (εκατον) [ρ]
mil- (mille)	thousand	kilo- chili- (χιλιοι) [,α]
primi- (primus)	first	prot- (πρωτος)
secund- (secundus)	second	deutero- (δευτερος)
tert- (tertius)	third	trito- (τριτος)
quart- (quartus)	fourth	tetar- (τεταρτος)
quint- (quintus)	fifth	pempt- (πεμπτος)
sex- (sextus)	sixth	ecto- (εκτος)
sept- (septimus)	seventh	hebdom- (εβδοματος)
oct- (octavus)	eighth	ogdo- (ογδοος)

non- (nonus)	ninth	enat- (ενατος)
deci- (decimus)	tenth	deca- (δεκατος)
centes- (centesimus)	hundreth	eka- (εκατοστος)
milles- (millesimus)	thousandth	(χιλιοστος)

sem- (semel)	once	eis- mia- en- (εις μια εν)
bis- (bis)	twice	dis- (δις)
ter- (ter)	thrice	estri- (εστρις)
quaterna- (quaternarius)	fourfold	tetrady- (τετραδυμος)

(singuli/singulorum)	single	haplo- (απλοος)
dupl- (duplex)	double	diplo- (διπλοος)
trip- (triples)	triple	tripo- (τριπλοος)

QUANTITY

all	omni- (L. omnis); pan- panto- (Gr. παντο); toti- (L. totus)
common	coeno- (Gr. κοινος); commun- (L. communis); vulgar- (L. vulgatus)
empty	ceno- (Gr. κιονος/κοινως); vacu- (L. vacuus); vani- (L. vanitas)
equal	equi- (L. aequus); iso- (Gr. ισος); pari- ; (L. parilis)
even-numbered	artio- (Gr. αρτιος)
few	oligo- (Gr. ολιγος); pauci- (L. paucitas); pauro- (Gr. παυρος)
full	mesto- (Gr. μεστος); pleni- (L. plenus); plero- (Gr. πληροω)
many	multi- (L. multus); myria- (Gr. μυριος); poly- (Gr. πολυς)
more	plio- (Gr. πλειον); pluri- (L. plurimus)
most	pleisto- (Gr. πλειστος)
odd-numbered	perisso- (Gr. περισσος)
part	mero- (Gr. μερος); part- (L. partire)
simple	haplo- (Gr. απλοος); simplici- (L. simplici-)
single	henico- (Gr. ενικος); haplo- (Gr. απλως)
solitary	eremit- (Gr. ερημια); eremo- (Gr. ερημος)
unequal	aniso- (Gr. ανισος)
very	aga- (Gr. αγα-); ari- (Gr. αρι-); za- (Gr. ζα-)
whole	holo- (Gr. ολος); integri- (L. integer)

DIRECTION AND LOCATION

above	ano- (Gr. ανω-); hyper- (Gr. υπερ-); pera- (Gr. περα); super- supra- (L. super); sur- (Fr. sur)
across	dia (Gr. δια); dochmi- dochmo (Gr. δοχμιος); peraeo- pereio- perio- (Gr. περαιος); trans- (L. trans)
against	anti- (Gr. αντι-); contra- (L. contra); enanti- (Gr. εναντα)
apart	dia- (Gr. δια); dis- (L. dis-)
around	ambi- (L. ambi-); amphi- ampho- (Gr. αμφισ-); circum- (L. cirum); peri- (Gr. περι)
away	a- ab- abs- (L.); aneu- (Gr. ανευ); ap- aph- (Gr. απ- αφ-); apo- (Gr. απο); de- (L.)
backward	ana- (Gr. ανα); au- (Gr. αυ); opisth- opistho- (Gr. οπισθεν); palin- (Gr. παλιν); post- (L. post); retr- retro- (L. retro); rursu- (L. rursus)

before	ante- antero- (L. anterius); prae- pre- (L. prae); pro- (Gr. προ-); prosth- prosthen- prostheno- (Gr. προσθεν)
behind	aefter- (AS.); histero- hystero- (Gr. ιστερος); opisth- opistho- (Gr. οπισθεν); post- postero- (L. posterior); retr- retro- (L. retro)
below	catant- (Gr. καταντα); hypo- (Gr. υπο); infra- (L. infra); subter- (L. subter); ypn- ypno- (Gr. υπνος)
beside	para- (Gr. παρα); praet- praeter- (L. praeter)
between	di- dis- (L. dis-); inter- (L. inter); meta- (Gr. μετα); metax- metaxi- metaxy (Gr. ματαξυ)
beyond	ultra- (L. ultra); praet- praeter- (L. praeter); per- pera- peraeo- pereio- perio- (Gr. περαιος)
crosswise	carsio- (Gr. καρσιος); chiasm- (Gr. χιασμα); decussi- (L. decusso); enallax- (Gr. εναλλαξ); lechri- lechrio- (Gr. λεχριος); loxo- (Gr. λοξος)
down	ap- apo- (Gr. απο); cat- cata- kata- (Gr. κατα); cato- (Gr. κατω); de- (L. de-); cathod- (Gr. καθοδος)
eastern	euro- (Gr. ευρος); heothino- (Gr. εωθινος); orient- oriental- (L. oriens)
far	aneu (Gr. ανευ); ap- apo- (Gr. απο); apuro (Gr. απουρος); ect- ecto- (Gr. εκτος); heca- (Gr. εκας); makr- makro- (Gr. μακρος); tele- (Gr. τηλε)
first	archi- archo- (Gr. αρχι-); primi- (L. primitus); princip- principali- (L. principalis); protero- proto- (Gr. προτερος); protisto- (Gr. προτιστος)
front	ante- antero- (L. anterius); fron- (L. frons); pro- (Gr. προ-); proso- (Gr. προσω); protero- proto- (Gr. προτερος)
in	apud- (L. apud); eis- (Gr. εις); em- (Gr. εμ-); en- (Gr. εν); enapo- (Gr. εναπο-); il- im- in- ir- (L.)
inner	endo- ento- (Gr. ενδον); interul- (L. interulus);
inside/within	ento- (Gr. εντος); em- (Gr. εμ-); en- (Gr. εν); endi- ento- (Gr. ενδον); eso- (Gr. εσω); intern- (L. internus); intra- intro- (L. intra); intrins- (L. intrinsecus);
middle	medi- medio- (L. medius); meso- (Gr. μεσος); medull- medulla- (L. meddula); perimeso (Gr. περιμεσος)
near	-ad (Gr. -αδ L. -ad); anchi- (Gr. αγχι-); apud- (L. apud); citer- (L. citer); contigu- (L. contiguus); engy- (Gr. εγγυς); epi- (Gr. επι); juxta- (L. iuxta); para- (Gr. παρα); paredro- (Gr. παρεδρος); peri- (Gr. περι); plesi- plesio- (Gr. πλησιος); prope- (L. prope); proxim- (L. proximus); schedo- (Gr. σχεδον); vicin- vicini- (L. vicinia)
northern	aquiloni- (L. aquilo); arctic- (L. αρκτικος); boreal- (L. boreas); septentrion- septentrional- (L. septemtrionalis)
opposite	ant- anti- (Gr. αντι-); anter- anteres- (Gr. αντηρης); contra- contro- (L. contra); enanti- (Gr. εναντα); hypenanti- (Gr. υπεναντιος)
out/going out	a- ab- abs- (L.); ec- ek- (Gr. εκ- L. ex-); ect- ecto- (Gr. εκτος); effere- (L. effero); exit- (L. exitus); exo- (Gr. εξο); exod- exodo- exodus (Gr. εξοδος); exorm- exormi- (Gr. εξορμη)
outside	ecto- hecto- (Gr. εκτος); exo- (Gr. εξο); extern- (L. externus); exoter- exotero- (Gr. εξωτερικος); extra- (L. extra-); extrin- (L. extrinsecus); fori- foris- (L. foris)
over	ant- anti- (Gr. αντι-); contr- contra- contro- (L. contra); hyper- (Gr. υπερ-); pel- (L. per); super- supra- (L. super); tran- trans- (L. trans); uper- (Gr. υπερ-); yper- (Gr. υπερ-)

second	deutero- (Gr. δευτερος); secund- (L. secundus)
separate	carpt- carptus- (L. carpere); chor- choris- (Gr. χορις); crino- (Gr. κρινειν); di- dia- (Gr. δια); divaricat- (L. divaricare); eccri- eccris- eccrit- (Gr. εκκρινω); excret- (L. excretus); singul- singular- (L. singularis)
side	lat- (L. latus); lateri- latero- (L. lateralis); pleur- pleura- pleuri- pleuro- pleurum- (Gr. πλευρα)
slanting	declivi- (L. declivis); devex- devexus (L. devexus); dochmo- (Gr. δοχμιος); epiphor- epiphoro- (Gr. επιφορος); fastigi- fastigium- (L. fastigium); lechri- lechrio- (Gr. λεχριος); loxo- (Gr. λοξος); obliqu- (L. obliquus); plagio- (Gr. πλαγιος); proale- (Gr. προαλης); proclivis (L. proclivis)
south	lips- (Gr. λιψ); merid- (L. meridies); mesembri- mesembria- (Gr. μεσημβρια); noto- (Gr. νοτος)
southern	austr- austral- (L. australis); notial- notio- (Gr. νοτιος)
southwest	(Gr. νωτος) noto-
top/sumit/apex	acri- acis- (Gr. ακρις); acro- (Gr. ακρον); apic- (L. apex); cara- (Gr. καρα); colophono- (Gr. κολοφων); corypha- (Gr. κορυφη); scopi- scopio- (Gr. σκοπια); vertex (L. vertex);
under	hypo- (Gr. υπο); infra- (L. infra); sub- (L. sub); sum- (L. sub-); ypo- (Gr. υπο-);
up/going up	ana- (Gr. ανα); anaba- (Gr. αναβασις); anarrhich- (Gr. αναρριχησις); ano- (Gr. ανω); ascend (L. ascendere)
west	dysi- (Gr. δυσις); lips- (Gr. λιψ)
western	dysmiko- (Gr. δυσμικος); hesperi- hespero- (Gr. εσπερος); occidental (L. occidens); scaeo- (Gr. σκαιος); vespertin- (L. vespertinus)

PARTS OF THE YEAR

early spring	Prevernal
late spring	Vernal
early summer	Aestival
late summer	Serotinal
autumn	Autumnal
winter	Hibernal
wintry/stormy	hiem -al, (L. hiemalis)
of today	hodiern, (L. hodiernus)
of the present year	hornotin, (L. hornotinus)
year/season/time	horo, (Gr. ωρος)
summer	theros (Gr. θεριος)
spring time	ver/veris
in the beginning of spring	primo vere

CHEMICAL ELEMENTS

actinium (Ac)   Gr. ακτις, ακτινος; a ray/beam (of the sun)

aluminium (Al)   L. alumen, aluminis; alum

americium (Am)   America. Made in 1944 in Chicago USA

antimony (Sb)   L. stibium (uncert. orig). Gr. αντι–μονος, not alone

argon (Ar)   Gr. αργον/αργος; lazy/idle/inactive. Argon is one of the least reactive elements.

arsenic (As)   L. arsenicum Gr. αρσενικον); yellow orpiment

astatine (At)   Gr. αστατος; unstable. Synthesized in 1940 at the University of California,

barium (Ba)   Gr. βαρις; heavy

berkelium (Bk)   Berkeley. Made in 1950 at the University of California, Berkeley, USA

beryllium (Be)   Gr. βερυλλιον; dim of βερυλλος; beryl

bismuth (Bi)   Ger. bisemutum

bohrium (Bh)   Made in 1981 at Gesellschaft für Schwerionenforschung (GSI) in Darmstadt, Germany and named in honour of Niels Bohr, the Danish physicist.

boron (B)   Per. burah; borax

bromine (Br)   Gr. βρμμος; stench. Bromine has an unpleasant smell.

cadmium (Cd)   L. cadmia Gr. καδμια; calamine

calcium (Ca)   L. calx, calsis; lime

californium (Cf)   California. Made in 1950 at the University of California, Berkeley, USA

carbon (C)   L. carbo, carbonis; coal, charcoal

cerium (Ce)   L. Ceres; goddess of agriculture (whose name was given to the first planetoid (asteroid) discovered

caesium (Cs)   L. caesius; bluish-grey

chlorine (Cl)   Gr. χλωρος; green. Chlorine is a green gas.

chromium (Cr)   Gr. χρωμα; colour

cobalt (Co)   MHG. kobalt; a fairy or demon or goblin of the mine. Miners working in the cobalt mines sometimes died unexpectedly. For this reason the miners thought that the mines contained evil spirits. The real reason for these unexpected deaths was that cobalt ores usually contained highly poisonous arsenic.

copper (Cu)   AS. coper, L. 'Aes Cyprium' metal of Cyprus, the ancient source of copper. The name became shortened to Cyprium and then 'Cuprum' from which copper gains its symbol.

curium (Cm)   Made in 1944 at Chicago and named in honour of Marie and Pierre Curie.

dubnium (Db)   Discovered in 1967 and named after the Joint Nuclear Institute at Dubna, Rusisia

dysprosium (Dy)   Gr. δυσπροσιτος; hard to get at

einsteinium (Es)   Made in 1952 at the University of California and named in honour of Albert Einstein.

erbium (Er)   Discovered in 1842 and named after the vilage of Ytterby, near Vaxholm in Sweden

europium (Eu)   Europe

fermium (Fm)   Made in 1952 at the University of California and named in honour of Enrico Fermi

fluorine (F)   L. fluor, fluis (fluere); flow, flux

francium (Fr)   France. Discovered in 1939 at the Curie Institute, Paris, France.

gadolinium (Gd)   Discovered by Jean de Marignac in 1880 and and named in honour of J. Gadolin; a Finnish Chemist

gallium (Ga)   L. Gallia, Gaul - France

germanium (Ge)	L. Germania; Germany. Discovered in 1886 by a German chemist – C.A. Winkler.
gold (Au)	L. aurum. AS. gold
hafnium (Hf)	L. Hafnia: Copenhagen
hassium (Hs)	Discovered in 1984 at Gesellschaft für Schwerionenforschung (GSI) in Darmstadt, Germany and named after the German state Hess, (L. Hassias).
helium (He)	Gr. ηλιος; the sun, first observed in the spectrum of the sun during the eclipse of 1868.
holmium (Ho)	L. Holmia: Stockholm
hydrogen (H)	Gr. υδωρ; water, -γεν; forming. Water is formed when hydrogen burns in air.
indium (In)	L. indicum; indigo
iodine (I)	Gr. ιοειδης; violet-coloured. Iodine is a grey solid at room temperature but gives off a violet coloured vapour when warmed.
iridium (Ir)	L. iris, iridis; a rainbow
iron (Fe)	L. ferrum, AS. iren
krypton (Kr)	Gr. κρυπτος; hidden
lanthanum (La)	Gr. λανθανω; I escape notice/I lie hidden
lawrencium (Lw)	Made at the University of California in 1961 and named honour of Ernest Lawrence, the man who invented the Cyclotron, in which the majority of man-made elements have been discovered
lead (Pb)	L. plumbum, AS. lead
lithium (Li)	Gr. λιθος; stone
lutetium (Lu)	L. Lutetia; the former name of Paris
magnesium (Mg)	L. Magnesia, a district in Thessaly (central Greece)
manganese (Mn)	It. manganese, a corruption of Magnesia
meitnerium (Mt)	Made in 1982 at Gesellschaft für Schwerionenforschung (GSI) in Darmstadt, Germany and named in honour of Lise Meitner, the Austrian physicist
mendelevium (Md)	Made in 1955 at the University of California and named in honour of the Russian Chemist Dimitri Mendeleef.
mercury (Hg)	L. hydrargyrus; liquid silver (quicksilver). Mercurius, Mercury – the messenger of the gods
molybdenum (Mo)	L. molybdaena; Gr. μολυβδος, lead. An ore of lead.
nobelium (No)	Discovered in 1958 at the Nobel Institute for Physics and later by others at Berkeley, California and named in honour of Alfred Nobel, the Swedish chemist who discovered dynamite, and founded of the Nobel Prizes
neodymium (Nd)	Gr. νεος διδυμος; new twin
neon (Ne)	Gr. νεος; new
neptunium (Np)	L. Neptunus; Neptune, god of the sea, but named after the planetNeptune.
nickel (Ni)	Ger. nickel; from 'kupfernickel' which means 'Old Nick's Copper' or 'False Copper'. Salts of nickel resemble salts of copper but when the ore was smelted a silvery metal (nickel) was produced and not the red copper metal as had been expected.
niobium (Nb)	Gr. Νιοβη, daughter of Tantalus. According to myth, father and daughter were always found together and were very similar. The two elements Niobium and Tantalum are usually found together in nature and their properties are very similar. Niobium was discovered in North America in 1801 and was originally named Columbium.
nitrogen (N)	L. nitrum, Gr. νιτρον; soda + Gr. -γεν; forming

osmium (Os)	Gr. οσμη; smell. It has a strong smell
oxygen (O)	Gr. οξυς; sour/acid + Gr. -γεν; forming. Most non-metals burn in oxygen to form acids.
palladium (Pd)	L. Palladium; a statue of Pallas (Gr. Παλλας), a name for Athena, goddess of wisdom
phosphorous (P)	Gr. φωσφορος; 'bringing light/bearer of light'. Also the ancient name for the planet Venus, usually the brightest 'star' in the night sky. Phosphorous glows in the dark and ignites spontaneously in air
platinum (Pt)	Sp. platina, plata; silver
plutonium (Pu)	L. Pluto, Gr. Πλουτων; god of the nether world, but named after the planet Pluto.
polonium (Po)	ML. Polonia; Poland. Discovered in 1898 by Marie Curie, who was Polish.
potassium (K)	NL. kalium, Du. potasch; pot + ash
praseodymium (Pr)	Gr. πρασιος διδυμος; green twin
promethium (Pm)	Gr. Προμηθευς; the titan who gave fire and the arts to man
protoactinium (Pa)	Gr. πρωτος; first + actinium (Gr. ακτις, ακτινος; a ray/beam (of the sun))
radium (Ra)	L. radius; ray (as in 'ray of light'). Radium was discovered in 1898 by Pierre and Marie Curie. It is radioactive and, when concentrated; glows in the dark.
radon (Rn)	rad- from radium + on (as in argon)
rhenium (Re)	L. Rhenus; named after the river Rhine in Germany
rhodium (Rh)	Gr. ροδον; rose/red
rubidium (Rb)	L. rubidus; reddish
ruthenium (Ru)	ML. Ruthenia; Russia
rutherfordium (Rf)	Synthesized in 1964 at the University of California, Berkeley, and named in honour of Ernest Rutherford
samarium (Sm)	from Samarskite, a mineral named in honour of Colonel Samarski – a Russian mine official
scandium (Sc)	L. Scandia; Scandinavia. Discovered and mined in Scandinavia
seaborgium (Sg)	Synthesized in 1974 at the University of California, Berkeley, and named in honour of Glenn T. Seaborg, an American nuclear chemist.
selenium (Se)	Gr. σεληνη; the moon
silicon (Si)	L. silex, silicis; flint
silver (Ag)	L. argnetum, AS. seolfor
sodium (Na)	Ar. natrum (sodium carbonate); ML. sodanum (a headache remedy), Ar. suda; headache
strontium (Sr)	Strontian, a small village in the Western Highlands of Scotland.
sulpher/sulfer (S)	From the Sanskrit word 'sulvere'; also from the Latin word 'sulphurium'; brimstone.
tantalum (Ta)	Gr. τανταλος; Tantalos, symbolic of eternal torment. Named after the Greek mythological king. It was discovered in 1802 and great difficulties were encountered in dissolving its oxide in acid to form salts.
technetium (Tc)	Gr. τεχνη/τεχνικος; craft/artificial
tellurium (Te)	L. tellus, telluris; the earth
terbium (Tb)	named after the village of Ytterby, near Vaxholm in Sweden
thallium (Tl)	Gr. θαλλιον; a little, young green shoot (the spectral line is green)
thorium (Th)	thorite, ON. Thor, the god of thunder. Named after Thor, the Scandinavian God of War and Thunder. It was discovered and named in 1828 and is used today as a nuclear fuel in nuclear weapons and reactors.
thulium (Tm)	L. thule; farthest north, an ancient name for Scandinavia

tin (Sn)	L. stannum, AS. tin
titanium (Ti)	Gr. Τιταν; one of the gods, symbolic of great strength and large size. Titanium is an extremely strong metal which resists attack by acids.
tungsten (W)	Sw. *tung sten*, 'heavy stone'. Ger. *wolf rahm*, 'wolfram'. The name comes from medieval German smelters who found that tin ores containing tungsten had a much lower yield. It was said that the tungsten devoured the tin 'like a wolf'.
uranium (U)	L. Uranus, Gr. Ουρανος; the god of heaven, but named after the planet Uranus. The element was discovered in 1789, shortly after the discovery of the planet.
vanadium (V)	ON. Vanadis, a name for Freya, the wife of Oden and the goddess of youth, love, beauty and the dead. The salts of vanadium have beautiful colours.
wolfram (W)	See tungsten.
xenon (Xe)	Gr. ξενος; stranger
ytterbium (YB)	named after the village of Ytterby, near Vaxholm in Sweden
yttrium (Y)	named after the village of Ytterby, near Vaxholm in Sweden
zinc (Zn)	Ger. zink
zirconium (Zr)	Fr. zircon, Ar. zarqun; gold-coloured

BIBLIOGRAPHY

ASKEW, R.R. (1988). *The Dragonflies of Europe*. Harley Books.

BARNES, R.D (1980). *Invertebrate Zoology*. 4th Edition. Saunders College, Philadelphia.

BENNET, H. (1947). *The Concise Chemical and Technical Dictionary*. W & G Foyle, Ltd.

BROWN, R.W. (1956). *Composition of Scientific Words*. Smithsonian Institute Press.

BURTON, M. (1962). *Systematic Dictionary of Mammals of the World*. Thomas Y. Crowell Company. New York.

CAMPBELL, B. & Lack, E. (eds.). (1985). *Dictionary of Birds*. The British Ornithologists Union.

CHIARELLI, A.B. (1972). *Taxonomic Atlas of Living Primates*. Academic Press.

GOTCH, A.F. (1995). *Latin Names Explained. A Guide to the Scientific Classification of Reptiles, Birds & Mammals*. Blandford.

HALTENORTH, T. & Diller, H. (1980). *Mammals of Africa Including Madagascar*. Collins

HARDE, K.W. (1984). *Beetles*. Octopus Books.

HIGGINS, L.G. & Riley,N.D. (1983). *A Field Guide to the Butterflies of Britain and Europe*. Collins.

IMMS, A.D. (1957). *A General Textbook of Entomology*. 9th Edition O.W. Richards & R.G. Davies eds. Methuen & Co. Ltd.

JEFFREY, C. (1977). *Biological Nomenclature*. 2nd Edition. Edward Arnold.

KINCHIN, I.M. (1994). *The Biology of the Tardigrades*. Portland Press.

KING, B., Woodcock, M. & Dickinson, E.C. (1975). *A Field guide to the Birds of South-East Asia*. Collins.

LIDDELL, H.G. & Scott, R. (1996). *Greek-English Lexicon*. 9th Edition. Clarendon Press, Oxford.

LONG, J.A. (1995). *The Rise of the Fishes*. The John Hopkins University Press.

MARSHELL, J.A. & Haes, E.C.M. (1988). *Grasshoppers and Allied Insects of Great Britain and Ireland*. Harley Books.

PAXTON, J.R. & Eschmyer, W.N. Consultant Editors (1998). Encyclopedia of Fishes. Academic Press.

PETERSON, R., Mountfort, G. & Hollom, P.A.D. (1983). *A Field Guide to the Birds of Britain and Europe*. Collins.

ROMER, A.S. (1945).*Vertebrate Paleontology*. 2nd Edition. The University of Chicago Press. Chicago.

ROTHSCHILD, Lord (1961). *A Classification of Living Animals*. Longmans, Green & Co. Ltd.

SIMPSON, D.P. (1994). *Cassell's Latin Dictionary*. 5th Edition. Cassell.

SIMPSON, G.G. (1945). *The Principles of Classification and a Classification of Mammals*. Bulletin of the American Museum of Natural History. Vol. 85.

SOKOLOV, V.E. (1988). Dictionary of Animal Names in Five languages. Amphibians and Reptiles. Russky Yazyk Publishers, Moscow.

SOKOLOV, V.E. (1984). Dictionary of Animal Names in Five languages. Mammals. Russky Yazyk Publishers, Moscow.

WATSON, L. (1985). *Whales of the World*. Hutchinson.

......

Made in the USA
Lexington, KY
25 November 2012